About Island Press

Island Press is the only nonprofit organization in the United States whose principal purpose is the publication of books on environmental issues and natural resource management. We provide solutions-oriented information to professionals, public officials, business and community leaders, and concerned citizens who are shaping responses to environmental problems.

In 1994, Island Press celebrated its tenth anniversary as the leading provider of timely and practical books that take a multidisciplinary approach to critical environmental concerns. Our growing list of titles reflects our commitment to bringing the best of an expanding body of literature to the environmental community throughout North America and the world.

Support for Island Press is provided by The Geraldine R. Dodge Foundation, The Energy Foundation, The Ford Foundation, The George Gund Foundation, William and Flora Hewlett Foundation, The John D. and Catherine T. MacArthur Foundation, The Andrew W. Mellon Foundation, The Joyce Mertz-Gilmore Foundation, The New-Land Foundation, The Pew Charitable Trusts, The Rockefeller Brothers Fund, The Tides Foundation, Turner Foundation, Inc., The Rockefeller Philanthropic Collaborative, Inc., and individual donors.

Let
the
People
Judge

The first duty of the human race on the material side is to control the use of the earth and all that therein is. Conservation means the wise use of the earth and its resources for the lasting good of men. Conservation is the foresighted utilization, preservation, and/or renewal of forests, waters, lands, and minerals, for the greatest good of the greatest number for the longest time.

Gifford Pinchot
Part XIII, "Let the People Judge," *Breaking New Ground*

Let the People Judge

Wise Use and the Private Property Rights Movement

Edited by

John D. Echeverria
and
Raymond Booth Eby

ISLAND PRESS
Washington, D.C. · Covelo, California

Correct ISBNs for this title:
1-55963-276-3
1-55963-277-1 (pbk.)

Copyright © 1995 Island Press

Acknowledgment for permission to include previously published material is expressed on p. 359

Library of Congress Cataloging-in-Publication Data

Let the people judge : a reader on the wise use movement / edited by
    John Echeverria and Raymond Booth Eby.
        p.   cm.
    Includes bibliographical references and index.
    ISBN 1-55963-300-X. — ISBN 1-55963-301-8 (pbk.)
        1. Environmental policy.   2. Environmental protection.   3. Wise
Use Movement—United States.   4. Environmental protection—Economic
aspects—United States.   I. Echeverria, John D.   II. Eby, Raymond
Booth.
GE180.L48   1995   93-43331
363.7—dc20   CIP

Printed on recycled, acid-free paper ♻ ∞

Manufactured in the United States of America

10 9 8 7 6 5 4 3 2 1

Contents

III. Resource Conflicts

IV. The Takings Issue

V. The Economics of Conservation

VI. People and Wildlife

VII. Effective Activism

VIII. Message and the Media

Preface

The purpose of this reader is to improve public understanding of the Wise Use movement and the related "property rights" challenge to the environmental movement. Although difficult to neatly characterize either in terms of their membership or goals, Wise Use and related ideologies generally attack environmental protection and conservation efforts as harmful to the economy and job creation, insensitive to the needs and desires of local communities, and inconsistent with certain traditional American values, including constitutionally protected property rights.

This reader collects the views of numerous individuals, including conservationists, scholars, writers, and businesspeople, on the Wise Use movement and the controversies that fuel the Wise Use debate. We have attempted to collect a wide range of different and sometimes sharply divergent thinking.

Some regard the Wise Use movement as a major threat to the environmental movement and to the achievement of environmental goals. The term "wise use" was coined by Gifford Pinchot, an early conservationist, and the Wise Use movement itself can be viewed as an effort to redefine and co-opt the traditional environmental movement. Indeed, one Wise Use leader has been widely quoted as stating that the movement seeks to put environmental groups "out of business." Certainly in terms of the sophistication of its political and media strategies, the Wise Use movement surpasses its historical antecedents, such as the Sagebrush Rebellion of the 1970s and early 1980s.

Others see the Wise Use movement as a natural and not entirely unhealthy response to the successes of the environmental movement over the last several decades. While environmental protection was once a fringe issue within the context of national and international concerns, it has become one of the central issues of our time. Protecting the environment today is not simply about preserving specific landscapes and habitats from development; rather, as the full scope of the threat of environmental degradation to the nation and the world has become clearer, environmental protection efforts now go to the heart of where and how we live, what modes of transportation we use, and what kinds of jobs we do. In a sense, the Wise Use debate simply reflects the breadth and ambition of the modern environmental movement.

In its emphasis—sometimes real, sometimes contrived—on defending the interests of individuals and rural communities, the Wise Use movement is a clarion call to environmentalists in general, and to major environmental groups in particular, about the need to continue to work toward solutions to resource conflicts in cooperation with local communities and individual citizens.

The pleasure of editing this reader has come from working with the many talented, thoughtful, and dedicated people who have agreed to the inclusion of their views. The views expressed in this reader are, of course, the authors' alone. While some of the contributions have been previously published in one form or another, most are original efforts or extensive revisions of earlier works that required substantial time and effort. We are grateful for those whose contributions make up this reader. We also thank Nancy Olsen and Heather Boyer of Island Press for their tireless assistance in bringing this volume to publication.

John D. Echeverria
Raymond Booth Eby

Let
the
People
Judge

Introduction

Freedom and Responsibility:
What We Can Learn
from the Wise Use Movement

Jon Roush

The question most important for our age is a familiar one. It is so familiar that it may seem either trite or unanswerable. Yet never has so much depended on the answer we devise. The question is, how should we reconcile individual freedom and social responsibility?

In a world of shrinking resources and growing demand, this question has gained urgency. In the past, people have disagreed about environmental regulation and management. Now they accuse one another of theft, fraud, and treason. They lobby and hire PR firms. They spend millions of dollars to prove that their opponents take food from children's mouths and lay waste to the earth. The roots of this conflict lie in some of our most prized institutions.

The so-called Wise Use movement illustrates the ways in which our institutions are dysfunctional. It springs from venerable American values, and it embodies our ambivalence toward freedom and responsibility. Because we live by incompatible values, we have created institutions that invite conflict.

In the Northern Rockies (where I lived until recently), people still take care of one another. They have pride in producing products that often come directly from the land. Here, many people can still *see* the places where their money comes from. Here, environmental issues are not just about economics and jobs. They are also about waking up every morning and heading out into the woods or the field. In nearby towns, many others derive their income from serving those who work the land. Environmental issues are about loyalty to friends and neighbors you've known since junior high school. They are about the freedom to enjoy a way of life. They are not abstractions, but concern specific places where people work, play, and dream.

Diverse people share this sense of place: vehement environmentalists, militant property rights advocates, and many who prefer not to take sides. The sense of place is stronger than many quarrels. As a rancher, I have worked well with people who know about my environmental ideas and disagree with them. As a consultant, I have interviewed countless people at all points of the spectrum. I have moderated focus groups of ranchers, farmers, loggers, miners, hunters, environmentalists, politicians, and businesspeople from rural areas and small towns. I have found near unanimity about the values of wildlife and wild places. Love for the earth is not exclusive to any class, occupation, or political persuasion. The difficulties lie elsewhere.

Some people who do understand the tie between community and the land are nevertheless opponents of conservation. To mobilize opposition to conservation, leaders of the Wise Use movement play on people's fears while evoking feelings of community. Environmentalists need to understand why that appeal succeeds.

Members of the Wise Use movement (for convenience, I will call them "WUMs") are a diverse lot. They do not always agree about goals and tactics, and they often compete for the same sources of money. What they share is hostility to laws and regulations protecting the environment. The hostility comes from two principles: Environmental constraints on private property are usually wrong, as are restraints on private use of public land and water.

WUMs claim to act from traditional American values, and we cannot dismiss that claim lightly. They proclaim values associated with John Locke, values that impelled the founding fathers. In this tradition, that government is best which governs least. The right to life, liberty, and the pursuit of happiness includes the individual's right to appropriate wealth from nature. If no one has claimed it, it's yours. In this view, government's role is to help convert natural resources into private property, and then to protect that property.

Locke believed this arrangement would produce benign results because people's "natural harmony of interests" would lead to a free and tolerant society. Although Alexander Hamilton and others disagreed, the Lockean vision prevailed. Its champion was Thomas Jefferson. Jeffersonian theory assumed that economic freedom would produce moral and social progress. That assumption shaped many American institutions throughout the nineteenth and twentieth centuries. It underlay the complex of laws that promoted the U.S. settlement of the West, like the Homestead Acts and the 1872 Mining Act. Lockean–Jeffersonian America pursued the vision of a society in which government protects private property and contracts, but does not interfere with them. That tradition drives the Wise Use movement.

Something has gone wrong with the scheme of achieving the good society through free markets. Jefferson did not foresee the transformed nature of American corporations. In Jefferson's day, the state chartered corporations for nonprofit functions—like towns, churches, and colleges. Or the state created corporations as monopolies for large economic projects with public benefits, like building roads and canals. These early corporations served clear public functions and were accountable to the public good. In the nineteenth century, legislatures and courts changed this idea radically. By the end of the century, corporations had attained the natural rights of persons. They were free to enter contracts without government influence.

Jefferson had feared the rise of "economic royalties"—persons whose economic power gave them political power. When corporations gained the Jeffersonian protection of individual freedom, the powers he had feared were born. Jefferson and others had seen small farmers, artisans, and merchants as democracy's hope. Jeffersonian freedom gave corporations an immense advantage over such citizens.

That irony raises a telling point about the Wise Use movement. WUMs claim to speak for the little guy. They claim to help the dispossessed worker or small landowner against forces threatening his property and livelihood. However, it is well documented that the decisions of large corporations have caused economic problems. In the Pacific Northwest, for example, decisions by logging companies have cost thousands of jobs. Then, why do the movement's leaders not include corporate behavior in their list of abuses?

One obvious answer is that the Wise Use movement is only partly a grassroots movement. Its message appeals to a broad array of people and interest groups. WUMs include cattlemen, loggers, miners, private-property owners within national forests, off-road-vehicle users, East Coast land developers, western water users, fishermen and shrimpers, recreational developers, and other users of natural resources. The diverse makeup of this group is one of its strengths. Politicians see it as a broad constituency. By supporting Wise Use interests, a politician can appeal to many groups at once. Politicians also like it because the issues involve big money. The WUMs favor the big-money side of the equation, and so the movement attracts big-money support. Many WUM groups are poorly camouflaged industry fronts.

Still, that does not explain everything. Corporations bankroll much of the movement, but they do not dictate its values. The movement's glue is a scrambled mixture of traditional values of personal freedom and claims to private rights. Ranchers want to protect grazing rights on public lands. Off-road-vehicle groups want more access to public lands. People living within national forests want protection against eminent domain and against restrictions on their use of their land. Loggers, miners, oil companies, and recreational-vehicle people share goals. They want to open public lands to logging, mineral and energy production, and motorized vehicles. Energy companies and irrigators want to strengthen states' control of water, to open the door for easier permitting for damming and diversion. Commercial fishermen oppose regulations that restrict their freedom to take any species of fish they wish, in any numbers, with any technology. The Wise Use movement is acquisitiveness riding on images of self-reliance and agrarian virtues.

Some WUM leaders have played on these images cynically. One, Ron Arnold, explained the strategy in a speech to Canadian timber executives in 1989. He advised them not to try to take their message to the public themselves. The public, he warned, will distrust the motives of big business. Instead, he told them to organize local grassroots organizations. He explained to the executives that a local citizens' group

> *can do things the industry can't. It can speak as public-spirited people who support the communities and the families affected by the local issue. It can speak as a group of people who live close to nature and have more natural wisdom than city people. It can provide allies with something to join, someplace to nurture that vital sense of belonging and common cause. It can develop emotional commitment among your allies. It can form coalitions to build real political clout. It can be an effective and convincing advocate for your industry. It can evoke powerful archetypes such as the sanctity of the family, the virtue of the close-knit community, the natural wisdom of the rural dweller, and many others I'm sure you can think of.*[1]

This cynical strategy is particularly reprehensible because it plays on the fears of working people like miners, loggers, farmers, and ranchers. They do have a lot to worry about, and the WUM message is one of false hope. Those archetypes that Ron Arnold mentioned so glibly—the sanctity of the family and the virtue of the close-knit community—are real and threatened. Still, they are not the values of resource-based corporations. Those corporations may create jobs, but not from a motivation to protect their workers' personal freedoms.

What does all this tell us? It does not tell us that corporations are evil. Although legally corporations are persons, in fact they are just one way to organize people for common goals. Whether they serve good or evil ends depends on their leaders and on the morality of institutions that control them. There have been countless instances of corporate support for environmental work. Many corporate leaders volunteer time and money to environmental causes.

There are many examples of constructive partnerships between corporations and nonprofits or government agencies. Yet individual partnerships and acts of conscience are not enough. We need institutions that reward farsighted action for the common good.

When I refer to "institutions," I am using the sociological definition of the word. An institution is a pattern of behavior enforced by social sanctions. The enforcing sanctions may be laws or customs. They express society's expectations of how people should behave in important transactions, processes, or relationships. For example, we use that definition when we speak of the institution of marriage. In common usage, people confuse organizations with institutions. Institutions might act through organizations, but the organizations themselves are not the institutions. The judges and clerks of the Supreme Court do not make an institution. They serve the laws and traditions of the institution of constitutional governance. If we mistake organizations for institutions, then we tinker with organizations when we should instead tackle underlying institutional problems.

Institutions program behavior. They embody codes of conduct for society's most important actions. Those codes have the force of custom. We rarely question them any more than we question the custom of shaking hands. It is just the way things are done. The more unconscious we are of them, the more powerful they are. When a judge is on the bench, he will not act as he does in the privacy of his home. He defers automatically to institutions of the law. Society has a stake in maintaining correct institutional behavior. The institution of marriage prescribes roles for husbands and wives, and violating those roles can bring censure from outsiders. Institutions embody ideas of right and wrong. They define and enforce moral and social order. Although they are human-made and change continuously, at any one time they *feel* eternal and immutable.

The two motives of the Wise Use movement—defending private property and the private use of public land—rest on venerable American values and institutions. They express ideas of Locke and Jefferson. They also conflict with some values and institutions that have shaped the environmental movement. For example, in "The Tragedy of the Commons," Garrett Hardin develops a central metaphor of the modern environmental movement. Hardin asks us to

> *picture a pasture open to all. It is to be expected that each herdsman will try to keep as many cattle as possible on the commons. Such an arrangement may work reasonably satisfactorily for centuries because tribal wars, poaching, and disease keep the numbers of both man and beast well below the carrying capacity of the land. Finally, however, comes the day of reckoning, that is, the day when the long-desired goal of social stability becomes*

a reality. At this point, the inherent logic of the commons remorselessly gen-erates tragedy.

As a rational being, each herdsman seeks to maximize his gain. Explic-itly or implicitly, more or less consciously, he asks, "What is the utility to me of adding one more animal to my herd?"[2]

Being rational, the herdsman makes a simple computation. He alone will receive the profit from that additional animal, while all the herdsmen share the costs of overgrazing.

. . . the rational herdsman concludes that the only sensible course for him to pursue is to add another animal to his herd. And another; and another. . . . But this is the conclusion reached by each and every rational herdsman sharing a commons. Therein is the tragedy. Each man is locked into a system that compels him to increase his herd without limit—in a world that is limited. Ruin is the destination toward which all men rush, each pur-suing his own best interest in a society that believes in the freedom of the commons. Freedom in a commons brings ruin to all.[3]

The solution, Hardin concludes, is not volutary action. That will not work. The solution, he says, is "mutual coercion, mutually agreed upon by the majority of the people affected."[4]

This prescription would not suit Thomas Jefferson, the Wise Use move-ment, or most Americans. They dislike coercion and place a high value on per-sonal freedom. Several studies have shown that middle-class Americans do not see work as something that is good in itself. It is a means to the freedom they think upper-middle- and upper-class people have. It is not wealth they envy but control over one's life. They value the work system because they think it gives them a shot at self-determination.

Our institutions emphasize economic opportunities for individual people and, by extension, for corporations. In exchange for this freedom of opportu-nity, we have accepted an increasingly precarious life. We have chosen a high level of individual consumption with a low level of public services. We like to own our homes, but we do not like to pay the taxes. We doubt that social safety nets and individual prosperity are compatible.

We have inherited two myths. In one, the United States has assured liberty and equality for all citizens; in the other, it has produced unequaled personal wealth. In the first myth, freedom requires an acknowledged responsibility to one another, which is revealed in a climate of tolerance, mutual support, and community. In the second myth, freedom is the power to do as you please. This myth equates freedom with independence, and it encourages people to succeed at one another's expense. It is such an appealing and credible myth that even the losers honor it, hoping they will become winners too.

For 200 years, we have tried to reconcile, or at least balance, the two myths. We talk, for example, not about equality but about equality of opportunity. The tension between the myths can be healthy: It helps us avoid excesses. Still, as the WUMs have shown, excesses do happen. Although WUMs talk the language of equality, they live the myth that equates personal gain with personal freedom. Their unbalanced enthusiasm for that myth causes problems when their fortunes turn sour or when the community asserts conflicting rights. When jobs get scarce, people who have embraced the myth of prosperity feel betrayed. Yet because the institutions of private gain are strong and pervasive, people do not blame them. They cannot ask for regulation or social services without admitting flaws in their own value system. So they look for scapegoats. Enter environmentalists.

Over the past 20 years, we have scaled back many public benefits. Yet during the same period, institutional supports for environmental protection have been increasingly generous. As newcomers on the institutional scene, with a motherhood halo, environmental causes have had a honeymoon period to overcome opposition. They have bucked the trend, but now the trend is catching up. The difficulties were almost inevitable. The environmental movement has positioned itself within our institutional order in ways guaranteed to create backlash.

An example of the institutional problems is the recent history of the Endangered Species Act. The act requires that federal projects be evaluated for their impact on endangered species and, if necessary, stopped. The act is not the powerful force its detractors claim it to be. Of more than 70,000 projects reviewed under the act, since late 1986, only 18 have been stopped. Still that number is likely to increase. As evidence mounts for the need to protect more species, the Endangered Species Act will inevitably become more influential and therefore more controversial.

A similar process occurs within government. The U.S. Fish and Wildlife Service and the National Marine Fisheries Service administer the Endangered Species Act. They have responsibility for second-guessing—or, in the polite language of the act, "consulting with"—other federal agencies. As they list more species for protection under the act, these two agencies will impinge more frequently on other agencies. The more diligently the government enforces the Endangered Species Act, the greater the chance of internal conflict and pressures to weaken the act.

The Endangered Species Act is an example of the way the conservation movement creates backlash because of its institutional structure. In *The Expendable*

Future: U.S. Politics and the Protection of Biological Diversity, Richard Tobin argues that the act creates its own opposition. To be widely popular, a government policy should call for small changes in current practices rather than changes in institutional behavior. It should conform to conventional opinion. It should not require people to change their way of living or cause them inconvenience. It also should offer clear, immediate benefits, and the benefits should outweigh the costs.

Policies protecting endangered species violate all the prescriptions for popular support. They demand that people change deep habits of environmental behavior. They restrict access to resources and limit their use. They demand that people not use available techologies and materials. They claim benefits that are obscure and hard to prove. They ask us to forego concrete benefits today for theoretical ones in an indeterminate future.

Environmentalists say the problem is that people refuse to take the long view. That refusal should not surprise us. Modern human beings evolved from people who survived by taking the short view. The Pleistocene world of constant personal danger and adequate resources was different from ours. Watching for saber-toothed tigers was more important than saving trees for future generations. Only recently, as the commons has become overcrowded, has conservation become a survival skill.

We have some evidence that people can rise above that inherited limitation. They can do it even when conditions get tough—read the history of the 1930s, for example. We conserve for the future when two conditions are met. People must share a commitment to a community and a vision of a better future. Movements rise on such commitment. Without a shared vision, short-term values and behavior will predominate.

To begin to build that commitment and vision, we need institutions that deal with poverty. Poverty drives environmental degradation. If affluent societies refuse to help people overcome poverty—at home and in developing countries—then those people might rationally decline to support environmental programs. Their world is the Pleistocene revisited; the short view is what matters. Within 12 years, the world will have to support one billion more people. Meanwhile, industries will rise and fall, and international turbulence in the job market will make employment even more unpredictable. In that environment, creating sustainable, gainful employment will be increasingly difficult. It will be possible only if we dare rethink some institutional habits. In a sustainable society, people may forego some individual gain, but institutions still could reward free enterprise. They could create opportunities and incentives for innovations that serve the vision of a sustainable economy.

The development of a sustainable society must include attention to questions of equity and freedom. Hardin's formula—"mutual coercion mutually agreed on by a majority of the people affected"—implies reciprocity. Mutual coercion is acceptable if a majority agree to it. Yet that is dangerous medicine. Tyranny of the majority has caused some of this country's most shameful missteps from the straight way of democracy. Many people sympathize with the WUMs because they correctly fear such tyranny. Our Constitution guarantees that a million people cannot deprive one person of property or freedom without due process.

As we gain political influence, environmentalists increasingly face the old challenge of *e pluribus unum,* but with a new twist. What are the limits of free, voluntary action in a world of accelerating scarcity? How far can voluntary commitment to community take us? At what point do we resort to coercion? The environmental crisis will deepen before it improves—can we imagine a unified society, in which social bonds still hold, without forced compliance and erosion of personal freedom? The most chilly utopias are those where the state imposes itself for our own good.

The institutions of free markets are useful but incomplete. They assume that if each of us pursues his or her own interests, our transactions with one another will yield the greatest good for the greatest number. Yet Adam Smith's invisible hand does not work for global warming, ozone depletion, or extinction. Although free markets are the most efficient way to produce many economic goods, they cannot resolve some large ethical questions. Individual consumers, acting in an international economy of bewildering complexity, cannot know enough to make appropriate choices. Nor will supply and demand set prices that will control consumption to benefit future generations. That could happen only if future generations have a secure voice in decisions about resources; being unborn, however, they cannot negotiate in free markets. Can we devise institutional ways to protect their interests without undue coercion?

We must resolve questions about mutual agreement. When so many environmental issues are local, planning must include local and regional people. Still, consent can be a trap. Parochial or short-term concerns can crowd out larger interests. We have seen that problem in the West, where states and counties have asserted local control over federal land. Legally, their claim is frivolous; psychologically, it is an important expression of frustration. We cannot have local people making unilateral demands on resources of national importance. Yet we also cannot have national policies forced down the throats of local people. We will not escape the dilemma until we create new institutional contexts for decisions about natural resources.

We already have created elements of a sustainable society. For example, in the late 1970s, California created tax incentives to supplement federal incentives for investments in renewable energy. The state also changed regulations to let producers other than electric utilities enter the electricity market. Today, California generates more electricity from wind farms and solar thermal power plants than the rest of the world combined. The state accounts for about one-third of the global development of geothermal energy. These sources, combined with biomass-fired power plants, produce electricity for four million households.

If such examples are not convincing, we have an even more compelling reason to credit the possibility of sustainability: The alternative is intolerable. No one—not even the most dedicated environmentalists—wants to go without food, shelter, and a livelihood. No one—not even the most dedicated industrialist or miner—wants to go without clean air and water and green places.

Our divisions and disagreements are not unalterable facts of human nature. We have created them. We have institutionalized our desire for personal freedom in laws, customs, and industries for exploiting nature. Meanwhile, we have institutionalized our desire for a livable habitat in a movement for environmental protection. We have failed to create institutions through which people can merge those two impulses by building sustainable communities.

The synthesis will require subtle changes in ideas of freedom. It must encourage local, voluntary actions that acknowledge the rights of strangers, those who live across oceans and across generations. It also must meet human needs for security and self-actualization. If we create the synthesis, the Wise Use movement will be a historical footnote. If we fail, expect a long, bitter winter.

Notes

1. "Loggerheads over land use." In Logging and Sawmilling Journal, reprinted in Deforestation and Development in Canada and the Tropics. Aaron Schneider, p. 132. Centre for International Studies, University College of Cape Breton, Cape Breton, Nova Scotia.
2. Hardin, Garrett. 1968. "The tragedy of the commons." *Science* 162, 1245.
3. Hardin, 1245.
4. Hardin, 1247.

I

The Wise Use and Property Rights Movements

The Wise Use movement emerged on the national scene with the publication of *The Wise Use Agenda* in 1989. Touted as both "the citizen's guide to environmental issues" and "a task force report to the Bush administration by the Wise Use movement," the book was a good likeness of the movement itself: a volatile mix of traditional conservative ideology blended with some revolutionary proposals to open public lands to greater private exploitation.

The takings, or property rights, movement is rooted in the libertarian ideology of Richard Epstein, a law professor at the University of Chicago, who argued in his 1985 book *Takings* that the Fifth Amendment to the Constitution requires public financial compensation for virtually any reduction in the use or value or private property due to regulatory action. Advocates of deregulation seized upon this novel legal theory as an indirect yet effective tool for achieving their goal.

Part I of this volume collects several articles providing an overview of the Wise Use and takings movements and the challenge they present to the cause of protecting the environment. Like the parts that follow, Part I is by no means encyclopedic. It is intended to provide selected background information on the origins and objectives of these related movements.

In "Cloaked in a Wise Disguise," Thomas A. Lewis describes the leaders of the Wise Use movement and its key objectives. He also explores how Wise Use leaders have embraced the takings issue as a way of broadening the base of their movement.

In "Stop the Greens," Eve Pell, with the Center for Investigative Reporting, examines the support that some corporations have provided to nominally grassroots groups with benign-sounding names in order to serve their corporate interests. Ms. Pell also describes what she terms as efforts by certain corporations to "co-opt" and "buy influence" with mainstream environmental groups.

Margaret Kriz, author of "Land Mine," explores the origins of Wise Use and the efforts of the environmental community to counter this new movement. She describes how Wise Use leaders have openly borrowed environmentalists' political organizing techniques, and relates some of the early conflicts between Wise Use leaders and the Clinton–Gore administration.

In "The 'Property Rights' Revolt," Marianne Lavelle, of the *National Law Journal*, focuses on the takings issue. She describes some of the efforts, particularly in the state legislatures, to enact takings legislation.

Cloaked in a Wise Disguise

Thomas A. Lewis

"I went to a meeting in Bozeman and there were 700 people there. You can't imagine the virulence of the outcry. I was Saddam Hussein, a Communist, everything else you could think of. One lady got up there, jaw quivering, used her time to say the Pledge of Allegiance, then looked at me and called me a Nazi."

Thus, early in 1991, Robert Barbee met the so-called "Wise Use Movement." Barbee, the superintendent of Yellowstone National Park, had gone to that meeting in Montana to discuss a plan for protecting the ecological integrity of the park and its surroundings. Congressional hearings had found that authorities at the region's two national parks, six national forests, and two wildlife refuges were managing resources in different, sometimes conflicting ways, seldom communicating with each other. Meanwhile, logging, drilling, mining, grazing, and development on the 11 million acres surrounding 2.2-million-acre Yellowstone park were increasingly threatening the ecosystem.

The response was a 76-page plan, titled "A Vision for the Future," designed by the managers of the region's national parks and national forests to bring unity to the handling of this remarkable natural area, and to "encourage opportunities that are economically sustainable." According to Bob Ekey of the Greater Yellowstone Coalition (a citizens' group favoring preservation of the area), "Nothing in the plan proposed to enlarge the park, or restrict or eliminate multiple use in areas around the park." But as expected, the reaction from loggers, miners, and cattlemen was negative. What was surprising was the strength of the reaction.

For example, of the 8,690 letters commenting on the plan, 5,625 were form letters opposing any limitations on industry. Of the 700 people at the public hearing described by Barbee, most were hostile and had arrived together on buses provided for them by groups opposed to the plan. Hundreds of angry people communicated with Secretary of the Interior Manuel Lujan and the area's Congressional delegation. Money and organization had been applied to create what looked like a spontaneous upwelling of outrage while, according to Ekey, polls showed strong public support for principles of the "Vision" document.

John Sununu, then President Bush's chief of staff, was quoted as describing the plan as a political "disaster" and demanding a rewrite. The document was pared from 76 pages to 11 and edited to remove any hint of opposition to commercial activity. For example, where the original "Vision" said that "projects permitted will have to be shown to be without potential to harm geothermal features," the revision said "development projects on adjacent national forests do not threaten geothermal features." The two key officials responsible for the draft—the regional forester and regional Park Service director—were transferred under protest to new jobs. Both soon left government service.

They, and their "Vision," were neither the first nor the last casualties of a new alliance of Americans who suggest that their government often is required to make a choice between economic prosperity and ecological health, and that government is usually intimidated by environmentalists into making the wrong choice. This alliance disparages the argument that a society can have both economic and ecological plenty as un-American.

The Wise Use alliance is rich and growing. In the four years since it coalesced, it has declared outright warfare against the environmental movement. It has also come up with an agenda of initiatives that, if implemented, could unravel the nation's system for protecting natural resources and the environment, as well as public health and worker safety.

"This is a classic example of a lie galloping across the range while the truth is still pulling its boots on," says National Wildlife Federation President Jay D. Hair. "The self-proclaimed 'Wise Use Agenda' is merely a wise disguise for a well-financed, industry-backed campaign that preys upon the economic woes and fears of U.S. citizens."

In recent years, the Wise Use alliance has loudly opposed federal and state legislation it did not like (such as bills to impose higher fees for grazing cattle on public lands), has won approval for federal and state laws it did like (such as an authorization for federal gasoline-tax money to be used to build off-road vehicle trails), has made powerful political friends (one of its founders is pictured on the cover of its national agenda with a smiling George Bush) and has intimidated government regulators. In the words of *U.S. News and World Report,* it represents the "first unified political challenge" to government's role as protector of natural resources "in the 20 years since the environmental movement took hold."

The appalling effects of uncontrolled pollution in the United States stimulated the imposition of a myriad of environmental regulations in the 1970s.

And it was outrage at the impact of some of the new laws on unrestrained development that triggered the so-called "Sagebrush Rebellion" in the late 1970s, in which western agricultural and business interests clamored for transfer of federal lands to state or private control in order to elude the growing pressures for environmental responsibility. Their uprising was raucous but not well organized, and with the election to the presidency of Ronald Reagan, the movement died out.

But beginning in the late 1980s, other events began to take shape that would further challenge unrestrained natural resource development. U.S. courts, acting on lawsuits brought by conservationists, upheld mandates of the Endangered Species Act and curtailed logging in ancient forests to safeguard imperiled animals like the spotted owl; tougher rules were adopted to protect the nation's dwindling wetlands. Opponents of such measures again strapped on their gunbelts, but this was no Sagebrush Rebellion. This time they had leadership, organization, and money.

Alan M. Gottlieb, 45, of Bellevue, Washington, had made a name and a small fortune as a direct-mail fund-raiser for conservative politicians and causes, especially his Citizens Committee for the Right to Keep and Bear Arms. He had a knack for writing letters that loosened purse-strings. And he had accumulated the names of millions whose purse-strings became especially slack when certain buttons were pushed. His career had not been unblemished, however. He served a year in prison in 1984 for tax evasion.

But Alan Gottlieb knew the direct-mail business and, in the late 1980s, he told *The New York Times* he needed another "evil empire" to stimulate giving. He decided to try out environmentalists in the role. The results were immediate and unambiguous. The environmental movement made the perfect bogeyman. So Gottlieb founded another of his tax-exempt creations, the Center for the Defense of Free Enterprise. His associate in that organization, Executive Vice-President Ron Arnold, took center stage with a theology of outrage for an anti-environmentalist crusade he dubbed the "Wise Use Movement."

Before joining Gottlieb in 1984, Arnold, 55, had been a public relations consultant to industry who saw, he says, company after company defeated by environmental regulations. "It was always the same," he explains. "The environmentalists would go to government and get a law or regulation passed, and the company that was about to be put out of business fought the government over the regulations. Nobody ever fought the environmentalists." In the 1980s, Arnold says, he decided "if things continued like they were going, the environmentalists were going to destroy all industry and all private property within 20 years." He determined the only way to avert this was to "systematically destroy the environmental movement," which he says is "polluted with a hatred of humans." To Arnold, this main proposition has two axioms: "Industry cannot save itself by itself" and "only an activist movement can defeat an activist movement."

Arnold does not speak of differences over public policy, but of a cosmic struggle between good and evil. A former activist in the Sierra Club, he speaks with the zeal of the converted. "This is a war," he told *The Baltimore Sun.* "We're trying to destroy the opposition."

The origin of the Wise Use name is instructive. Arnold concluded the best way of opposing environmental activism was to adopt its techniques. For inspiration, he turned to the words of Gifford Pinchot, the first U.S. Forest Service chief. Pinchot, in 1907, had coined the word conservation, defining it as "the wise use of resources." Arnold saw that the phrase had a nice ring, and "took up only nine spaces in a newspaper headline." The Wide Use campaign had a name.

While Gottlieb and Arnold became their cause's most visible proponents, they were hardly the only ones. Another principal is Charles Cushman, executive director of the National Inholders Association (of owners of private property in federal parks and other facilities) and organizer of a group dedicated to opening public lands to private profit. Cushman describes himself as a "tank commander" in the war against environmentalists, and insists it is not merely a war, but "a holy war between fundamentally different religions. The preservationists are like a new pagan religion, worshiping trees and animals and sacrificing people."

Meanwhile, in 1986, Nevada attorney A. Grant Gerber founded another group, the Wilderness Impact Research Foundation. He declared that preservationists are anti-Christian and anti-scientific, that environmentalists are "pantheists, like the Druids," and that the Sierra Club practices "weird science and earth religions." Gerber's foundation is an important partner in the Wise Use campaign.

Another ally in the "cause" was the Blue Ribbon Coalition of Pocatello, Idaho. This was an alliance of some 200 local clubs of dirt-bike, snowmobile, and all-terrain vehicle users who wanted public lands opened up to them. Their case was stated by a past president, Henry Yake, who commented, "Wilderness has no economic value."

These groups and about 200 other organizations, companies, and individuals participated in a conference in Reno, Nevada, in August of 1988. More than 100 papers were presented there, and these were later published as a "Wise Use Agenda." This document called for a number of initiatives, including: opening "all public lands including wilderness and national parks to oil drilling, logging, and commercial development"; immediate oil and gas development of Alaska's Arctic National Wildlife Refuge; liquidation of all old-growth forests; and privatization of public rangelands. It advised breaking up the National Park Service and launching a "20-year construction program of new concessions" in all national parks.

"This isn't a battle between two 'religions,'" says George Frampton Jr., president of The Wilderness Society. "It's an assault by commercial interests trying to preserve their traditional freedom to plunder the West without restriction—indeed, with taxpayer subsidies. They claim they lead a grass-roots movement, but they are in fact speaking for industry and their grass is watered by corporate money."

Since 1988, the Wise Use campaign has developed three principal themes, says Arnold: "The private-property movement; pro-jobs economic development; and multiple-use of federal lands."

Their so-called multiple-use lobby was instrumental in defeating the Yellowstone "Vision" statement. It also succeeded in getting a Congressional amendment passed in 1991 authorizing use of as much as $30 million a year from the Highway Trust Fund for building recreational trails, much of it for off-road vehicle use.

The pro-jobs arm of the campaign argues at every opportunity that employment is more important than ecology. Cowboys, for example, must work, whether or not overgrazing is destroying their range.

The intensifying debate over property rights has become truly national in scope. The Wise Use campaign contends government has no right to interfere in how land is used and it cites the U.S. Constitution. The Fifth Amendment says that private property shall not be "taken for public use without just compensation." Its traditional meaning is that the U.S. government, unlike a monarchy, has no sovereignty over the land and has to pay for any private property it takes for a road, an army base, or public building. But in the view of the Wise Use alliance, any government regulation that reduces the value of property constitutes a taking and requires compensation.

If taxpayers had to pay people to obey laws, we could afford few laws. The idea, observes attorney Albert Meyerhoff of the Natural Resources Defense Council, "presents an extremely serious threat to much of the environmental reform legislation that has been enacted over the past 30 years." It also, adds NWF attorney Glenn Sugameli, "threatens health, safety, labor, civil rights, and consumer laws."

Yet the notion has support in the executive and legislative branches of the federal government. President Reagan issued an executive order, still in effect, that requires all federal agencies to follow guidelines that review the effect on private property values of any regulations they promulgate. The Congressional Research Service has stated that these guidelines are flawed because they misinterpret Supreme Court rulings and exaggerate the risk of a taking.

Even so, the Senate twice approved a bill to codify the executive order, and the Bush administration proposed a bill requiring agencies to pay such compensation from their budgets. While waiting for legislation to get through Congress, Wise Use leaders wanted action to redefine the Constitution. In the late 1980s, they found a court willing to do it.

The United States Claims Court is a little-known tribunal in Washington, D.C., which has the job of settling land-dispute and other claims for compensation against the U.S. government. By the late 1980s, it was dominated by Reagan appointees and sympathetic to the idea of a new definition of taking. It awarded a New Jersey developer who was prevented from building on 12.5 acres of wetlands (5 percent of a 250-acre parcel bought for $300,000) damages of $2.68 million. It held that a Florida quarrying company, stopped from mining 98 of its 1,560-acre tract because of a threat to groundwater, deserved more than $1 million in compensation. The largest judgment went to Whitney Benefits, a Wyoming coal owner awarded some $150 million because it was prohibited from strip mining in a protected area. Appeals are pending on all of these cases.

The effect of such judgments, in the words of Rhode Island Senator John Chafee, ranking Republican on the Senate Environment and Public Works Committee, "could be ruinous. The courts appear to be whittling away at the existing structure of environmental protection." Pace University law professor John Humbach calculated that in cases he studied, it cost the taxpayers "more than $60 million in 'compensation' in order to protect fewer than 1,500 acres of river bottoms and wetlands."

The individual claimants were no doubt satisfied with their windfalls, but the Wise Use alliance was after a still-bigger prize: A definitive ruling from the U.S. Supreme Court that would establish their principle of regulatory takings. It was hardly a new idea; one of the first litigants to claim compensation for regulation was a Kansas brewer put out of business in the 1880s by a state Prohibition law. The high court ruled against him.

Similarly, in *Hudson Water Company v. McCarter,* the Supreme Court ruled in 1907 that a state has the right "to protect the atmosphere, the water, and the forests within its territory, irrespective of the assent or dissent of the private owners of the land most immediately concerned." And in a 1978 case, *Penn Central v. New York,* the Court branded "quite simply untenable" the idea that property owners "may establish a 'taking' simply by showing they have been denied the ability to exploit a property interest." But the Court has also warned that "if regulation goes too far it will be recognized as a taking."

In March 1992, the Court heard oral arguments in a case that had the potential to elicit a landmark ruling on the subject. Developer David Lucas had paid about $1 million for two oceanfront lots on a South Carolina barrier island (although the land was known to have been submerged many times). Because of dangers to human lives and inland property, the South Carolina Coastal Council in 1988 prohibited permanent buildings beyond a certain setback line near the ocean. Lucas claimed the "economic viability" of his lots was destroyed and that his loss constituted a taking. In June, the Court sent the case back to the state for reconsideration. The Court also reaffirmed that property ownership is not a license to harm people and that the Constitution does not require taxpayers to pay ransom to landowners who use property to create nuisances that endanger public health or the environment.

"Private property is sacred in society," says NWF President Jay D. Hair, "but not when an individual's use of his or her property causes a neighbor's basement to flood or pesticides to concentrate in surrounding farmers' wellwater."

Ron Arnold and the so-called Wise Use alliance, says Hair, "do not understand the environmental movement, or the human values at its core. They are people who would convert our natural heritage to short-term wealth and damn the consequences." Law professor Humbach takes a similar view, calling the Wise Use alliance "the last powerful gasp of a land-use ethic that is becoming obsolete."

APPENDIX

You Can't Judge a Group by Its Cover

Some of the participants in the Wise Use campaign are actual associations of people that share beliefs, hold meetings, and sponsor events. But environmental regulations are also under attack from a different kind of entity which has few members, but which has high visibility and expensive activities.

These hybrid groups bear names that make them sound environmental, usually with the addition of a benign-sounding qualifier, such as "sensible" or "responsible." However, their aims are neither benign nor environmental. They call themselves "committees," "citizens," and "coalitions," but often are merely the creations of a public-relations agency or law firm, using funds provided by corporate clients. Some of the groups have come and gone quickly; others are more permanent. Following are examples of such groups, their public stances and real identities:

- The Information Council on the Environment (ICE) started a 1991 advertising campaign claiming Minnesota is getting colder, contrary to theories that pollution is causing global warming. When the media reported that ICE was created and funded by coal and utility companies, and that Minnesota's average temperature is rising, the ads and ICE melted away.
- The Marine Preservation Association of 15 oil companies said in its charter that what it meant by marine preservation was to "promote the welfare and interests of the petroleum and energy industries."
- The National Wetlands Coalition, on whose logo a duck flies over cattails, is a leading opponent of attempts to preserve wetlands. It is sponsored by oil and gas companies, with help from developers.
- The Environmental Conservation Association is a coalition of farm associations, industries, builders, and other developers that is lobbying U.S. officials to water down legislation protecting wetlands.
- The American Farm Bureau Federation is actually an insurance company for farmers that has developed a strong anti-environmental campaign to promote development of wetlands and public lands. It claims to represent its policy holders.
- The American Council on Science and Health, created and funded by chemical firms, argues that consumers should not be worried about the health effects of pesticides and food additives.
- Californians for Food Safety was created by the Western Agricultural Chemical Association to fight restrictions on the use of its members' products.
- Endangered Species Reform Coalition is a group sponsored by utility companies and other industries to promote efforts to weaken the Endangered Species Act.
- Nevadans for Fair Fuel Economy was created by a Washington, D.C., consulting firm, which was hired by auto makers to oppose fuel-efficiency requirements sponsored by Nevada Senator Richard Bryan.
- Alliance for a Responsible CFC Policy was initiated by chemical and petroleum companies to fight the phaseout of CFCs and to oppose limits on their CFC replacement, HCFCs, also considered harmful to the atmospheric ozone layer.
- U.S. Council on Energy Awareness spends an estimated $18 million a year to advertise the benefits of nuclear power. The money comes from utilities and reactor builders.

Stop the Greens

Business Fights Back by Hook or by Crook

Eve Pell

Can you tell what these groups do?

The Wilderness Impact Research Foundation? The Oregon Committee for Recycling? Californians for Food Safety? You might be surprised.

The Wilderness Impact Research Foundation advocates grazing and other commercial uses on public lands—lands that environmentalists want to preserve. The Oregon Committee for Recycling, an industry front, lobbied against a recycling initiative on the state ballot. Californians for Food Safety was created by the Western Agricultural Chemical Association, producers of pesticides, who successfully opposed the state's Big Green proposition in 1990.

These and other groups, sometimes funded by corporate polluters, constitute one prong of a wide-ranging counterattack against the environmental movement. With profits threatened by new demands to protect the environment, many corporations have adopted an array of tactics designed to erode the strong popular support gained by environmental, health, and consumer advocates. "I've been involved for about 10 years," said Patty Frase, who directs the Arkansas Environmental Congress. "There's no question about it; companies are getting slicker and meaner."

"Businesses have figured out how to deal with conventional environmentalists," added Will Collette, a long-time activist now working with the Citizens Coal Council in Washinton, D.C. "Just see how Big Green went down the toilet."

A spokeswoman for the U.S. Chamber of Commerce agrees that industry is striking back. "The tables have turned," said Mary Bernhard. "In the past, businesses have tried to mediate. But there's a renewed commitment now on the part of the business community to be more proactive when we are right." Businesses are now using the very techniques that environmentalists have used against them. Asks Bernhard, "Environmentalists don't like it when things turn against them, do they?"

The new business tactics range from slick and sophisticated to heavy-handed and intimidating. Worse, some environmentalists now worry that the fight against them has escalated to include violence, arson, and agents provocateurs.

MONEY TALKS

Industry's simplest method of countering the work of the green crusade is to co-opt its institutions and buy influence. In recent years, as corporate donations to environmental groups have increased, corporate executives have even turned up on those organizations' boards of directors. Critics, such as Greenpeace and many grassroots organizers, claim the corporations are trying to buy off the groups that oppose them; why else, they ask, would businesses donate to a political movement that has cost them billions of dollars in lawsuits, fines, and new regulations?

Consider the case of Waste Management Inc. (WMI), the nation's largest operator of toxic waste dumps. In 1987, when his company began giving thousands of dollars to the National Wildlife Federation (NWF), WMI's CEO, Dean Buntrock, was elected to NWF's governing board—even though WMI, a worldwide conglomerate, had an unsavory record of price fixing and millions of dollars in fines for violating environmental laws. The company appeared to profit from this environmental connection when NWF set up a cozy breakfast meeting between EPA administrator William Reilly, after which Reilly advocated a change in EPA waste disposal policy that was favored by Waste Management.

Two years later, WMI joined the influential Environmental Grantmakers Association (EGA). Since these funders help determine the strategy of the environmental movement by deciding who gets grants and who doesn't, some EGA members—who support citizens groups fighting WMI disposal sites around the country—bitterly opposed admitting the corporate giant. WMI spokesman William Y. Brown maintained at the time, "The only criterion for inclusion in the group should be a program of giving grants to environmentalists. EGA should be a diverse organization."

The struggle polarized the association, which later expelled WMI for "a pattern of abusive corporate conduct" and "endangering and degrading the environment."

But then in 1990, the grantmakers admitted Chevron, the large oil company that is a leading industrial air polluter in the San Francisco Bay area and the Los

Angeles basin. That same year, Chevron contributed more than $800,000 to defeat the Californian environmental initiative nicknamed Big Green—nearly as much money as it gave to environmentalists.

According to spokeswoman Pam Maurath, EGA has decided to let in another oil company—Arco—and now "finds no reason not to readmit Waste Management," which has applied for readmission. Some activists and foundation executives find this reprehensible. "Do people use charitable contributions to buy legitimacy?" asked Michael Picker of the Boston-based National Toxics Campaign, spoofing a controversial Chevron ad. "People do."

SLAPPS: HARASSMENT IN THE COURTS

In Squaw Valley, California, developers filed a $75 million lawsuit against daredevil skier Rick Sylvester and several others who spoke out against a planned resort. In Bowie, Maryland, a homemaker who organized opposition to a planned shopping mall faced an $8 million suit filed last May be the mall's general contractor. In New York State, the small town of North Salem was paralyzed after two developers sued the town council, its planning board, and the officers of a local citizen's group.

These are SLAPPs—Strategic Lawsuits against Public Participation—say two University of Denver law professors who have studied more than 400 of them. The professors, Penelope Canan and George Pring, note an alarming increase in such lawsuits, which are directed largely against environmentalists. SLAPPs are not mere nuisances: the average amount sought is $9 million, and the lawsuits drag on for an average of 36 months.

Some businesses seek to censor information. Shell Oil, for example, sued plumbers' union attorney Raymond Leonardini after he gave the California legislature lab tests that indicated potential health problems with Shell's plastic pipe. Leonardini advocated further testing of the product, which the company had hoped to market for use in homes.

"If Shell could have gotten a change in the plumbing code, that could have meant a *million* contracts for them," said Canan. "The corporation didn't want Leonardini to participate in the decision-making process." Not only did Shell ultimately lose the case, but Leonardini won a $5.2 million award from the company for malicious prosecution after he filed a SLAPP-back suit.

Last May, a Missouri woman who had been SLAPPed in 1988 for criticizing a medical-waste incinerator won an $86.5 million judgment against the incinerator's owner for wrongfully suing her. [*The parties settled the case prior to appeal—Eds.*]

Despite such counter-suits, the tide of SLAPPs rolls on. Rick Sylvester, the skier, explained how he felt about being sued: "It's like having a monster move in with your family."

FALSE FLAGS

In 1990, Senator Richard Bryan (D-NV) sponsored a bill that would require automakers to increase fuel efficiency. He soon began getting letters from members of a group called "Nevadans for Fair Fuel Economy," urging him to change his stand and saying that consumer demand, not government regulation, should determine how fuel-efficient vehicles ought to be.

What Bryan did not know was that "Nevadans for Fair Fuel Economy" was the brainchild of a Washington political consulting firm hired by the Big Three domestic automakers to help defeat his bill. When he found out the truth, he was furious. "Your corporate efforts, executed through this Washington-based firm, were not above board," the angry senator wrote the Big Three. "Nowhere did you say that this purported Nevada-based organization was, in truth, organized by and for the automobile manufacturers. . . . In effect, your firm came into my community under a false flag."

The use of this tactic was taken considerably further by a Jacksonville, Arkansas, company identified by the EPA as a Superfund polluter. Vertac Inc., which under its earlier name of Hercules manufactured dioxin for the Department of Defense, set up a purported citizens group in 1989. The company sponsored a raffle with prizes, taking the names and addresses of those who signed up and listing them as members of the Jacksonville People with Pride Cleanup Coalition. This new organization successfully applied for an EPA grant under a program designed to assist citizens' groups that wished to monitor Superfund site cleanups. Suspicious Jacksonville environmentalists learned of the group's corporate origins through a Freedom of Information Act request and protested to the EPA. The grant was rescinded.

BRASS KNUCKLES

"If the troubles from environmentalists cannot be solved in the jury box or at the ballot box, perhaps the cartridge box should be used." The speaker was former Interior Secretary James Watt, talking to a cattlemen's dinner in June, 1991, according to *Outside Magazine.*

William Holmes, retired president of a timber company, also delivered a vitriolic speech at a California logging conference in May 1991. Holmes called for a "Hate Them" campaign against environmentalism "with the single objective of destroying it as a political force." The campaign should be "headed up by tough street-wise gunslingers who know how to head for the jugular," he advised, exhorting his audience to make it a "fun program" and prepare to "kick somebody in the crotch." Holmes suggested that funding for this group be "disguised" so it could not be traced to the timber industry.

Such fevered rhetoric, say activists, helps to fuel a worrisome trend of threats and violence against the environmental movement. Activists in California, Arkansas, Ohio, and other states have reported "hate crimes"—offices trashed, arson, cars run off the road, rock throwing, and anonymous threats. Paula Siemers of Lower Price Hill, Ohio, has been harassed for the last two years since becoming a leader of the Urban Appalachian Council, which protests industrial air pollution there. Her house was twice set on fire and repeatedly pelted with rocks. Notes in her mailbox, she says, read, "Shut up!" and "You were warned!" In August, a gang of teenagers calling her "the pollution bitch" threw rocks at her, knocking her unconscious.

Anna Marie Stenberg of Fort Bragg, California, runs a day care center. She also works with grassroots groups opposing the logging practices of the Georgia Pacific Lumber Company there. The week of a large rally against the company, she reports, 11 timber company employees pulled their children from her day care center. Whereas once her center's capacity was full, with 50 families on a waiting list, now only four children are enrolled and Stenberg says she will soon be out of business. Stenberg says she has also received numerous death threats over the phone and once found a Molotov cocktail on her doorstep.

Greenpeace researcher Pat Costner no longer even has a doorstep. When she returned to her home in Eureka Springs, Arkansas, she found only a smoldering ruin. Costner, an expert on the effects of toxic chemicals, has been conducting and gathering research for 15 years. Greenpeace was about to publish a report she had written against waste incineration entitled, ironically, "Playing with Fire."

"This was a hit at Greenpeace," charges Sheila O'Donnell, a private investigator hired by the organization. "We found a gas can and evidence that it was arson." Later, after Costner had moved into a trailer on the site, her telephone line was cut. The search for a suspect continues.

SOWING DISSENSION?

Adrienne Anderson, a community organizer, has worked with neighborhoods hit by corporate pollution for 16 years. She now runs the Denver office of the National Toxics Campaign and never lacks for problems. Areas of Denver have been badly contaminated by lethal substances—including radioactive waste, solvents, and other toxic byproducts of weapons production. Some communities believe that these substances have caused cancer clusters and other health effects, so residents have filed lawsuits against Martin Marietta Corporation and Rockwell International, seeking compensation. [The Martin Marietta suit was dismissed and the Rockwell International suit ended in a settlement—ed.] Yet Anderson has not achieved success with the National Toxics Campaign. "Here, there is always something weird," she said. "We can't build a mass-based movement." She has been harassed, she says, by thefts from her office, mysterious power outages, and associates who turn against her. Though Anderson cannot prove it, she believes that infiltrators paid by industry have mounted a counter-organizing effort to sabotage her work. In late August, she reports, her director of canvassing received two telephoned death threats. The National Toxics Campaign hired private investigator Bob Carey of Boston, who found troubling leads but thus far no proof.

THE COUNTER COUNTER-OFFENSIVE

Whether or not corporations are perpetrating violence, one thing is certain: many American businesses, whose profits are threatened both by foreign competition and by demands to protect the environment, are fighting back hard. And environmentalists now have to respond with SLAPP-back suits, private investigators, and publicity to embarrass corporations that have set up bogus citizen's groups.

Robin Lee Zeff and Peter Montague of the Environmental Research Foundation in Washington, D.C., have created a pool of information about "corporate bad actors" for use by community environmental groups.

"The corporations can't win by arguing technical issues any more," said Zeff. "People know the problems with landfills and incinerators. So if corporations can't get what they want by being honest, then they play dirty."

Land Mine

Margaret Kriz

Tammy Johnson had a touch of bitterness in her voice as she talked about the state and national environmental organizations that are waging a legal battle to stop the expansion of the Golden Sunlight Mine in her hometown of White-hall, Montana.

"The company had gone through the public meetings and all of the permitting process to expand the mine," Johnson, whose husband works as an electrician at the mine, recalled in an interview. "A lot of us had put our lives on hold waiting to see if the permit would be issued. When it was, we did things like buy cars, remodel our homes."

At the eleventh hour, however, the National Wildlife Federation and two local environmental groups went to court to short-circuit Vancouver-based Placer Dome Inc.'s plans to enlarge its open-pit gold mine. The environmental groups charged in a lawsuit that the company's mining operation had allowed millions of gallons of cyanide-laced water to leach into the ground and would disturb a 4.5-square-mile region of the Bull Mountains. The lawsuit, which aims to force the company to conduct an environmental impact study, is pending.

The mining families were fearful that they might lose the main source of employment in their southwestern Montana community and angry that they'd become pawns in a legal tug-of-war. They channeled their frustration into forming their own organization, Citizens for a Responsible Environment, and joined the lawsuit as interveners on behalf of the mining company.

"At first we formed the group just as a knee-jerk reaction to this lawsuit," Johnson, who's the group's vice president, said. "But once we got involved, we discovered just a whole world out there we didn't know existed. We started paying attention to a lot of the political issues surrounding not only mining, but other natural resource industries. What we discovered was that in the whole environmental debate, the human element was being left out."

In trying to protect her husband's job, Johnson became an activist in a burgeoning new land rights movement, sometimes broadly referred to as the Wise

Use movement, which contends that jobs and property rights are more important than environmental protection.

Organizing in rural communities across the nation, the land rights movement is strongest in regions where environmental activists have been blamed for
undermining—or even wrecking—local economies.

"The people see environmental policy as promoting a massive land grab to
shut down all natural resource use, first on the federal lands and increasingly on
the private lands," R. J. Smith, a visiting scholar at the conservative Competitive Enterprise Institute who's working with the Wise Use groups, said in an interview.

Local communities are becoming politically active "because the federal regulatory regime on public and private lands is in the process of putting whole industries out of business or damaging them severely," said Myron Ebell, the
Washington representative of the American Land Rights Association and the
National Inholders Association, two Wise Use groups that organize at the
grassroots level.

Johnson has now taken on national issues, campaigning against legislation to
amend the 1872 Mining Act that would require miners to pay royalties on minerals extracted from federal lands and would establish environmental cleanup
standards for mining companies. She has traveled to the nation's capital to fight
efforts to designate 1.6 million acres of Montana lands as wilderness, off-limits
to development. And her group is actively opposing the reintroduction of
wolves into Yellowstone National Park.

Grassroots groups such as Johnson's are the most visible part of a growing
and far-flung network of local citizens' organizations, industry-financed lobbying committees, and conservative think tanks and legal foundations that are
pressing for sweeping changes in the way government seeks to protect the
environment.

The conservative-backed land rights movement is made of hundreds—
maybe even thousands—of local, regional, and national organizations, most of
them based in the western United States. Some of the organizations—the
American Farm Bureau Federation and the Idaho Mining Association, for example—are clearly financed by regulated industries. Others survive on the contributions of local citizens who work at companies or in industries that are affected by federal environmental laws and regulations.

Here are brief profiles of some of the organizations that are pushing for the
continued commercial use of federal lands and the expansion of private property rights.

Alliance for America. Organized in 1991, this national umbrella organization of land and property rights groups holds an annual Washington lobbying

campaign for its 400 members, which include everything from the National Cattlemen's Association to the Adirondack Park and Local Government Review Board. Most of its key officials also work for member organizations or trade associations. Its 1993 budget is $115,000.

Blue Ribbon Coalition. This national organization, which represents manufacturers of off-road recreational vehicles, also lobbies on behalf of the mining, oil, and timber industries. It opposes designating additional federal lands as wilderness areas and wants the federal government to finance more dirt bike trails in national parks. The coalition is based in Pocatello, Idaho, and is said to have 500,000 members. Nearly half of its $185,000 annual budget comes from Japanese manufacturers of off-road vehicles.

National Inholders Association. This Battle Ground, Washington-based organization was founded in 1978 by Charles Cushman to protect the rights of "inholders" who own land in or near national parks and forests. The association, which puts its membership at 16,000, declines to release financial information. Its claim to fame is Cushman himself, a flamboyant speaker and community organizer who's wet-nursed dozens of state and local land rights groups.

Oregon Lands Coalition. The Salem-based coalition is among the largest of the regional land rights groups, with 80,000 members and 61 chapters— many of them linked to agricultural, ranching, and timber interests—and an annual budget of $145,000. Having cut its teeth during the battle over preserving the forest habitats of the northern spotted owl in the Pacific Northwest, the coalition champions efforts to limit federal protections for endangered species.

Western States Public Lands Coalition/People for the West! The best-financed of the conservative-backed land rights groups, the coalition and its subsidiary were formed by mining companies in an effort to improve their industry's public image. The Pueblo, Colorado-based coalition, which has 200 corporate members and an annual budget of $1.7 million, is currently fighting efforts to strengthen the 1872 Mining Act. It's also helping to organize grassroots groups in communities that are dependent on grazing, logging, and mining on federal lands.

The crusade is far broader than the Sagebrush Rebellion of the 1970s, the ranchers' movement that petered out after President Reagan took office. It reaches into groups that represent farming, fishing, logging, mining, oil and natural gas, ranching, recreation, and real estate interests.

The land rights movement is also tapping into a growing distrust of the federal government and a belief that environmental activists have gone too far in protecting animals and plants. It is feeding—and feeding on—the fears of workers and homeowners that they might lose their jobs and land as a result of what they see as extremist environmental protection laws, according to Don Judge, the executive secretary of the Montana AFL–CIO.

"The folks in the Wise Use movement would really like to portray this as a great debate between jobs and the environment," Judge said in an interview. "It's essentially a corporate-funded effort to drive a wedge between the workers and environmentalists. They're taking advantage of people's genuine and legitimate fear of economic dislocation."

LEARNING FROM THEIR ENEMIES

If it's true that imitation is the sincerest form of flattery, the leaders of the nation's major environmental organizations ought to be blushing these days.

For two decades, the nation's biggest environmental groups used emotional public education campaigns, grassroots organizations, and a seemingly endless barrage of lawsuits to win over the public to their causes. But in recent years, surveys show, they have increasingly come to be perceived as catering to a largely urban, well-to-do constituency that wants to preserve western public lands as their summer playgrounds.

In the meantime, the land rights movement has turned to grassroots organizing—the stock-in-trade of its adversaries—in an effort to overturn some landmark environmental protection victories. Its campaign is built on the environmental community's Achilles' heel: its seeming disregard for the economic and human costs of aggressive environmental protection measures.

"Honest to God, these environmentalists don't have any concept of where their clothing comes from or their food or housing," Harry McIntosh, a vice president of Alliance for America, said in an interview. "They don't understand that we need these extractive industries."

But Judge argues that extremism is a two-way street. "There's a legitimate argument to be made that the environmental extremists are not concerned about the impact their actions have on workers in the communities," he said. "But just as clearly there are those out there whose agenda is profit, and they're exploiting the concern that workers have about the long-term stability of their communities and their jobs."

When the land rights movement emerged in the late 1980s, environmental activists belittled it as an industry-financed flash-in-the-pan. In the past five years, however, the movement has exploded throughout the nation as hundreds of new, grassroots groups have been organized, with some of them scoring legal and legislative victories at the state and federal levels.

The movement has been further energized by Interior Secretary Bruce E. Babbitt's push to strengthen federal controls on mining, grazing, and logging on federal lands. Much as former Interior Secretary James G. Watt's radical proposals invigorated the environmental community during the Reagan administration, Babbitt is being portrayed by many land rights groups as the Clinton administration bogeyman who's hell-bent on shutting down industries that use federal lands.

The environmental community is waking up to the challenge just as leaders of the land rights movement are mounting a broad campaign to rewrite federal environmental laws that they contend harm citizens' economic well-being and violate their constitutional property rights.

The land rights activists plan to flex their lobbying muscle not only on western lands legislation, but also on dozens of other environmental issues awaiting Congressional action—everything from wetlands protection to the Superfund law. They are aligning themselves with conservative lawmakers in both parties and with sympathetic lawmakers from western states. "The people who belong to the Wise Use and property rights movement vote overwhelmingly conservative, and that's generally Republican," Ebell said. "The movement is much stronger across rural America. It's in public-lands states in the West."

Some land rights groups, including Alliance for America, a national umbrella organization, also vow to become more active in the 1994 Congressional elections. They take credit, for example, for having helped to unseat Rep. Jim Jontz (D-Ind.), a vocal advocate of environmental protection measures, in 1992.

FORGING A UNITED FRONT

Encouraged, organized, and, in some cases, financed by industry, the land rights groups generally fall into two categories: those that promote private property rights and those that support resource extraction on public lands. But the two wings of the movement have begun to join forces in lobbying Washington, presenting a unified front that is fast developing into a political force.

The property rights groups, most of them based east of the Mississippi River, argue that environmental activists and overzealous government regulators have used federal laws and regulations to take private land without adequately compensating property owners. They want to expand the rights of property owners to gain compensation when the government restricts the use of their lands.

"It's an attractive mom-and-apple-pie argument," said John Echeverria, a lawyer for the National Audubon Society. "I don't think there is any fair-minded American who doesn't respect private property rights. But in this case, their objective isn't to protect property, but to stop the government from regulating the land."

In early October, property rights groups were instrumental in weakening legislation that seeks to establish a national biological survey to map the country's native animals, plants, and ecosystems. Opponents of the survey, which is one of Babbitt's pet projects, contend that it would be used to indentify endangered species and to stop private property owners from developing their land.

"The national biological survey is obviously an attempt to create the data that is going to be used to regulate endangered species protection, grazing, wetlands, and to affect other public land management issues," Rep. W. J. (Billy) Tauzin (D-La.), who championed some of the amendments favored by the property rights groups, said in an interview.

Property rights groups are also taking the lead in pushing legislation that would dramatically change the 1973 Endangered Species Act and federal wetlands protections.

The other wing of the movement, which includes Johnson's Montana mining workers group, argues that the Clinton administration is threatening their lifestyles by trying to restrict grazing, logging, mining, recreation, and other activities on federal lands. It began in the Pacific Northwest, in communities that have been the sites of battles between environmental activists and the timber industry over logging in national forests that are home to the endangered northern spotted owl.

FISH STORIES

In 1986, the Klamath Indian Tribe, supported by the Oregon Natural Resource Council, an environmental group, petitioned the Interior Department's Fish and Wildlife Service to list two fish—the short-nose sucker and the Lost River sucker—as threatened or endangered species, eligible for special federal protection under the Endangered Species Act. The fish live in a handful of waterways, including Klamath Lake and the Klamath River, that run between southern Oregon and northern California.

The council's routine request triggered a series of actions that continue to send shock waves through the national environmental community.

In response to the council's request, the Interior Department's Fish and Wildlife Service agreed to add the fish to its list of protected plants and wildlife species. Once the fish were granted federal protection, Interior's Bureau of Reclamation moved to guard their dwindling populations by cutting the amount of water that farmers and ranchers could divert from the waterways.

That didn't sit well with Marion F. Palmer, a farmer in Modoc County, California, who relies on water from the Klamath River to irrigate his crops. Less water meant smaller profits. Blaming his smaller profits on the Oregon Natural Resource Council, Palmer sued the group for $40,000.

Palmer's lawsuit charges that the council provided federal regulators with false and distorted information on the fish and that its officers acted "to deceive the general public and to extract [financial] contributions."

The case, which is pending in the Modoc County Superior Court, is a vivid example of the creative tactics that property owners are adopting to fight environmental activists and federal environmental protection laws.

A group of Wise Use activists also showed up at the Oregon Natural Resource Council's recent annual meeting, taking pictures of speakers and the audience and tape-recording speeches. "They're taking a lot of the tactics used by grassroots environmentalists and turning them against people like us," Jim Middaugh, a spokesman for the council, said.

The Oregon Lands Coalition, for example, sponsors workshops that aim to teach Wise Use activists "how to beat national environmental groups at their own dirty little game." A recent seminar included "pit bull" sessions on using injunctions to stop environmentalists and writing "intent to sue" letters to government agencies and environmental groups.

Many land rights activists, however, don't openly advocate such radical approaches. The 400 representatives who descended on Washington in September as part of the Alliance for America's "Fly in for Freedom," for example, preached moderation, not extremism. "We are for taking into account the social and economic factors in making environmental decisions," said Kathy Kvanda of the California Forestry Association, who coordinated the lobbying effort. "We are certainly not for seeing any species go extinct or our history, through the national parks, disappear."

And many local land rights groups are seeking to distance themselves, at least publicly, from the founders of the Wise Use movement and its most vitriolic speakers, such as Ron Arnold, whose Center for the Defense of Free Enterprise is the movement's premier think tank and training center, and Charles Cushman, the executive director of the National Inholders Association. Cushman's group, which was formed to represent "inholders" who own property within or next to national parks, operates a massive communications network and helps to organize local community activists.

Despite their efforts to cast themselves as moderates, many land rights activists clearly harbor a dark view of their adversaries. McIntosh of the Alliance for America warned that environmental activists "are working to bring their brand of socialism to the forefront because they've got a lot of people in the administration." And several others joked that environmentalists are like watermelons: green on the outside and red—Communist—on the inside.

National environmental organizations have responded to the threat by publicizing evidence that some of the land rights groups are heavily financed by conservative and corporate interests. But they say that the money trail is often difficult to trace because companies and industry groups frequently mask their financial involvement by paying for the professionals who organize at the grassroots level and by underwriting activists' trips to Washington.

By the time the professional organizers have come in and defined the nature of the issues, local people believe that they're fighting for their jobs," said an investigator for a think tank that's tracking the land rights movement. "When people believe that's what's going on, you bet they're going to be committed to the cause."

Both Greenpeace and the Wilderness Society have helped to finance analyses of the land rights groups, which Greenpeace refers to as "anti-environmental organizations."

The National Audubon Society highlighted the struggle between the environmental and land rights movements in a public television special it produced titled *Backlash in the Wild*. The report included a dramatic segment on a New Hampshire property rights group's drive to stop the federal government from classifying a local river as "wild and scenic" and thus eligible for special government protection.

REBELLION OR REVOLUTION?

The land rights activists and their adversaries agree on at least one thing: that the movement has the potential to spill out of the environmental arena.

The Montana AFL-CIO's Judge, for example, fears that the movement has a hidden agenda. "We see this as a broad issue," he said. "The folks that have been involved in the Wise Use movement are also people or corporations that have been promoting politicians and policies that are detrimental to workers, not just on issues of environment but on issues like worker compensation, unemployment compensation, taxation, and public employees."

That view is shared by Jack Sheehan, the legislative director of the United Steelworkers of America. Sheehan described attempts to force the government to compensate landowners when it restricts the use of private property as "an effort to oppose the regulatory activities of the federal government in the environment area and the workplace."

On the other hand, Bruce Yandle, a professor of economics at Clemson University, predicted that the conservative-backed movement is ushering in the next generation of land rights controls in the United States—and potentially the return to the common-law approach of protecting the environment.

Under that philosophy, which is embraced by conservatives and libertarians, individuals whose rights to clean water or air have been violated must directly sue the offending polluters for violating their property rights—that is, their right to a clean environment.

"I have more faith in judges and juries to protect property rights," Yandle said. "It's a cleaner process outside of the political arena."

For the land rights rebellion to turn into a full-fledged political revolution, however, its leaders will have to win the hearts and minds of people who now look to the movement only for solutions to local problems.

"People didn't really have an outlet before this," Johnson said in explaining why her Montana citizens group has attracted so much attention. But she added that most Americans find neither extreme acceptable.

"I think what's missing," Johnson said, "is that the country can't do without natural resources or the environment."

The "Property Rights" Revolt

Environmentalists Fret as States Pass Reagan-Style Takings Laws

Marianne Lavelle

The cowboy caucus had a friend in the White House with Ronald Reagan and later with his trailmate George Bush. But when the Republicans rode off into the sunset, the caucus took matters into its own hands.

The cowboys planted their feet in Utah's capital, Salt Lake City, and in March threw a rope around the desert tortoise and all other endangered species that would tread on plans for real estate development in the state's scenic southwest.

In the past 10 months, three states—Utah being the most recent—have passed the kind of legislation that the true believers of the Reagan–Bush era only dreamed about. Utah followed neighbor Arizona and a state on a moister frontier, Delaware, in adopting laws that attempt to rein in environmental regulation. And in 23 other state capitals this year, virtually identical bills have been introduced—most of them for the first time.

These bills fight the growth of green regulations using a concept developed by the legal theorists of the Reagan revolution—the idea that government restrictions to protect land, air, and water are tantamount to condemnation. The theory is that environmental regulations often amount to takings of private property as defined by the Fifth Amendment of the U.S. Constitution, and property owners who are thus deprived are entitled to compensation from the taxpayers.

Neither the Reagan nor Bush administrations ever fully succeeded in turning this idea into a bona fide government program, although President Reagan did sign an executive order calling for takings assessments of all governmental regulations in 1988, which has had a limited impact.

Congress repeatedly has rejected legislation that would codify the executive order. And in the courts, the private property movement has little success winning rulings that support its interpretation of the Constitution. The advent of the Clinton administration, of course, has reduced the likelihood that additional sympathetic judges will be appointed to the bench or that presidential clout will help move a federal bill through Congress.

Local environmentalists admit that in some cases, the state bills—garnering support with difficult-to-bash titles like "The Private Property Rights Act"— have caught them by surprise.

"The best I know is this is 100 percent grassroots activity by all kinds of people that have property interests," says John J. Rademacher, general counsel of the American Farm Bureau Federation, whose members support takings legislation because they often are prevented by environmental regulations from making changes to their land or selling it for development.

The seeds of this movement, however, are being planted in a nationally coordinated way, with the help of such conservative Washington, D.C.-based groups as the American Legislative Exchange Council and Defenders of Property Rights. "What we're seeing is a concerted, multifaceted effort to use the state forum to pursue the anti-environmental agenda," says John D. Echeverria, chief legal counsel of the National Audubon Society.

CITY VERSUS COUNTRY

Only a few states have considered takings legislation before this year—such as Maryland, surrounded on one side by the policy machine of Washington, D.C., and on the other side, by the environmentally precarious Chesapeake Bay. In April, the Maryland bill died in committee for the third time.

Utah, on the other hand, never had taken up the issue until its lawmakers and governor considered and endorsed the bill within the short span of the 45-day legislative season of 1993. The political climate was ripe in Salt Lake City, where one-third of the state House turned over with the November election, and tension between the rural ranching counties and the populous urban areas has reached a fevered pitch.

A vocal minority of new representatives from the state's rural counties, calling themselves the "Cowboy Caucus," succeeded in cutting city project spending and in giving ranchers more freedom to shoot the wildlife that prey on their animals or crops. But it was around another issue that Cowboy Caucus leader Met Johnson, a Republican rancher, built his campaign last year. He promised to obtain passage of a "Private Property Rights" bill.

"The impact of these federal regulations has been terrible on our lifestyle, custom, culture, and economic stability," says Mr. Johnson. "And the state has followed suit, to our dismay."

In Mr. Johnson's corner of Utah near the town of St. George, connected to Las Vegas and Los Angeles by an interstate highway, plans for big real estate development have been limited by enforcement of laws such as the Endangered Species Act. Particularly galling to landowners was that Utah's own Division of Wildlife Resources opted during the past several years to protect from development 20,000 more acres than the federal government said were necessary to preserve the habitat of the desert tortoise and the region's unique plant life.

The new law can't undo the protections Utah already has put into place for the desert tortoise and plants, says Mr. Johnson, but it could make it difficult to take similar steps in the future.

"LOOK BEFORE YOU LEAP"

The bills passed in Utah, Arizona, and Delaware are the milder of two forms of takings legislation under consideration in state capitals across the nation. Modeled on the Reagan executive order, this type requires state agencies to study whether they risk liability under the takings clause of the Fifth Amendment before they undertake any new regulatory program. The approach mimics the mechanism of the original green law, the National Environmental Policy Act, which since 1970 has required federal agencies to study the potential environmental impact of all their major programs.

"I have a hard time seeing why anone would object to this type of statute—it's really a 'look-before-you-leap' law," says Nancie G. Marzulla, general counsel of the D.C.-based Defenders of Property Rights, whose husband, Roger, was one of the principal architects of the Reagan administration's takings policy under Attorney General Edwin Meese. "It's not setting new standards," she says. "It's reflecting the law as it is."

The main developments in the law to which Ms. Marzulla refers have occurred in the U.S. Claims Court in Washington, led by Reagan-appointed Chief Judge Loren A. Smith, who has stated publicly that he believes the takings clause was meant to provide a check on government regulatory programs. The biggest case, *Whitney Benefits Inc. v. U.S.,* 926 F.2d 1169 (1991), resulted in a $60 million judgment against the government.

But environmentalists say that outside of the Claims Court decisions of the past few years, the courts repeatedly have found that states have the power to regulate private property in the public interest for goals such as environmental protection, historic preservation, and human rights.

And, in a disappointment to private property rights advocates in what was facially a favorable decision, Justice Antonin Scalia in 1992 left the door open for government regulations that diminish private property value substantially— as long as they are rooted in the principles of nuisance law (*Lucas v. South Carolina Coastal Commission,* 112 S. Ct. 2886). The 5–4 majority that voted for this limitation on regulation is precarious, because of Justice Byron R. White's retirement and because Justice Anthony M. Kennedy's concurrence said that the nuisance law standard was "too narrow a confine for the exercise of regulatory power in a complex and interdependent society."

Mr. Echeverria of the Audubon Society says that the Reagan executive order and the takings laws now being considered in the states ignore this background. "The existence of these proposals has had an influence on people's understanding or belief of what the takings clause means," says Mr. Echeverria. "And they are based on an interpretation of the takings clause that is inconsistent with existing law."

A RADICAL PROJECT?

Even former Solicitor General Charles Fried, now at Harvard Law School, viewed the effort by his former Justice Department colleagues to use the takings clause as an "aggressive, and it seemed to me, quite radical project," he said in his 1991 memoir.

"The grand plan was to make the government pay compensation as for a taking of property every time its regulations impinged too severely on a property right," Mr. Fried wrote. "If the government labored under so severe an obligation, there would be, to say the least, much less regulation."

The Reagan-era takings advocates are continuing their work—but now as advisers to the state capitals: Ms. Marzulla and her husband, Roger, along with his former special assistant in the Meese Justice Department, Mark Pollot, now of the San Francisco office of Chicago's Keck, Mahin & Cate, and University of Chicago conservative economics and law theorist Richard Epstein.

Mr. Pollot, who drafted the Reagan order, says that private property rights advocates around the country have been concerned with the idea of protecting the order—which, because Congress has never given it the force of law, can be eliminated at any time by President Clinton's pen.

50 PERCENT SOLUTION

But Mr. Pollot and other takings law advocates are pushing for state legislatures to go a step further than the executive order. He has drafted a new, stronger proposed takings law at the request of the American Legislative Exchange Council, a D.C.-based organization of state legislators who call themselves pro-business and pro-free enterprise, and who claim 2,400 members.

The idea is that a property owner should be able automatically to obtain compensation if he or she can show that his or her land lost 50 percent of its value as a result of a new zoning law, or wetlands regulation, wildlife habitat preservation plan, or other regulation. The federal courts never have established any "trigger point," and in fact, Justice Scalia said in *Lucas* that a 95 percent loss of property value still may not constitute a taking—depending upon the facts of the case.

"The court has refused to set down principles governing what constitutes a taking, and with every case it does this ad hoc analysis," says Mr. Pollot. "We all agree that if you have a 30-acre parcel of land, and the government wants to build a government office building on 10 of those acres, there's no question it has to condemn those 10 acres and pay you the fair market value. How do you get to the situation where when there's a wetland on 10 of those 30 acres, and the government wants it set aside so we can enjoy it and takes away the other uses of the land, that the property owner doesn't have to be paid the market value?"

Environmentalists strenuously oppose the 50 percent idea as a major expansion in the concept of takings as it has developed in the courts, and one that could result in a flood of claims against the government that would most certainly put a brake on regulation. "You can always find an appraiser who will say your land would have been worth so much," says Glenn Sugameli, counsel to the National Wildlife Federation.

The model "50 percent" bill has been introduced in 10 states, including coastal Delaware, which already passed the milder takings bill last year. In Arizona, takings advocates hope to introduce the "50 percent" bill, because implementation of the weaker bill passed last June is on hold at least until 1994. Environmentalists there, originally caught by surprise by the speed with which the bill moved through the legislature, succeeded in garnering 50,000 names within 90 days of its passage to petition for a statewide referendum on what they have labeled "the worst anti-environmental law ever passed in the United States."

Mr. Rademacher of the Farm Bureau, which fought for the Arizona law and others, responds to the charge by saying, "There's a claim that the environment will suffer if you let people use their land lawfully, the way they want to.

"These state laws are saying we are going to pay strict attention to constitutional requirements of compensation," he says. "It may be that it takes a legislative act such as that in Arizona to get the attention of government in this present day of regulatory excess."

Environmentalists believe bills like this send a quite different message.

Says Dana Larson of Arizona Common Cause, which is fighting for repeal of the state's new takings law, "Because a lot of [conservatives'] access at the federal government has been lost, they realize that if they are going to have success on these kinds of deregulatory issues, it's going to be on the state level. And a lot of times, the states are unprepared, and unaware of what the agenda's full and real impact is likely to be."

II

Conservation Leaders
Speak Out

Some have dismissed the Wise Use movement as extremist and lacking in credibility and genuine grassroots support. Others perceive its leaders as effective organizers on behalf of an anti-environmental agenda. In either case, most environmental leaders and other thoughtful commentators see the Wise Use movement as a demonstration of the need to reaffirm, rejuvenate, and broaden the traditional environmental movement.

The boom-and-bust character of western resource development and the historical origins of the Wise Use movement are the focus of T. H. Watkins' "Wise Use Discouragements and Clarifications." Watkins, editor of The Wilderness Society's *Wilderness*, describes what he sees as the shallow public support for the Wise Use movement and argues against "untrammeled" private access to public resources.

In "People for the West!—Challenges and Opportunities," a speech delivered in September 1991 to the annual convention of the Montana Wilderness Association, Jim Baca, former New Mexico Land Commissioner and former director of the Federal Bureau of Land Management, expresses alarm at the rise of People for the West! as the chief advocate for western mining firms. Borrowing the tactics of the environmental movement, People for the West!, according to Baca, has done an effective job of rallying grassroots support for the outdated Mining Act of 1872.

Creating a positive, credible conservation message is the topic of a speech to the 1992 annual meeting of the Natural Resources Council of America by James Gustave Speth, former president of the World Resources Institute and current director of the U.N. Environmental Program. He contends that the time is ripe for a new phase in the development of environmental policy and action.

Change in the environmental community's agenda and message is the focus of "Taking Back the Rural West," by Philip Brick of Whitman College. Brick argues against the traditional wilderness ethic and calls for a more inclusive natural resource conservation strategy. Instead of fighting legal battles in win/lose situations that polarize communities, take years to settle, and cost millions of dollars, he contends that conservationists should negotiate solutions that meet citizens' real needs and in the process rebuild the grassroots support for conservation.

Wise Use

Discouragements and Clarifications

T. H. Watkins

Ron Arnold makes no bones about it: he would like to eviscerate every environmental organization in the United States. "We're going to put you guys out of business," he warned the environmental community on network television in April of 1992. "We're going to take your money and members away from you." Arnold, president of the Center for the Defense of Free Enterprise, may sound a little ridiculous when he lets loose with outbursts like that, but he is just one of the noisiest of many leaders who speak for the newest incarnation of an old and dangerous impulse in America—an attempt to cloak the exploitation of the natural world in the garb of "free enterprise" and concern for "ordinary Americans," a movement that already has done a lot of damage and will continue to do a lot of damage before it inevitably collapses under the weight of its own excess. Until then, the movement has found a good horse and intends to ride it until it drops.

This time around it is called the Wise Use movement, and it travels under a lot of high-sounding names: Center for the Defense of Free Enterprise, People for the West!, Multiple Use Land Alliance, National Wetlands Coalition, The Blue Ribbon Coalition, and many more—about 250 more, in fact. Generally right-wing in its political leanings, with a touch of fundamentalism thrown in for good measure, the movement is supported, both philosophically and financially, by such corporate interests as the mining, timber, petroleum, livestock, and agribusiness industries. Waving the flags of economic freedom and rugged individualism and decrying the "oppression" of government regulation, the leading lights of this ideological adventure have been shouting that an orgy of ultraliberal concern for land and wildlife has stifled economic growth, obliterated jobs, and otherwise enfeebled the American Way. It is time, they say, to take the government off the public lands, get it out of the business of regulating private-land use, and free the people to pursue their happiness unhindered by the dead hand of Washington's extreme environmentalists.

Despite their unmistakable corporate connections, Wise Use leaders like to celebrate their emergence as a true social movement, a widespread grassroots response to economic and cultural tyranny. They would like us to think that their movement has the same kind of validity as the explosion of populism in the Midwest of the 1890s or the Ghost Dance excitement among Native Americans during the 1880s, when a Paiute shaman called Wovoka led a widespread and short-lived nativist movement that believed that the Indians, armed only with ritualistic dances and rites and shielded only by "holy" shirts that were invulnerable to bullets, ultimately would rise up and take their ancestral lands back from the white invaders.

Unfortunately, the comparison of today's Wise Use movement to such a genuine, if tragic, expression of nativist anguish would be odious—valid only if the American textile industry had organized the Ghost Dance effort, manufactured and sold the holy shirts to Wovoka and his followers, then carried him and his people around the West by bus to spread the word. (The final destination, of course, would have been Wounded Knee Creek, South Dakota.) In fact, there is little that could be described as "grassroots" about the current movement. It is, instead, a spectacularly cynical and self-serving manipulation of human fears and uncertainties in the name of greed—corporate greed, for the most part.

Nor is there anything new about the movement, save for its glaze of sophistication and professionalism. Both its philosophy, which is pretty thin, and its press releases, which are pretty thick, are part and parcel of an old antagonism between the "boomers," who would use up the natural resources of this nation for short-term gain, and those who insist on having a decent respect for the long-term health and prosperity of all Americans. It is a phenomenon that has affected land-use decisions in many parts of the country, from the remaining forestlands of northern New England to the eroding barrier islands of the mid-Atlantic coast; but it is in the states of the trans-Mississippi West where the flames of battle have been most visible, past and present.

In 1878, for example, government explorer and naturalist Major John Wesley Powell concluded more than a decade of study in the poorly watered regions west of the one-hundredth meridian. He published his findings in one of the most important documents in our history: *Report on the Lands of the Arid Region of the United States.* In this report, Powell pointed out the simple fact that there was not and never would be enough water in the West to sustain the dreams of growth that western politicians and corporate adventurers entertained, and that such land laws as the Homestead Act of 1862 were unworkable in a land of aridity. Neither idea was greeted with enthusiasm by the boomers of his day, nor did they like it much when Powell was appointed director of the

U.S. Geological Survey and closed most of the public lands of the West in order to conduct a survey of potential areas that might (or might not) be irrigated as part of a careful plan of regional development. The boomers' best friend in Congress, Senator William ("Big Bill") Stewart of Nevada, promptly persuaded his colleagues to gut Powell's budget for both the irrigation survey and the Geological Survey itself.

For another example, it was boomers like Stewart and his friends who rose up in outrage when President Grover Cleveland, acting on the advice of an 1896 forest commission, established 21 million acres of new forest reserves, on which all mining, timbering, and other exploitive uses were forbidden. The act was, the *Cheyenne Tribune* trumpeted, "a dangerous and ridiculous farce"; the *Denver Republican* headlined its story "A Menace to the Interests of the Western States" and the *San Francisco Chronicle* insisted that the whole idea of forest reserves was the notion of "wiseacres" and "amiable theorists." This early version of the charge of "elitism," which would become so much a part of the rhetoric of our own time, had its desired effect: Congress managed to subvert the President's action by sundry legislative devices.

It was the same breed of boomers who, at the turn of the century, railed (vainly, this time) against Chief Forester Gifford Pinchot when he insisted on protecting the timber in the national forests from rapacious cut-and-run loggers who cheerfully would have stripped the mountains clean. They howled again when Pinchot refused to let cattlemen and sheepmen graze the mountain meadows and foothill grasslands down to the nubbin.

It was the boomers who cried "socialism" when the Reclamation Act of 1902 stipulated that federally funded irrigation water in the West would be made available only to small family farms. And it was the boomers who bent the law to their own ends, using it to water corporate farms the size of small European countries—factories in the field nurtured by taxpayer water and harvested by cheap imported labor.

It was the boomers who told President Herbert Hoover in 1929 that the public lands of the West not already in national forests or national parks should be turned over to the states. Hoover agreed. The individual states, he said,

> *are today more competent to manage [these lands] than is the Federal Government. . . . For the best interests of the people as a whole, and people of the western states and the small farmers and stockmen by whom they are primarily used, they should be managed and the policies for their use determined by state governments.*

That the state governments in question had been in the pockets of the livestock industry for decades ensured that any such management would allow cattlemen and sheepmen to use the land pretty much as they wished; and since the industry had never demonstrated the slightest interest in the long-term health of the land when balanced against the opportunity to make as much money as possible as swiftly as possible by running as many cattle and sheep as possible on as much of the land as possible as often as possible, the American grasslands almost certainly would have been obliterated within a generation or two.

The New Deal of Franklin Roosevelt arrived before Congress could finish deliberation on various bills of transfer, and the New Dealers, chief among them Interior Secretary Harold Ickes, were firm believers in the doctrine of federal ownership, federal management, and long-term stewardship. The boomers were not silenced by the arrival of the New Deal, but they were generally muffled during the next thirteen years, until Roosevelt was dead and Ickes was out.

At which point they arose again, punctuating the postwar Congresses with cries that both the lands of which Hoover had spoken and the entire national forest system should be given to the states. This time, they ran up against a buzzsaw in the form of journalist Bernard DeVoto, a transplanted westerner who occupied the "Easy Chair" column of *Harper's* magazine and knew a boomer's scam when he saw one. Even as Senator Allan Robertson of Wyoming introduced land-transfer legislation in Congress in January 1947, DeVoto launched a major attack in the pages of the magazine:

> *The public lands are first to be transferred to the states on the fully justi-fied assumption that if there should be a state government not wholly com-pliant to the desires of stockgrowers, it could be pressured into compliance. The intention is to free them of all regulation except such as stockgrowers might impose upon themselves. Nothing in history suggests that the states are adequate to protect their own resources, or even want to, or suggests that cattlemen and sheepmen are capable of regulating themselves. . . . And the larger intention is to liquidate all the publicly held reserves of the West.*

The boomers failed again; the pressure against the proposal engineered by DeVoto and a small army of conservationists was too much for Congress to resist. The boomers were defeated yet again when the proposal was raised once more in 1948, and again in the mid-1950s, when proposals to build hydroelectric and irrigation dams that would have flooded much of Dinosaur National Monument came up against an increasingly sophisticated and vig-orous opposition.

But, as Wallace Stegner has written, "There are discouragements as well as clarifications to be found in the study of history. It demonstrates with precision who the adversaries are. Always are." The boomers did not go away; instead, they rose up once again with the arrival of President Ronald Reagan, and his team of trickle-down, free-market economists. Trailing soon after came Interior Secretary James Gaius Watt, who during his confirmation hearings gave us the eternal questions: "What is the real motive of the extreme environmentalists? Is it to weaken America?" In such fertile ground did the so-called Sagebrush Rebellion of the early 1980s briefly flourish, calling for the sale of all public lands, for the evisceration of the Bureau of Land Management, for the commercial development of national parks, for the clear-cutting of the national forests, for oil and gas drilling and hard-rock mining in wilderness areas, for the removal of grazing restrictions, for an end to wilderness designations and wild and scenic river designations, and, finally, for an end to government regulations of any and all kinds, but especially those that would prevent a private landowner from doing anything he or she might want to do with his or her property, and the environment be damned.

Sanity prevailed just long enough for James Watt to vanish from the public scene and for the conservation community to prevent, in one bitter battle after another, the worst that the Sagebrush Rebellion and its friends in Congress and the Executive Branch could do. The presidency of George Herbert Walker Bush stifled the boomers briefly by cloaking itself gently in the mantle of environmentalism; but when the cloth began to unravel in the hands of such as Interior Secretary Manuel Lujan, the boomers were ready for another crusade. They called it Wise Use.

For all their energy and persistence, the boomers' movements of the past were pretty loose affairs, poorly organized, riven by internecine strife, plagued by an inability to present themselves and their arguments in anything but shrill, sometimes slightly lunatic, vituperation. Moreover, the industries for whom the boomers spoke—minerals, timber, agriculture, oil, gas, livestock—had rarely joined as one voice to fight the good fight.

No longer. Wise Use leaders like Ron Arnold of the Center for the Defense of Free Enterprise and Charles Cushman of the Multiple Use Land Alliance (headquarters, Battleground, Washington) pride themselves on having learned the importance of public relations from the environmental community itself. They know how to work the press, engineer media "events," and cloak their rhetoric in smooth-sounding sentiments regarding the sanctity of the Constitution and the economic realities of life in the West.

They have learned with some considerable skill how to engage a wide variety of public-land users, from off-road-vehicle enthusiasts to hunters and anglers, inflating the fears of such people that federal regulations and land classifications are going to eliminate their use of the lands. They are even more proficient at playing on the legitimate concerns of local people who are worried about their economic future—timber-dependent communities faced with economic transition, for example. Many such communities have already been devastated by the loss of timber jobs because of mill modernization and the flight of timber companies to the cheaper environs of the South; but by the time the Wise Use public-relations effort is completed (ably aided by the timber industry and, in recent years, such administration officials as Manuel Lujan), the blame for job loss is laid entirely at the door of "extreme environmentalists" who would lock up the land from all development and who, as Ron Arnold insists, care not a tinker's damn about human beings who get hurt when such inferior species as the northern spotted owl or the marbled murrelet are saved. "Environmentalism," he says, "is the new paganism. It worships trees and sacrifices people."

What is more, many, if not most, of the plethora of Wise Use organizations are being funded almost entirely by the industries whose philosophies they parrot and whose needs they service. Take, for instance, the Denver-based People for the West! (the exclamation point comes attached to the title), a self-described "Grassroots Campaign Supporting Western Communities," one of whose principal goals is keeping the giveaway General Mining Law of 1872 uncorrupted by any kind of reform that would impose royalties on the extraction of hard-rock minerals from public lands or the sale (at $2.50 or $5.00 per acre) of said lands to anyone who "proves up." This "grassroots" group boasts of no fewer than 191 corporate sponsors, virtually every single one of which is a mining company or a company that services mining companies.

So we should make no mistake—whatever they choose to call themselves, no matter who they claim to represent, such groups are after just one thing: untrammeled access to the resources of the public lands, access that has never been a right but only a privilege, access that should be, though seldom has been, governed by principles of stewardship, not exploitation. It is not even much of a secret. Consider the so-called *Wise Use Agenda,* an unashamed and utterly serious tract edited by Alan M. Gottlieb of the Center for the Defense of Free Enterprise. Among the 25 goals articulated in the *Wise Use Agenda* is a call for civil penalties against anyone who would legally challenge "economic action or development on federal lands"; the protection of private-property rights by eliminating all restrictions on development; freeing up the national parks, national wildlife refuges, and all designated wilderness areas to mining and oil and gas development; allowing almost unrestricted off-road-vehicle access to all public lands of any kind; clear-cutting all remaining ancient forests in the Pacific Northwest and elsewhere and replanting them as tree farms; amending the Endangered Species Act to exclude "nonadaptive" species like the California condor and any endemic species not strong enough to spread in range, while giving economic considerations equal weight with species extinction in all decisions resulting from the enforcement of the act; and repealing or weakening virtually every other environmental protection law on the books.

The movement still may seem crude and even laughable in its extremism, but we cannot underestimate its impact or its power. Its leaders have too much money and have learned too much about public relations for environmentalists to dismiss them as little more than special-interest clown acts. The Blue Ribbon Coalition, for example, managed to persuade Congress in December 1991 to pass the National Recreational Trails Fund Act, which gives as much as 70 percent of $30 million in gasoline tax money to trails reserved to or dominated by off-road-vehicle users. That leaves only 30 percent for foot trails and horse trails—yet ORV owners account for only 11 percent of all trail users.

For another example, People for the West! put so much pressure on federal officials that a management plan for the Greater Yellowstone Ecosystem, produced with the cooperation of the Forest Service, the National Park Service, and other federal land-managing agencies, was reduced to pablum. This plan was supposed to establish long-needed controls on logging, grazing, mining, and other extractive uses of the public lands around Yellowstone National Park; instead, it will permit the continuing abuse of one of the nation's most important ecosystems. And when the National Audubon Society produced television specials critical of the cattle and timber industries, boycotts were threatened by many anti-environmentalist groups—and the sponsoring companies for both programs promptly withdrew their advertising.

Even with a new presidential administration clearly dedicated to the wise management of federal lands and the protection of the environment in all its variety, these organizations now have money and power and they know how to use both—to buy television, radio, and print ads; pack hearings halls and meeting rooms; hire the best legal firms in Washington, D.C., to represent them; manipulate the press with "spontaneous demonstrations" and broadcast outrageous charges so repeatedly that they begin to be accepted as unvarnished fact. It has worked before, and it will work again.

How, then, to fight them? At the risk of seeming simpleminded, I will insist that truth is still the best defense, as it was when Benny DeVoto leveled the howitzer of his splendid prose against the boomers of the postwar years. As we confront the boomers of the modern age, it would serve us well not to lose sight of the essential message—which is not merely about specific trees being cut in specific forests and the loss of specific jobs, or about a specific endangered species being protected at the expense of someone's God-given right to build an equal opportunity golf course, or about any specific conflict between the warriors of progress and the warriors of preservation. We should fall back on what we must know in our bones, if we know anything at all. The essential message that must be hammered home again and again, even as we fling the facts of the matter in the faces of the Wise Use boomers, is this: The short-term economies of extraction, waste, and plunder that have characterized the human use of the American land have brought more ruin to individual lives than anything any environmentalist ever promoted.

The term "boom and bust" does not define balance—because the boom is always temporary and the bust is always permanent. You cannot regrow oil, or gas, or coal, or gold, or silver lost to extraction, or barrier islands and wetlands lost to real estate. While you can regrow a treelike substance on a tree farm, you cannot regrow the true complexity of a forest or the intricate web of species that comprises an uneaten grassland or an unfilled wetland. You cannot regrow a critter or a plant that has been driven to extinction—not even in the laboratory; not yet, anyway—and you cannot replace biodiversity with glitzy biospheres steaming under geodesic domes somewhere in the desert Southwest.

And yet it is on all these irreplaceable things that the true health of our economy as a nation and as a species depends. Without adequate reserves of natural resources preserved and maintained for future need, there is no secure economy. Without the genetic richness of diversity, wild creatures decline in strength and reproductive ability. Without wild species to enrich the gene pool of the future, life on this planet will grow thin and attenuated, a steadily diminishing number of species living off a steadily diminishing resource base. Existence for all species, including the human species, will be brutish and brief. Men, women, children, corporate board members and environmental activists, bureaucrats and bootblacks, Wise Use mavens and Earth First! tree-sitters, white-collar and blue-collar, rich people, poor people, miners, farmers, cowboys, housebuilders, backpackers, dirtbikers, left-wingers, right-wingers—all of us, without exception, will be bound together in the great democracy of planetary ruin.

People for the West!

Challenges and Opportunities

Jim Baca

I would like to begin my assessment with the hopefully provocative assertion that People for the West! (hereinafter referred to as PFW) may very well be the best thing to happen to land-oriented environmentalists since James Watt . . . depending on our response.

I must caution that the current manifestation is more pernicious than previous raids. Our adversaries have learned from the mistakes of the Sagebrush Rebellion and the Watt Era. Our responses must be more sophisticated and well considered than before in order to counter a well-orchestrated effort to isolate, trivialize, and marginalize environmental concerns and environmentalists themselves.

The objective of PFW's efforts is to assure industrial access to cheap resources with a minimum of environmental restraints. PFW is the mining-oriented head of the Wise Use Hydra.

Unfortunately, the PFW effort in New Mexico has been very successful to date. In reviewing their publications, it is apparent that PFW has focused on New Mexico, along with Montana, because of the importance of our congressional delegations to mining-law reform. It also appears they have chosen New Mexico as a proving ground for their model, because it is on the cusp politically between liberalism and conservatism and between environmentalism and exploitation.

Although the main focus of PFW thus far has been to preserve the 1872 Mining Law, their successes have stalled many items on the environmental agenda in New Mexico. Even though PFW is funded almost exclusively by the mining industry, they have had to reach well beyond the mining-law issue, because the mining industry realizes it cannot generate the grassroots potential for victory by itself.

PFW is actively appealing to ranchers, loggers, ORVers, sportsmen, ethnic minorities, and organized labor. Most politicians in New Mexico, both state and federal, are backpedaling furiously from environmental initiatives. As a result of PFW organizing, New Mexico BLM Wilderness is stalled indefinitely, and the proposed Jemez and Rio Grande National Conservation Areas appear dead, at least temporarily. A draconian "takings bill" is a real possibility in our state legislature. The New Mexico congressional delegation championed the defeat of the proposed grazing fee hike.

Whether or not PFW is a valid reflection of grassroots sentiment (PFW is widely regarded in New Mexico as having about as much relation to genuine grassroots as astroturf does to biological processes), politicians are running scared and voting accordingly.

PFW has been so successful in its one year of existence largely because the environmental movement has given its adversaries a huge window of opportunity. Quite bluntly, the environmental movement has for all practical purposes abandoned the grass roots and let them atrophy. There is very little real engagement between environmentalists and others who should be under our umbrella, or at least be neutral. Recruitment of activists is minimal. In addition to failing to engage potential allies, the environmental movement is not doing a great job of activating our traditional constituencies. Many of our stalwarts (volunteer and professional) are burned out. The agenda of the mainstream environmental movement is not inclusive enough. It must make strategic alliances across class and ethnic barriers in order to thrive and revive. About the only real dynamism and excitement is in some of the environmental thrusts in ethnic and working-class communities.

In contrast, PFW makes no secret that it is employing the tactics environmentalists have historically used to their great advantage, albeit with a palpable overlay of cynicism. "Ecotactics," by the Sierra Club, is cited in some of their literature as a tactical model!

PFW is going door to door with petitions in rural and minority communities. They are courting mayors and county commissioners on a one-to-one basis. They have assembled formidable phone trees and letter-writing events in a relatively short time. They seek out and court the aggrieved and disenfranchised. Whenever there is a mill closing, for whatever reason, PFW is there directing peoples' anxieties and fears toward the convenient scapegoat of the environmental movement. PFW has identified a "them" (which is us) and has proceeded to demagogue with a vengeance.

I had the opportunity to observe PFW in action during congressional hearings on mining-law reform held in Santa Fe last May. They staged a rally and picketed the hearings, and were less than polite to witnesses and representatives who disagreed with them. They had an impressive turnout, which I estimated to be around 400 (even though it wasn't close to the 1,000 they claimed). Some of the demonstrators were school kids bused in from rural school districts. Many of the demonstrators were mining company employees (some weren't quite sure why they were there), bused in from around the region, although there appeared to be a significant number of loggers and ranchers. In contrast, there was a small scattering of cowed environmentalists. The contrast wasn't lost on politicians, absent and present.

PFW's manipulation of symbolism is as expert as it is perverse—downright Orwellian, in fact. My hunch is that they have retained PR consultants who specialize in creating Astroturf grassroots movements. They seem to have taken a page from the racist Washington, D.C., bottle bill defeat, when bottlers poured money into the churches to encourage the message that "white people just want to make you pay more for sodas."

The simple fact is that their rhetoric is playing well with their targets and the media. Their masthead states that PFW is dedicated to "Fighting to Keep Public Lands Open," but nothing could be more antithetical to open public lands than patenting! Two of their dominant themes are "community stability" and "strength of the family," which is rather ironic since the industry funding PFW has frequently undermined those worthy values through boom-and-bust cycles, pollution, union busting, and pay cuts.

They lay the blame for most any problem imaginable at the feet of "elite environmentalists, who care more about owls than people." PFW is succeeding in many of its attempts to reach out to minorities, labor, and just plain folks, because industries that have traditionally been viewed as their adversaries are seen as a lesser evil than environmentalists. This is partly because environmentalists do sometimes come off as elitist; but more importantly, it is because the environmentalists are not countering.

We are losing the battle for the hearts and minds of a large segment of the populace, at least in New Mexico, opinion polls notwithstanding. If the trend continues, the political landscape in the West will be considerably more hostile to environmental protection than it is now.

For several reasons, the cornerstone of any PFW counterstrategy should be reform of the 1872 Mining Law. Its environmental travesties are obvious. It is so egregious that, if we can't win this one, we better hit the showers: they are giving us a fat, slow pitch. The mining industry is the major underwriter of PFW, which, as we have seen, is undercutting our whole agenda. We need to cut off that infusion of funds to our most fundamental opposition. Most importantly, the PFW model is being tested on this issue and we must prove it ineffective early on or deal with very ugly consequences over the long term.

We must intensify our PR efforts—our message is not getting across well enough. Not only must we counter the falsehoods of PFW and the "Wise

Users," we must put forth cogent and compelling analyses of the benefits of mining-law reform, in the short term, and of wilderness and environmental protection generally (a la Dr. Power's Utah analysis and the TWS economic analysis of the Four Corners Region).

We must translate and aggressively market these conclusions to the general public in terms they understand: jobs, taxes, and quality of life. We must encourage positive programs and initiatives wherever possible (e.g., actively support ecologically acceptable timber sales for small operators and personal use, over "mega-sales"). This, of course, brings us to longer-term strategies.

Even if PWF is vanquished on the mining-law issue, the lessons of the battle should be heeded. In order to maintain their effectiveness into the 1990s, national environmental groups should begin to assess their relationship to the grassroots in hopes of achieving a greater symmetry between the grassroots and centralized administration and lobbying. I believe that the 1990s will witness a strategic shift by extractive industries, and the right generally, to the grass roots (by "grass roots" I mean the mobilization of large numbers of people on behalf of a particular issue). It seems as though our adversaries have realized that they have reached the limits of direct mail and traditional lobbying techniques.

The other side has learned from our successes and have regrouped to aim at our core agendas. The formation of People for the West! could wind up being a blessing in disguise, by putting us back in touch with our own grass roots.

Address to the
Natural Resources Council
of America

James Gustave Speth

Receiving the Natural Resouces Council of America's Award of Honor this evening means a great deal to me, and I thank you.

I have reflected on why I am so moved by this award. At age 50, I have had to become a little reflective, and I have even asked myself recently, "what am I, really?" I guess what I have been, when it is all said and done, is an environmentalist. And so it means a lot to me to get this award from you, my fellow environmentalists.

Working for a sustaining, nurturing environment, and all that that means, and all that that requires, is a high calling. I can imagine none better. It has been a great 22 years for me, and I look forward to another 22. I've just got to figure out how to do it!

I know also that I am receiving this award not so much for my own work but for the efforts of the people with whom I have worked at the Natural Resources Defense Council, the Council on Environmental Quality, and particularly the World Resources Institute, where I have had 10 wonderful years. It has been my great good fortune to work closely with outstanding people over this period, and I accept the award on their behalf too.

The others you are recognizing tonight are extraordinary company. And it is a special honor to be paired with Al Gore. We talk a lot about the need for policitical leadership. Al gives it. He is my political leader.

Andrea has asked me to speak for a few minutes, and I will. But I'll be brief. I will just offer a few reflections on where I think we stand today.

First, our environmental situation today is worse than people think, both nationally and globally. The rates of deterioration around the world are alarming, as is the anti-environmental backlash here at home. Environmentalists are accused of gloom and doom about the future. No. Gloom and doom about the future is completely inappropriate. But the present is another matter.

What seems to be missing is not recognition of real problems, but the will to do something about them. The agenda has been built; the urgency has not. We do not need environmental extremism to carry the day; environmental realism would do the job if we could find more of it, particularly among our political leaders.

There's lots to be done to address these challenges; I certainly do not need to inventory them for this group. But whatever the demands we environmentalists place on society, there are demands we must place on ourselves, on the environmental programs we have helped to create, on the very concept of environmentalism.

One of these, one that many of you preach every day, is to demand of ourselves that we get it right. That we get it right through a commitment to openness, self-criticism, and accuracy. If we do get it right, we will continue to build credibility. And in this business, credibility isn't the main thing; it's the only thing.

But there's another demand we must place on ourselves: the demand, to borrow a line from Ezra Pound, to "make it new," to renew and revitalize environmentalism itself.

We now have the opportunity, I believe, to launch a new phase in the development of environmental policy and action. For Americans it is nothing less than the opportunity to build a sustainable society, with a sustainable economy and sustainable lifestyles, here at home.

There is no greater contribution the U.S. can make to the global environment than to show our own commitment to sustainability and to hold out to the world a model of economic development that the world can share—safely.

"Making it new," first of all, means revisiting and revamping many of the environmental programs and approaches of the past two decades. And it means finding new approaches outside the traditional areas of environmental law and regulation.

The environmental laws and programs we launched mostly in the 1970s will not get the job done, in my view. They will not put America on the path to sustainability. They have accomplished much but have peaked in effectiveness, and they are no match for the challenges ahead.

In a nutshell, we can say that environmentalism began on the periphery of the economy—capturing pollution at the end of the pipe, saving landscape at the end of the road. It was "outside" the economy. Now it must be brought inside. Environmentalism must spread as creed and code to permeate to the core of economic activity. Economic and environmental policies, and our nation's economic and environmental goals, must be brought together in the new synthesis we call sustainable development.

In part, what is required is nothing more than a rapid acceleration and expansion of an old pattern. Those who brought the first challenges to big dams quickly found that they had to become expert on water policy. Challenges to offshore drilling and the breeder reactor led to energy policy. Over the years, as we have pursued environmental concerns, and looked deeper for underlying forces at the roots of the problems, many of us have felt a little like an investigative reporter following a story and discovering linkages and ramifications and even whole new areas. Like international debt. And trade and GATT, of all things.

What began as early fights over local highways reached a new level of maturity in the accomplishments of the transportation coalition honored here tonight. The result has been the much-needed overhaul of national transportation policy. Again, we have moved from particular, often site-specific controversies to broad new areas of policy action.

Now we must turn the environmental spotlight to still newer areas, such as national economic revitalization and competitiveness policy, technology policy, tax and deficit-reduction issues. Military-to-civilian conversion. U.S. foreign policy and the whole of our relations with the developing countries. The arcane worlds of the U.N. system and the multilateral development banks. And there is the need for much greater work with major nongovernmental actors like corporations, consumers, and educators at all levels.

Environmentalists must lead in all these areas and others, bringing the values of sustainability and equity into the picture. But clearly we will not get very far on our own. The arenas for action are too numerous; the demands for true expertise are too great. So "making it new" also means making new friends and alliances and breaking down the barriers that separate us from other communities. It means adopting a more inclusive concept of environmental leadership and what it means to be an environmentalist.

We will need everyone's effort. The community leader with a vision of a sustainable city. The corporate executive who now sees that the company's future depends on environmental performance. The activist who knows how to get things done in the Congress or in the courts. The think-tank intellectual with a new insight or the analysis that makes the difference. We need the whole spectrum—from those with purity of purpose to those whose search for sales and profits has made them green.

We need to bring environmentalists and business leaders together; labor and environment together; economists and ecologists together; upper-income preservationists and lower-income pollution victims together.

I am convinced there is a community out there that can eventually coalesce, if we work to build it. It is the community of those who care enough about tomorrow's world to sacrifice today. It is the community of those who want to invest in order to secure a just and sustainable future. A society that genuinely cares about the future will invest at home *and* abroad, in jobs *and* in the environment. Such a society will invest in our cities, our schools, *and* our environment. And it will know that we cannot neglect the desperate needs of the poorer countries, lest we merely create a fool's paradise here at home and lose our souls in the process.

Perhaps the most basic question facing America today is: are we such a society? What Edward Gibbon said about the Athenians sounds too much like the U.S. now:

> *In the end, more than they wanted freedom, they wanted security.*
>
> *They wanted a comfortable life and they lost it all—security, comfort and freedom. . . .*
>
> *When the Athenians finally wanted not to give to society but for society to give to them, when the freedom they wished for most was freedom from responsibility, then Athens ceased to be free.*

The one great thing that the environmental community knows—profoundly—is that tomorrow counts, and that we must shoulder responsibility for building a sustainable and just future. That's why we're worth having around.

Thank you.

Taking Back the Rural West

Philip Brick

The American West has been at war with itself over land resource issues. In the battle for the future of the West, it seems chic to be radical. Environmental radicals declare there will be "no compromise in defense of Mother Earth" and vow to make the West "cattle free in '93." On the other side of the fence, Wise Use radicals claim to "put people first" (before owls, grizzly bears, and wolves) and promise "cows galore in '94." Both sides are convinced that any compromise on key western issues such as timber, mining, and grazing will have apocalyptic consequences. The polarization of the debate has brought public-land policy to a virtual standstill. Is such paralysis necessary? Both environmental interests and the concerns of rural Americans would be better served by putting aside the radical rhetoric and working together toward goals that need not be mutually exclusive. Polls clearly demonstrate that concern for the environment is not limited to urban America. But to reach rural Americans, the goals and tactics of the environmental movement must change.

Environmentalists blame the Wise Use radicals for polarizing communities across the West. Although described as a "virus" by environmental groups, the Wise Use message has found resonance in small towns throughout the West. To date, the greatest success of the Wise Use movement has been to frame public-resource debates in terms of jobs versus the environment, thus ensuring a constituency committed to fight any environmental regulation. Wise Use rhetoric reaches deep into rural communities, recruiting the working class in areas hard hit by economic transitions in resource-extraction industries such as mining and forest products. In some small towns dependent on the survival of a timber mill or mine, Wise Use groups have successfully recruited entire communities. Environmentalists tend to scoff at these grassroots groups, charging that they are merely paid puppets of industry and not true grassroots movements. But doing so seriously underestimates the rage on the range and the potential power of committed Wise Use activists to torpedo environmental progress in the West. The anger and frustration in the rural West is real—we tend to dismiss both the extent to which sympathy for the Wise Use agenda has captured certain constituencies in the rural West and the degree to which the environmental community is responsible for this.

Despite its contempt for Wise Use "suicide squads," the environmental community has only itself to blame for the rise of Wise Use sentiments. Within the environmental movement, it remains an article of faith that increasingly radical approaches are required to deal with ever greater environmental threats. According to conventional wisdom, increasingly strident demands expand the environmental agenda and make so-called mainstream organizations appear more reasonable. Environmentalists and Wise Use advocates alike are fond of quoting David Brower in this regard: "I founded Friends of the Earth to make the Sierra Club look reasonable. Then I founded the Earth Island Institute to make Friends of the Earth look reasonable. Earth First! now makes us look reasonable. We're still waiting for someone to come along and make Earth First! look reasonable."

Although it is clear that Earth First! makes the Sierra Club look more reasonable, it is less clear whether Earth First! makes the environmental community appear any more reasonable, especially in small towns across the West. Wise Use advocates have made a virtual cottage industry out of reprinting selected excerpts from radical environmental rhetoric, which are used to energize those who feel threatened by much needed reforms on public lands in the West.

It would be far too simple, however, to argue that the rise of Wise Use groups is a simple backlash to an increasingly strident environmental agenda. The movement's rise is instead the result of two causes that run much deeper: the social and economic transformation of the West coupled with the misplaced priorities of the environmental movement.

Far-reaching social and economic changes are sweeping the West. People in search of the good life are coming to the West (or leaving California) and moving to rural communities from Montana to New Mexico, where open space and a clean environment are almost a birthright. Fax machines, video conferencing, and decentralized work environments emerged as staples of American business in the 1980s, helping make the out-migration possible. Concerned with preserving the kind of environment that drew them to the West in the first place, the new emigrants have sought to change long-standing public-land priorities that favor extractive-resource interests and threaten quality-of-life values. But many long-time residents of the West, often depending on extractive industries for their livelihood, see the invasion of relatively wealthy outsiders as a threat to their very survival. At the same time, extensive mill and mine modernizations have resulted in still fewer high-paying jobs, increasing rural insecurity and pessimism.

What results are uncompromising land-use conflicts with thinly veiled over-tones of class and a polarization of insiders and outsiders. This helps explain why the notion that "people are important too" is central to the success of Wise Use rhetoric. The importance of class and an insider–outsider consciousness comes through in a number of statements from Wise Use organizers. As Ron Arnold put it, "people's livelihoods should be every bit as sacred as the coffee-table-book preferences of rich Ph.D.'s living at the top of the food chain." Or consider Wise Use hero Bruce Vincent's story. Vincent organized local resistance to a federal plan to reintroduce the grizzly bear into his native Montana:

> *That's what lets them [environmentalists and federal land-management bureaucrats] think they can do this to us—turn our homes into their play-grounds, destroy the economy of our communities, wipe out our families—because we're worthless, because, in their eyes, what we do and how we live has no value. But we're not disposable. We're not some inconvenience society brushes aside like a piece of lint simply because of where we live or what we do for a living.*

In most Wise Use stories, environmentalists are invariably characterized as un-caring elitists and outsiders. In many cases, they are. Amid changing social and economic conditions in the West, the environmental movement has shown as-tonishing insensitivity to the plight of those who live near the areas they hope to save, handing the Wise Use movement a committed constituency on a silver platter.

American environmentalism has never really come to terms with the con-tradictions of class and ideas within its ranks. The movement's commitment to preserving wilderness is part of the problem. The idea of wilderness has always been advanced by those who can afford it, not by those who live in it. Not only does the emphasis on wilderness make most environmental groups outsiders in rural America, it pits the interests of urban, upper-middle-class aesthetics against working-class livelihoods. As Luis Torres writes,

> *Environmentalists' efforts to align land-based people to their causes have been mostly unsuccessful because they continue to overlook some of the basic flaws in their movement. Primary among these is their continuing failure to present themselves as anything other than the latest wave of outsider elitists imposing their will without regard for the needs of others and without a clear understanding of the relationship and interdependency between the people and the lands in question.*

Just as it grew increasingly important for the environmental movement to become involved in rural communities undergoing wrenching transformations, the movement instead became more and more remote from the grass roots, focusing its energies in Washington, D.C. Instead of worrying about the loss of employment in rural communities, most of the large environmental groups focused on national environmental legislation. Although such legislation is indispensable, one wonders if the priorities are not backward. The "Big Ten" of the environmental movement raise a lot of money through direct-mail solicitation, and the material that accompanies the request for $25 or $50 typically raises alarms about issues far from home for most contributors. For example, threats to the Arctic National Wildlife Refuge in northern Alaska were a key issue in direct-mail appeals in the late 1980s and early 1990s. Meanwhile, rural communities closer to home became ever more frustrated and polarized. By confusing lobbying and direct-mail campaigns with real political organizing, we have helped create a backlash that was just waiting for Wise Use organizers to exploit its fury.

The environmental community has reacted to the growing Wise Use movement with horror and indignation. The first impulse has been to make every effort to discredit its leadership and the "phony puppets of industry" at the grass roots. As one executive of a major environmental organization wrote, "we must immediately launch a broad-based, aggressive public education campaign to thoroughly expose the Wise Use movement for the land-abuse movement that it really is." Although Wise Use connections to industry and unsavory right-wing organizations may raise the ire of Audubon or Sierra Club members, they are unlikely to change the minds of those who have joined Wise Use groups. Instead of trying to discredit their message, the environmental movement must reoccupy the territory all but ceded to Wise Use organizers. Ron Arnold once promised his followers that they would "enter the environmentalist's domain and take it away from them." It is time for environmentalists to turn the tables and enter the rural communities where Wise Use organizers have been so effective. To do so, the two strategic flaws that helped create the Wise Use backlash in the first place must be addressed.

First, new environmental values and goals that go beyond the concept of wilderness are needed. The idea of wilderness has served the environmental movement well in the twentieth century, but it will not be adequate in the twenty-first century. Overemphasis of wilderness not only polarizes the haves from the have-nots, it also is an increasingly inappropriate instrument to protect global biodiversity. Wilderness advocates argue that setting aside islands of diversity will ensure the survival of endangered species and permit natural evolution to proceed, insulated from the pervasive influences of humankind. Increasingly, however, we are discovering that the "islands" are not big enough. Instead of helping to change social and economic trends inconsistent with a sustainable economy and ecology, the idea of wilderness reinforces such trends.

In the search for new approaches, we might begin to think like Chico Mendes, our own hero of the struggle for sustainable development in the Brazilian rainforest. Mendes fought to protect the forest from logging and pioneered the concept of extractive reserves to preserve both the forest and the natives who live in it. Apparently, extractive reserves are more attractive to us when they are in Latin America and not here. Committed to the idea of wilderness, we too often simply argue that eco-tourism can replace extractive-resource activities in the West without considering the effects that tourism can have on the land and on the cultural economy of small communities. In some cases, tourism can be more harmful to the land than carefully managed grazing or sustainable timber harvesting.

Second, the environmental community must get down to some serious political organizing at the grass roots, emphasizing the vital connections between a healthy and sustainable environment, economic opportunity, and the stability and integrity of rural communities. The environmental community cannot hope to be successful in rural communities until it becomes part of those communities, working to integrate environmental values with high-quality, sustainable economic opportunities. To do so, we must broaden our concept of what constitutes legitimate grassroots activism. Traditionally, real grassroots activism has meant local people standing up against the powers that be, not with them. But to make sure that environmental protection does not come at the price of economic opportunity, new alliances between local environmentalists and their former enemies are both necessary and possible. All over the West, local environmentalists are sitting at the same table with industry, federal agencies, and concerned citizens in watershed working groups. These "consensus groups" are working to generate sustainable plans for the truly wise use of public resources, ensuring both quality jobs and environmental protection.

Instead of an army of lawyers and lobbyists trying to maximize gains from the legal and political system, a new environmental movement based in the rural West is beginning to focus on nonwilderness, land-use planning *before* the disputes become so intractable that they must be resolved in an often arbitrary political or legal process. By working together in consensus groups with federal land managers and industry representatives, a new breed of local environmentalist is taking back the West, town by town, watershed by watershed. People in the West are weary of land-use conflicts that seem to produce nothing but more conflict. The side that gets down to the real work of building communities and planning for sustainable economic development will win the confidence of rural constituencies. Ultimately, the Wise Use challenge has forced the environmental movement to come back home to the grass roots, but home to a different kind of activism, one engaged in consensus problem solving and better prepared to meet tomorrow's challenges.

III

Resource Conflicts

Part III focuses in detail on some of the key resource issues over which environmentalists and Wise Use leaders have locked horns in the last several years. Some of the contributors to this part critique the methods and goals of the Wise Use movement while others focus on finding a middle ground in order to resolve these conflicts.

Polarization of public opinion on the grazing issue is the topic of "Mapping Common Ground on Public Rangelands," by William E. Riebsame and Robert G. Woodmansee of the University of Colorado at Boulder and Colorado State University, respectively. Examining the different perspectives that underlie the debate over grazing on public lands, the authors propose new approaches to finding solutions that will serve the interests of both conservationists and ranchers.

In "Wise Use in the West: The Case of the Northwest Timber Industry," Tarso Ramos of the Western States Center traces the development of the Wise Use movement in the context of the Pacific Northwest timber controversies, focusing on the Wise Use leader Ron Arnold. He examines in critical detail the sometimes contrived character of the grassroots support for the Wise Use agenda.

Turning attention to what has long been considered the most "inexhaustible" resource, our oceans, Carl Safina of the National Audubon Society and Suzanne Iudicello of the Center for Marine Conservation, in "Wise Use below the High-Tide Line: Threats and Opportunities," describe efforts by Wise Use activists to bring the fishing industry into the movement. They describe some of the issues that have attracted elements of the fishing community to the Wise Use camp, as well as the opportunities for environmentalists and the fishing industry to forge effective alliances on many issues of common concern, such as water pollution and loss of spawning habitat.

Returning to dry land, Florence Williams, a freelance journalist, describes, in "Sagebrush Rebellion II," the "county movement," a scattered effort across the country to fundamentally redefine the legal relationship between federal and local governments with respect to management of federal public lands. Modeled on a Catron, New Mexico, ordinance, these local legislative initiatives seek to subject federal management decisions to local review and control.

Thomas Michael Power's "Not All That Glitters," a report commissioned by the Mineral Policy Center, explores the case for reform of the nation's outdated hard-rock mineral law. This piece also describes the status of reform bills pending before the 103rd Congress.

Mapping Common Ground on Public Rangelands

William E. Riebsame • *Robert G. Woodmansee*

INTRODUCTION

As environmentalists turn their attention to landscapes neglected in past preservation efforts, and as themes like ecosystems management replace narrowly focused land- and species-management traditions, the western grasslands and deserts are becoming a new hot spot in the campaign for an ecologically healthy landscape in the West. Because the vast majority of the West's grasslands and deserts are in the public domain and are grazed by domestic livestock, grazing reform has moved higher on the agenda of environmental groups.

As with many environmental issues, the debate over public-lands grazing has polarized. Environmentalists claim that much of the federal rangeland is overgrazed and that low grazing fees and lax agency oversight have given ranchers de facto control over the land and made them careless of the resource. Grazing supporters, including ranchers, range professionals, and the key federal agencies—the Bureau of Land Management (BLM) and the U.S. Forest Service (USFS)—argue that grazing is a legitimate and productive endeavor on many public lands, that ranchers respect the land as the basis for their own well-being, and that most of the western range is improving through carefully planned management.

Despite this customary drawing of lines in the sand over public-lands grazing and the traditional jousting among interest groups at the 1993 grazing hearings held by Interior Secretary Bruce Babbitt (see *High Country News,* May 17, 1993), there are some indications that ranchers and environmentalists can find common ground on grazing issues and can create new approaches to problem solving that avoid the gridlock standard to so many environmental issues.

THE GRAZING DEBATE

Some 270 million acres of western federal lands—an area larger than all of Colorado, Wyoming, Montana, Utah, and Nevada—are used for livestock grazing through a permit process established by the Taylor Grazing Act in 1934. That act launched the Grazing Service, precursor to today's BLM, and created a grazing permitting and management process that mostly reflects livestock interests and uses (the USFS uses a similar grazing-allotment process). Like western water and mining law, many aspects of grazing policy produce inefficient and damaging resource uses: grazing allotments are tied to private ranches rather than opened for bidding among competing interests; cattle numbers are set at unrealistically high levels; ranchers who voluntarily reduce grazing pressure for environmental or other reasons receive no fee reduction and even risk losing their permit; fees are formulated to protect the livestock industry rather than to cover administrative costs or make money for the treasury; and roughly half the grazing fees collected are plowed back into range improvements for livestock, under the guidance of grazing advisory boards not representative of many other land users. Most of these facets of grazing policy are targeted for reform by environmental organizations.

The need for reform hinges on a widespread sense that the range is being abused. But, rangeland condition is hotly debated. Agencies were forced to monitor range quality more carefully under NEPA and a 1974 benchmark court case, *Natural Resources Defense Council Inc. v. Morton,* which required environmental impact statements and increased monitoring of grazing plans. Since then, a series of range assessments, based on various technical methods, have indicated that roughly half of the public range is in a condition that most ranchers and many environmentalists would consider reasonably good; that another quarter is degraded in one way or another, with some of these lands improving and others stable or declining; and that a final quarter is being seriously damaged under current grazing practices.

Critics also argue that grazing fees are too low, an undeserved subsidy that encourages resource abuse. Though it remains on the agenda of most environmental groups, the fee issue is sometimes played down in an attempt to focus on ecological aspects of grazing and to avoid the appearance of seeking broader social reforms or redistributions of wealth.

Our experience at grazing hearings and other venues in which ranchers and environmentalists interact is that both sides generally agree that the western range has been abused in the past—that vegetation, wildlife, and water quality have been hurt—and that the grazing-fee formula is outdated. However, even with this toehold on some common ground, they cannot agree on whether modern grazing methods are worsening or lessening range degradation, nor can they agree on a new method for valuing the rangeland resource. The issue is weighed down, on both sides, by slavish clinging to symbolism and tradition, fear over loss of control and independence, and unwillingness of the two sides to work together.

FINDING COMMON GROUND ON THE WESTERN RANGE

Different perceptions, backgrounds, and perspectives on range issues (Fig. 1) inevitably produce conflict in the absence of mechanisms for dialogue and participation. The grazing debate has reached an especially polarized stage, with livestock interests, arguing that they are the best stewards of the land, squared off against the "cattle-free" and "rest-the-West" proponents, who feel that only wholesale elimination of grazing can restore rangeland ecologies.

Like many environmental debates, the grazing battle is driven by fundamentally divergent views of the "correct" relationship between environment and society. The debate is anchored at one extreme by ecologists who believe that humans have too long dominated nature, bending environment to their needs and damaging the well-functioning natural system that was in place long before human technology emerged. This biocentric view holds that civilization must be changed to emulate and work with, not against, natural systems, and that it is time for humans to reduce their demands and impacts on nature. At the other extreme are the utilitarians who view nature as a resource to be used, even improved upon, to meet human needs and desires. One side sees

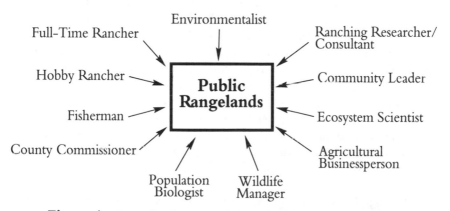

"What You See Depends on Where You Sit"

Figure 1 Rangeland sustainability—land-based viewpoints.

domestic cattle as poor substitutes for the natural grazers that evolved on the great western grasslands; the other sees the cow as an efficient machine for harvesting natural resources and creating the wealth on which modern society is based.

Our task here, to suggest how some common ground can be created despite these quite different philosophical stands, requires that we disappoint both sides of the polarized argument. These ideological positions are so fundamentally different that they are best simply acknowledged by both parties and then set aside in the search for shared values and goals and for pragmatic solutions to real ecological and social problems. Our experience is that when ranchers and environmentalists openly discuss their perceptions of grazing and other issues, they are surprised by the number of common goals they share, a realization that can quickly lead to agreement on broad environmental aspirations. For example, The Colorado Resource Round-Table, a coalition of ranchers and environmentalists, developed this statement of shared landscape vision for the state:

> *The landscape is the integration of ecological and social development and must be managed to maintain the sustainable health of rural, urban, and wild lands. Development must be environmentally harmonious with its surroundings and aesthetically pleasing. Areas of wilderness, wildlife habitat, and recreational spaces must be maintained. Landscapes must be designed so as to maintain healthy ecosystem processes, including vegetation succession, water and nutrient cycling, and animal well-being.*

Although this statement is too general to reflect the coalition members' thoughts on sticky questions like the role of predators in a "healthy ecosystem" or just how much urban development a landscape can absorb, the process of coauthoring it helped them identify some common concerns and goals, as well as enabling them to get to know one another better. A small stepping stone was thus established for creating more extensive and specific common goals.

It is important to note that the "common ground" we speak of is not simply a compromise landscape; the prospect of impending compromise encourages extremists to stake out more polarized positions, reckoning that the ultimate agreement will be closer to their starting point. Rather than compromise, we envision a new territory mapped out by all groups seriously interested in rangeland sustainability, a *terra incognita* to be carefully explored by joint scouting parties seeking both ecosystem health and social well-being.

We believe that progress in this direciton requires two starting principles:

1. Ecological health is a prerequisite for social well-being, and grazing that degrades the landscape, even slowly, is simply not socially or ecologically

acceptable. Grazing, more than most other resource systems, is founded in working with ecosystems, not overcoming them. In this way, it is potentially more sustainable than mining, foresty, or farming as they have emerged in twentieth-century America. But, grazing in much of the western United States is not ecologically or socially sustainable as currently practiced.

2. The recognition of both society's need to harvest some natural resources and the social legitimacy of grazing, along with recreation and other activities, on federal lands. Environmentalists denigrate their cause by scorning the human dignity and social utility of ranching as livelihood and lose credibility by appearing to oppose all resource uses rather than offering ideas on how modern resource systems can coexist with whole ecosystems.

These two principles provide a starting point for coalition groups to seek a new vision of environment and society on the western range. That goal, in our view, can be created by making the emerging ideas of ecosystems management and sustainability central to the debate. The challenge is to map out a strategy of federal-land use, grazing practices, and administration that independent resource and environmental experts, as well as the general public, would judge to be ecologically sustainable and socially equitable for the long haul. The first step in this effort is to help define, and then to meet, the emerging standards of sustainability and how it can be achieved through ecosystems management.

SUSTAINABLE RANGELANDS

The emerging notion of environmental sustainability is both simple and complex. Simply put, it means the maintenance of ecosystems that constitute the natural environment and provide what humans have defined as natural resources. The notion of sustainable development adds a stronger utilitarian factor: environment must be sustained, but so must human development. Sustainability takes on more biocentric or utilitarian qualities, depending on who does the defining. Environmentalists give priority to natural processes and elements, seeing human civilization—especially industrial society—as an interloper threatening the environment. Utilitarians see human needs, and social definitions of environmental values, as the legitimate criteria for measuring sustainability.

A more ecologically based definition of sustainability starts with natural systems and their integrity and then identifies how human society—by reducing its resource needs and gleaning those it does need, while conscientiously maintaining ecosystem integrity and process—can fit in. In our view, grazing on western rangelands, public and private, requires that society carefully match its resource needs to those that can be extracted from the land without a net loss of biological productivity, resource quality, or underlying biodiversity.

Ecosystems management and sustainability depends on the actions of both ecological and social systems. The four main ecological elements are (1) soil, (2) climate and water, (3) energy, and (4) biodiversity. How these factors interact to affect ecosystem health is reasonably well understood in theory but unevenly applied to the actual management and monitoring of public rangelands. The main social factors in sustainability are less well understood but include at least five other ingredients: (1) economic viability, (2) individual behavior, (3) community and cultural goals, (4) institutional legitimacy and competency, and (5) policy and legal power. These factors interact in complex ways. Past economic and policy goals—chiefly aimed at creating economic wealth and national power from America's natural resources—bequeathed a mixed legacy of healthy and degraded rangelands and good and poor management traditions. Behavioral problems (e.g., laziness, greed, and ignorance) and institutional impediments (e.g., agency inertia, lack of support for field personnel, and politics) made the problems worse.

Together, ecological and social elements constitute a chain of sustainability, and, like any chain, this one is only as strong as its weakest link. If water is sufficient, but soil organisms are missing, then vegetation cannot be sustained at a site. Moreover, if the institutional system for managing rangelands is incompetent, politically unstable, or culturally unacceptable, it simply will not function well. In a world in which cultural and ecological systems are so intertwined, social dysfunction ultimately leads to ecological dysfunction, and vice versa. The goal of ecosystems management, then, must be to maintain viable ecological and social systems.

ACHIEVING RANGELAND SUSTAINABILITY

The challenge to grazing interests of all ilks is to devise a way to adjust social needs and maintain ecological intergrity, which will require some sacrifice on both sides of the grazing debate. Ecosystems must be restored and maintained, and grazing, while permitted in many places, must be adapted to ecosystem processes. This cannot happen overnight, and the perfect prescription for sustainability does not exist; rather, we are in transition from an old model to a new one, with the shape of the new one—ecosystems management—not yet clear. Fortunately, the ecological and social situation on western U.S. rangelands is not as desperate as, say, in the Sahel of Africa. There are ecological and social problems to be addressed—some lands should not be grazed at all, too much public grazing land is controlled by too few ranchers, and fees need to be raised to cover at least the costs of grazing administration and environmental protection. The great challenge, we believe, is to meet high standards of both ecological health and social equity—that is, restore whole ecosystem structures and functions without jeopardizing the well-being of current rangeland users and communities. In some cases this will mean reduced grazing—perhaps none—and alternative resource and economic activities. In others, it will mean grazing adapted to local and regional ecological conditions, maybe even more cattle in some areas at certain times.

Several obstacles will slow the transition from polarized debate to ecologically and socially sustainable rangelands:

1. the legacy of past abuse
2. lack of ecologically based rangeland data and monitoring
3. the difficulty of finding socially equitable modifications of current grazing systems
4. accessibility of the rangeland management process

Legacies of the Past

The move to sustainable rangeland use will not be easy for some areas because of the historical legacy of ecologically unsound practices and the simple severity of the current climate. This negative legacy is only now—and not in all areas—being remediated by more careful management and stewardship; and some fraction of the public range either ought not to be grazed at all by domestic livestock or should be grazed only under very special circumstances and strict adherence to time and spatial limitations. A seasoned range scientist, Jerry Holechek, estimated in the May–June 1993 issue of the *Journal of Soil and Water Conservation* that perhaps 10 percent of federal range ought not to be grazed. Our reading of the literature and range assessments, combined with personal observation, suggests something more like 20–25 percent, mostly in the Southwest deserts, which simply cannot abide grazing levels needed to make ranching economically viable. Particular landscapes elsewhere in the West—many riparian and alpine areas, for example—also cannot abide current grazing pressure, though we desperately need better ecological assessments to make such determinations.

Lack of Ecological Analysis

The system of rangeland quality measurement is flawed, having been developed to assess range condition from a cow's point of view (i.e., in terms of forage for domestic livestock) not in terms of broader ecosystems. It appears that much of the western range is improving as a result of better grazing management, but the ecological status of western rangelands is simply not sufficiently well established to guide new grazing approaches. Except in the most obviously degraded cases, we lack the information needed to judge land condition and alter land uses to preserve and restore ecosystem function. Even the most obvious prescription—reduced grazing—is not right for all western rangelands. Agency attention has been squandered on growing administrative burdens, while underfunding, lack of ecologically trained field staff, and, of course, the constant need to deal with controversy and opposing interests have kept the agencies from focusing on land stewardship. An ecologically based monitoring and management system is needed quickly. Both the USFS and BLM have proposed ecosystems-based approaches, but progress has been too slow. Interior Secretary Babbitt's proposed "National Biological Survey" should be assigned the task of assessing ecological potential for all major public-land holdings, including rangelands, in the next few years, while a concerted effort is made to give ecological and social meaning to the idea of ecosystems management.

Ranchers and environmentalists must get involved in actual rangeland monitoring if both sides are ever to agree on how to interpret range condition. A few pilot efforts at collaborative monitoring have emerged; for example, Colorado Trout Unlimited is working with agencies and permittees to monitor riparian areas. Members establish monitoring sites and visit them each year before and after the grazing season. But the history of public planning, from cities to wilderness areas, shows that participatory assessment is key to success and that broad participation reduces interest-group bias. Collaborative monitoring produces much more than data: environmentalists, ranchers, and agency personnel spend time together on the land and develop the new working relationships needed in the shift to ecologically and socially sustainable rangelands.

The catch here is that growing public interest in range management may force policy decisions on grazing plans, fees, and alternative land uses before the information is available to point toward sustainability. Environmentalists will argue that lack of information is a smoke screen, while some scientists will never be satisfied that sufficient information exists to change current practices. To reduce conflict in the transition to sustainable rangelands management, agencies will have to prove their sincerity by taking immediate, sometimes drastic, steps to reform grazing practices on lands that are obviously in trouble (i.e., where no additional ecological analysis is needed to demonstrate that a problem exists). With the worst lands launched toward faster recovery, a more meticulous ecological approach can be taken elsewhere.

Rangeland Equity

Quick and decisive action on the most degraded lands again raises questions of social equity: How much social dislocation are we willing to accept in the transition to ecosystems management and sustainability on rangelands? The notion of common ground requires that social, as well as ecological, values be considered. Unfortunately, social science has trouble defining important terms in the equity equation: What is fair market value for a public-lands grazing permit? Do parties who lose access to public-lands resources deserve some form of compensation? How can historical uses and large differences between public and private grasslands be taken into account during the transition to new ecosystem approaches? What is the link between social and ecological community health?

Antigrazing activists argue that people have had the upper hand for too long and that the natural environment must now be given time to rebound; if there is sacrifice to be made, it must be by people, not environment, and the welfare of ranch families and rural communities has less standing than that of ecosystems. We believe, however, that a shift toward ecosystem sustainability must take account of impacts on people currently using the ecosystem as a resource. Indeed, socially inequitable solutions will be self-defeating, leading back to the old gridlock. A historical social contract with American society allowed, even encouraged, ranchers to use public lands for their own profit and the benefit of the food supply and national economy. While this contract needs to be reformed, care must be taken not to discard human values in the search for ecological improvement. This is tricky territory: What about the young rancher trying to do a good job on degraded land? Is it sufficient that the land is recovering, or should all degraded lands, no matter what their trend, be released from grazing?

Social equity is also the principal factor in the grazing-fee debate. In all likelihood, fees will be increased in the near future, expanding the funds available for range monitoring and management and maybe reducing some grazing pressure. The effect of a fee hike on rural communities is uncertain; some studies indicate that it would change grazing economics very little, while others suggest that it would put many ranches out of business. Fees should be increased, but by how much is a crucial question. Those who argue for "market value" fail to recognize that there is no true market in a system based on a common property resource like the federal lands. We argue, instead, for a better "societal value," one that recognizes the social value of rangelands and grazing and covers the costs of managing them. We are especially concerned that false market pricing will create a fee hike that actually knocks out some ranchers who are the best land managers: those who have invested more in range protection (fencing riparian areas, deferred grazing) and who are voluntarily managing land for values other than maximum economic return. A large increase might reduce the viability of more rural communities, forcing them into alternative (sometimes less desirable) economic development schemes. There is also social logic in setting the fee so as not to reduce the economic viability of associated private-land holdings that now act as de facto buffers against subdivisions and other developments.

Access to the Policy Process

While it will demand great effort from all rangeland interests, more participatory grazing planning and monitoring is needed. Arizona State University law professor Joe Feller has fought for the participation of affected interests in all significant range-management decisions; environmentalists should get involved in grazing policy and monitoring as well. The Sierra Club's Public Lands Committee already sends activists out to assess problem allotments, using its guidebook *How Not to Be Cowed*. This should be expanded to both good and bad allotments. All rangeland interests need to hone their skills at assessing resource quality; true participatory and ecologically sound land management requires that all groups learn about, and apply, principles of landscape ecology.

A more open policy process is also needed. The old grazing advisory boards must be replaced with multiple-use committees reflecting a broader community of rangeland users.

MAPPING COMMON GROUND ON THE WESTERN RANGE

Much of the problem with public-lands grazing, we think, is nicely expressed in the hackneyed phrase "what we have here is a failure to communicate." Some of that failure is purposeful: antigrazing activists avoid interacting with ranchers and other rural folk so as not to be compromised; ranchers don't want to be seen with "the enemy" and can't imagine that they have anything to learn from environmentalists. But each side should have the strength of conviction and open-mindedness to look the other in the eye and explore their differences and similarities. This is the only way to fairly determine how much each must contribute to bring human use into compliance with ecological sustainability.

Unfortunately, only a few meeting grounds for such dialogue now exist—in grazing working groups that have sprung up around the West, like Arizona's 6×6 process (*High Country News,* September 21, 1992); the Oregon Watershed Improvement Coalition (*High Country News,* March 23, 1992); and the Colorado Resource Round-Table. These are discussion groups of ranchers and environmentalists coming together to get around the gridlock caused when institutionalized interests, like national livestock and mainline environmental groups, fight it out in the courts and on Capitol Hill.

Such grassroots efforts need time and additional energy to succeed and spread elsewhere. Working groups of ranchers, environmentalists, and agency personnel can be formed by anyone with a real interest in rangeland issues. These working groups are creating a new approach to western grazing, inventing a new social contract among producers, consumers, environmentalists, and others simply by getting them to know one another; they are spending time on the land and starting from agreed-upon principles rather than from the rigid rhetoric of preservation versus exploitation. The history of western public-lands use, especially the dismal record of interest groups squaring off against one another, shows that only a shared process of regional, social, and ecological goal setting will solve grazing conflicts. This grassroots process must be aided by federal agencies that take participatory planning and monitoring seriously, that accept ecosystems and biodiversity goals as equal to, even more basic than, commodity goals, and that practice scientifically, not politically based, management.

Because of broader participation in public rangeland management, rich ideas are emerging, such as working-group agreements to actually manage grazing allotments under the current system and trading grazing permits that can be used or left ungrazed by groups willing to pay, as proposed in Karl Hess' book *Visions on the Land* (Island Press). Charles Wilkinson, a thoughtful observer of western culture and landscape, argues in his book *Crossing the Next Meridian* (Island Press) for a rebirth of community-scale planning and stewardship based on watersheds or other natural units. This is starting to show up not only in the grazing working groups, but in coordinated resource management (CRM) projects around the West that bring together a wider representation than the grazing advisory boards ever did. Some CRM projects, such as on the Sun Ranch in Wyoming and Axial Basin in Colorado, have yielded measurable improvements in critical areas like riparian vegetation and overall biodiversity, as well as new connections among people. Many ranchers are adopting holistic resource management (HRM) or similar grazing and ranch management schemes that call for more balance between livestock production and social and ecological goals. These are encouraging developments, though they have weaknesses. Many CRM teams still need more environmental representation, and they often get hung up over the role of predators in a healthy landscape; and HRM adherents seem overly optimistic about the positive benefits of intense grazing. Yet, CRM, HRM, and the working groups are steps in the right direction.

We also need some relief from the institutionalized gridlock over grazing issues. Both environmentalists and ranchers have criticized the incipient working-group process (*High Country News,* December 28, 1992). Environmentalists fear that concerns for ranching culture and social equity—which often emerge when people get to know one another—will weaken the resolve to give nature its due. The formalized institutions of both environmentalism and the livestock industry may even prefer to keep the battle in the courts and Congress, fearing that local and regional groups may reach agreements that do not support their national agenda.

Grassroots efforts to reinvent public rangeland management need support, and some breathing room, from the "establishment" of national environmental organizations, livestock associations, and even agencies and range professionals pursuing an old agenda. Geographical differences in rangelands across the West mean that local and regional solutions may be best. We definitely need a common ecological inventory and assessment by the agencies and range professionals, and we need them as participants in the discussion process. We need the support of nongovernmental organizations, but, we also need some relief from the long tradition of hierarchical decision making. National organizations often lose touch with local and regional needs as they fight battles in the rarified atmosphere of national policy. Their mandates tend to be applied universally, regardless of regional differences of culture, ecology, and social need. Too often, simple care for land and people at the local and regional scale is seen by agency, industry, and environmental bigwigs as idealistic, unprofessional, and unpolitic. If they are to create common ground in range issues, local people require room to maneuver, as well as relief from the barrage of lawsuits and the institutionalized environmentalism and utilitarianism that squash grassroots solutions.

NEXT STEPS

Armed with new ideas, new lines of communication, a few success stories like those from the working groups and CRM projects, a few people, in a few places, are forging a new social ecology on the great western rangelands. The well-being of both sides in the grazing debate is centered on the land itself, which provides the most obvious place to start mapping a broader common ground. More environmentalist and rancher working groups must be formed, and they should go out on the land and explore it together. The land acts as a sounding board for our ideals and our biases, and people trying to understand how it works, and how to live on it, will start with much in common.

Our prescription for creating common ground in the grazing debate includes these steps:

1. More grazing working groups—mapping parties of environmentalists and ranchers, as it were—must be formed right away. The few ongoing roundtables and coalitions must expand their efforts and spawn new groups. Their discussions should not start with standard grazing issues; rather, they should explore broad environmental and social goals and then work down to specifics. They should choose local rangelands to explore, monitor, and even manage jointly.

2. Policy makers at all levels, local to national, should take part in this process and withhold major change until the working groups have fashioned new approaches aimed at sustainable, regionally viable management and monitoring. The scouting parties cannot function if they believe that national institutions and agencies—industrial, governmental, and environmental—will simply continue business as usual.

3. Rangeland management success stories must be written up and widely shared. Several integrated land-management efforts are functioning on the ground right now, and while the degree of their success will be debated, our sense is that an authentic shift toward sustainability is occurring in a few cases, which deserve attention from grazing working groups, environmental leaders, and policy makers.

4. Finally, environmentalists must work toward a new social contract with the rural interests that they so often find themselves fighting. The rural West is changing, but urban environmentalists have tended to distance themselves from rural communities and society. While they have fought the good fight to preserve public lands, rural well-being has declined, and new, often urbanlike and less desirable developments are sprouting up on private rural lands. Environmentalists may soon find themselves supporting, rather than fighting, ranching in the West as a line of defense against creeping urbanization and suburbanization. A rural environmentalism is growing in the West, and it should be embraced and fostered.

The overarching need is for collaborative, conscientious involvement in a new and more open process. The old institutions, like grazing advisory boards, must be replaced with a broader community of interests. Finding common ground, and moving toward rangeland sustainability, will take meetings and more meetings, and time out on the land. Perhaps most important, it will take more openness. Public-lands ranchers cannot seclude themselves behind the ranch gate or in producer organizations, agency folks must get out of their offices, and environmental activists cannot continue to distance themselves from the rural society that their advocacy affects. A sustainable western range will come only from our joint efforts.

Wise Use in the West

The Case of the Northwest Timber Industry

Tarso Ramos

Throughout the West, the "Wise Use" movement is leading campaigns to defend the rapacious policies of natural resource industries. Much like the extractive practices of the corporations that finance them, these campaigns are leaving deep scars on the West. While industry involvement in the political and social arenas is not a new phenomenon, the Wise Use movement represents a fundamental departure from typical industry lobbying efforts. Drawing strength from some of the same leaders of, and the same sentiment as, the Sagebrush Rebellion,[1] the Wise Use movement involves a much broader coalition of ideological and economic interests that stand to profit from the deregulation of industry and the weakening of environmental regulations than did its older cousin. More important, this coalition has tapped corporate coffers to fund pro-industry community organizing against environmental protections. This effort has spawned pro-business citizens groups in communities throughout the West and the nation, has dominated local politics with an industry agenda, and has built power at the state and national levels.

"BEGINNINGS"

The start of the Wise Use movement is commonly dated to the 1988 Multiple Use Strategy Conference sponsored by the Center for the Defense of Free Enterprise (CDFE). That event brought Sagebrush-era "rebels" together with representatives from natural-resource corporations and leaders of right-wing organizations—some 250 persons in all[2]—for three days of strategizing. Soon after, CDFE president Alan Gottlieb edited and published "the results" of the conference in a paperback volume titled, *The Wise Use Agenda: The Citizen's Policy Guide to Environmental Resource Issues.*[3] Described on its cover as "A Task Force Report to the Bush Administration by the Wise Use Movement," the book includes a "letter of transmittal" to then-President Bush from "the Wise Use Movement," a list of the top 25 movement goals, letters to Bush from various Wise Use groups (as well as a telegram of support from Bush to one of these groups),[4] and an "Index of The Wise Use Movement": 224 organizations and individuals that "attended or supported the Multiple Use Strategy Conference in August 1988 at Reno, Nevada, where the Wise Use movement mandated the publication of this agenda."[5]

In his introduction to *The Wise Use Agenda,* CDFE Executive Vice President Ron Arnold describes these conference participants as the "founders of the Wise Use Movement." Claims Arnold, "They were not single-minded preservationists and they were not single-minded apologists for industrial development. They were representatives of a new balance, of a middle way between extreme environmentalism and extreme industrialism."[6] However, the "Index of The Wise Use Movement" (as well as the "top 25 goals"[7]) suggests a different orientation. The index includes resource corporations (e.g. Boise-Cascade, Du Pont, Exxon U.S.A., Georgia Pacific, and Louisiana-Pacific); various industry trade associations (e.g. Associated Logging Contractors of Idaho, National Association of Wheat Growers, Nevada Cattlemen's Association, Nevada Miners & Prospectors Association, Timber Association of California, Washington Contract Loggers Association, Western Forest Industries Association, Western Wood Products Association, the Williamette Forestry Council); and a number of right-wing groups, such as the National Center for Constitutional Studies.[8]

Far from embracing environmental "balance," the Multiple Use Strategy Conference represented an effort to forge an alliance between right-wing activists, many of whom were active in the Reagan Administration, and resource companies intent on eliminating environmental regulations. The rhetoric of "balance," which includes slogans like "putting people back into the environmental equation" and "man and nature together: a world that's whole," is part of a carefully calculated public relations strategy to win public support by disguising the true aims of the movement. Instead of openly attacking environmentalism, which has popular appeal in the United States, Wise Use leaders like Ron Arnold have instead claimed the mantle of environmentalism for themselves and branded their adversaries as "radical preservationists." The rhetoric employed by Wise Use leaders at their own conferences is more revealing. Arnold told a 1991 meeting of 150 members of the New Mexico

Wool Growers Association that environmentalists are "nature fascists" out to "destroy industrial civilization." Not to worry, said Arnold, "We're going to destroy them, like they're trying to destroy you!"[9]

Arnold notes that four "distinct constituencies" attended the 1988 Multiple Use Strategy Conference. By his calculation, the largest of these was "executives of public interest membership organizations dealing in some way with environmental or resource issues."[10] Next in size was "unaffiliated individuals." Both groups were dominated by right-wing activists. According to Arnold, the third-largest constituency was "trade group and government representatives" (e.g., right-wing county commissioners drawn to the "home rule" legal strategies of the National Federal Lands Conference[11]), followed by "industrial firms focused around natural resource extraction and conversion."[12] The domination of the Multiple Use Strategy Conference by activists reflected both Arnold's underdeveloped relationships with industry and his emphasis on building an activist movement. At an unscheduled strategy session at the conference on spreading the movement through the West, Arnold told those present, "Issues don't matter. *Mastery of activism* is all that matters. I want to create Killer Activists."[13] Arnold encouraged activists to sponsor similar events in their home states, so as to quickly spread the Wise Use movement.[14] In adjourning the Multiple Use Strategy Conference, Wyoming State Rep. Marlene Simons declared, "This is the start of the Wise Use movement. Now get the hell out there and go to work!"[15]

Following the 1988 Multiple Use Strategy Conference, the Wise Use movement began to develop as a tangible and increasingly powerful political force. The conference itself became an annual event that attracted both Wise Use activists and their allies in business and politics. While maintaining an uneasy truce with "environmental president" George Bush, the Wise Use movement established firm ties with Vice President Dan Quayle's Council on Competitiveness, which functioned as industry's back door into the White House. At the 1992 conference, Quayle assistant and Competitiveness Council Executive Director David McIntosh addressed a luncheon ceremony where Louisiana–Pacific CEO Harry Merlo was presented with an "Industrial Achievement Award."[16]

Although the Center for the Defense of Free Enterprise's 1988 Reno conference and the subsequent publication of *The Wise Use Agenda* officially launched the Wise Use movement, for Ron Arnold and other key activists the movement had been a long time in the making. Nearly ten years before the Multiple Use Strategy Conference, before Ronald Reagan had appointed James Watt to head the Department of the Interior, or even had been elected president, Arnold proposed the strategy that, with a few modifications, would guide the Wise Use movement as it took shape in the late 1980s.

THE ARCHITECT OF WISE USE

As he himself is fond of pointing out, in the late 1960s and early 1970s, Ron Arnold was an environmental activist. He was recruited to the Alpine Lakes Protection Society (ALPS) in 1969 while visiting an outdoor show in Seattle. The volunteer staffing an ALPS literature table engaged Arnold in conversation and quickly perceived that he was capable and bright. The year-old conservation group was working to create a national recreation area for the Alpine Lakes region of Washington state and Arnold offered to contribute his talents to their efforts. Arnold, who at the time was working as a draftsman for Boeing,[17] set to work producing a slide show for the group in early 1970. Before long, he was invited to serve as an ALPS trustee.[18] He completed the slide show—by all accounts impressive—in the fall of 1970 and the following spring was appointed "publicity chairman" for the group.[19] Later, Arnold produced a second slide show for ALPS and helped write the text for a map of the Alpine Lakes region.

According to former ALPS members, Arnold's slide shows were seen by many thousands of people and helped to generate strong support for protection of the Alpine Lakes region, including some 5,000 favorable responses during a Forest Service comment period. As ALPS amassed support for its agenda, several timber companies created a coalition to fight protection of the Alpine Lakes. It is perhaps a testament to the effectiveness of Arnold's slide shows that the industry group quickly produced its own slide show on the Alpine Lakes issue.[20]

Despite his industriousness, however, Arnold was not exactly an impassioned environmentalist. Although he served as an ALPS trustee and belonged to the Sierra Club, some of his colleagues at ALPS found him to be unknowledgeable about basic environmental issues. According to one, he was given to long, philosophical discussions that suggested deeper convictions regarding free enterprise and private property rights than protection of the natural environment. Some ALPS activists even suggest that Arnold assisted the group as a means to develop his portfolio and attract commercial clients.[21] But whatever his initial commitment to the environmental cause, Arnold started selling his skills to timber companies—much to the dismay of his colleagues at ALPS.

This development may have been precipitated by Arnold's losing his job at Boeing during a major downsizing there. Following his layoff, Arnold started his own media-relations firm, Northwood Studios. According to Ben Hayes, a founder and one-time president of ALPS, Arnold was hired by Weyerhaeuser to produce training films, and later did work for a Portland-based timber company.[22] In 1977, he was hired to defeat a proposed expansion of Redwoods National Park.[23] He failed in that endeavor, but became known as a hired gun for industry.

Over the years, Arnold hired himself out to both timber and pesticide companies.[24] He wrote an eight-part series of articles attacking the environmental movement entitled "The Environmental Battle" that ran in *Logging Management* magazine from February, 1979 to June, 1980.[25] The seventh installment in the series, "Defeating Environmentalism," contains the blueprints for what would eventually become the Wise Use movement.[26] In that article, Arnold urged the timber industry to adopt the cornerstone of the Wise Use strategy: "combine our traditional approaches with the same activist techniques that have been so devastating in environmentalist hands." Advising industry to take a lesson from community organizer Saul Alinsky and go outside the experience and expectations of its adversaries, Arnold insisted that "the forest industry can ultimately win [the battle against environmentalism] only by expanding its experience and by striking back with its own brand of activism."[27]

Arnold identified pro-industry citizen activism as the key to defeating the environmental movement. "Citizen activist groups, allied to the forest industry," he wrote, "are vital to our future survival. They can speak for us in the public interest where we ourselves cannot. They are not limited by liability, contract law or ethical codes. They can provide something for people to join, to be part of, to fight for." For "our" part, he argued, "[i]ndustry must come to support citizen activist groups, providing funds, materials, transportation, and most of all, hard facts."[28] Arnold proposed that careful investment in and cultivation of existing industry-identified, though not necessarily activist, citizen groups, such as Women in Timber chapters, could yield not only a grassroots constituency (lending new legitimacy to perennial industry claims of advancing the best interests of society) but a pro-industry counter-culture to compete with and overtake the environmentalist counter-culture. With this objective in mind, Arnold set about devising a strategy for industry activism that involved electing officials, promoting citizen activism, and shaping public opinion with such tactics as "good works in the public interest" and a large-scale pro-industry publication program that included classroom-targeted materials.[29] To be successful, Arnold's strategy would require an alliance of industry and activists.

Arnold penned this treatise from the Seattle suburb of Bellevue, Washington, which lies just across Puget Sound from the Olympic Peninsula and its large national park, old-growth forests, and the town of Forks, the self-proclaimed "logging capital of the world." Undoubtedly, his subject was of considerable interest to his audience of "logging managers," for whom the increasing success of the environmental movement in the 1970s had become a political and financial threat.

In 1980 Arnold became executive vice president of the Center for the Defense of Free Enterprise, joining CDFE president Alan Gottlieb, a well-known direct-mail fund-raiser for a variety of right-wing causes.[30] At CDFE, Arnold pursued the strategy he laid out in *Logging Management Magazine,* working to cultivate Women in Timber and other pro-industry "citizens" groups. A prolific writer and newspaper columnist, Arnold's fervent anti-environmentalism and connections with right-wing political networks[31] landed him a contract with the Free Congress Foundation to bolster the image of besieged Interior Secretary and Sagebrush Rebellion leader James Watt with a flattering biography, published in 1982.[32]

In 1981, a dispute between Dow Chemical Co. and the Environmental Protection Agency over the forest herbicide 2,4,5-T brought Arnold to a meeting of the Society of Weed Sciences in Wilsonville, Oregon. Arnold came to report that there was "evidence of collusion if not of actual conspiracy" between the EPA and nine Alsea, Oregon, women who had experienced mysterious, spontaneous abortions and identified the Dow-manufactured chemical 2,4,5-T sprayed on neighboring forests as the probable cause. Arnold, who said that he had conducted research into the matter, cited the testimony of a witness hired by Dow as evidence that half or more of the abortions could be attributed to "lifestyle" choices, such as cigarette and marijuana smoking, use of hallucinogenic drugs, drinking raw milk, and eating venison.[33] "In my opinion," he concluded, "there is no connection between 2,4,5-T and spontaneous abortion." Masking his industry orientation behind his history as an environmental activist, Arnold portrayed himself as sympathetic to the Alsea women: "I came from the counter-culture, I'm a friend of these people." He added, perhaps less disingenuously, "But they are too simplistic about who they're dealing with."[34]

Arnold used the Center for the Defense of Free Enterprise to build relationships with right-wing think tanks, legal centers, and activist groups that today participate in the Wise Use movement.[35] However, despite Arnold's years of work for the forest products industry, timber companies did not immediately line up to support his 'industry activism' strategy. One ALPS member who in the mid-1980s had occasion to work on a joint environmental/industry project, "Keep Washington Green," claims that the timber industry looked on Arnold as a "dangerous maverick."[36] In his articles for *Logging Management,* Arnold himself remarked that the experience of organizations that represented "the first stirrings of a genuine pro-industry citizen activist movement" demonstrated that "any such constituency first has to fight industry almost as hard as it fights environmentalists." "Trade associations in particular," he noted, "jealously guarded their power turf from the new interlopers."[37] It would take more than a compelling argument to lure industry to the Wise Use agenda and Arnold's posse of right-wing activists. Not until the timber industry faced major internal crises, in addition to ongoing challenges from the environmental movement, was it moved to take action on Arnold's unorthodox ideas.

The Northwest timber industry effectively pursued short-term profit over long-term stability through much of the 1980s, liquidating private timber holdings,[38] restricting reinvestment to the automation of a few mills, and otherwise reducing labor costs wherever possible. Over that decade both employment and real wages in Oregon's timber industry, the largest in the country, dropped by around 20 percent. In 1989 a decline in the demand for forest products sent shock waves through timber towns, as some statewide firms closed down and national conglomerates like Georgia–Pacific moved to exploit a lower-paid, non-union workforce in the South. Throughout the Northwest these shifts produced a large pool of unemployed and underemployed timber workers and struggling small business owners who over generations had come to depend on the timber industry for their livelihoods, but who now feared for their economic futures. At the same time, environmental groups were becoming increasingly successful in garnering public support for their campaigns to save the region's remaining ancient forests. Faced with a gloomy economic forecast and the likelihood of massive popular resentment from workers as well as environmental groups, some timber firms signed on to the first industry-wide Wise Use organizing experiment, spearheaded not by Ron Arnold, but by veterans of Oregon's Sagebrush Rebellion.

THE EMERGENCE OF WISE USE: THE OREGON PROJECT

From the steps of the Oregon state capitol building in Salem on May 21, 1989, Wise Use organizer Barbara Grannell addressed an audience of over 1,000 who had gathered to protest a U.S. district judge's injunction against logging in spotted owl habitat and to demonstrate support for the timber industry. The listing of the spotted owl as an endangered species had precipitated a series of legal and legislative battles over logging in owl habitat and particularly the old-growth forests that the bird was found to favor. The spotted owl crisis was a windfall for Grannell, whose mission was to create broad-based support for unrestricted industry access to public forest lands. It provided a scapegoat for a crisis precipitated in no small part by irresponsible industry practices such as overcutting, automation, and log exportation. Grannell assured those assembled that they would soon replace the owl as Oregon's leading newsmaker, and she presented members of the state's congressional delegation with stacks of petitions bearing some 158,000 signatures which called for the "continued use of federal lands within Oregon for commercial timber harvesting at historic and sustainable rates."[39] Among those sharing the stage with Grannell were Richard Butrick, president of Associated Oregon Industries, Oregon Representative Bob Smith, a staunch supporter of the timber and ranching industries, and Senator Bob Packwood, a sometime wilderness advocate, who called for saving mill jobs with a raw log export ban.[40] In her closing remarks Grannell declared, "This is only the beginning of what Oregon's communities are prepared to do. This is only the beginning of the Oregon Project and similar projects in other western states."[41]

The rally was followed by others. These demonstrations often featured logging-truck caravans that stretched for fifteen miles, brandishing yellow ribbons and parading through towns in the heart of Oregon's timber country, or circling the state capitol building with their horns blaring.[42] The yellow ribbon had become the official symbol of the pro-industry movement. It was meant to represent solidarity with timber communities "held hostage" to an extremist environmental agenda and could be seen on lapels and car antennas and in store windows in timber-dependent communities.[43] These events were coordinated by Grannell's Oregon Project, a campaign of the Pueblo, Colorado-based Western States Public Lands Coalition (WSPLC), and also by a growing number of local pro-industry "citizens" groups that appeared in seemingly spontaneous response to the timber crisis that industry and its allies attributed to scarcity caused by environmentalist "lock-ups."

The WSPLC was directed by Grannell's husband Bill, a former Oregon state legislator and original Sagebrush Rebel.[44] Bill Grannell was best known for spearheading an unsuccessful 1981 effort to transfer federally owned public lands in Oregon to state control, as well as for some difficulty that same year with the Oregon Government Ethics Commission.[45] When following that legislative session Grannell announced his decision not to seek reelection, *The Oregonian* noted that the outgoing representative was regarded by one colleague as "manipulative—inclined to maneuver people for private agendas that are not always revealed."[46] This is an equally apt characterization of the WSPLC and its first Wise Use campaign, the Oregon Project.

The Grannells, who had recently moved to Colorado, founded the WSPLC in the summer of 1988.[47] Later that same year they set up shop for the Oregon Project in the offices of Associated Oregon Industries and began selling seats on the WSPLC board of directors at $15,000 each to a host of Oregon timber firms.[48] The way the Grannells tell it, at the suggestion of Senator Mark O. Hatfield they were invited back to Oregon by the Association of Oregon & California Counties, which is a coalition of county governments that rely on revenue from federal timber sales on local lands once owned by the Oregon and California Railroad.[49] By April, 1989, the Oregon Project claimed the endorsement of 11 county governments, four members of Oregon's congressional delegation (AuCoin, Hatfield, Packwood, and Smith), a number of business associations representing timber and banking, two timber-related labor unions (the International Woodworkers of America and the International Brotherhood of Lumber and Sawmill Workers), and the Confederation of Oregon School Administrators.[50]

As the Grannells launched their pro-timber industry campaign, Ron Arnold was active in attempting to open the Alaska National Wildlife Refuge to oil drilling (item number two on *The Wise Use Agenda*), working with the Canadian timber industry to develop the "Share" movement, a Canadian equivalent to Wise Use, and otherwise expanding the Wise Use movement to include other issues and groups.[51] While Arnold and the Grannells operated more or less independently of each other, they appear at times to have coordinated their efforts. For instance, a CDFE-sponsored Oregon Wise Use Conference featuring Senator Bob Packwood, Jim Geisinger (president of the Northwest Forestry Association), and representatives from a variety of local and national Wise Use organizations was scheduled for the day before the May 1989 WSPLC Salem rally where Packwood and other elected officials were presented with petitions collected by the Oregon Project.[52] More important, the Grannells and Oregon's timber industry implemented the fundamental elements of Arnold's strategy.

An Oregon Project brochure circulated in April 1989 boasts "Across western Oregon a rare phenomenon is happening, which if it takes root in other states in the west [*sic*] could bring about a revolution in the management of federal public lands. The phenomenon [*sic*] is grassroots, community organizing."[53] Aided by the cooperation of timber industry managers and the chilling experience of mill closures (15 in the first months of 1989 alone), the Oregon

Project began adding pro-industry "citizens" groups to their coalition of industry and local governments.[54] Adopting a key tactic of the Wise Use strategy, these groups attempted to overcome the widespread appeal of the environmental movement by characterizing themselves as the "true" environmentalists and their environmental opponents as "radical preservationists" more concerned with the welfare of birds and bugs than with the survival of human beings.

In one case of pro-industry organizing, a saw operator at Roseburg Forest Products started the group Timber Resources Equal Economic Stability, or TREES. His employer gave him time away from work to organize the employees and paid some of his expenses. Plant supervisors called workers off the shop floor to hear his presentations and implored them to defend their jobs by taking action in defense of the timber industry by joining pro-industry groups and by writing letters to the editor attacking environmentalism.[55] Fortunate to have jobs in a contracting industry, employees found it difficult to refuse these suggestions or to decline to attend rallies when they were given the day off for that purpose and were provided with transportation to the event. Four months after its founding, TREES claimed some 1,100 timber workers among its membership.[56] Such methods, viewed by some workers as job blackmail, became commonplace.[57] On at least one occasion, several timber firms side-stepped the usual coercion by simply purchasing individual memberships, at $12 each, for all their employees in a pro-industry organizing group.[58] Using such tactics, the timber industry could produce bodies at pro-industry rallies as well as names on the rolls of pro-industry citizen organizations like TREES, Workers of Oregon Development (WOOD), Protect Industries Now Endangered (PINE), and Communities for a Great Oregon. The intent of the Wise Use strategy devised by Arnold, however, was to win converts and thereby create an actual pro-industry citizens' movement, not just the appearance of one. This has proven a more difficult task, though not for any lack of effort.

One cause of the difficulty has been the problem of convincing working people that their interests lie with industry. The timber industry's legacy of automation over the 1980s created a wave of unemployment in timber communities and did little to facilitate trust between employer and employee. The conflicting interests of workers and industry sometimes took an even more palpable form. During a 1989 strike at Roseburg Forest Products, where TREES was organized, scabs flying the emblematic yellow ribbon from their car antennas drove across the picket line,[59] which sent a clear message to the strikers that Wise Use was not a movement for the workers. Although this event had an initial chilling effect on grassroots support for the Oregon Project and other pro-industry efforts, many timber workers found themselves with few options.

A fundamental element of the Grannells' strategy was to stress the dependence of county budgets, schools, families, and communities on federal timberland harvests.[60] To this same end, the timber industry has launched any number of "educational" campaigns targeted at mills, schools, and television audiences. Some of these predate the Oregon Project. In the early 1980s, Associated Oregon Loggers and Willamette Industries contributed a combined total of $6,000 to the production of a pro-resource-industry textbook. The book, titled *Get Oregonized,* treated such controversial issues as coyote eradication, private grazing on public lands, and clear-cutting favorably, while expressing skepticism about wilderness designation.[61] Other funders for *Get Oregonized* included the Oregon Wheat Commission ($9,000), the Federal Land Bank ($6,000), the Oregon Beef Council ($3,000), the Oregon Seed Council ($2,000), and the Oregon Farm Bureau Federation ($1,250).[62] Critics from environmental and educational groups decried the book's biases as well as the numerous factual and grammatical errors discovered in the text.[63] But, in what one reporter described as "a battle for the hearts and minds of Oregon schoolchildren,"[64] over 100 volunteers with timber and farming organizations lobbied the state and local school districts to use the book. By January 1985, *Get Oregonized* was being used in fourth grade classes in ten Oregon school districts,[65] and in March of the following year the state board of education gave the book its stamp of approval.[66] While the Oregon Environmental Council and the Portland Audubon Society brought an unsuccessful appeals suit against the board of education,[67] the director of the *Get Oregonized* project produced and distributed a second textbook, *Global Oregon,* aimed at tenth-graders.[68]

In 1989, the timber industry tried another tactic to win the hearts and minds of schoolchildren, while circumventing the textbook review process. That year a Sweet Home, Oregon, outfit named Common Sense Inc. produced a storybook/songbook and audio cassette titled *Timbear's Unibearsity.* The story is narrated by the title character, a bear not unlike the Forest Service's Smokey, dressed in pants, suspenders, and hardhat. Timbear takes his readers/listeners on a tour of the woods ("Now this is where I work, right here in a renewable natural resource"), including a logging site where various machines are identified by name and function ("Yarders are no more than powerful winches, much like your fishing reel, and their drums are shaped like mom's thread spools"), and a clearing where an old logger pays his last respects to a tree he intends to fell ("farmers and loggers are the same, you see. Loggers' plants, they're just bigger—and we call them trees").[69] According to Ted Ferrioli, president of the Springfield, Oregon, timber industry public relations firm Community Relations Associates, following the *Get Oregonized* experiment, the industry began producing "supplemental" education materials instead of textbooks in order to circumvent school board review. Supplemental materials can be used at the discretion of schoolteachers. Ferrioli claims that the strategy has worked well in public schools, which are often short on supplies and whose instructors, burdened with large classes, welcome the opportunity to distribute materials that keep students occupied.[70]

Ferrioli's Community Relations Associates (CRA) was founded in 1986 for the sole purpose of promoting the timber industry. Among its activities, CRA publishes *Timber!,* a newsletter that defines the terms of debate over environmental issues for an audience of timber-dependent communities in the Pacific Northwest. In it, readers are told that biodiversity is a key forestry principle of *Timber!* underwriter Weyerhaeuser—that is, the company plants different species of monoculture forests appropriate to the various regions in which it owns tree farms. In keeping with industry "greening" efforts and attempts by Wise Use activists to portray themselves as environmentalists who simply aim to "put people back into the environmental equation,"[71] in 1992, *Timber!* changed its name to *Forests Now and Forever.*[72]

Other industry "educational" materials are designed to translate Wise Use ideology into results at the voting booth. In late 1988 the Northwest Forest Resources Council, a coalition of 11 Pacific Northwest forest-products companies and timber associations that depend on federal timber, bought and distributed 25,000 copies of a 48-page voters' pamphlet-like primer on pro-timber activism titled *A Resource Book for People Affected by Log Shortages.* The pamphlet was distributed by the Oregon Project.[73]

By the summer of 1989 WSPLC had raised $180,000 for itself, and the Oregon Project boasted chapters in half the counties in the state, as well as an invitation to send "official observers" to Governor Neil Goldschmidt's Forest Summit.[74] The influence of the Oregon Project was manifest in other ways. A year after the 1989 Salem rally, Senator Bob Packwood, now firmly in the Wise Use camp, addressed the largest rally that had ever been held in Portland's Pioneer Courthouse Square and told the crowd of 10,000 timber industry supporters that he "had reached his limit of patience" with advocates of more wilderness.[75] The Portland event was sponsored by a pro-industry group called the Yellow Ribbon Coalition, part of a new coalition formed by Oregon Project leaders. As in Salem the previous year, the group's namesake could be seen on lapels and trucks, and even as bows in the hair of rally goers. More than 300 companies around the state gave employees the day off to attend the gathering, and transportation to Portland was provided by many employers and pro-industry groups.[76] Oregon State AFL-CIO president Irv Fletcher, who had been invited to speak to the crowd, at the last minute declined to do so when rally organizers prohibited him from speaking in favor of a raw log export ban, insisting that he limit his remarks to the spotted owl.[77] The goal of an export ban would be to save jobs by requiring domestic milling of Northwest timber. Large exporters like Weyerhaeuser oppose a ban because it would cut into their very profitable trade in raw logs to Pacific rim countries, including Japan.

With tactics ranging from intimidation to sophisticated public relations campaigns to solid grassroots organizing, Oregon's Wise Use movement mobilized a grassroots base for a timber industry agenda. It also successfully recast the debate over environmental protections and sustainable forest practices in the news media and the political arena to a polarized "us against them" contest in which the cost of protecting the natural environment was increasingly perceived to be the protection of individuals and communities.

THE OREGON LANDS COALITION

The network of pro-industry groups that the Oregon Project helped to develop evolved into the Oregon Lands Coalition (OLC), founded by, among others, Valerie Johnson, chapter president of Oregon Project–Portland. Johnson, of the D.R. Johnson timber family, is on the family payroll as a full-time Wise Use organizer.[78] The OLC split with the WSPLC when it became clear that the Grannells wanted to extend the Oregon Project to other states while maintaining tight control over Oregon's Wise Use movement.[79] The Grannells returned to Colorado, where fears ran high that an impending congressional debate over reform of the 1872 Mining Law might impinge on the immensely favorable terms for mining on public lands,[80] and turned their attention to the mining industry. With the success of the Oregon Project behind them, the Grannells convinced executives of major mining corporations that they could produce a groundswell of grassroots opposition to any reform of the 1872 Mining Law. The result was a five-state pro-mining campaign called People for the West!, which has since expanded beyond its original target states of California, Colorado, New Mexico, Arizona, and Montana.

The OLC rapidly expanded into an umbrella organization representing over 60 groups statewide, including natural resource industry associations (the

Eastern Oregon Mining Association, Associated Oregon Loggers, Oregon Cattlemen's Association, Oregon Sheep Growers Association), an insurance consortium (Oregon Farm Bureau), labor union locals (Association of Pulp & Paper Workers Locals 1, 3, and 166), a pro-pesticide group (Oregonians for Food and Shelter), and a variety of "grassroots" organizations such as the Yellow Ribbon Coalition and TREES.[81] OLC activities are funded by a host of businesses and individuals, including half of the timber firms that bought seats on the WSPLC board of directors, and many other timber companies, including industry giants like Weyerhaeuser.[82] OLC supporters Bohemia, Freres Lumber, Boise-Cascade, and Seneca Sawmill have been involved in the Wise Use movement since at least 1988, when all attended or supported the Multiple Use Strategy Conference organized by Ron Arnold, and other early Wise Use groups are represented in the coalition. For instance, OLC backers Sun Studs, Seneca Sawmill, and Sterling Hanel of Hanel Lumber Co. were part of the task force that provided funding and printing for CDFE's *The Wise Use Agenda*.[83]

Ron Arnold appears to work more closely with the OLC than he had done with the Grannells, who seemed more comfortable with industry than with right-wing activists of Arnold's ilk and also may have sought to defend their "turf" from other Wise Use leaders. Still, the relationship is not always a comfortable one. As Arnold's ties to the Reverend Sun Myung Moon's Unification Church became more widely known following press revelations starting in 1989, the OLC publicly distanced itself from CDFE. Still, as recently as October 1992, Arnold told a Portland newspaper, "I love the OLC. They've been very successful in promoting what I call our bumper-sticker philosophy: Man and nature can live in productive harmony."[84] He even claimed to plan strategy with OLC leaders. In fact, the OLC's public distancing from Arnold may have been for appearances only. In response to press probes into the coalition's "moonie connection," OLC public relations officer Jackie Lang arranged media training for members with none other than Washington, D.C.-based Accuracy in Media, which is parent to the infamous right-wing campus "watchdog" group and *The Wise Use Agenda* signator Accuracy in Academia.[85] And in 1993 the OLC-affiliated Alliance for America co-sponsored CDFE's Wise Use Leadership Conference.[86]

Like the Oregon Project that preceded it, the OLC organized rallies and orchestrated telephone and letter campaigns to target particular pieces of legislation and individual elected officials. The OLC has gotten involved in a wide spectrum of resource industry issues, but its main timber policy objective is the same as that of its predecessor: unrestricted access to the public lands timber base. A principal impact of OLC organizing has been the polarization of debate on environmental issues to an extent that erodes the middle ground, where solutions to tough political problems are generally negotiated. To cite one example, during the 1991 legislative session the OLC mobilized its network to press both houses of the Oregon legislature for a joint memorial to Congress in support of the Community Stability Act, which was created by OLC leaders and staff members of Representative Bob Smith (R-OR), who introduced it in Congress.[87] Although the act, which would have prioritized economic stability over environmental protection, was dead on arrival in the legislature, the OLC fought hard for the memorial, itself a sure loser and of little potential impact on Congress, even in the implausible event of its passage. The OLC used the memorial's defeat as evidence for its claims that environmentalists have undue legislative influence and to stir up the already widespread public resentment of the political process.

SPREADING THE MOVEMENT: NEAR AND FAR

Washington State's Olympic Peninsula has been a hotbed of Wise Use activity since the beginning of the movement. Both Ron Arnold and Charles Cushman, Arnold's associate at the National Inholders Association, have been promoting Wise Use-type activity there since before the 1988 Reno conference. On July 1, 1989, shortly after Barbara Grannell addressed timber-industry supporters in Salem, Cushman spoke before a capacity crowd in the Spartan High School gym in Forks, Washington. This "Support for Life" rally began with the singing of the National Anthem, followed by a sermon from an Assemblies of God minister who prayed that "the voice of the grassroots of logging be heard. . . . Bless this rally." Cushman, a familiar face to some who knew him from a 1981 fight against Wild and Scenic Rivers designation, urged rally participants to move their message from the Peninsula to the urban centers and the political mainstream, and warned against compromising with environmentalists, who, he warned, will just keep coming back for more. Cushman shared the stage with Washington Senators Slade Gorton and Jack Metcalf,[88] Mountain States Legal Foundation President Perry Pendley, Wise Use "county movement" spokeswoman Karen Budd, and others.[89]

Timber-dependent communities on the Olympic Peninsula have been especially hard-hit by reductions in public land harvest levels and have seen unemployment surpass the 20-percent mark in several areas. To these communities the Wise Use movement has offered an opportunity to take action and with it a sense of hope, however false. Timber workers in Forks, once the self-proclaimed "logging capital of the world," seized national headlines in the summer of 1992 when 20 of them cut blown-down trees in protected spotted owl habitat into standard mill lengths.[90] The action was led by Larry Mason, a native New Englander who moved to Forks in 1987 and by 1989 scraped together enough money to open an old-growth timber mill just as environmentalists succeeded in blocking the harvest of old-growth in owl habitat.[91] Without a supply of old-growth, Mason's investment was worthless. The group had announced its direct action plans to the local press days before and newspapers carried photographs of one logger waving a large U.S. flag and of the protesters being taken off to jail. Mason, who heads the Washington Commercial Forest Action Committee, was among those arrested. Less than two weeks later, 16 people went back into owl habitat to repeat the tactic.[92] The actions were successful in attracting national attention, and in the fall the Bush administration called for lifting restrictions against harvesting blown-down trees in federally managed forests.[93]

Washington pro-timber-industry activists like Mason have been linked to the larger Wise Use movement by the OLC network, mainly through its national umbrella group, the Alliance for America. The Alliance was created by OLC and other Wise Use activists in 1991 to give a national presence to the movement and forge alliances between various Wise Use constituencies.[94] The Alliance organizes annual "Fly-In-for-Freedom" lobbying trips to the nation's capital[95] and has spread the influence of the OLC as far afield as New England.[96] Mason serves on the group's steering committee, and another prominent Olympic Peninsula activist, Barbara Mossman, is editor of the Alliance for America newsletter. Mossman also heads a group called American Loggers Solidarity[97] and serves as area representative for TREES, an OLC member group. With the assistance of Alliance activists, in 1992 Mossman helped to start The Umbrella Group (TUG), a Washington statewide coalition of Wise Use organizations akin to the Oregon Lands Coalition. The first TUG convention was held in August of 1992 and attracted major Wise Use figures such as Karen Budd, Charles Cushman, and Alliance president David Howard.

Involvement in the national Wise Use movement has provided Washington pro-timber industry activists with resources to fight against environmental protections. In line with Ron Arnold's prescriptions, industry has provided citizen groups like Mason's Washington Commercial Forest Action Committee with technical assistance and industry "facts" on resource issues. For instance, the Alliance for America distributes a "Grassroots Activist Handbook" which includes a directory of other pro-industry groups, listings of sympathetic reporters, articles on key Wise Use issues (timber, mining, grazing, etc.), as well as a basic primer on political action reprinted from materials produced by an industry lobby called the American Forest Resource Alliance.[98] The slicker and more elaborate *Loggers Activist Manual* is available through the Washington Contract Loggers Association, also active on the Peninsula.[99] Published by the American Pulpwood Association (APA), this over 300 page action kit comes in a fancy three-ring binder broken into 19 sections that includes sample ad copy and letters to the editor, information on how to get Wise Use messages into the schools, responses to common questions, and sample speeches.[100] The kit also comes with a video tape featuring Libby, Montana logger and Wise Use leader Bruce Vincent, whom the APA has adopted as the poster boy for its loggers activist program. According to the APA's 1991–93 strategic plan, this program includes distribution of the kits, logger activism workshops, and a loggers activist awards program.[101] Vincent is extremely popular on the industry-sponsored lecture circuit and has travelled extensively throughout Montana, Idaho, Washington, and Oregon. His industry-backed evangelism has taken Vincent to Canada and even Australia.[102]

The tactics that these logger activist guides promote help to create the social and political polarization that perpetuates the stalemate on public timber harvests, which, in a cyclical manner, further exacerbates social and political polarization. This state of affairs has proven enormously profitable for private timber holders such as Weyerhaeuser, which was saved from economic decline by the rise in lumber prices produced by the public timber supply crisis.[103] If corporations like Weyerhaeuser are the beneficiaries of the crisis, it is natural that they should seek to prolong and direct it. As it happens, Weyerhaeuser's John Manz serves as vice chairman of APA's strategic planning committee, which integrated logger activism into the association's 1991–93 strategic plan.[104]

Mason is aware that his interests and those of large timber corporations are not identical. For instance, he has noted that "[t]he direct and most immediate response to the court injunctions on the spotted owl was windfall profit to corporate profiteers and increases in the most irresponsible harvest [practices]. . ."[105] Yet Mason seems impervious to the fact that a combination of non-sustainable rates of timber harvest, log exports, and his own activism—and not just the listing of the spotted owl—are driving corporate profits while small mills like his are starving to death. In the all-or-nothing war of Wise Use, Mason is helping Weyerhaeuser to get it all, whereas he is getting nothing.

WISE USE IN THE ELECTORAL ARENA

Today the pro-timber industry campaign initiated by the Grannells in Oregon has expanded into a growing regional network involving Oregon, Washington,

California, Idaho, and Montana. Representing the state with the largest timber economy and the oldest pro-industry activist network, leaders play a prominent role in the Wise Use movement. And, on environmental issues, Oregon remains one of the most polarized states in the country.

Such polarization has left rural legislators with progressive-to-moderate positions on environmental issues extremely vulnerable. As environmentalism has become a dirty word and endorsement by an environmental organization has become a thing to avoid, in some instances these public officials have either backed away from pro-environmental positions or lost to Wise Use-supported-opponents.[106] This shift contributed in 1990 to the transfer of control for the first time in 20 years, of the Oregon House from Democrats to Republicans, who typically rate lower with environmental groups and higher with industry than their Democratic counterparts. With the Senate and governorship in Democratic hands, this change has resulted in political deadlock on environmental and other critical issues as the generally Republican anti-environmental candidates backed by Wise Use factions have proven to be opponents of labor, women's groups, civil rights organizations, and other champions of progressive causes.

Wise Use has proven to be a remarkably partisan force not just in Oregon, but across the West and the nation. This is particularly evident in the timber industry, which, if measured in campaign contributions, is the most pro-Republican industry in the country in both national and statewide races. In 1990 timber gave 74 percent of its national campaign dollars to Republicans, and was even more partisan at the state level, where it was also a potent political force. In Oregon in 1990, 85 percent of timber contributions went to Republicans, and 68 percent of timber-supported candidates won their races. In Washington state 79 percent of timber contributions went to Republicans, in Montana 86 percent, and in Idaho an incredible 93.6 percent went to GOP candidates, with 60 percent of timber-backed candidates winning election. In Idaho and Oregon, timber was the third largest contributor to political campaigns.[107] Timber financing of elections and Wise Use pro-timber industry-campaigns have worked hand in glove to erode legislative support for environmentally sustainable forest practices.

In 1992 a group of timber firms, including many OLC supporters, bankrolled two efforts to recall Democratic Governor Barbara Roberts.[108] The OLC named Roberts "public enemy number one" for her open support of the Endangered Species Act.[109] Particularly irritating to the OLC was Roberts' opposition to its efforts to exempt 44 public lands timber sales in spotted owl habitat from protection under the act. Bureau of Land Management director Cy Jamison's request for the exemptions resulted in the convening of the so-called God Squad in January 1992.[110] With the pro bono assistance of the Mountain States Legal Foundation, the OLC intervened in the hearings on the behalf of the BLM.[111] It also secured the extension of public hearings and turned out 1,200 demonstrators for a rally in Portland.[112] Roberts held her ground and the OLC, feeling its strength, decided to take her on. While both recall efforts failed to garner the signatures required to put the issue to a vote, the campaigns diverted the human and financial resources of the governor's office, damaged Roberts publicly, and seriously weakened her chances at a second term.

For their part, Oregon's Republican delegates have been a source of financial as well as political support for the Oregon Lands Coalition. The state's three Republican congressional delegates, Representative Bob Smith and Senators Mark Hatfield and Bob Packwood, each donated luncheon meetings to the OLC's 1992 auction. Coalition funder Sterling Hanel of Hanel Lumber paid $495 for lunch with Smith, while Sears store owner[113] and OLC co-chair Evelyn Badger bought a $325 lunch with Packwood, and the meal with Hatfield also went for $325. The event raised a total of $40,000 for the group.[114]

The 1992 electoral season saw heavy Wise Use involvement in statewide, congressional, and presidential races. At the congressional level, the most unseemly Wise Use involvement in the electoral arena may have been in Montana, where reapportionment left Republican Representative Ron Marlenee and Democratic Representative Pat Williams contesting a single congressional seat. Marlenee, a Wise Use ally, received the strong-armed support of the timber industry. In one instance, workers at Plum Creek Timber's Columbia Falls, Montana, plant found their pay envelopes stuffed with flyers urging them to attend an anti-wilderness rally sponsored by the Western Environmental Trade Association's Ad Hoc Coalition, a Wise Use group. The flyer contained two pages of suggested slogans for signs to be carried at the rally, including "No more Williams, wilderness, or wolves," and "You'll need a job, Pat." In response to a complaint filed by a representative of the Western Council of Industrial Workers, a county attorney ruled that the flyers violated Montana election laws and imposed the maximum penalty against Plum Creek, which pleaded guilty to the crime.[115] Despite these shenanigans, Williams won the election handily. However, in legislative races Montana progressives suffered a serious setback in the House, which turned from a 61–39 Democratic majority to a 47–53 minority. Political observers assert that Wise Use was a significant factor in about half of the 14 seats lost. The practice of attaching (literally) worker participation in Wise Use activities to their livelihoods by stuffing pay envelopes with propaganda is not unique to Plum Creek or the Ad Hoc Coalition. The OLC, for instance, has used its newsletter to publish flyers labeled "PAYROLL STUFFER" in bold typeface.[116]

In 1992, the Alliance for America worked to defeat environmental advocates in Congress. For instance, the group flew members into the congressional district of Indiana Representative Jim Jontz to organize opposition to his stand on Northwest timber issues.[117] When Jontz lost his bid for reelection, the OLC claimed victory.[118] The Alliance for America also opposed Representatives Peter Kostmayer of Pennsylvania and Gerry Sikorski of Minnesota, who were likewise defeated at the polls.[119]

The 1992 presidential race also was influenced by the Wise Use movement, particularly around timber-related issues. As the Clinton/Bush/Perot race wore into its final months, Bush sought to undercut Clinton's strong support in the Northwest by adopting the rhetoric and seeking the support of the Wise Use movement. In September, as Wise Use activists were rallying in the streets of Washington, D.C., and meeting with Bush aides at the White House,[120] the president made a quick swing through the Northwest, visiting the small timber towns of White City, Oregon, and Colville, Washington.[121] In White City, he told timber workers in a local lumberyard, "The balance has been lost. It is time to make people more important than owls. It is time to put the mills back to work."[122] One strongly pro-industry local paper commented on Bush's visit: "After more than two years of vague calls for balance, Bush has abandoned his previous position and squarely aligned himself with timber supporters. The president's remarks . . . exceeded the wildest dreams of those who have been looking to the White House for leadership on this divisive issue."[123] Bush's relationship with Wise Use involved more than rhetoric. For instance, earlier in that same month, Bush ordered federal agencies to expedite the process of harvesting dead timber on public lands, circumventing the normal comment and appeals processes.[124] Following his change of posture, Wise Use timber groups strongly supported Bush. The president's White City stop was coordinated by OLC leaders[125] and Ron Arnold claims that Dan Quayle's office requested his Wise Use mailing list for last-minute campaign support.[126]

Perot, too, adopted a Wise Use framework for discussing timber issues, telling a reporter, "I'm pragmatic. If there's a choice between survival and protecting the planet, we will pillage and plunder the planet, if it gets that basic. . . Let's assume you don't have a job and I don't have a job and the only thing we can do is cut every tree in the area and ship it to Japan to feed our children. We're going to want to cut every tree in the area and ship it to Japan to feed our children . . . Nobody will think about the spotted owl if they're starving, except maybe to eat him."[127]

THE "GREEN" ADMINISTRATION

During the presidential campaign, the OLC had repeatedly attacked the Clinton–Gore ticket as overly "green."[128] In a move designed in part to undermine the Bush campaign's Northwest strategy, presidential candidate Bill Clinton had promised that, if elected, he would convene a summit on the Northwest timber crisis as a first step towards solving it. On April 2, 1993, President Clinton arrived in Portland for the promised event. With him were Vice President Al Gore, Interior Secretary Bruce Babbitt, Labor Secretary Robert Reich, Environmental Protection Agency Administrator Carol Browner, and other top administration officials.

In the months between Clinton's election and the forest summit, Wise Use timber groups continued their attacks on the Clinton administration (particularly on his cabinet appointments) and at the same time engaged in a public relations and lobbying offensive designed to win them entry to the summit. To this latter end, pro-timber-industry groups in five states formed the Forest Values Task Force, which worked to coordinate the Wise Use presence in and outside the event.[129] Wise Use figures who gained entrance to the conference included Larry Mason, executive director of the Forks-based Washington Commercial Forest Action Committee, and Nadine Bailey, a pro-timber-industry activist from Northern California.[130] Representatives of timber firms involved in Wise Use activity, such as Plum Creek Timber, were also present.

Outside the conference, both environmental and industry groups staged large demonstrations. While environmentalists made the larger showing, industry managed to gather nearly 10,000 individuals. (Environmentalists staged a rally and concert that drew many times that number.)[131] Mills throughout the Northwest shut down so that employees could attend the event, and many companies provided transportation. In Idaho, OLC backer Boise Cascade shipped 150 of its workers to Portland. Larry Mason successfully petitioned his local school board to close schools and to allow school children to attend the event.[132]

Three months later, when the administration's forest plans were released, Wise Use leader Charles Cushman organized a demonstration in Portland in which loggers burned black coffins labelled with the names of Northwest timber towns.[133] Many environmental groups were little happier with the administration's compromise solution.[134] Even before the administration made its designs public, rumors that Clinton intended to significantly reduce harvest levels on federal lands had already elicited attacks from industry groups.[135] By the summer of 1993, Charles Cushman was promoting a "Clinton Free Zone" campaign featuring a contest for the first town to ban the president. Cushman and other Wise Use activists also organized efforts to block the nomination of environmentalists to positions within the administration.[136]

Ironically, the Clinton administration may provide opportunities for the Wise Use movement unavailable under Bush. The so-called greening of the Clinton administration has given Wise Use an identifiable political target. It has, apparently, also provided a fund-raising opportunity. Alan Gottlieb, president of the Center for the Defense of Free Enterprise, claims that Clinton's appointments have resulted in a 40 percent increase in his organizational revenue.[137] By comparison, the impression that a "green" administration is in power has made it difficult for many environmental groups to reach their fund-raising goal. Some observers have compared the situation to the financial boon environmental groups experienced in the early 1980s following the Reagan administration appointment of James Watt to Secretary of the Interior and Anne Burford to Administrator of the Environmental Protection Agency.[138] The comparison may be taken further: the Wise Use movement is an insurgent force that is gaining momentum, not unlike the environmental movement during Watt's heyday. And evidence suggests that the political winds are now favoring Wise Use.

WISE USE AND OTHER RIGHT-WING POPULISMS

The 1992 recall campaigns against Oregon Governor Barbara Roberts yielded some new and dangerous alliances that, while short-lived, are nonetheless alarming. The second campaign won the endorsement of the state's premier religious-right organization, the Oregon Citizens Alliance (affiliated with Pat Robertson's Christian Coalition[139]), which garnered 25,000 of an estimated 155,000 signatures collected for the effort.[140] While some backers of the recall campaign bristled at the involvement of the OCA, the Committee to Save Oregon Jobs, an industry front-group that coordinated timber industry involvement in the second effort, defended OCA participation.[141] Since that time the OCA, which led the notorious 1992 Measure 9 campaign to deny civil-rights protections for lesbians and gay men, has launched its first explicitly anti-environmental ballot initiative—an attack on the state land-use planning board[142]—and OCA chapters in neighboring states likewise have announced that they will become involved in environmental issues.[143]

The OCA network is not an isolated example of Wise Use/religious right crossover. Another instance comes from Idaho, where former Sagebrush Rebel and current Wise Use leader[144] Helen P. Chenoweth is also a board member of both the Idaho Family Forum and the Rutherford Institute,[145] and a trainer for the Idaho Christian Coalition.[146] In July, 1993, Chenoweth announced that she would run for Congress in Idaho's 1st Congressional District, a seat held by Democrat Larry LaRocco. That same month, Chenoweth spoke at the Wise Use Leadership Conference in Reno, Nev., where she told the audience, "We are in a spiritual war of a proportion we have not seen before . . . A war between those who believe that God put us on this earth and those who believe that God is nature."[147] Among those backing Chenoweth's campaign was prominent Wise Use leader Charles Cushman, who had appeared at several "endangered species salmon bake" fund-raising dinners for the would-be congressperson.[148] In November 1994, Chenoweth successfully unseated incumbent LaRocco.

The potential for growing convergence between the Wise Use movement and the religious right should not be ignored, nor should the significance of such convergence be trivialized. While many Wise Use leaders are uneasy about associating with groups perceived as religious extremists, the movement nevertheless has made environmentalism an emotionally charged wedge issue that, like reproductive choice, gay and lesbian civil rights, and affirmative action, can be exploited by various right-wing groups to split their opposition and attract new members. The Christian Coalition, formed from Pat Robertson's failed 1988 presidential campaign, has built a still-expanding grass-roots political machine that has, in a very short period of time, developed a presence in communities across the United States. As the Coalition and other religious right groups field candidates for local, state, and national office, they are bound to exploit the anti-environmental backlash created by the Wise Use movement.[149] The conservative Christian doctrine of dominion theology provides a spiritual basis for such political opportunism and blends nicely with Wise Use "putting people first" rhetoric.[150] Wise Use ally Representative Bob Smith, for one, has cited the book of Genesis as the basis for his position on natural resource issues. Moreover, the religious right generally supports the anti-regulatory, pro-industry principles that drive much of the Wise Use agenda.

Wise Use itself is nothing if not opportunistic, and Wise Use organizers may be the beneficiaries of other "populist" movements emerging in the West. At the Center for the Defense of Free Enterprise's 1993 Wise Use Leadership Conference, Charles Cushman suggested that Wise Users in his home state of Washington join United We Stand, Ross Perot's organization. The West was the cradle of Perot's support during his 1992 presidential bid and Wise Use organizers like Cushman will likely attempt to turn the economic insecurity and political disaffection of Perot voters, as well as the ballot eligibility of United We Stand, to the advantage of their own Wise Use deregulation campaigns. The "tax revolt" taking place in the West and other anti-government campaigns may also bolster Wise Use efforts.

To an extent, such overlap is facilitated by institutional relationships between Wise Use and other right-wing groups. For instance, Wise Use legislative efforts are promoted by the American Legislative Exhange Council (ALEC), which introduces right-wing bills into statehouses across the country through a network of conservative legislators. ALEC is largely responsible for the dissemination of Wise Use "regulatory takings" legislation as well as bills on HIV and AIDS, anti-labor "right-to-work" laws, and other pieces of the New Right agenda.[151] ALEC's task force on natural resources includes representatives from such environmentally sensitive corporations as Waste Management, Amoco, Shell, Texaco, Union Pacific Railroad, Chevron, America Petroleum Institute, American Nuclear Energy Council, and Coors, among others.[152] Philanthropic patronage also ties Wise Use to broader right-wing activity. Ron Arnold and Alan Gottlieb's Center for the Defense of Free Enterprise has received financial support from the Coors (beer-brewing) family, whose philanthropy helped to establish the Mountain States Legal Foundation, the Heritage Foundation, and the Free Congress Foundation—all pillars of the New Right and/or the religious right.[153] Coors also has supported the vehemently antiunion National Right-to-Work Committee.[154] In turn, at least one timber industry backer of Wise Use, Boise Cascade Corp., has supported this Coors-established network with a foundation grant to the Heritage Foundation.[155]

The right-wing ecumenical character of Wise Use leadership is apparent at the movement's conferences, where speakers have declared their opposition to statehood for Washington, D.C., compared the struggle against "radical preservationists" to the cold war fight against communism, and called for "splitting the real Teamsters, the real Carpenters, the real AFL-CIO away from their own lunatic fringe leadership."[156] One speaker at the 1993 Wise Use Leadership Conference censured his colleagues for openly expressing their GOP sympathies, remarking that Republicans had done as much as Democrats to lead the country down the road towards socialism.[157] The growing influence of the Wise Use movement has attracted the entire spectrum of the U.S. right wing, including extremist factions like the John Birch Society and followers of neo-fascist Lyndon LaRouche. (Birchers and LaRouche followers, for instance, actively participate in Wise Use conferences and include Wise Use issues in their journals.[158]) Indeed, the handling of the Center for the Defense of Free Enterprise's "Moonie" connection illustrates that ties to the ultra right are viewed within the Wise Use movement as little more than public relations problems. For most of these individuals and organizations, the fight against environmental protections is part of a larger struggle against an overbearing and unduly liberal or even leftist government, and includes anti-labor, anti-feminist, and anti-civil rights fronts. Environmentalism, in the words of Alan Gottlieb, has simply become "the perfect bogeyman" for society's ills.[159] It would be more accurate to say that it has been made into a bogeyman through the well-financed and carefully coordinated activities of figures like Gottlieb and Ron Arnold.

CONCLUSIONS

This chapter has provided only a sketch of Wise Use activity in the Northwest timber industry, and, for pragmatic reasons, has focussed heavily on Oregon and to a lesser extent Washington. However, the timber industry is only one of many theaters of Wise Use engagement. Since at least the time of the Multiple Use Strategy Conference, Wise Use has pursued a coalition strategy, arguing that natural-resource industries and the communities dependent on them have a common interest as "resource providers" as well as a common enemy: the environmental movement and its "proxies" in government. This emphasis on coalition is everywhere evident: The OLC, born from the pro-timber-industry Oregon Project, has a broad agenda that reflects its mining, grazing, and development constituents; in Boundary County, Idaho, Women In Timber has spearheaded a "county rule" campaign coordinated not by the timber industry, but by a different wing of the Wise Use movement;[160] in Washington, Wise Use leader Charles Cushman has championed the "causes" of ranching, mining, timber, and development; timber interests have worked cooperatively with the movement's growing "property rights" wing, which is winning a suburban as well as a rural movement, the takings lobby, the property-rights movement, and other pro-industry activities—all contribute to the effectiveness of timber industry organizing.

Within the timber industry, Wise Use also represents a coalition of different and sometimes contradictory interests. Large corporations with private timber holdings, small and mid-sized firms dependent on public timberlands, and right-wing organizers seeking to develop an activist base are all part of the Wise Use coalition—and even this breakdown simplifies the true situation. This chapter has attempted to differentiate some of these factions and to draw attention to the social as well as the political implications of the movement. As Ron

Arnold argued in his articles for *Logging Management* magazine, the activist nature of Wise Use campaigns make them enormously effective vehicles for resource corporations. And such activism presents a different kind of challenge than have other industry-backed anti-environmental initiatives.

It is extremely important to expose publicly the corporate and right-wing ideological interests behind Wise Use activism. However, exposure alone cannot defeat the Wise Use movement any more than the environmental movement can be erased by corporate public relations efforts. Effective opposition to Wise Use must involve building an alternative movement that promotes sustainable ecologies *and* economies as part of a larger vision of social and economic justice as well as environmental conservation. Environmental groups must be part of the effort, a large part even, but only a part. The growing influence of the Wise Use movement stems as much from the failure of progressiveness to work successfully in coalition as from the movement's own coalition-building efforts. Wise Use, which in the long run will prove as onerous to workers and communities as to environmental groups, has very deliberately isolated environmentalists from their natural allies in the labor, women's, civil rights, and other progressive movements. The environmental movement has been complicit in this isolation. If progressives cannot or will not come together under the assault of large corporations and the right wing, they can expect to experience a steady erosion of their support and influence from the divide-and-conquer campaigns of Wise Use and other reactionary forces.

Notes

1. The term "Sagebrush Rebellion" refers to the efforts of conservative western state legislators during the late 1970s and early 1980s to transfer control of federally managed public lands to state government. Many had privatization as their ultimate goal. The most outspoken champion of these efforts at the federal level was Reagan administration Secretary of the Interior James Watt.
2. Alan Gottlieb, ed, *The Wise Use Agenda: The Citizen's Policy Guide to Environmental Resource Issues.* (Bellevue, WA: The Free Enterprise Press, 1989), p. ix.
3. Ibid.
4. The National Conference on Federal Lands, also known as the National Federal Lands Conference, the principal force behind the "county rule" or "home rule" strategy of the Wise Use movement. For a comprehensive examination of the NFLC, see Jeff Fox and Marc McAllister, *The Wise Use Movement in Utah.* (Portland, OR: Western States Center, 1994). See also, *A Report on the County Movement, with Emphasis on its Activities in New Mexico,* prepared for the Wilderness Society by the Southwest Environmental Center, 9/30/92.
5. Gottlieb, *The Wise Use Agenda*, 157.
6. Ibid., ix.

7. These include passage of something called the "Global Warming Prevention Act." This act proposes to harvest all old-growth stands on Forest Service lands, arguing that this "oxygen-using forest growth" should be replaced with "young stands of oxygen-producing, carbon dioxide-absorbing trees to help ameliorate the rate of global warming and prevent the green-house effect." Other items include immediate development of the petroleum resources in the Arctic National Wildlife Refuge (ANWR), a timber harvest act "designed to recapture accrued undercuts from previous years when the annual allowable harvest level has not been achieved," extension of patent protections on new pesticides, amendment of the Endangered Species Act to challenge the protection of "non-adaptive species such as the California Condor," and the granting to "pro-industry advocates" of "standing to sue on behalf of industries threatened or harmed by environmentalists." Gottlieb, *The Wise Use Agenda,* 5–18.

8. The National Center for Constitutional Studies, formerly the Freeman Institute, seeks, among other things, to institute biblical law in the United States. The organization and its director, W. Cleon Skousen, have been supported by the Unification Church through its CAUSA group, which has paid for hundreds of state lawmakers to attend Skousen's constitutional seminars. Skousen advances international conspiracy theories akin to those of the John Birch Society. These theories implicate international bankers, Presidents Nixon and Eisenhower, and others in a plot to take control of the world using "Communist revolution" and other objectionable tactics. See David Postman, "Skousen under Fire as He Spreads Ideology," *Anchorage Daily News,* 25 January 1987. See also Robert Gottlieb and Peter Wiley, *America's Saints: The Rise of Mormon Power.* (Toronto: General Publishing Company, 1984), p. 91.

    Other right-wing organizations listed in the "Index of the Wise Use Movement" include Accuracy in Academia, which in the 1980s promised to use students to monitor Marxist influences in U.S. classrooms; the American Freedom Coalition, to which Arnold and Alan Gottlieb have strong ties, and which is a political arm of Reverend Sun Myung Moon's Unification Church and was formed in cooperation with Christian Voice, a religious right organization; California Farm Bureau Federation, which, like the national Farm Bureau Federation, has a broad right-wing political agenda that includes anti-labor, anti-women and anti-environmental positions; Center for the Defense of Free Enterprise, Arnold and Gottlieb's group and sponsor of the 1988 Multiple Use Strategy Conference; Mountain States Legal Foundation, formerly headed by James Watt and currently under the leadership of New Right activist Perry Pendley; National Inholders Association, headed by Charles Cushman, who, among other things, has been an active participant in organized efforts involving white supremacists and others to undermine the sovereignty and treaty rights of Native American nations; National Rifle Association, in which CDFE's Alan Gottlieb has been very involved and which adopted an anti-wilderness position in the 1980s; and the Northwest Legal Foundation and the Pacific Legal Foundation, which have served as the legal arm for right-wing activists on a variety of issues For Cushman's anti-Indian activities, see Rudolph Ryser, *The Anti-Indian Movement on the Tribal Frontier.* (Kenmore, WA: Center for World Indigenous Studies, 1992).

9. Jon Krakauer, "Brown Fellas," *Outside Magazine,* December 1991, p. 70.

10. The public interest organizations from which these "executives" were drawn were generally of a similar orientation to those described in note #8. But of the two hundred and some organizations listed in the "Index of the Wise Use Movement," over fifty are recreational-vehicle user clubs or recreational-vehicle trade associations. The former are mostly local snowmobile or all-terrain-vehicle (ATV) groups, many of which may have been signed on

to the *The Wise Use Agenda* through their association with the Idaho-based BlueRibbon Coalition, an anti-environmental group which claims to represent recreation groups from across the country. The BlueRibbon Coalition is headed by Clark Collins, a key Wise Use leader who calls environmental organizations "hate groups."

11. For a comprehensive examination of the NFLC and the "home rule" legal strategy, see Jeff Fox and Marc McAllister, *The Wise Use Movement in Utah.* (Portland, OR: Western States Center, 1994). See also, *A Report on the County Movement, With Emphasis on Its Activities in New Mexico,* prepared for the Wilderness Society by the Southwest Environmental Center, 9/30/92.

12. Gottlieb, *The Wise Use Agenda,* p. ix.

13. "Wise Use," *Counterpoint,* August 1988, p. 9. In 1988 *Counterpoint* was the publication of the Counterpoint Foundation of Tigard, Oregon. More recently, it is published by the Tamarack Foundation, which uses the same post office box as its predecessor.

14. Ibid.

15. Ibid.

16. For coverage of the 1992 Wise Use Leadership Conference, see Dean Kuipers, "Setting the Woods on Fire: Dan Quayle's Favorite Environmentalists," *LA Weekly,* July 3–9 1992, p. 24. See also William Poole, "Neither Wise Nor Well," *Sierra Magazine,* November 1992, p. 59.

17. Arnold notes that he worked for a "publication group" at Boeing. Ron Arnold, "So, Who Is This New Columnist, Ron Arnold?", *Bellevue Journal American,* 8 March 1983.

18. Arnold became an ALPS trustee on 2 June 1970, filling a board seat vacated by Brock Evans. Minutes from 2 June 1970 trustee meeting. University of Washington archives. Alpine Lakes Protection Society. Acc. #1740-12, folder #13.

19. The following notation appears in the minutes from the 15 September 1970 ALPS trustee meeting: "We had a preview of 'A Forever Place, The Alpine Lakes.' Truly beautiful piece of art. It will be ready to travel in three weeks; keep your eyes open for excellent chances for exposure. *We have it; let's book it!*" University of Washington archives. Alpine Lakes Protection Society. Acc. #1740-12, folder #13.

In March 1971, the ALPS board of trustees approved sale of Arnold's slide show for $100 a set. The following note appears in the minutes of its April 1971 meeting: "[trustee Ben] Hayes raised question of personal profit by trustees. Raised in context of selling slideshow, potential profit by Arnold. Ron doesn't intend to keep the profits." Minutes from 13 March and 17 April 1971 APLS trustee meetings. U.W. archives. Alpine Lakes Protection Society. Acc. #1740-12, folders #13 & 14.

20. Ben Hayes, ALPS founder and trustee, in an interview by author, 6 August 1993.

21. From interviews by author.

22. Ben Hayes, in an interview by author, 6 August 1993.

23. Ron Arnold, "So, Who Is This New Columnist, Ron Arnold?"

24. Paul E. Merrell and Carol Can Strum, "Civil Rights—The Pest?", *The Journal of Pesticide Reform,* Winter 1986, p. 22. For Arnold's work for the timber industry, see, for example, "Closure," United Press International, 9 July 1985.

25. These articles were later edited and published by Arnold as *Ecology Wars: Environmentalism As If People Mattered* (Bellevue, WA: Free Enterprise Press, 1987). CDFE president Alan Gottlieb wrote the introduction. The book is described on its jacket as "A Free Enterprise Battle Book."

26. Later Arnold would find a label for the movement in the writings of Gifford Pinchot, the first head of the Forest Service. Arnold is quoted as saying, "Wise Use was catchy, and it

took up only nine spaces in a newspaper headline, just about as short as 'ecology.' It was also marvelously ambiguous. Symbols register most powerfully when they're not perfectly clear." Krakauer, "Brown Fellas," p. 68.

27. Ron Arnold, "Defeating Environmentalism," *Logging Management Magazine,* April 1980, p. 39.

28. Ibid., pp. 40–41. This formula has been followed very closely by industry funders of Wise Use organizations and campaigns, who oftentimes are more likely to make "in kind" contributions of training seminars, transportation, printed materials, paid leave time for employees, public relations assistance, etc., than direct financial contributions. Among the incentives for this approach, such indirect contributions are considerably more difficult for Wise Use opponents to document. On a different note, it is interesting that Arnold uses the collective "our" in speaking about the role of industry in developing activist groups.

29. Ibid., p. 41

30. In addition to his reputation as the best right-wing direct-mail fund-raiser outside of Washington, D.C., Gottlieb is a convicted tax felon. [See Loretta Callahan, "Organizations, financing murky," *The Columbian* (Vancouver, Wash.), 17 May 1992, p. A11.]

31. Arnold demonstrates his familiarity with a variety of right-wing organizations in "Defeating Environmentalism."

32. See Ron Arnold, *At the Eye of the Storm: James Watt and the Environmentalists* (Chicago: Regnery-Gateway, 1982). An Associated Press article on the publication of the book notes that "Arnold conceded the book is ideological rather than objective, written from a conservative viewpoint sympathetic to Watt's goals." William Kronholm, "Conservative Book Portrays 'Real James Watt'." Associated Press, 9 November 1982. The Free Congress Foundation was created, in part, by Paul Weyrich, known as the "godfather of the New Right." Weyrich helped to create a number of other prominent right-wing institutions, including the Heritage Foundation and the American Legislative Exchange Council, and also is one of the key architects of the religious right.

33. Russ Bellant notes that Arnold's attacks on environmentalists in his 1982 *At the Eye of the Storm: James Watt and the Environmentalists* "bear an uncanny resemblance to the propaganda of the neo-Nazi Lyndon LaRouche. Arnold's book", he adds, "even cites a LaRouche follower as a source for some allegations of drug ties to environmentalism. LaRouche met with Watt in 1981 after Watt became Secretary of the Interior and former LaRouche group members have claimed that Watt nearly hired LaRouche as a consultant." Russ Bellant, *The Coors Connection: How Coors Family Philanthropy Undermines Democratic Pluralism* (Boston: South End Press, 1991), p. 89.

34. Tom Ferschweiler, "Did Sprayed Forest Chemical or Lifestyle Cause Abortions?" United Press International, 29 October 1981.

35. In addition to utilizing Gottlieb's political contacts and fundraising acumen, Arnold took advantage of communications media networks developed by the Center for the Defense of Free Enterprise. According to the dust jacket of Arnold's 1987 *Ecology Wars,* Arnold's weekly newspaper column was "distributed" by the American Press Syndicate (a CDFE project that claims the involvement of some 400 newspapers with an audience of eight million readers), and a weekly radio show hosted by Arnold, "Economics 101 on the Air," was carried by 400 radio stations across the country (presumably on CDFE's American Broadcasting network, which claims more than 600 participating radio stations and an audience of six million).

36. Ben Hayes, in an interview by author, 6 August 1993.

37. Ron Arnold, "Defeating Environmentalism," p. 40. Arnold's Wise Use strategy had to be carefully marketed to an industry audience that was, initially, more than a little reluctant.

38. In places like western Montana, large private timberland holders Plum Creek and Champion International abandoned sustained-yield forestry in the 1980s, choosing instead to liquidate their holdings. The massive overcutting that resulted will cost jobs as forests dwindle, and will create enormous pressure to step-up harvesting on public lands even though federal policy requires that the Forest Service compensate for cuts on private lands by "locking up" adjoining federal forests. See, for instance, Richard Manning, *Last Stand: Logging Journalism, and the Case for Humility* (Salt Lake City: Peregrine Smith Books, 1991).

39. Those congressional delegates were Senator Bob Packwood, Representative Bob Smith, and Representative Peter DeFazio. Holly Danks, "Timber industry backers rally in Salem," *The Oregonian,* 22 May 1989. It is unlikely that many at this rally perceived the contradiction between "historic and sustainable rates" of timber harvesting.

40. Holly Danks, "Timber industry backers rally in Salem."

41. "Rally Huge Success," *The Oregon Project Weekly Report,* 24 May, 1989, p.2.

42. See, for example, Dana Tims, "Eugene reverberates with rumble of log trucks," *The Oregonian,* 4 June 1989.

43. In the summer of 1990 the mayor of Roseburg, Oregon proclaimed that city a "Yellow Ribbon Community," prompting the resignation of a prominent environmentalist from the city council. Foster Church, "A Time of Passionate Convictions," *The Oregonian,* 26 October 1990.

44. Foster Church, "'Sagebrush Rebels' Get Cool Reception," *The Oregonian,* 27 May 1981, p. C1. Despite serving as one of its principal champions in the Oregon legislature, Grannell has since denied his connection with the Sagebrush Rebellion, writing of the Western States Public Lands Coalition, "[W]e have no other political biases other than continued use of federal public lands. We are not part of the 'sagebrush rebellion' or any other ultraconservative organization. . ." From a letter to Don Judge, executive secretary of the Montana State AFL-CIO, dated 9 September 1989.

45. Leslie Zaitz, "Grannell Faulted in Draft of Opinion," *The Oregonian,* 16 June 1981, P. B1. See also, Leslie Zaitz, "Second Lobbyist Bought Grannell Corporation Stock," *The Oregonian,* 23 June 1981, p. B4.

46. Foster Church, "Grannell, Powell Handle Revenue Panel Tasks with Aplomb," *The Oregonian,* 14 March 1982. Church also paraphrases a "legislative observer" who remarked that Grannell was somewhat inclined "to favor tax policies that might favor special interests to the detriment of the state as a whole."

47. According to a biographical sketch published by the WPLC, Barbara Grannell worked in Oregon as legislative staff, field director for a 1985 sales tax campaign, and owner of a small real estate business, and is familiar with "such diverse groups as the League of Women Voters, educators, and the Association of Oregon Industries." Western States Public Lands Coalition, "Barbara Grannell Biography," undated. The WSPLC biographical sketch for Bill Grannell claims that from 1982 to 1988 he was "a lobbyist for county governments, serving in Oregon as the Executive Assistant to the Association of Oregon Counties. . . In Colorado he served as Director of Lobbying for Colorado Counties, Inc. In 1986, Bill spent the year in Washington, D.C., representing the western states counties." According to this same document, since 1987 the Grannells had been publishing "Federal Land Payments—a monthly report," which they circulated to "counties, school districts, state and federal officials and to industry." Western States Public Lands Coalition, "Bill Grannell Biography," undated.

48. Bohemia Inc. of Eugene, South Coast Lumber Co. of Brookings, and Hanel Lumber, of Hood River each gave $15,000 to the Oregon Project; C&D Lumber Co., D.R. Johnson Lumber Co., and Herbert Lumber Co. gave a total of $15,000; Roseburg Forest Products and Sun Studs gave a joint gift of $15,000. Church, "A Time of Passionate Convictions."

49. The Grannells' account is recorded in Alan R. Hayakawa, "More Sophisticated Sagebrush Rebels Broaden Base," *The Oregonian,* 25 June 1989, p. C1.

50. "The Oregon Project: A Special Project of the Western States Public Lands Coalition," undated. (Circulated in April 1989.)

51. See, for example, George Frost, "Development Council Taps Conservative Alliance for ANWR Fight," *Anchorage Daily News,* 1 March 1989. The article begins, "Alaska's Resource Development Council is enlisting support from a new breed of New Right activist for its push to open the Arctic National Wildlife Refuge to oil exploration." Arnold travelled as part of an American Freedom Coalition (AFC) junket to Alaska involving AFC Environmental Task Force director Merril Sikorski, Grant Gerber from the Wilderness Impact Research Foundation, and Barbara Keating-Edh of Consumer Alert. See also Claude Emery, *Share Groups in British Columbia* (Canada: Library of Parliament Research Branch, 10 December 1991).

52. The Oregon Wise Use Conference was no doubt one of the statewide Wise Use conferences planned at the 1988 Multiple Use Strategy Conference. Flyer titled "Partial List of Speakers Scheduled to Appear at the Oregon Wise Use Conference Saterday [*sic*], May 20, 1989," dated 24 April 1989.

53. "The Oregon Project: A Special Project of the Western States Public Lands Coalition," undated.

54. Kathie Durbin, "Timber Towns in Oregon Fight Back," *The Oregonian,* 22 May 1989.

55. Gene Lawhorn, "Hopelessness and Hate in Our Timber Communities," *The Portland Alliance,* July 1991, p. 2.

56. Church, "A Time of Passionate Convictions."

57. Lawhorn, "Hopelessness and Hate in Our Timber Communities."

58. Ibid.

59. Church, "A Time of Passionate Convictions."

60. Hayakawa, "More Sophisticated Sagebrush Rebels Broaden Base."

61. Kathie Durbin, "Critics Assail Pro-Industry Bent of Textbook," *The Oregonian,* 9 January 1986, p. C1.

62. Ibid. *Get Oregonized* was developed from within the agricultural industry and one of the main champions of the project was the group Agriculture in the Classroom. The American Farm Bureau Federation and its state chapters are actively involved in a variety of Wise Use efforts. Kathie Durbin, "Textbook Emphasizes the Division of the State," *The Oregonian,* 14 February 1986, p. D11.

63. Among other errors, the book had the Platte River running in the wrong direction. Kathie Durbin, "*Get Oregonized* Editor Gets Mixed Signals," *The Oregonian,* 16 April 1986, p. B8. Oregon's largest newspaper was among those who editorialized against the textbook: "Textbook Still Not Ready," *The Oregonian,* 2 March 1986, p. B2.

64. Durbin, "Textbook Emphasizes the Division of the State."

65. Robert E. Shotwell, "Home-Grown Textbook Helps Fourth-Graders to 'get Oregonized'," *The Oregonian,* 27 January 1985, p. C1.

66. Kathie Durbin, "'Oregonized' Text Adopted," *The Oregonian,* 7 March, 1986, p. A1.

67. Associated Press, "High Court Orders Textbook Case Axed," *The Oregonian,* 1 October 1988, p. C5.

68. Associated Press, "Text Looks at 'Global Oregon'," *The Oregonian,* 10 August 1987, p. B3.

69. Odean Hall, author, John Christianson, artist, and Jeff McMahon, voice, *Timbear's Unibearsity* (Sweet Home, Oregon: Common Sense Inc., 1989). According to materials produced by the national Wise Use umbrella group, Alliance for America, these and other "educational" materials are available through WOOD, a member group of the Oregon Lands Coalition.

70. Ted Ferrioli, in a presentation to the convening conference of The Umbrella Group (TUG), held in Ellensburg, Washington, 22 August 1992. At this same conference, Wise Use leader Charles Cushman was introduced as a consultant to school districts.

71. "Putting People Back into the Environmental Equation" is the slogan of the Alliance for America.

72. The change occurred with vol. 6, issue 6., undated. With the subsequent issue, the title was modified further to *Forests Today and Forever.*

73. Durbin, "Timber Towns in Oregon Fight Back."

74. "Efforts To Get in Summit Succeed," *The Oregon Project Weekly Report,* 15 June 1989, p. 1.

75. Jeff Mapes, "Protest Draws Thousands," *The Oregonian,* 14 April 1990, p. A1.

76. Ibid. See also Lawhorn, "Hopelessness and Hate in Our Timber Communities."

77. Mapes, "Protest Draws Thousands."

78. Robin Franzen, "Giving Voice to the Timber Workers," *The Oregonian,* 21 January 1993.

79. According to *Oregonian* reporter Foster Church, "the statewide Oregon Project dissolved when organizers became dissatisfied with the degree of control the Grannells demanded." Church, "A Time of Passionate Convictions." For the Grannells' intentions to expand their efforts, see "What's Next for the Oregon Project?", *The Oregon Project Weekly Report,* 24 May, 1989, p. 2.

80. Under the 1872 law, which was written with the aim of encouraging settlement in the West, vast tracts of federally managed land can be purchased by mining companies at between $2.00 and $5.00 per acre, and companies are not required to pay any royalties on the minerals they extract.

81. OLC member groups are listed on the back page of each issue of *The Seedling,* a publication that appears six times a year produced by the Oregon Lands Coalition.

82. A thank-you letter to "individuals, Coalition groups and businesses that have provided support through financial or in-kind contributions" appeared in the 10 July 1992 issue of the Oregon Lands Coalition newsletter, "Network News." The letter included a list of OLC supporters.

83. Gottlieb, *The Wise Use Agenda,* pp. xv–xvi. Also named among the book's financiers is the Kirby Foundation. Recent beneficiaries of Kirby Foundation grants include Wise Use ally Accuracy in Media ($60,000) and the Christian Anti-Communism Crusade in Long Beach, California. In Susan E. Elnicki and Bohdan R. Romaniuk, eds., *Foundation Reporter: Comprehensive Profiles and Giving Analyses of America's Major Private Foundations* (Rockville, MD: The Taft Group, 1991), pp. 408–409.

84. Rachel Zimmerman, "Wise Use Adds Environmentalists to the List of Bogeymen," *Willamette Week,* 15–21 October 1992, p. 1.

85. Ibid.

86. CDFE conference flyer.

87. Margaret L. Knox, "The Wise Use Guys," *Buzzworm: The Environmental Journal,* Nov/Dec 1990, p. 33. For the OLC's efforts, see "CSA Memorial headed for 66th Legislature," *The Seedling,* February 1991, p.1.

88. For Metcalf's right-wing political activities, see Ryser, *The Anti-Indian Movement on the Tribal Frontier.*

89. Notes from rally.

90. Associated Press, "Loggers Arrested in Protest over Forest Service Rules," *Skagit Valley Herald* (Mount Vernon, Wash.), 8 July 1992.

91. William Dietrich, *The Final Forest* (New York: Simon & Schuster, 1992), p. 236.

92. Associated Press, "16 Arrested in Forest Protest," *Lewiston Tribune* (Lewiston, Idaho), 23 July 1992.

93. "Bush OKs Limited Blowdown Harvest," *Peninsula Daily News* (Port Angeles, Wash.), 10 September 1992.

94. An Alliance for America brochure states that the objectives of the group include: "1. To achieve representation in all 50 states. 2. To create a comprehensive communications network. 3. To hold members of Congress accountable for extreme environmental votes. 4. To establish an identity in the national press. 5. To develop and maintain communications with the U.S. Congress as well as state government legislatures." The brochure goes on to claim that the Alliance quickly made significant strides toward achieving these goals, such as establishing 50 state representation within the first seven months of operation.

95. Associated Press, "Logger and Fishermen Picket CBS," *Statesman-Journal* (Salem, Ore.), 15 October 1992.

96. For a look at Alliance for America activities in New England, see William Kevin Burke, *The Scent of Opportunity: A Survey of the Wise Use/Property Rights Movement in New England* (Cambridge, Mass.: Political Research Associates, 1992).

97. American Loggers Solidarity publishes a newsletter titled *The Woodbox.*

98. The American Forest Resource Alliance has offices in Washington, D.C. and Portland Oregon. It's executive director, Mark Rey, has worked with the Bureau of Land Management and the National Forest Products Association. Rey, who works closely with the right-wing Mountain States Legal Foundation, advocates bringing organized labor into the Wise Use movement. Following a presentation on "legislative awareness" that he gave at the August, 1992, convention of TUG in Washington State, Rey was asked by a man in the audience whether he approved of the term "coercive utopian" to describe environmentalists. Rey replied that he favored "asshole" or "obstinate son-of-a-bitch."

99. The Washington Contract Loggers Association is headed by Bill Pickell, whose wife, Ellen, runs Tree Farm Services, a signatory of *The Wise Use Agenda.*

100. *Loggers Activist Manual: An Idea Book on How to Influence Public Opinion in Your Local Community,* second ed. (Washington, D.C.: American Pulpwood Association, 1993).

101. "1991–93 Strategic Plan" (Washington, D.C.: American Pulpwood Association, 1991) Vincent heads the organization Communities for a Great Northwest. In 1993 the APA's Forest Activist Award went to Nadine Bailey of the Trinity County Concerned Citizens in Hayfork, California. Bailey was presented with the award at the group's annual meeting, where Valerie Johnson of the OLC and former Washington Governor and Wise Use icon Dixie Lee Ray were also in evidence. American Pulpwood Association, *Pulpwood Highlights,* February 1993.

102. Rob Diotte, "'Big Lie' Misleading Public on Environment: American Says Democracy Works, Urges People to Use It," *Alberni Valley Times* (Port Alberni, British Columbia), 8

June 1993, p. 1. When Vincent failed to appear at the 1993 Wise Use Leadership Conference as scheduled, conference organizers explained that he was in Australia spreading the Wise Use message.

103. Bill Richards, "How the Owl Helps: Surprise—The Threatened Species Is Actually Making Business Better for One Timber Company," *Mail Tribune* (Medford, Ore.), 9 August 1992.

104. "1991–93 Strategic Plan." Vincent heads the organization Communities for a Great Northwest.

105. Quoted in William Dietrich, *The Final Forest: The Battle for the Last Great Trees of the Pacific Northwest*. (New York: Simon & Schuster, 1992), p. 188.

106. For the impact of Wise Use on the legislative arena, see David Mazza, *God, Land and Politics: The Wise Use and Religious Right Connection in 1992 Oregon Politics*. (Portland: Western States Center, 1993.)

107. Campaign contribution figures are from *Timber Industry Contributions in Western States*. (Helena, Montana: Western States Center, 1993).

108. The single best account of the recall efforts is David Mazza, *God, Land and Politics: The Wise and Religious Right Connection in 1992 Oregon Politics* (Portland, Oregon: Western States Center, 1993).

109. Oregon Lands Coalition *Network News,* 21 February 1992.

110. The God Squad is the Endangered Species Committee (dubbed the "God Squad" for its authority to allow the extinction of a species). It is comprised of representatives from the departments of Interior and Agriculture, the Army Corps of Engineers, the Environmental Protection Agency, and other persons nominated by the governors of the affected states, in this case, Oregon and Washington.

111. Kathie Durbin, "Lands Coalition Leads Fight for Timber Jobs," *The Oregonian,* 27 January 1992, p. B1. It should be noted that Jamison developed a good working relationship with the OLC and was a scheduled speaker at a September, 1991, rally in Washington, D.C. organized by OLC leaders. Of his role in attempting to exempt the timber sales from ESA protection, OLC spokesperson Valerie Johnson has said, "Cy Jamison went to bat for us." Alliance for America 1991 "Fly-In-For-Freedom" schedule, dated 17 September 1991. Johnson quote is from the above-cited Durbin article.

112. Kathie Durbin, "Lands Coalition Leads Fight for Timber Jobs."

113. Alliance for America 1991 "Fly-In-For-Freedom" schedule.

114. Alan K. Ota and Roberta Ulrich, "Hatfield, Packwood, Smith Aid Oregon Lands Coalition," *The Oregonian,* 29 March 1992.

115. See "Plum Creek Admits Political Interference," *Western Horizons* (Newsletter of Western States Center and Montana State AFL-CIO's Wise Use Public Exposure Project), April 1993, p. 5.

116. In the OLC newsletter *Network News,* undated. The materials in the newsletter indicate that it was published in the winter of 1993.

117. Alliance for America news release, dated 28 October 1992.

118. Scott Sonner, "Voters Oust Three Top Environmentalists," *The Oregonian,* 6 November 1992.

119. See Associated Press, "Timber Groups Celebrate Loss of 3 Key Foes," *Statesman-Journal* (Salem, Ore.), 5 November 1992.

120. Associated Press, "Help Promised for Timber Industry," *Wenatchee World* (Wenatchee, Wash.), 17 September 1992. According to the AP story, around 140 members of the

Alliance for America met at the White House with Bush advisor on economic affairs Michael Boskin and other officials.

121. Presidential candidate Bill Clinton's announcement that he would hold a summit on forest issues in the early days of a Clinton administration may have kept Bush from making a more significant tour of the Northwest.

122. Kristine Thomas, "Bush Seeks Jobs Balance," *News-Review* (Roseburg, Ore.), 15 September 1992, p. 1.

123. Jeff Mize, "Timber Supporters Happy with Bush's New Stand," *News-Review* (Roseburg, Ore.), 16 September 1992.

124. Staff, "Bush OKs Limited Blowdown Harvest," *Penninsula Daily News* (Port Angeles, Wash.), 10 September 1992.

125. Marc Cooper, "Fear Brings Perfectly Decent Oregonians into the OCA Fold," *Willamette Week*, 15–21 October 1992, p. 1.

126. Zimmerman, "Wise Use Adds Environmentalists to the List of Bogeymen."

127. Quoted in "Verbatim," *The Oregonian*, 13 July 1992, p. B1.

128. See, for example, the Coalition's *Network News*, dated 17 July 1992, which leads with an article attacking Gore as an "environmental hypocrite."

129. Kathie Durbin, "Activists Urge Wise Scope of Forest Goals," *The Oregonian*, 17 Febuary 1993, p. B7. OLC chair Valerie Johnson and Larry Mason of the Washington Commercial Forest Action Committee were both involved in this "new" coalition.

130. Mason, described by the OLC as "one of our Alliance for America friends," has served on the steering committee for that group. He has also led "loggers civil disobedience" by cutting up blowndown trees in Spotted Owl habitat on the Olympic Penninsula. Associated Press, "Loggers arrested in Protest over Forest Service Rules," *Skagit Valley Herald* (Mount Vernon, Wash.), 8 July 1992.

131. Ted Nelson, "Timber Workers Rally at Forest Summit," *The Observer* (LaGrande, Ore.), 3 April 1993.

132. Staff, "Briefly," *Peninsula Daily News* (Port Angeles, Wash.), 17 March 1993.

133. Associated Press, "Owl Ruling Riles U.S. Loggers," *Vancouver Sun* (Vancouver, B.C.), 2 July 1993.

134. See, for instance, Carol Ann Riha, "Clinton Acts on Timber," *Herald and News* (Klamath Falls, Ore.), 1 July 1993.

135. For instance, in the 14 May 1993 issue of its newsletter, *Network News,* the OLC declared that "The Decision To Lock Up Pacific Northwest Forests Was Made Long Ago . . . & All The Clinton Administration Is Doing Now Is Fussing Around About How To Do It."

136. Such nominations included former League of Conservation Voters President Bruce Babbitt to head the Department of the Interior, former Wilderness Society President George Frampton to oversee agencies responsible for fish, wildlife and parks, and former Wilderness Society board member Jim Baca, to head the Bureau of Land Management. In response to Babbitt's grazing reform campaign, the Wise Use Movement launched a "fire Babbitt" campaign.

137. Rob Taylor, "Conservatives Thriving on Greening of Clinton," *Post-Intelligencer* (Seattle, Wash.), 3 March, 1993.

138. Ibid.

139. See, for example, Sura Rubenstein, "Robertson Coalition Strong for Measure 9," *The Oregonian,* 18 September 1992, p. D4.

140. For the recall campaigns against Barbara Roberts, see Mazza, *God, Land and Politics*.

141. "Recall Committee Disavows Help of OCA," *The Oregonian*, 28 July 1992, p. B3.

142. Paul Neville, "Land Use Process Target by OCA," *The Register Guard* (Eugene, Ore.), 25 February 1993, p. 1.
143. For instance, in a press conference announcing the formation of the Citizens Alliance of Washington, the OCA's Lon Mabon stated, in the words of one press account, that the group will "push 'family values' by promoting politicians and efforts to limit welfare programs, protecting the right to bear arms and reversing what the group sees as environmental extremism in land use controls." Associated Press, "Anti-Gay Group Makes Its State Debut," *Daily News* (Longview, Wash.), 30 January 1993. Similarly, the Idaho Citizens Alliance has declared its intention to become involved in land-use issues.
144. Chenoweth is former vice president of the Boise-based Consulting Associates, former director of the Idaho Republican Party, and former chief of staff to Idaho Senator and Wise Use ally Steve Symms. Helen Chenoweth biography, undated.
145. Ibid.
146. Chenoweth conducted a workshop on "influencing public policy" at an Idaho Christian Coalition leadership conference held 19–20 February 1994 in Boise. Dallas Chase, "ICC— Another Religious Extremist Group in Idaho," *Diversity* (Boise, Idaho), March 1993, p. 4.
147. Chenoweth was echoing a favorite saying of Ron Arnold, that "Environmentalism is a new paganism that worships trees and sacrifices people." See, for example, Krakauer, "Brown Fellas," p. 70.
148. Bill Loftus, "An Endangered Dish," *Lewiston Tribune* (Lewiston, Idaho), 29 October 1993.
149. For a look at religious right organizing in the West, see *The Covert Crusade: The Christian Right and Politics in the West* (Portland, Oregon: Western States Center and the Coalition for Human Dignity, 1993).
150. For a thorough examination of the rise of the Christian right as well as a discussion of dominion theology, see Sura Diamond, *Spiritual Warfare: The Politics of the Christian Right* (Boston: South End Press, 1989). Put simply, dominion theology asserts a strict hierarchy in which man has authority over the earth and all its creatures.
151. American Legislative Exchange Council brochure, *Building a Winning Team: 1992 National Orientation Conference*. The idea of regulatory takings emerged from the Justice Department of Reagan-era Attorney General Edwin Meese III and was codified as Executive Order 12630 in 1988. The February, 1991 issue of ALEC's newsletter, *The State Factor,* carried a speech given by Warren Brookes of the *Detroit News* to ALEC's 1990 annual meeting, entitled "The Attack of the Killer Watermelons: Flat Earth Science & Zero Risk." "Watermelon" is a favorite right-wing term for "environmentalist," and is generally followed by the explanation "green on the outside and red [as in a communist] on the inside." Wise Users frequently advance the idea that the environmental movement represents the last bastion of socialism.
152. Wendell Cox and Samuel A. Brunelli, "Environmental Partners: A State Legislator's Guide to Public-Private Partnership" (Washington D.C.: American Legislative Exchange Council, 1992).
153. Bellant, *The Coors Connection,* p. 89. The evolving roles of these organizations at times makes their proper classification difficult. CDFE has also benefitted from the financial support of the Unification Church network.
154. Bellant, *The Coors Connection*. pp. 82–83.
155. Bohdan R. Romanivl, ed., *Corporate Giving Directory 1994*. (Washington D.C.: The Taft Group, 1994).
156. The latter quote is from John Hosemann, chief economist of the American Farm Bureau Federation, speaking at the Environmental Conservation Organization (ECO) convention

held 18–20 February 1993 in Reno, Nevada. The Farm Bureau Federation is a principal sponsor of anti-union "right-to work" legislation. At the 1993 Wise Use Leadership Conference, Perry Pendley picked up on the religious right rhetoric of Pat Buchanan's 1992 speech at the Republican National Convention and claimed that "There *is* a culture war in this country," in which a major battle should be that against "socialistic" environmentalists. At this same event, Putting People First chair and conference emcee Kathleen Marquardt derided the idea of statehood for Washington, D.C.

157. Dan Budd, former Wyoming state senator and father to Wise Use leader Karen Budd-Falen.

158. The Birch Society covers Wise Use issues in its publication *The New American* and the LaRouche-affiliated *Twenty-First Century Science and Technology* magazine dutifully covers Wise Use conferences and seems particularly enamored of Wise Use figure Dixie Lee Ray.

159. Timothy Egan, "125 Groups Put Their Anti-Environmental Eggs in One Basket to Fight 'The Perfect Bogeyman,'" *New York Times News Service,* January 1992.

160. The "county rule" movement is most ardently advanced by the National Federal Lands Conference, based in Bountiful, Utah. NFLC is a signatory of *The Wise Use Agenda* and Ron Arnold sits on the group's advisory board. The most vocal spokesperson for NFLC is Karen Budd, a Cheyenne, Wyoming attorney associated with the Mountain States Legal Foundation and protege of James Watt.

161. Interestingly, David Howard, first president of the OLC-affiliated Alliance for America, is executive director of "Land Rights Letter," the premier organ of the property rights movement.

Wise Use below the High-Tide Line

Threats and Opportunities

Carl Safina • *Suzanne Iudicello*

In 1991, more than 100 people from 40 co-sponsoring organizations staged a "fly-in for freedom" rally in Washington, D.C. Concerned Shrimpers of America, an organization of Gulf of Mexico shrimpers, figured significantly in the demonstrations and lobbying that comprised the event. Concerned Shrimpers had become members of the steering committee of Alliance for America, a group working to weaken the Endangered Species Act. The shrimpers wanted conservationists off their backs.

The shrimpers' beef, to coin a surf-and-turf mixed metaphor, had been their adamant resistance to turtle excluder devices, or TEDs. TEDs, which are required by federal regulation on most Southeastern U.S. shrimp boats, allow sea turtles to escape from shrimp trawl nets. A trawl net is a bag-shaped net pulled behind a boat, scooping up sea life in its path. After being towed for awhile, sometimes several hours, the trawl is winched back aboard the boat and the contents in the terminal end of the net bag are dumped on deck. In the southern United States, the contents include about 10 percent shrimp and 90 percent unwanted marine life, mostly juvenile fish that are shoveled overboard, dead. Occasionally a turtle is pulled aboard. Occasionally, the turtle has drowned by the time the net surfaces.

All sea turtles occurring in U.S. waters are listed as either threatened or endangered under the Endangered Species Act. In 1990 the National Research Council estimated that shrimp trawling in the southern United States, which annually killls up to 55,000 sea turtles, is responsible for the deaths of more sea turtles than all the other sources of human-caused mortality combined. The Council noted that "Declines of Kemp's ridleys . . . and of loggerheads . . . are especially clear" and that "[t]rawl-related mortality must be reduced to conserve sea turtle populations, especially loggerheads and Kemp's ridleys." But the Council noted that "[s]hrimping can be compatible with conservation of sea turtles if adequate controls are placed on trawling activities, especially the mandatory use of turtle excluder devices at most places at most times of year."

A TED is a shunt, often consisting of a slanted metal grate and a hinged exit door, sewn into the trawl just ahead of the terminal net bag. There are a variety of TED designs, but the idea is that turtles hit the grate and slide out the door to freedom, while shrimp pass through the grate and are caught. TEDs can cost as little as $35 to $50 to as much as $300, and most are fairly easy to install. Although the Wise Use movement in its Alliance for America literature has termed the Endangered Species Act (ESA) "a law out of control," TEDs seemed to conservationists and fishery managers a perfect example of an ESA success story. TEDs fulfill the mandate of the ESA to prevent takes of critically endangered species with little or no impact on the industry.

Problem was, a small but vocal and active cadre of shrimpers hated TEDs for a variety of reasons, ranging from the fact that some TED designs lost part of the shrimp catch under certain conditions (e.g., if the grate clogged up with seaweed) to simple resentment of conservationist meddling and federal bureaucratic mandates. When it began to look as though the National Marine Fisheries Service would mandate use of TEDs year-round in all southern shrimp fisheries (this did occur in 1992, but only after threat of litigation on the part of conservationists), shrimpers responded with a variety of actions and joined the movement whose avowed purpose is to break environmental regulation that interferes with natural-resource-based private business activities. Concerned Shrimpers had more to be concerned about than just turtles and TEDs. Incidental bycatch of millions of juvenile fish in shrimp nets has devastated several species of fish and incurs very high costs to other fishers because these same juveniles would be worth a considerable amount as adults. It seemed a matter of time before shrimpers' juvenile-fish bycatch would come under increasing fire, increasing scrutiny from enviro-meddlers, and increasing regulation from bureaucrats.

The hookup of shrimpers with Wise Use people from the Northwest was widely perceived (and alternately applauded and dreaded in the Wise Use and marine conservation communities, respectively) as the beginning of a grand marriage between terrestrial and aquatic enviro-bashing natural-resource users, spanning the length and breadth of the United States of American, from sea to depleted sea.

Many people in both the terrestrial and fishing groups feel overburdened by federal regulations. Further, certain fishing practices have recently come under attack by conservation groups that have begun to perceive that marine fish are among our most mismanaged and severely depleted wildlife. This has caused some organized fishing groups to portray environmentalists as one of the causes of their problems and thus to see terrestrial Wise Users as people with whom they share something in common. Complaints that environmentalists are out to "shut fisheries down" and that conservation concerns about fish are over-shadowing the importance of the livelihood of small communities and fishing families have become standard rhetoric in the industry press. They have a familiar ring. The Wise Use message spin that it makes sense to put human needs before the needs of lesser creatures has surfaced with some regularity in fishing circles. Indeed, one theme that recently has been repeated by the industry from the most sophisticated national associations to small, regional fishing co-ops and coalitions is the message that fishers—from hand trollers to factory trawlers—are "producing food for the world," placing them in the same bucolic context as farmers rather than as resource users who kill fish.

Although the honeymoon between shrimpers and their landward kindred spirits has matured into a surviving marriage, and though a flirtation continues on the part of a few fishing associations, neither has resulted in an all-out rush to the altar by commercial fishing groups. The reasons are several, and they vary around the coastal perimeter of the country. In many areas there is an inherent tension between the Wise Use movement's agenda and the problems of commercial fishers. One prime reason is that habitat loss is responsible for a major share of the declines in fish abundance that are hurting fishers, and fishers are smart enough to see the direct link between falling catches, lost and degraded rivers and coastal wetlands, and the private landowners who are log-ging, grazing, destroying wetlands, and spraying pesticides in watersheds under the Wise Use banner.

Further, many commercial fishers are simply not well networked. The free, independent, iconoclastic, and ofter self-styled curmudgeonly personal-ities that are drawn to the open sea are not traditionally "joiners" and hob-nobbers. And they spend much of their time away from home and away from phones. Even the heads of several of the most prominent fishermen's organi-zations we polled had never heard of the Wise Use movement or were only dimly aware of it.

Still, the courtship continues. At the moment it is relatively one-sided, with Wise Users doing the calling and fishers listening politely but generally not get-ting into bed. In February 1993, the National Fisheries Institute (NFI), the major U.S. lobbying and advocacy association for seafood distributors, spon-sored a forum on the Endangered Species Act, Marine Mammal Protection Act, Magnuson Fishery Conservation and Management Act, and Clean Water

Act. Wise Users came a-courting, saying that fishers needed to join them to make the case against ESA.

Despite these overtures, the forum demurred, partly because of the habitat-destruction problem that is part and parcel of the Wise Use agenda and partly because a number of big commercial fishing organizations that were involved in the forum already had recognized the Wise Users as habitat destructionists. At an April 1993 meeting in Portland sponsored by the Pacific States Marine Fisheries Commission, fishermen said openly that they had more in common with the environmental movement than with the Wise Use people, because problems caused by logging, hydropower development, agriculture, and mining were significant threats to the salmon that they relied on for a living. Certain West Coast salmon fishers' organizations have noted in their literature that the Endangered Species Act holds some promise for restoration of salmon populations and the salmon fishery, which is currently on the ropes primarily because of just those activities that Wise Use holds high and defends. Tension between fishers and landowners has occasionally erupted into the open, as in a civil rights suit in Louisiana, where fishers are suing private landowners for charging fishermen fees to use waterways.

This is not cause for complacency, however. Fishers are beset by an array of serious problems and are being squeezed as never before. Some are attracted to the Wise Use, anti-regulation perspective. In June 1992, Fishermen of the Eastern Tropical Pacific, representing the fleet that catches dolphins while catching tuna, attended the Wise Use Leadership Conference in Reno, Nevada, complaining at length that environmental regulations were forcing many ships out of the fleet. The Fishermen's Coalition of Coronado, California, is listed among citizens groups in the *Guide to the Property Rights Movement,* a publication of the *Land Rights Letter.* Some fishers see Wise Use as the next place to turn if the conservationists' marine fish agenda becomes too demanding or strident. The American High Seas Fisheries Association, in a letter objecting to language in a Marine Fish Conservation Network pamphlet, complained that the sentence "Conservation and management measures to prevent overfishing and rebuild depleted fish populations must be given priority over any other considerations" suggests ignoring human needs, "and this is the genesis of the Wise Use movement."

In certain areas, fishers' access to severely depleted fish and shellfish populations is increasingly restricted by federal regulations, and conservation groups have in the last two years become prominent on the fishery scene. Wise Use literature is continuing to try to establish the link between rights of access to private lands and rights of access to fishing grounds. The *Land Rights Letter* has denounced the fishery activities of the New England–based Conservation Law

Foundation, which sued the National Marine Fisheries Service for failing to develop a plan to rebuild several severely overfished, depleted populations off New England. The *Land Rights Letter* said that "the resulting plan would have put Maine lobstermen out of business in droves and led to a storm of protest," and that "ongoing CLF legal activism continues to incite the wrath of Maine fishermen. Political leverage based on the failure of the government to recognize private property rights—in these cases . . . fishing rights—is a common theme in environmentalist strategy nationwide." While CLF's suit and the rebuilding plan it attempted to force did in fact ignite a storm of protest from the fishers who had been mining the fish to their lowest levels ever, the affected fishery did not include lobsters and had nothing in particular to do with Maine. And despite the fact that fish and fishing grounds are publicly owned and access is a privilege, the *Land Rights Letter* referred to fishing rights as private-property rights.

That a system of open access to public resources is referred to as private-property rights bodes ominously for future interpretations of a new way to manage fisheries based on privatizing access to federally set fishing quotas through the use of salable shares known as individual transferrable quotas, or ITQs.

PROPERTY RIGHTS IN MARINE FISHERIES: WAVE OF THE FUTURE?

Protection of property rights is, if not the heart and soul of the Wise Use movement, certainly its lungs and larynx. Indeed, the *Land Rights Letter*'s slogan is "For Americans dedicated to preserving our heritage of private property rights."

Currently, there is little to indicate that the Wise Use movement has made much progress in most marine fisheries despite its efforts. But the potential for private-property rights becoming important in the ocean context is on the near horizon in the form of government giveaways of fishing rights that then can be sold.

The government argues that these ITQs are not property rights but rather access rights. However, most conservationists, economists, and some courts are not so sure. If you can buy and sell an ITQ, it can be, and has been construed to be, a private-property right.

Although they can be structured in myriad ways, depending on the fishery in question, the ITQ is basically a right to a guaranteed share of fish. Based either on historic participation in a fishery or on an auction system where fishers bid for rights, the government divides up a catch quota among successful bidders/users. All others are excluded from the fishery. Those fishers holding a share can then fish it, tie up at the dock and have someone else fish it, or sell it.

Proponents claim that the system will prohibit new entrants into a fishery where the vessel capacity already matches (or exceeds) what is needed to catch the allowable quota. Another argument is that the system will avoid "derby"-style fisheries, where short season openings have resulted in a rush of vessels competing for the quota. The most glaring example is the halibut frenzy in Alaska, where recently more that 5,500 boats jammed the two 24-hour openings with tragic results—the deaths of seven fishermen. The government contends that privatization will simplify management and regulation by reducing the number of vessels that need to be monitored. Ultimately, the argument goes, the buying and selling of quota shares will improve fishing efficiency until all the marginal people are out of the business and only the best catchers hold all the shares.

Government resource economists have been touting ITQs since the mid-1980s, and privatization has been a major element of the National Marine Fisheries Service management strategy for several years. As of mid-1993, 10 fishery management plans (out of 43) either had or planned to place fisheries under ITQ management.

Conservation groups entered the ITQ debate only recently, and reviews are mixed. While there are numerous conservation, fiscal, and social-justice issues that can be raised in opposition to ITQs, we examine here only the property rights implications of the system and the fertile ground they provide for the Wise Use movement.

The economic theory driving the rush to privatization was first popularized in 1968 by Garrett Hardin in his essay "The Tragedy of the Commons." The notion is that open or unrestricted access to public resources leads to entry of more and more users until they exceed the capacity of the commons. On the other hand, the theory goes, users who own the resource will, because of their own rational, economic self-interest, take better care of it.

This incentive to maximize profit and, concomitantly, prevent waste or destruction of the resource is one basis of support for privatization expressed by the Competitive Enterprise Institute, which, though it claims no connection with the Wise Use movement, certainly shares some of its views about the benefits of private property and the burdensomeness of governmental regulation. Spokespersons for the Institute have appeared at various fish forums in recent years espousing ITQs as a means to attain in the ocean that market-based efficiency the Institute espouses in terrestrial contexts. Kent Jeffries, director of environmental studies for the Institute, argues in a 1992 publication titled *Who Should Own the Ocean?* that a property rights regime could improve not only fisheries management but also ocean management on every front, from pollution prevention to conservation of the great whales. A market-based model, argue Jeffries and economists like John Ward of the National Marine Fisheries Service, could more efficiently allocate the resources needed to catch fish if the property rights to do so were clearly defined, transferrable, and enforceable.

While the theory may sound seductive, practical application appears less promising from the conservation point of view. Property rights that are defined, transferrable, and enforceable create new territory for Wise Use action. Transformation of public resources into a private-property right opens opportunities for assertions of the takings clause of the Fifth Amendment to the Constitution, a favorite litigation ground for Wise Users. What would be unthinkable above high tide line—say, giving away the south slope of Gates of the Arctic National Monument to XYZ Ski Resort Company complete with XYZ's right not only to make money from selling lift tickets but also to later sell the slope—has caused barely a ripple in the community when done in the ocean context. Why should it?

First, the government argument that ITQs do not create a private-property right doesn't wash, since the fundamental characteristic of "property" is the right to exclude all others—a clear outcome of ITQs. Even in systems where the transferability was eliminated, as in a program on Canada's east coast, government officials freely admit that quota shares are bought and sold like any other private property. Second, conservationists could well lose the well-established principal that fish belong in common to all citizens. Writing in 1895 to uphold the power of a state to pass wildlife laws, the Supreme Court said government ownership of fish and wildlife in common is "exercised . . . as a trust for the benefit of the people and not as a prerogative for the advantage of the government . . . or for the benefit of private individuals as distinguished from the public good" [*Geer v. Connecticut,* 161 U.S. 519 (1895)]. This notion has been amplified over time with regard to the ocean, particularly through the Public Trust Doctrine, to stand for the idea that certain lands such as tidelands and waters are exempt from private ownership and must be held by the state for the full use and enjoyment of the general public.

Third, as non-owners, conservationists would have to rely on traditional means—property suits in nuisance or trespass cases, suits based on specific legislative mandates, or citizen actions where sufficient standing could be established—to assert the public interest should something go awry. For example, what mechanism would remain in an ITQ fishery to reduce the quota or call for emergency in-season management measures? It has been difficult enough with the government as steward. What could go awry? Take the case of ITQs in New Zealand, where the shares were based on actual tonnage. When the government tried to step in to reduce the quota for biological and conservation reasons, the fishers asserted that they had a property right to the entire share. Not only did the court agree, it made the government *buy the shares back;* and when the government could not afford to repurchase the amount necessary to reduce the catch to sustainable levels because the price of fish had gone so high, overfishing continued unchecked. Although it could be argued that the New Zealand case is peculiar because the quota share was for tonnage rather than percentage of a quota set by government, it is worth considering the consequences of creating even an expectation of a catch right.

Finally, were conservationists to be successful in an action to reduce a quota or cut short a season, it could be expected that property rights advocates would step in to assert their interest as well. As one ITQ proponent wrote recently, "The allocation of ITQs is not merely an awarding of fish, but an allocation of the entire wealth of the resource." It does not seem a stretch that regulating fishing operations in a way that reduced the catch would be a taking, comparable to regulating land use in the coastal zone.

Despite the efforts of some to characterize fishing as agriculture and catching fish as "harvest," it seems appropriate to sum up the property rights argument against privatizing America's fisheries in the words of noted water law commentator Joseph Sax. He suggests that because fishing, unlike agriculture, "partake[s] so much of the bounty of nature, rather than of individual enterprise that [it] should be made freely available to the entire citizenry . . . and that it is a principle purpose of government to promote the interests of the general public rather than to redistribute public goods from broad public uses to restricted private benefit."[1]

Capture is by no means the only problem facing living marine creatures. A serious long-term threat is the degradation and loss of marine habitats. Along the coast, where many marine creatures spawn or spend the early part of their lives, habitat loss and degradation has begun to limit the productivity and recovery potential of marine areas, especially estuaries. An estuary is a mixing zone between fresh water and seawater. Typical estuaries are the vast coastal bays of the East Coast and the tidal portions of rivers.

At the coast, hurting habitat hurts business. Seventy-five percent of U.S. commercial landings consist of species dependent on coastal estuaries for part of their life cycle. The annual economic value of estuarine habitats to U.S. fisheries is about $14 billion. Coastal wetlands are still being filled at a significant rate by private owners. Consequently, fish runs are declining and shellfish beds are being destroyed or polluted. Coastal habitat is disappearing in direct proportion to human population growth, and because coastal areas are desirable places to live, human population growth there is four times the national average. This greatly increases development pressures and adds additional urgency to the need for protecting remaining habitats before they are destroyed.

There exists an opportunity for the conservation community to do something novel: link arms with the people who make money taking a living resource, in this case commercial fishermen. Coastal fishers, many of whom are colorful people with long local traditions and long-established communities, are being pushed off the end of the earth by developers, polluters, and wetlands wreckers.

This issue has a very large human and social component that has not yet been elevated to public view. Commercial fishers are the last hunter–gatherers on a continent that has not been accommodating the needs of hunter–gatherers since Columbus landed. Fish are our only major food source whose supply still depends on natural production in a wild environment. This is why fishing is fundamentally unlike agriculture and livestock raising, and why fishing depends on productive, healthy, abundant habitat. Fish are wildlife, not commodities.

A demonstration that conservation groups can fight vigorously on behalf of people who use natural resources would help the cause of conservationists. Who says conservationists are antipeople and antibusiness? Demonstrating that wrecking nature bankrupts local economies by having those who are hurt financially do much of the speaking on their own behalf would be a powerful message, if heard. The conservation community could help fishers get their own message across. Conservationists have the skills, fishers have the problems, and both camps have the common goal of preserving habitat and the quality and productivity of coastal waters into the future. The two could work together to protect, enhance, and restore coastal habitats and their related fisheries, producing economic benefits for the nation and coastal culture. Enabling a financially vested fishing constituency to work with environmentalists for common goals would not only be powerful for the task of habitat conservation, it would also help blunt the Wise Use movement in local areas by establishing as opponents of the movement local grassroots business interests that depend on healthy habitat. For example, because logging can destroy salmon-spawning habitat, salmon fishers depend on healthy forests in the Northwest; and by some estimates there are several times as many fishers as loggers in the Northwest. At the very least, even if there are fewer fishers than Wise Users, the appearance of fishers in the debate changes it from an environment-versus-jobs debate to one about jobs versus jobs.

The Wise Use movement frequently has used a grassroots approach. One view of this, ironically, is that it is an effort by vested interests to copy the strategies that have worked so well for public-interest grassroots groups, exemplified by conservationists and environmentalists themselves. Wise Users usually portray the "little guy" as struggling to survive under attempts by well-funded adversaries who would ruin their ability to work the land, thus taking away their rights to make a living. Usually, but not always, this involves activity on privately owned land; at other times it involves rights of access to publicly owned land. Below the high-tide line, because hurting habitat hurts business and hurts fishers' access to clean, productive waters in which to work, conservationists have an opportunity to co-opt this Wise Use, little-guy-as-underdog approach. Untapped opportunities exist for the conservation community to begin building strong ties and active working relationships with fishers and coastal fishing communities against common adversaries, such as developers and polluters of coastal wetlands, estuaries, and rivers. Conservationists could work with fishers, act as a conduit for providing scientific data on the effects of fish and fishery economics of wetlands filling, coastal construction, pesticides, and other factors that degrade habitat and undermine fishing communities. Conservationists could help facilitate fishers' speaking on their own behalf and help mobilize a grassroots self-defense effort of fishing people whose income and way of life are directly linked to healthy marine habitat.

This inverse Wise Use, pro-conservation, grassroots/business approach could be applied on local or regional scales, centered around particular estuary systems. This could take the form of estuary-based campaigns to secure habitat, stop development, stem pollution, clean the water, and restore biological productivity. It could also take the form of infrastructure development initiatives to build up sewage-treatment capacity and thus provide money and jobs ashore. Other pro-fishing business initiatives on which conservationists and working fishers could collaborate are in efforts to give the National Marine Fisheries Service veto power over Army Corps permits to alter coastal habitats; to streamline the numbing array of overlapping jurisdictions that allow real coastal protection to fall through the cracks; to guard against oil pollution caused by drilling and spills; to watch closely over marine environmental impact analyses and construction permitting; to strengthen pollution controls; to clean up contaminated sediments; to end the diversion of river water for agriculture, dams, and cattle; and to eliminate construction and insurance subsidies in coastal areas and timber subsidies in watersheds.

Because fisheries are so varied and their problems and pressures so mixed, the response of fishers to the Wise Use movement has ranged from embrace to repulsion. There are issues to be wary of, but there also are intriguing opportunities to adapt the Wise Use approach to neutralize its own efforts below the high-tide line.

Notes

1. Quoted in Donohue, Charles, T. E. Kauper, and P. W. Martin, 1983. Property: An Introduction to the Concept and the Institution, 342. West, St. Paul, Minn.

Sagebrush Rebellion II

Florence Williams

Until two years ago, Catron County, New Mexico, population 2,500, was a typical rural western community. The cattle and timber industries accounted for most of the tax base, with the bulk of land in the arid county owned by the federal government. So when the Forest Service announced it wanted more elk and fewer cattle, and that it also intended to cut timber sales to protect the Mexican spotted owl, people got mad.

"The problem was that our civil rights were being violated," says Richard Manning, a cattle rancher and one of a growing number of western activists arguing that federal grazing permits confer a constitutionally protected property right.

Manning, who is heralded by his peers in the cattle industry as a "rawhide American hero," did more than complain. In the summer of 1990, he talked his local county commissioners into drafting emergency ordinances designed to protect the county's cattle heritage and limit the power of federal officials.

"No one ever heard of Catron County until we passed the ordinances," Manning told a rapt audience of 300 ranchers in Colorado last year. "Within 24 hours, Washington, D.C., knew where Catron County was."

Catron County is no longer alone. By the end of 1992, dozens of counties in Montana, Idaho, Wyoming, New Mexico, Utah, Nebraska, and California had quietly codified their frustrations into local laws that could hinder the way the federal government administers the public lands and resources in these counties.

"A quarter of the counties in the West are involved," estimates Karl Hess, a Las Cruces–based planning consultant who initially helped Catron write the county plan that goes hand in hand with the new ordinances. "Eight months ago, this didn't exist."

The new ordinances and land-use plans attempt to weaken the Endangered Species Act, the Clean Water Act, the Wild and Scenic Rivers Act, the Wilderness Act, and the National Forest Management Act by stating that local governments must approve all federal actions in their counties. Codes create criminal sanctions for federal officials who violate county demands. For example, forest rangers in Catron County, and now elsewhere, can be arrested for "arbitrarily" reducing a rancher's cattle on public land.

"The ordinances scared the hell out of us," says Mike Gardner, a Forest Service district ranger in Reserve, the county seat. "I've got small children. It would be tough to tell my kids why I'm being arrested. It was intimidating."

The assumption underlying the ordinances is that grazing permits are the "intangible" property of the permittee. Manning and his followers say the number of cattle allowed on a federal permit directly affects the value of his private ranch.

Federal agencies insist that grazing permits have always been a privilege, not a right, and that the government has supremacy over decisions on public land. In fact, the U.S. Justice Department and the Office of General Counsel for the Forest Service quickly responded that Catron's ordinances were null and void, and they threatened to prosecute county officials if the local laws were enforced.

"The county cannot in any way proscribe or dictate land management functions undertaken by the Forest Service," wrote agency attorney James Perry to Catron County commissioner Buddy Allred. Says Wilderness Society attorney Jim Norton: "The resolutions are really almost silly because they're so illegal and unconstitutional. They're only trying to intimidate federal officials and browbeat them into putting up more timber, grass, and mining than they otherwise would."

County officials elsewhere seem confused. In Granite County, Montana, which passed the same ordinances this winter, county attorney Al Bradshaw says he's not even sure whether the ordinances are legal. "I guess that since it hasn't been tested, it's kind of shaky water whether it would be upheld." Manning summed up Catron County's experimental approach: "If there's no law that says you can't do it, do it." He says the courts have yet to rule on the county's legal arguments, and even if they lose court battles, the antigovernment sentiment sweeping the counties may yet start a revolution.

As many as 45 rural counties in six states are currently drafting Catron's ordinances into their own emergency interim land-use plans, says consultant Hess, a self-avowed libertarian and free-market proponent.

Although Hess assisted Catron County, he later parted ways with local officials and has since disassociated himself from the Catron-style movement. "My argument all along has been that federal control is harmful to local communities and the environment. But I disagree vehemently with Catron

County's use of my language to disguise their own hidden agenda, which is to continue government subsidies for mining and ranching at the expense of the environment."

The antiregulation ordinances in Catron's model plan were written by Karen Budd, a Wyoming attorney and former assistant in James Watt's Interior Department. "You're kidding yourself if you think there's not a war going on for the West," Budd tells her audiences of ranchers. "The war is about philosophy. Your county commissioners can protect your rights a lot better than the federal government can."

Budd says she wants there to be greater local control over decisions made on federal lands. "My parents own a ranch," explains the blonde, fifth-generation Wyomingite, 33. "It's a medium-size ranch, not a corporation, just dad and his brother. I saw it eroding." Budd does not mean physically eroding; she means her family's control of the land. "It used to be you'd sit down with the local [ranger] and take care of any problems you had on a local level. Now, they just tell you what you to do." Budd says ranchers are losing their ability to influence range and other public-land decisions that affect them. "We want a fair fight. We just want our ranch protected."

Budd's weapons are the courts. She hopes to test the local ordinances she has written for some 45 western counties demanding equal status to the feds on public-land decisions there.

In her thriving private practice, Budd represents some of the most controversial figures to hit the public land in a decade. One client from Nevada, Wayne Hage, is suing the Forest Service because it confiscated his cattle after he refused to reduce their numbers on his grazing allotment (*High Country News,* September 9, 1991). With Budd's help, Hage argues that his federal permit amounts to his private property and cannot be taken away from him without due process or compensation.

Budd also represents Catron County rancher Richard Manning in a suit designed to force the Forest Service to use consistent guidelines across different states when writing allotment management plans. Her client Budd Eppers hopes to go to the Supreme Court testing the legal principle of the "split estate," which allows mineral, grazing, and water rights to pass to heirs even if the land belongs to the government.

She often cites Executive Order 12630, signed by President Reagan in 1988, which says federal agencies must consider the effects of their decisions on private property. She wants economic-impact studies done for decisions affecting grazing land.

These arguments anger some federal attorneys, who say the Supreme Court has already ruled in support of the government's authority over its own lands. Says Forest Service attorney Mary Ann Joca in Sante Fe: "I consider these nonissues. Permits are not private property." As for Executive Order 12630, Joca says it is not subject to judicial review (meaning it is not a law, just a directive), and even if it were, most Forest Service regulations predate it.

"[Budd] has these bizarre theories," continues Joca. "She gets people to believe they have ancient rights predating national forests. It's a little sad because she gets these guys all psyched up. I give her credit for creativity."

Other observers and participants compare the new county-planning movement to the Sagebrush Rebellion of the late 1970s and early 1980s, whose backers demanded that the government turn over its land to state or private hands.

But the county movement goes beyond trying to influence public land decisions, says Wyoming rancher and activist Dick Hiser, who is trying to get his native Carbon County to enact a similar plan. "Many things on the horizon from the federal government are going to have an impact on private property," speculates Hiser. He says the Endangered Species Act and other laws restrict certain private-land uses. "We need to safeguard and strengthen ourselves on the homefront."

"This is really a more sophisticated Sagebrush Rebellion," notes Larry Mehlhaff of the Sierra Club in Wyoming.

Son of Sagebrush has some environmentalists worried. "The scary thing is they want to butcher environmental protection," says Scott Groene, an attorney with the Southern Utah Wilderness Alliance. "It's disconcerting to have elected officials trying to do that."

Assisting in the county-planning movement is an organization based in Bountiful, Utah, called the National Federal Lands Conference. Run by right-wing ideologues who have stated they hope to dismantle the environmental movement, its motto is "property is sacred if liberty is to exist." One of the conference's advisors, Ron Arnold, also heads the Center for the Defense of Free Enterprise in Bellevue, Washington. "We're going to run the environmentalists out of business," he said in a recent *Time* magazine.

The National Federal Lands Conference has given seminars throughout the West with Karen Budd and Dick Manning, among others. A recent meeting in Steamboat Springs, Colorado, attracted nearly 300 ranchers. The organization also distributes materials and publishes strategies for defeating environmentalists, whom it calls "entrenched radicals." The movement appears most popular in states with pending wilderness bills, such as California, Montana, and Utah. In Beaverhead County, Montana, commissioner Robert Peterson told the local newspaper: "Any wilderness is killing us. It takes away our timber and hurts our whole economy."

The Utah Office of Planning and Budget, responsible for assisting counties in preparing land-use plans, hopes to water down attempts to replicate Catron's plan. "We don't think this is the right approach to be used for comprehensive planning," says state planning director Brad Barber. "We're not supportive of these interim plans. They're not very useful, and don't provide real direction or planning for the future. We don't want to have a predetermined agenda."

Salt Lake City attorney Ralph Becker, who consults for federal agencies, agrees. "These plans . . . are policy statements, not planning. In no way do they resemble planning," he says.

Indeed, many residents of Grand County, Utah, which contains the town of Moab, say they are horrified by the rhetoric in their county's draft plan. Included in the draft document, lifted almost word-for-word from Catron County, are statements that support the controversial 1872 Mining Law, demand a weaker definition of wetlands, and condemn the designation of wilderness. As an alternative to following federal guidelines for protecting endangered species, Grand County commissioners also propose writing their own guidelines.

Karen Budd argues that such unconventional measures are necessary to gain local control of resources and preserve the "heritage" of commodity production in the West. She says existing federal regulations contain provisions for local governments to participate in public-land planning. The best way to do this is for the locals to codify their definition of "custom and culture," she says. "NEPA [the National Environmental Policy Act] says the government must use all practicable means to protect our national heritage," explains Budd. "Most people think of Indian bones and dinosaurs, but it could be just any use that's occurred over long periods of time. Wouldn't five generations of ranching be a form of custom and culture?"

Budd says if counties define their custom and culture through these plans, then the federal agencies must work with them and respect their needs. In fact, she says the counties and feds have equal standing. "Only in this way," she says, "can a local government fight to protect its economic base and the private property and rights of its citizens."

The federal land managers in Catron County disagree. They say the existing channels of communication, such as the public-hearing process of NEPA, are adequate for airing the county's concerns. "All they had to do was come and talk to us," says Gila National Forest planner Delbert Griego. "We are not a faceless institution."

But forest ranger Gardner concedes the Catron plan has made him more aware of the county's needs. "Dealing with the county is a little tense, but I go to every county commission meeting now." Gardner also says he hasn't cut any grazing permits since the ordinances passed.

When Catron County rancher Manning speaks to crowds of rural westerners, he stresses the power of local law and political activism. He says the movement is more than county-level planning, that it must have the force of numbers to be successful.

In Steamboat Springs, ranchers packed a conference room at the Sheraton to hear Manning, Karl Hess, and Karen Budd. Perched on the coat racks were dozens of cowboy hats.

"Our constitution as we know it is being arbitrarily and capriciously changed through policies and regulations," said the tall, slightly bent Manning. "If you don't lock your custom and culture into law, you're through, you're history. We've been asleep too long."

In Steamboat, where ranchers say a recent Forest Service approval of a new ski development will hurt them, Dick Manning received a standing ovation.

POSTSCRIPT

At least one lawsuit has recently been filed that could make or break the validity of the new county regulations. In Boundary County in northern Idaho, the local ordinances are being challenged by environmental groups and private citizens. North Idaho Audubon, Bonner's Ferry Forest Watch, Boundary Backpackers, and 19 individuals filed suit in state court in early March 1993 against the county. They argue that the county's ordinances violate federal and state constitutional provisions, specifically including the federal supremacy clause giving the government authority to manage public lands. [*On January 27, 1994, the state court ruled that the Boundary County ordinance was unconstitutional—Eds.*]

Local activist Dave Bodner says the Boundary ordinances threaten to dismantle federal efforts to protect endangered species, enforce clean-water standards, and regulate timber production. The ordinance most offensive is the one stating that federal agents may be subject to fines and arrest for regulating federal lands without prior negotiation with county officials. One of the plaintiffs is a U.S. Forest Service official.

Not All That Glitters

Thomas Michael Power

Hard-rock mining on federal land is currently governed by a law passed 121 years ago, the 1872 Mining Law. In 1872, the West was seen as an uninhabited wasteland that needed to be converted to commodity production in order to facilitate settlement. The federal lands were seen almost exclusively as potential sources of commodities whose extraction would generate economic activity.

Much has changed since then. The frontier has closed; the West has been settled. Those federal lands are now seen as much more than a store of extractable commodities. These public lands provide the environmental base upon which the current settlement of the West depends: recreational opportunities, wildlife, high-quality water, scenic beauty, and intact ecosystems.

Mining Law reform seeks to protect that environmental base, which has also become an important part of the region's economic base. It does this in several important ways:

First, it removes a distortion which has been built into the current mining industry economy by the federal government subsidizing extractive activities on federal land. The federal government currently gives away the mineral resources it owns and the land supporting mining operations at a near zero price. Since other mineral owners do not engage in this type of noneconomic behavior, mining activities are artificially shifted toward federal public lands.

Second, Mining Law reform seeks to allow the many nonextractive values associated with these lands to be seriously considered and protected when decisions are made about opening federal lands to hard-rock mining. These other values often are the dominant values associated with our public lands but now often have to be ignored because the 1872 Mining Law is blind to them.

Third, Mining Law reform seeks to ensure that mining on federal land is carried out in a responsible way and that the mining site is reclaimed at the end of the mining activity. This ensures that mining companies pay the full costs of producing their outputs, rather than impose those costs on other sectors of the economy.

Finally, Mining Law reform seeks to repair the ongoing damage being done by past mining activities that left scarred landscapes, safety hazards, and toxic mineral sites behind when they were abandoned. These sites threaten the usability of western lands and water supplies. These elements of Mining Law reform are found in two bills, H.R. 322 and S. 257, which were submitted to the 103rd Congress in January 1993. This chapter analyzes the economic impact of these proposed reforms, which will be collectively referred to as the Reform Bills.

ECONOMIC CONTEXT

The American West has been in an important economic transition for almost two decades now. As the West's traditional extractive industries, mining, timber, and agriculture, have gone through painful declines that have displaced tens of thousands of workers, the rest of the West's economy has shown considerable vitality, adding millions of new jobs.

The positive movement of the overall economy in the opposite direction to that taken by the traditional extractive base does not represent an economic contradiction or anomaly. It represents very conventional and familiar economic development: The frontier dependence upon a few unstable raw-material industries has been replaced by a sophisticated and diverse economy. Rather than rely upon the export of a few unprocessed raw materials and imports of almost everything needed to live in the West, the economy has developed so it can not only fill many of its own needs but can export sophisticated goods and services to the rest of the national economy.

The development of this modern diversified economy has been driven by the relocation of people and businesses to the higher-quality living environment offered by the western landscape. This environmental-driven economic vitality is, also, not a new or uniquely western phenomenon. The economic development of our suburban areas and of the Sun Belt over the last 50 years was driven by the same pursuit of higher-quality living environments.

The Reform Bills seek to protect the West's high-quality living environment by seeing that the full range of values associated with federal public lands are considered when management decisions are made, which protects the current and future economic base of the region.

IMPACT OF REFORM

Mining Law reform will create jobs. The Reform Bills would require the federal government to behave as a responsible landowner and ask those mining companies who wish to extract minerals to make a reasonable payment for that privilege. Almost all other mineral landowners, private, state, and tribal, already do that. The federal government already does it for energy resources. Such payments are a normal cost of engaging in the mining business, which the federal government has neglected to collect in the past. Collecting such royalty and claim holding fees now will simply end a distortion in the mineral economy that discouraged development on nonfederal lands and redirected it to federal lands.

The revenues generated by these royalties and fees would largely be used, according to the Reform Bills, to support reclamation of abandoned mine sites and state and local government programs. In that sense, these royalties and fees collect the part of a mining company's profits that in the past was created by the federal subsidy and redirects that money to needed projects in the West. Those investments in mine reclamation will directly create jobs. They will also enhance the attractiveness of the West as a place to live, work, and do business by reclaiming ugly and dangerous abandoned mining sites and by supporting state and local government programs with something other than tax dollars.

For those mining operations on federal lands, these new royalties will effectively increase the cost of operations. This could have a negative impact on the viability of those mines. However, an analysis of both the cash costs associated with gold-mining operations and the longer-term total costs (including a competitive return on investment) indicates that very little of current production would be threatened by the proposed federal royalty. In the near term, because almost all operations have cash costs well below gold prices even with the royalty included, there would only be a one- or two-percent decline in production.

In the longer term, when a competitive return on mining investments must also be earned, the impact of royalty charges would be somewhat larger but still very modest, about a three percent. These potential declines in gold production should be compared with the six-percent-per-year annual growth in the production of gold over the last decade.

The net effect of the reclamation programs and the royalty payments is positive. The employment associated with the reclamation programs more than offsets the potential declines in mining employment due to the federal royalty. The reason for this is that the reclamation programs will be funded not only by the royalty payments but also by the mine claim rental fees. Since those fees primarily fall on the owners of nonoperating mineral sites, they do not depress mining employment but do create jobs when they are invested in mine reclamation. Overall, the Reform Bills would make a significant contribution to the ongoing economic vitality of the West.

ADAPTABILITY OF THE INDUSTRY

The hard-rock mining industry, out of necessity, has had to be very resilient and adaptable. It has always faced an uncertain market where the price it can receive for its product can fluctuate widely. In just six months in 1993 the price of gold moved from $325 per ounce to $410, an $86, or 26 percent, change. It then began to move quickly downward. Between 1987 and 1992 gold prices fell by $225 in real terms, a 40 percent decline.

It is in the context of market fluctuations of this size that the very modest eight percent royalty proposed in the Reform Bills has to be considered.

The gold industry was not disrupted and thrown into disarray by these large declines in gold prices, declines as large a $200 per ounce. In fact, despite these large price declines, the industry dramatically expanded to record levels of production. Between 1987 and 1993 production expanded by 140 percent while gold prices fell by over $200 per ounce in real terms. In this context, the impact of a federal royalty that would have a quantitative impact of about $15 per ounce when corrected for tax effects is unlikely to represent a significant change.

THE ROLE OF MINING

In order to estimate the likely impact of Mining Law reform on the economies of the western states, one needs to look closely at the role that federal hard-rock mineral deposits play in those economies. Despite the folk images perpetuated by western films and novels that suggest that metal mining is a central economic activity in the West, it actually plays a very tiny role in the overall economy. Only about one western job in a thousand is directly tied to metal mining in the West.

Furthermore, it is not correct to assume that all metal mining in the West is dependent upon federal land that would be affected by Mining Law reform. Copper mining, for example, largely takes place on private land. Many of the largest gold mines, for instance most of the Newmont operations in Nevada and Homestake operations in South Dakota and California, also rely almost exclusively on private lands.

The U.S. government's General Accounting Office, after surveying hard-rock mining companies, estimates that only 30 percent of gold production comes from federal lands and only about 15 percent of total hard-rock mining production comes from such lands. If the current rush to patent and transfer to private ownership most of the current producing mines succeeds, this federal percentage will decline further.

Since only one in a thousand western jobs is in metal mining and only one in six of *those* jobs relies upon federal land, Mining Law reform has the potential to affect only a tiny sliver of total western jobs, 3 out of every 10,000 jobs (0.025 percent). The actual impact, at worst, will only be a tiny fraction of these jobs. It should not be surprising, then, that the potential negative impact of Mining Law reform on the western economies is tiny.

IV

The Takings Issue

Our society has long held that private-property ownership confers certain rights. But we also have traditionally recognized that property owners have a responsibility to respect the rights and interests of others and the community as a whole. The Fifth Amendment to the U.S. Constitution prohibits government action, including regulatory activity, that results in the "taking" of private property "without just compensation." Yet the courts have recognized that the public, acting through its elected representatives, has a right to limit property uses, sometimes severely, to prevent harm to the environment and otherwise protect the public welfare.

As described by John D. Echeverria of the National Audubon Society, in "The Takings Issue," the takings question has assumed increasing prominence in recent years as developers and landowners—in public pronouncements and in court—have aggressively attacked environmental and other regulations as a violation of the Fifth Amendment. This trend has been abetted by a marked conservative shift in the composition of the U.S. Supreme Court as well as the lower federal courts.

In "The Value of Land," Neil D. Hamilton offers the perspective of a farmer and law professor on the property rights debate as it relates to the agricultural community. He contends that the policy debate over future management of our natural resources should not be subverted into a political debate over property rights; he argues instead for respect of every citizen's ethical duty of stewardship of the land.

"The Takings Debate and Federal Regulatory Programs," by Audubon's Sharon Dennis, examines recent developments in the takings debate at the federal level, including proposals pending in Congress on the issue and recent decisions by the U. S. Court of Federal Claims.

In 1992 the U.S. Supreme Court appeared to chart a new approach to takings law, at least in the unusual case where a regulation denies a property owner all economic use of his or her land. In *"Lucas v. South Carolina Coastal Council: An Enigmatic Approach to the Environmental Regulation of Land,"* Tim Searchinger of the Environmental Defense Fund dissects the landmark decision and discusses what it may portend for the future direction of takings law.

Beyond legal doctrine, the takings issue raises fundamental social and moral issues about the appropriate balance between rights and responsibilities in a civilized society. In "'Absolute' Rights: Property and Privacy," Mary Ann Glendon of Harvard University Law School attempts to establish a "communitarian balance" on the property issue.

The Takings Issue

John D. Echeverria

Since 1940, the U.S. population has doubled to approximately 250 million, and it is expected to reach nearly 400 million by the middle of the next century. We Americans, in our methods of transportation, patterns of settlement, and other aspects of modern culture, consume natural resources at an extraordinary pace, especially in relation to lesser-developed countries. The large and growing demands on the U.S. resource base have inevitably led to conflicts among different uses and interests. These burgeoning conflicts suggest the need for greater individual restraint in the use of natural resources for our own individual well-being and to protect the community as a whole.

On the other hand, protection of individual property rights is also an important American value, enshrined in the U.S. Constitution. For many, the right to use one's property, like the right of free speech or freedom of religion, is an essential ingredient of the liberty that each American enjoys. The tradition of respect for private property is particularly strong in the case of land.

A crucial challenge facing the conservation community in the years ahead is to define the place of private-property rights in the context of ever-increasing resource competition. Our goal must be to develop innovative techniques that harness the task of environmental protection and restoration to the cause of increased efficiency in resource use. We also must forge a more balanced understanding of the relationship between the individual's right to hold and use property, especially land, and each citizen's responsibilities to the community in a free society. Ultimately, conservationists will only succeed in achieving our vision of an environmentally sustainable society if we respect private property as well as encourage careful stewardship of land and other resources.

THE TAKINGS CLAUSE

The crux of the tension between environmental protection and individual liberty is expressed by the Fifth Amendment to the U.S. Constitution, which states: "nor shall private property be taken for public use, without just compensation." The exact purpose of this provision is a matter of historical debate. But it is clear, at a minimum, that the Fifth Amendment was adopted to ensure that government would pay financial compensation when it takes private property for some public purpose, such as for a school, a road, or a park. The Fifth Amendment does not deny the government's broad authority to "take" private property for a public purpose; it simply guarantees that the individual property owner will be compensated by the public that benefits from the taking.

In the early part of this century, in *Pennsylvania Coal Co. v. Mahon* [260 U.S. 393 (1922)], the U.S. Supreme Court ruled that government regulatory action, like out-and-out public seizure of private property, can amount to a taking in violation of the Fifth Amendment. The Court did not establish clear standards for identifying a "regulatory taking"; rather it simply stated that regulation, when it goes "too far," will be deemed a taking.

According to the modern advocates for expanding landowners' rights, government regulatory action that reduces the value of private property is indistinguishable from seizure or occupation of property by government. When the government prohibits filling of a wetland, bars development of critical wildlife habitat, or perhaps even restricts pollution, so the property rights argument goes, the property has in effect been "taken" for a "public use," and just compensation is due.

This argument has the force of simplicity. The protection against takings in the Fifth Amendment, like other guarantees in the Bill of Rights, is designed to prevent the government from singling out a particular individual to bear a burden that in fairness should be borne by the public as a whole. If the public needs a road, the Fifth Amendment ensures that the majority does not meet this public need simply by seizing an individual's land without paying compensation. Similarly, according to property rights advocates, if the public wants to protect endangered species, for example, individuals whose property uses are restricted as a result of this effort should not be required to bear the burden alone.

IN DEFENSE OF REASONABLE REGULATION

While the property rights argument has undeniable force, it is sometimes taken to a simplistic extreme. Property rights are not and never have been absolute in this country.

Most important, the extreme versions of the property rights argument ignore that the primary purpose of government regulation is to protect private and public rights, including property rights. Pollution-control laws protect property owners against harmful activities by their neighbors, wetlands laws prevent downstream flooding and property destruction, and wildlife laws preserve the world's genetic storehouse for all of mankind, including future generations. In reality, most public regulation represents society's best effort to resolve the often conflicting rights we all hold. Absent mutually protective regulation, individual claims to private property and other rights would be meaningless.

As the Supreme Court has long recognized, a property owner's rights are held subject to the condition that the owner not use the property in a way that is harmful to his or her neighbors or to the general public. A property owner obviously has no constitutionally protected right to maintain a use of property that would constitute a public or private nuisance. Beyond that, at least so long as a regulation does not render property valueless, the general public, acting through its elected representatives, has broad latitude to identify uses and activities it deems harmful and then to prevent or limit them without creating a right to compensation.

Furthermore, while regulation can obviously restrict the value of property, it is also undeniable that reasonable regulations also frequently help maintain or even enhance property values. Land subject to a comprehensive zoning scheme may be reduced in value in the sense that greater economic profit could be extracted from the land if the restrictions were removed. On the other hand, zoning also protects land values by protecting property owners from neighboring activities that would reduce the value of their property. These types of reciprocal benefits, which arise in a variety of regulatory contexts, demonstrate the irrationality of the claim that every adverse effect on property values should create a right to compensation from the government.

Finally, as Justice Oliver Wendell Holmes observed in *Mahon* in 1922, government "could hardly go on" if compensation were required for every adverse effect that government action has on property values. Our government frequently and routinely affects property values, for example, by changes in federal budget priorities, as a result of worker-safety laws, through regulation of the manufacture and distribution of toxic substances, by funding the construction of harbors and roads, and so on. There are simply not enough lawyers and accountants in the world (much less the public desire to pay them!) to keep track of each minute effect on property values resulting from regulations designed to advance the public welfare.

There are, in addition, several more general economic, political, and social arguments that can be raised in opposition to efforts to expand the scope of the Fifth Amendment. First, the takings argument focuses only on the adverse effects of governmental actions on property values and generally ignores the ways in which governmental actions sometimes enhance property values. If the public has increased the value of a parcel of land, for example, by constructing an interstate highway or creating a public park nearby, does a landowner have a fair claim to compensation because government regulation prevents him from fully exploiting this enhanced value?

The property rights debate also raises important questions about the proper allocation of decision-making authority in our society between judges (who, in the federal court system, are unelected and life-tenured) and the more politically responsive legislatures. A broad reading of the Fifth Amendment would increase the power of the judiciary to second-guess legislative enactments by authorizing judges to examine whether regulations further a valid purpose, to weigh the costs and benefits of the regulation, and to determine whether the means selected in a particular regulatory program are well tailored to the goals of the program. At the same time, a broader reading of the takings clause would impede the ability of elected representatives to enact and implement environmental and other measures that they believe are in society's best interest.

Finally, the prospect of a broader reading of the takings clause raises important questions of equity. Numerous recent studies have shown that federal tax and fiscal policies in the 1980s resulted in a substantial redistribution of wealth in this country from lower- and middle-income families to upper-income corporations and individuals. If the Supreme Court were to adopt a more expansive interpretation of the Fifth Amendment, the result would again be a redistribution of wealth in favor of those who already have the most resources. Property rights that today are subject to various kinds of restrictions that protect the public welfare would be expanded in scope, enlarging the ability of owners to use their property for personal gain, or at least providing them monetary compensation if they are prevented from doing so. On the other hand, the beneficiaries of regulation—those protected from pollution by wetlands regulations, for example, or future generations that will benefit from the preservation of biological diversity—would lose, either because they would be denied the benefits provided by the regulations or because more public funds would be needed to support existing programs.

THE PROPERTY RIGHTS MOVEMENT

Wrapping themselves in the banner of Fifth Amendment property rights, a loosely organized but effective network of organizations is working hard to defeat a wide spectrum of environmental, public-health, and consumer-safety laws through the legislative and executive branches at both the federal and the state level, as well as through a broad-based public education effort. One key goal of the coalition is to convince the Supreme Court to adopt an expanded interpretation of private property protected by the Fifth Amendment.

The membership in the coalition is diverse. Its intellectual leaders include Richard Epstein of the University of Chicago, Roger Pilon of the Cato Institute, and numerous other conservative academics and students associated with the Federalist Society. Leading proponents include prodevelopment groups such as the National Association of Home Builders, the International Council of Shopping Centers, and the National Farm Bureau. A variety of nonprofit advocacy organizations, such as Defenders of Property Rights, Pacific Legal Foundation, and others focus largely, if not exclusively, on the so-called protection of property rights.

There also is a substantial grassroots network that supports the expansion of private-property rights. These include, for example, the Maryland-based Fairness to Landowners Committee, the Maine Freedom Fighters, the Independent Landholders Association, the Property Rights Alliance, and many others. The property rights movement is closely related to the Wise Use movement, which in its origins focused on western public-lands issues. As public interest in the property rights issue has grown, the Wise Use activists have increasingly adopted the language of private-property rights. In the view of some, property rights arguments offer a new, more defensible coloration for the Wise Use movement.

While the property rights argument has principled advocates as well as popular support, it also is clear that some have seized on the takings issue because they see it as an effective tool for advancing an antigovernment, antienvironmental protection agenda. For example, officials within the Reagan administration fixed upon the takings clause precisely because they thought that a broader reading of the Fifth Amendment would help serve their deregulatory agenda. Charles Fried, who served as U.S. Solicitor General from 1985 to 1989 and subsequently recounted his professional experiences in a book entitled *Order and Law: Arguing the Reagan Revolution, A First Hand Account,* writes:

> *Attorney General Meese and his young advisors—many drawn from the ranks of the then fledgling Federalist Society and often devotees of the extreme libertarian views of Chicago Law Professor Richard Epstein—had a specific, aggressive, and, it seemed to me, quite radical project in mind: to use the takings clause of the Fifth Amendment as a severe brake upon federal and state regulation of business and property. The grand plan was to make government pay compensation as for a taking of property every time*

its regulations impinged too severely on a property right. . . . If the gov-
ernment labored under so severe an obligation there would be, to say the
least, much less regulation.

There can be little doubt that an expanded reading of the takings clause
would in fact increase the cost of existing environmental programs and reduce
the level of environmental protection Americans currently enjoy. The cost of
federal wetlands, endangered species, and a variety of other programs would
increase enormously if the public were required to pay every property owner
affected by such regulations. For example, it has been estimated that the cost of
acquiring the most ecologically significant wetlands in this country could run
as high as $50 billion, 100 times the federal government's annual expenditures
on all land conservation purchases.

For several different reasons, the property rights argument is enormously
attractive to those who seek to roll back the existing level of environmental
protection. Perhaps most important is the opportunity to seek radical legal
change offered by the ascendancy of conservative thinking on the federal
bench and, in particular, on the Supreme Court. Today, seven of the nine sitting justices on the Court were appointed by Republican presidents. Because
the courts today represent the single most conservative branch of the federal
government, constitutional arguments advance the conservative agenda as well
or better than more broadly political arguments.

Starting in the late 1980s, the transformation of the federal judiciary began
to bear fruit on the property issue. In *First English Evangelical Lutheran Church
of Glendale v. County of Los Angeles* [482 U.S. 304 (1987)], the Supreme Court
rejected the contention, adopted in various states, that invalidation was the
appropriate remedy for a regulation determined to effect a taking; a property
owner is constitutionally entitled, the Court ruled, to financial compensation,
at least from the regulation's promulgation until it is rescinded. In *Nollan v.
California Coastal Commission* [483 U.S. 825 (1987)], the Court invalidated as
a taking a construction permit condition requiring a property owner to grant
a public easement across his beachfront property on the grounds that the condition was not "substantially related" to a legitimate state interest. And, most
recently, in *Lucas v. South Carolina Coastal Council* [112 S. Ct. 2886 (1992)],
the Court created a presumption that regulation that renders property valueless constitutes a taking, subject to certain exceptions centered on state property and nuisance law.

The Fifth Amendment has been ripe for conservative judicial activism
because the Supreme Court has so far failed to articulate a clear standard for
when payment of compensation is required. The Court has frequently

observed that it has no "set formula" for deciding when a regulation constitutes a taking. While this case-by-case approach may be justified in part by the nature of the takings inquiry, it also reflects the absence of a coherent theoretical structure that yields clear legal rules. The present doctrinal confusion invites judicial innovation.

The property rights argument also has political appeal, largely because it allows property rights advocates to treat environmental, land-use, and other regulatory issues as involving a debate over means rather than ends. The fundamental issue, they say, is not whether protecting endangered species or preserving wetlands is an important or worthy goal. Rather, the issue is whether those who suffer economic injury as a result of these programs deserve "compensation" from the general public. Equipped with the takings argument, opponents of environmental regulation need no longer allow themselves to be portrayed as advocates of destroying endangered species or wetlands. If the majority wishes to pursue environmental goals, so-called property advocates say, then the majority should pay for it.

Finally, the property rights argument is attractive to opponents of environmental regulation because a victory would be both far reaching and long lasting. The Supreme Court is the final arbiter of the meaning of the Constitution. Thus, the Court's interpretation of the Fifth Amendment is binding on federal and state legislatures as well as on the lower courts. Absent a constitutional amendment (a very rare event indeed), the Supreme Court's reading of the Fifth Amendment is final. The Court rarely changes its mind, and then only with reluctance, generally after a substantial shift in the ideological makeup of its membership. Thus, if the Supreme Court expands protection for private-property rights under the Fifth Amendment, the results of that decision will be with us for many years to come.

THE CONSERVATIONIST AGENDA

There are two main themes that conservationists need to keep in mind in responding to efforts to expand upon the existing property protections provided by the Fifth Amendment.

First, conservationists must never abandon the high ground they can rightfully claim as their own by opening themselves to the charge of being against property rights. Environmental regulation is fundamentally about the protection of property rights, including not only private land but also common rights in air, water, and the world's biodiversity. Wetlands regulations, for example, are firmly rooted in the ancient legal doctrine that no person has a legal right to divert the natural flow of water across his or her land in a way that harms neighbors' property. Similarly, the effort to preserve endangered species seeks to protect, in part, the rights of future generations. In short, conservationists are at least as much concerned about the protection of individual rights as any person or firm resisting reasonable government regulation designed to safeguard the environment.

Second, conservationists need to understand the widespread public frustration with the too frequent arbitrariness and inefficiency of government regulatory programs. Indeed, conservationists themselves frequently bear the brunt of bad government. There is simply no principled defense for unresponsive, heavy-handed, time-consuming regulatory action, no matter what the goal to be achieved. While supporting sound and valuable regulatory action, we should also consistently join forces with others who support good government.

The Value of Land

Seeking Property Rights Solutions to Public Environmental Concerns

Neil D. Hamilton

Understanding the growing debate between private property and the ability of government to protect the health, safety, and welfare of society is essential in shaping the next generation of environmental policies for agriculture. When asked if I would be uncomfortable advocating the proregulatory view as a counterpoint to others who will take the popular "property rights" approach, my response was I have no trouble presenting what I believe is a historically accurate view of both American law and political reality for natural resource policy. I find no conflict doing so as a farm owner because I have no misconception my ownership empowers me to use my land any way I choose, free from concerns of my neighbors or insulated from the society in which I live.

I don't view the discussion as being are you for private property or for more powerful government. We all enjoy the freedom and economic potential offered by private property, just as we all benefit by a strong government. The issue is what balance does the Constitution require between individual property rights and society's power to restrict how land is used. The environmental community should not feel threatened by the "property rights debate," but instead should welcome the opportunity to clarify both the value of environmental policies and the government's role in protecting important public interests. It also provides the opportunity to identify alternative methods of protecting natural resources without imposing all the costs on either landowners or the public.

The agricultural community has a fundamental stake in the debate because farmers own most privately held land in the nation. Whether it is wetland protection, controlling soil erosion, or preventing water pollution, important public goals cannot be achieved without affecting the actions of landowners. As a result judicial rulings on the "taking issue" will greatly shape future laws by defining the range of regulatory actions possible without compensation. In 1979 the Iowa Supreme Court ruled it was not a taking for the state to require landowners to spend money to implement soil conservation because soil was a vital resource the state had the power to protect. The court upheld Iowa's innovative soil loss limits that make it the duty of every landowner to protect the soil. Consider how the state's agricultural future could be threatened if the court had ruled the state had no power to require soil conservation without compensation.

WHAT IS TAKINGS

As an initial matter it is important to recognize the taking issue has no application to the basic components of federal conservation policy. Requiring a conservation plan to remain eligible for farm program benefits or losing payments for violating swampbuster are not takings. Farm program participation is voluntary and eligibility is controlled by contract. Similarly the taking issue is not in issue when property has been sold to or acquired by the government through eminent domain. In the first situation the sale is voluntary and in the second, compensation is all the Constitution requires, assuming the acquisition is for a legitimate public use.

It is understandable that laws restricting use of private property may be viewed with hostility by landowners. Everyone has heard claims that wetland laws or local zoning ordinances are unconstitutional takings. But are they? Just because the "taking" label is used so frequency does not mean the laws in question are unconstitutional. The right to use private property has never been absolute in our country. Property rights have always been subject to the power of courts to limit uses to protect the interests of other landowners; that is the basis of nuisance law. Property rights are also subject to the power of government to enact reasonable restrictions to protect public health, safety, and welfare, known as the police power.

That is not to say restrictions may not be takings. There is a natural inclination for government to try to achieve through regulation what it cannot afford through acquisition. Laws that function by making extensive restrictions on land, for example habitat protection under the Endangered Species Act, are more prone to taking challenges than environmental laws, such as the Clean

Water Act, which have a history in public nuisance law. The purpose of the takings clause of the Fifth Amendment is to prevent confiscations of private land for public use. Courts have held governments can go too far in restricting use of private property, but defining the limits on the reach of the "police power" has been a difficult question for our courts. Even the U.S. Supreme Court has noted its inability to develop a set test for determining when takings occur.

Where property is physically occupied by the public it is clear the owner must be compensated, as is true when all economic use has been restricted to render the property valueless, unless the use was historically considered a threat to the public. But what about situations when land is not physically taken, instead the use is restricted as is possible with many environmental laws? Is an agricultural zoning law to prevent converting land to houses a taking? Courts consider many factors when deciding a taking claim: the nature of the restrictions and whether they promote a use of legitimate state interest, the impact on the property value and the owner's reasonable expectation to use it, and the nature of the public benefit being protected or the evil being prevented. Courts generally find restrictions valid if they promote a public interest and the owner is left with some economic use. Only in extreme situations will a court find a taking.

The limits on the "police power" are hard to define for other reasons. First, the nature of private property, or what society will respect as distinctly private, is influenced by legislative action and changes over time. When the public made production of alcoholic beverages illegal during Prohibition, the owner of a closed brewery could not claim a taking, no more than could slave owners argue their property had been taken when slavery was abolished. But clearly the brewery and the slaves were "property" at one time. Second, the range of activities seen as adverse to public health also changes. The environmental regulations developed in the last 20 years demonstrate this, as does society's rapidly changing attitudes toward smoking.

Perhaps the best example of changing attitudes toward property is the dramatic shift in policies for wetlands. From our earliest history, wetlands were considered undeveloped swamps, wastelands that should be drained for economic use, and drain them we did. But in recent years the important values of wetlands, such as flood control, water purification, and wildlife habitat, have been recognized. As a result federal and state laws now prohibit draining wetlands, the laws having shifted dramatically, perhaps faster than public awareness of the value of wetlands. Wetland protection has unleashed a storm of controversy by owners who claim their lands are being taken. South Carolina's beach-protection law was held to be a taking because the court found it rendered the property "valueless," but this is an unusual situation. Protecting a wetland on a farm is probably not a taking if some economic use is possible, or if the expectation to convert the wetland was unreasonable and not reflected in its cost.

This does not mean the government can decide what today is private property may tomorrow be taken for use by the public through regulation. Government regulations and changes in society's attitudes and laws will be evaluated by courts applying the Fifth Amendment. In recent years a growing and vocal "property rights" movement has emerged in the U.S. arguing for a strict interpretation of the taking clause. Laws such as the Endangered Species Act and wetlands protection are the prime targets. The stated goal is to protect private property, but the real goal is to rewrite American law to place private desires to develop land paramount to public welfare, and require compensation whenever regulations reduce values.

This goal is reflected in the Hayes proposal to reform federal wetland law. The goal was not simply to provide greater clarity in using functional values to identify wetlands, an issue still facing the nation. The real goal of the law was to require full compensation to landowners for any wetland designated as being important enough to protect. In other words, if the government wouldn't pay, it was powerless to regulate the use. That portion of the bill marked a radical departure from the historic ability of government to regulate private land uses which threaten public health.

It is important to recognize that the property rights movement is laden with individuals and organizations whose larger goal is promoting a conservative political agenda to limit the power of government. This is not to discredit all supporters of the movement. Many are well-intentioned individuals driven to action by personal experience with government officials exercising the police power in new and aggressive ways, some of which may in fact be takings. But the property rights debate is not just a question of constitutional law but a clash of political ideology and the direction of national resource protection policy.

Environmental restrictions on use of agricultural land, such as buffer strips to protect water quality from pesticide application, or requiring a nutrient management plan as may be proposed in the Clean Water Act, are controversial. Some may allege they take private property, but is that plausible? How do these laws differ from a city zoning ordinance which determines if a developer can build on a tract of land or a building code that requires apartments to be constructed to meet fire safety standards? Just as the necessity to have sprinklers increases the cost of the building, the requirement to control wastes may add costs to the farming operation. The mere fact property use is restricted does not result in a taking.

The property rights debate focuses on the impact regulations have on private expectations to develop property. But where in the debate is the public interest considered? If public concerns are not heard, then shouldn't the debate also consider the role regulations, such as zoning or expenditures for roads, play in adding value to property? Is the flip side of protecting private property the government exacting a larger share of the income from property to compensate the public for its investments? I doubt proponents of property rights would seek this compromise.

The point is, we are all part of the public. That is why the result in the Iowa soil conservation case makes sense. If the government had to compensate owners for every restriction, or pay the cost of complying with any regulation, government would not be able to function. If your goal is less government, you might welcome this and argue the public will just have to choose which issues are important. But if you are concerned about protecting the sustainability of our resources, then expanding "takings law" to limit the power of government may result in environmental anarchy, with individuals free to act without regard for public health or welfare. The quality of life in America would be eroded, public health endangered, and the value of all property lessened. The police power was created to avoid this result. Trying to answer issues of public health and environmental protection on the basis of private economics will not work unless the cost of environmental damage on public health or the public role in creating the value and context of private property are adequately valued.

Each member of society is benefited and burdened by regulations—this reciprocity of benefits and burdens is what makes the exercise of the policy power constitutional. Consider right-to-farm laws, a popular form of law enacted by all 50 states to protect farmers from nuisance suits brought by those who move nearby. But right-to-farm laws work by restricting the rights of neighbors to bring nuisance suits to protect their property. Are the laws unconstitutional takings or reasonable exercises of the policy power to protect agriculture from the intrusion of nonfarmers? What you see depends on where you sit. Land use planning to protect farmland may be viewed as unconstitutional land use control by another.

There are risks if the farm community stakes its response to public desires for environmental protection on an extremist position which in essence says, "If the public wants me to protect the environment on my land, then pay me." One risk is the position may be judicially incorrect. Court rulings show considerable precedent exists for regulating farming practices. Another risk is the clamor about "property rights" and "takings" fails to recognize the benefits agriculture receives, in the form of public sharing of conservation costs and more direct subsidies in various farm programs and tax breaks such as homestead credits and special use valuations. By focusing on claims the public cannot limit use of private property, farmers may risk a political and social backlash that may cause the public and lawmakers to reexamine support for agriculture.

A final risk is by diverting the debate on environmental protection to a referendum on "property rights," the agricultural community will miss an opportunity to help create alternatives to accommodate both the public's and landowner's desires. A good example of private–public compromise is the use of conservation easements. Purchasing conservation easements is an effective compromise between regulatory approaches that attempt to force the landowner to do the same thing but without compensation or public acquisition of the property. Conservation easements leave the property in private ownership and available for other economic uses not incompatible with the easements, while placing responsibility for funding on the public which reaps many of the benefits. In this regard, the work of the American Farmland Trust, which focuses its efforts on market-driven and economic approaches to preserve farmland rather than on land use controls, is an important guide to what can be done.

The potential to use conservation easements is illustrated by the Wetlands Reserve Program (WRP). More than 2,700 farmers expressed interest in bidding 466,000 acres into the program and final bids were recently approved for 46,000 acres, showing permanent approaches can work. Unfortunately, the irony is only one month after the sign up Congress eliminated funding for the second year. Regardless of the state of WRP, we need to continue searching for ways to accommodate economic activity on private land while protecting resource values. We face a similar test as we develop policies for land under CRP contracts.

In conclusion, we cannot let the policy debate over what society needs to do to protect natural resources and the economic and social health of our future be subverted into a political debate over private property. Private property is important and will always underpin our economy, but defining private property is a political not a legal question. The shared obligations of all citizens, and our ethical duty of stewardship to the land, as articulated by Aldo Leopold, require property rights be balanced with the power of government to restrict use of private property. Fifty years ago the Iowa Supreme Court rejected a taking challenge to the constitutionality of a law requiring advance notice to terminate farm tenancies. It said:

It is quite apparent that during recent years the old concept of duties and responsibilities of the owners and operators of farmland has undergone a change. Such persons, by controlling the food source of the nation, bear a certain responsibility to the general public. They possess a vital part of the national wealth and legislation designed to stop waste and exploitation in the interest of the general public is within the sphere of the state's police power.

The question for us today is what is the content of that responsibility?

The Takings Debate and Federal Regulatory Programs

Sharon Dennis

Twenty years ago, the Council on Environmental Quality commissioned a study to explore the "interrelationship between environmental quality and constitutional law." The result, an influential treatise on Fifth Amendment takings entitled *The Taking Issue,* sought to define the constitutional balance between private-property rights and environmental protection. *The Taking Issue* framed the takings debate solely in terms of challenges to state and local programs. Since that report, Congress has enacted a number of comprehensive federal environmental statutes, including the Federal Water Pollution Control Act Amendments, the Surface Mining Control and Reclamation Act, the National Trails System Act, and the Endangered Species Act. The comprehensive scope of federal environmental measures has brought the federal government into the center of the takings debate, with critics charging that these laws sometimes run afoul of the takings clause of the Fifth Amendment.

Although constitutional challenges are routinely resolved in the courts, the takings controversy has played out in all three branches of the federal government. The first part of this chapter briefly traces how the executive, legislative, and judicial branches have dealt with the takings issue in recent years. The second part then explores the interplay of these forces in three areas of particular concern to the environmental community: wetlands conservation, mining controls, and endangered species protections.

THE FEDERAL GOVERNMENT'S APPROACH TO TAKINGS

The Reagan Executive Order

In 1988, President Reagan issued Executive Order 12630, which requires all federal agencies to conduct detailed reviews of all actions that "may affect the use or value of private property," ostensibly to avoid actions that might result in an unconstitutional taking of private property. The order and its accompanying guidelines purport to interpret the law of takings in an effort to help agency officials prepare takings impact assessments, or TIAs.

The Reagan executive order has been the subject of a great deal of criticism. In its review of the document, the nonpartisan Congressional Research Service (CRS) determined that the order exaggerated the possibility that government regulatory action may result in a taking. For example, the phrase "regulations imposed on private property that substantially affect its value or use . . . may constitute a taking" was found by the CRS to be "overbroad, both as to 'value' and as to 'use'." A provision requiring that health and safety measures be "undertaken only in response to real and substantial threats to public health" was viewed by the CRS to be "a quantum leap beyond" the Supreme Court standard. Finally, CRS observed that the guidelines implementing the order would require agencies to consider the takings implications of a much larger range of policies and actions than would pose a serious likelihood of a taking.

The actual impact of the executive order on agency actions has been unclear. Assuming TIAs are being prepared, they are not publicly available. Thus it is hard to see whether and to what extent takings concerns have affected agency decisions. However, the order and its accompanying guidelines are apparently viewed by some as an authoritative source of takings law. In 1991, for example, the Department of Interior proposed a rule that would have used the attorney general's guidelines to steer the analysis of takings claims arising from prohibitions on mining on federal land. Despite the controversy surrounding the order and the guidelines, the proposed rule stated that the guidelines "are widely regarded as a useful summary of current takings law." In addition, the U.S. Court of Appeals for the District of Columbia Circuit cited the attorney general's guidelines in *Nixon v. United States* for a proposition of takings law concerning personal property that is arguably inconsistent with court precedents, including the Supreme Court's decision in *Lucas v. South Carolina Coastal Council*.

As of this writing, the Reagan executive order remains in effect, although President Clinton could rescind or replace the order if he chose.

Federal Takings Legislation

Advocates of expanded protection for private-property rights have always understood that the Reagan regulatory review process could be wiped out with the stroke of a pen if a president were so inclined. As a result, some lawmakers have sought to make the process permanent by codifying Executive Order 12630 into law. In 1990, for example, Senator Steve Symms introduced an amendment to the farm bill that would have prevented the four federal agencies with jurisdiction over wetlands from implementing regulations until the attorney general certified that the agencies were in compliance with Executive Order 12630 or similar procedures. The amendment was defeated.

In 1991, Senator Symms introduced the Private Property Rights Act (S. 50). The act would have prohibited any new regulation from becoming effective until the attorney general had certified that the issuing agency was in compliance with Executive Order 12630 or a similar measure. The Senate passed the Symms takings bill as an amendment to the surface transportation bill. At the insistence of House conferees, however, the Symms provision was stripped out of the measure in House–Senate conference. In 1992, the Symms bill passed again in the Senate, this time as an amendment to the EPA-to-Cabinet bill. The EPA bill failed to become law during that session, however. Companion legislation introduced in the House of Representatives did not move either year.

On January 23, 1993, Senator Robert Dole (R-KS) took up the battle where Senator Symms left off by introducing the Private Property Rights Act of 1993 (S. 177). The Dole bill differs from the Symms bill in one critical way: It would incorporate the actual language of Executive Order 12630 into law, thus binding President Clinton and future administrations to the express language of President Reagan's executive order. Senator Dole offered his takings bill as an amendment to the EPA-to-Cabinet bill when the Senate considered the latter in May 1993. The Senate debated the merits of the bill, but Dole subsequently withdrew the measure because, as he put it, he feared that the Democrats would "gut" his bill. Senator Dole subsequently succeeded in attaching a variation of this takings amendment to the Safe Drinking Water Act, which failed to pass the House of Representatives.

The real action on takings during the 103rd Congress occurred in the House of Representatives. In November, a subcommittee of the House Committee on Agriculture held a hearing on H.R. 561, a bill introduced by Representative Gary Condit (D-CA) that is roughly comparable to the Dole bill in the Senate. Representatives of the Farm Bureau and the National Cattlemen's Association joined David Lucas, the plaintiff in the well-known Supreme Court case of the same name, in calling for a legislative redefinition of the Fifth Amendment's takings clause. An academic, an official from the Maryland State Attorney General's office, and public-interest activists responded by arguing that H.R. 561 and similar takings bills would be extremely costly and would threaten important health, safety, and environmental laws.

No takings bill moved in the House, but the threat of takings amendments lurked ominously during consideration of certain environmental bills. For example, Representative Billy Tauzin (D-LA) tried repeatedly to add a takings amendment to a bill to create a National Biological Survey (NBS) in the Department of the Interior. The Tauzin amendment would have required compensation anytime certain federal agency decisions relying upon data collected by the survey caused property values to decline by 50 percent or more. The House did not vote on Tauzin's controversial measure because it was not germane to the NBS bill.

Similar amendments arose in connection with the House version of the EPA-to-Cabinet bill. In addition to takings amendments, the EPA bill was a magnet for proposals to require a cost–benefit analysis of all regulations proposed by the new Department of the Environment, and to require the department to conduct a comparative-risk analysis of its various activities. The House Rules Committee deemed most of these anti-regulatory measures "not germane," thus preventing debate on the amendments. When support for the bill waned, Congressional leaders opted to shelve the bill rather than face a bitter floor vote.

In 1994, Congressman Tauzin introduced H.R. 3875, the Private Property Owners Bill of Rights. The bill was similar to Tauzin's proposed amendment to the NBS bill, requiring taxpayer payments when all or even only a portion of a property's value declines by 50% or more as a result of wetlands or endangered species protections. Tauzin filed a petition to discharge his bill from the usual committee process and bring the bill to the House floor for an immediate vote. While over 150 members signed the petition, Tauzin did not succeed in getting the 218 signatures necessary for a discharge.

In the closing days of the 103rd Congress, the House rejected, by a vote of 234 to 187, a payment-type takings amendment to the American Heritage Areas bill offered by Rep. Tauzin.

The United States Court of Federal Claims

While the president contemplates the fate of the executive order and Congress debates takings bills, the courts remain the primary forum for resolving actual takings disputes. One of the key federal courts responsible for handling takings cases is the U.S. Court of Federal Claims. The Claims Court has jurisdiction over all regulatory takings suits against the U.S. government for just compensation of more than $10,000. Decisions of the Claims Court are reviewed by the U.S. Court of Appeals for the Federal Circuit and, in rare instances, the U.S. Supreme Court.

The chief judge of the Claims Court is Loren A. Smith, who was appointed by President Reagan in 1985. Chief Judge Smith, a self-described libertarian/conservative, has been a forceful advocate for expanded protection of private-property rights, both on and off the bench. Smith argues that the takings clause of the Fifth Amendment provides a necessary restraint on government regulation. The chief judge earned a degree of notoriety when certain of his decisions broke with a long line of cases rejecting takings claims against the federal government. In two separate challenges to the wetlands provisions of the Clean Water Act, for example, the takings claimants were awarded $1 million and $2.7 million, respectively. In a challenge to the Surface Mining Control and Reclamation Act, a coal company received a judgment of $60 million. Each of these cases, which are described in detail below, has been criticized for misapplying precedent and ignoring the important goals of environmental regulation.

Other Claims Court judges have been less likely to find a taking as a result of environmental regulation. For example, in a 1992 case, the court refused to compensate a developer whose sales of wetlands property were stalled for a two-year period as a result of a cease and desist order issued by the Army Corps of Engineers. The decision was recently affirmed by the Federal Circuit Court.

The court also refused to compensate property owners who claimed that the National Trails System Act effectively confiscated railroad right-of-ways that would have reverted to the property owners once the railroads stopped using them. This case is presently on appeal.

THE TAKINGS BATTLEGROUND

In recent years, takings challenges to federal environmental programs have frequently been raised in connection with the regulation of wetlands and surface mining. The habitat protection provisions of the Endangered Species Act (ESA) are also coming under fire by those who believe that such measures interfere with private-property rights. This section explores how the takings controversy has played out in the wetlands and mining contexts and looks ahead to possible challenges to the ESA.

Wetlands

Wetlands provide a key battleground for the takings controversy. Wetlands are important because they filter pollutants from adjacent waters, prevent flooding and erosion, and provide habitat for migratory birds and other wildlife. The Army Corps of Engineers is authorized under the Clean Water Act (CWA) to regulate the development of wetlands through a permit system (the "section

404" permit system). Three factors determine whether a permit will be issued: The relative private and public need for the proposed project, the feasibility of locating the project elsewhere, and the degree to which the proposed project would either harm or benefit the public and private interests involved. The Corps is authorized to deny a permit when development would have a significant adverse effect on the environment.

Agribusiness, realtors, and the oil and gas industries have been particularly vocal critics of the CWA and its wetlands provisions. They complain that the section 404 program prevents property owners from using their land, in effect taking private property without just compensation. These interest groups argue that the CWA authorizes a massive federal land grab under the guise of environmental protection. In fact, the Corps denies very few section 404 permit applications outright. In 1992, only 500 of a total of 15,000 permit applications were reportedly rejected.

Nevertheless, efforts to enhance the CWA's private-property protections are under way. A bill introduced in the 103d Congress by Representative Jimmy Hayes, the Comprehensive Conservation and Management Act of 1993 (H.R. 1330), would begin by eliminating federal jurisdiction over approximately half of the nation's wetlands. The bill would then classify the remaining wetlands in terms of their ecological value. "Low-value" wetlands would be deregulated, and regulations would be relaxed for "medium-value" wetlands. A taking would be deemed to have occurred as a result of a "high-value" designation, and the owner of such property would be entitled to obtain the fair market value for that property from the U.S. government by virtue of the classification alone. The Congressional Budget Office has estimated that a buyout of just high-value wetlands would cost taxpayers an estimated $10 to $45 billion.

Takings do not figure in the Wetlands Reform Act of 1993 (H.R. 350), a bill introduced by Representative Don Edwards. The premise of the Edwards bill is that sound public policy requires that economic incentives be made available for the conservation of wetlands on private property. For example, the bill would amend the Internal Revenue Code to encourage charitable donations of wetlands to private conservation trusts.

Surprisingly, while the rhetoric continues to heat up in Congress on wetlands and takings, the number of takings lawsuits against the Corps appears to be declining. In 1993, there were 23 active wetlands takings cases against the Corps pending before the Federal Claims and Federal Circuit Courts, down from approximately 30 in previous years.

In the past, under Chief Judge Loren Smith, the Claims Court has sometimes proven sympathetic to property owners challenging wetlands restrictions. In *Florida Rock Industries v. United States,* a company sought a section 404 permit in order to operate a limestone quarry in a South Florida wetland. The permit was denied when the Corps determined that the cumulative impact of additional mining in the area would harm the environment. The Claims Court disagreed, finding that any pollution would be of a "pro forma" nature: "Rock mining of the type at issue here is not considered a nuisance in this area. It certainly is not considered one several thousand feet away, where rock mining is proceeding happily apace."

The court then considered the degree of economic harm resulting from the Corps' activities. Evidence suggested that the property could fetch as much as $4,000 per acre based on the possibility that the existing controls would be lifted at a later date. The Claims Court rejected this figure as too speculative and determined that the land's value was actually only $500 per acre. According to this calculation, the permit denial was responsible for a 95 percent diminution in value. The court determined that the land had in fact been taken and awarded the company $1 million in damages.

The Federal Circuit of Appeals recently reversed the trial court ruling on the ground that it improperly ignored the speculative market for the land in question.

In *Loveladies Harbor Inc. v. United States,* a developer was denied permission to dredge and fill a wetland for a residential development. Again, the trial court refused to believe that the proposed activity presented an actual threat of harm. As a result, the private interest in development was held to be superior to the public interest in wetlands preservation, reversing the usual outcome in takings challenges to wetlands regulations.

The court's findings concerning the company's economic injury were equally controversial. The permit denial affected a 12.5-acre portion of a larger 250-acre landholding. Precedent arguably required the court to consider the economic impact of the denial on the larger unit, the so-called parcel-as-a-whole doctrine. Instead, the court focused only on the 12.5-acre unit and determined that the value of that land had been virtually eliminated, or taken, by the permit denial. Damages in excess of $2.7 million were awarded.

The Federal Circuit Court of Appeals recently affirmed the trial court ruling in the *Loveladies* case.

Recently, in *Tabb Lakes v. United States,* the Claims Court criticized the *Loveladies* trial court decision for its departure from established precedent and reaffirmed the use of the parcel-as-a-whole doctrine in evaluating economic harm. Tabb Lakes was a developer who owned a large tract of land planned for residential use, some of which contained wetlands. Sales of certain building lots were temporarily halted when the Army Corps of Engineers discovered that the company's operations were proceeding without the requisite federal permits. However, sales were eventually allowed to proceed when litigation determined that the Corps lacked jurisdiction over the wetlands portions of Tabb Lakes' property. The Claims Court rejected the company's temporary taking claim. Since sales had been made during the period of the Corps' order, economic value remained in the parcel as a whole. The Federal Circuit Court affirmed the Claims Court's decision in *Tabb Lakes.* In a strongly worded decision, the chief judge observed that the economic impact of a regulation must be measured in relation to the property as a whole, and that a mere diminution in the value of private property does not constitute a taking.

Mining Regulation

Mining is a second area in which the takings controversy has raged. The 103rd Congress took up the 1872 Mining Law, which still provides for the sale of public lands for hard-rock mining activity for only $2.50 per acre. The Senate passed a bare bill, planning to work out the numerous cumbersome issues involved in mining reform during conference with the House of Representatives. The House passed a bill, H.R. 322, that would require miners to pay a royalty for hard-rock minerals, implement a leasing system for mining on public lands, and require far more accountability in cleaning up mining sites. The 103rd Congress ended without any resolution of the differences between the Senate and House bills.

H.R. 322 included a takings amendment offered by Representative Joe Skeen, which would require takings judgments resulting from implementation of the mining bill to come from a new mine reclamation fund rather than from the general Judgment Fund. The Skeen amendment represents a troubling new development because it would require that takings judgments be paid directly from an agency's budget. Not only would this amendment unreasonably deter the agency from initiating reasonable regulatory action, it would enormously complicate the federal budgeting process.

The Endangered Species Act

Unlike section 404, the Endangered Species Act (ESA) has not been the target of many takings claims. But as the ESA makes greater and more visible strides in protecting the habitat in which endangered species live, property owners will no doubt anticipate more of a squeeze, making more claims likely.

The focus of the few reported cases involving wildlife and takings concern complaints by individuals whose property has been damaged by protected wildlife. For example, in *Christy v. Hodel,* a grizzly bear entered a rancher's property and preyed on the rancher's sheep. Because the ESA prohibited Christy from shooting the protected bear, the rancher argued that his livestock had been taken and demanded just compensation. This argument was not unlike that made in a 1917 takings case over damage to timber caused by beavers protected under state law (*Barrett v. State of New York*), or a 1954 case over damage to crops caused by birds protected by the Migratory Bird Treaty Act (*Bishop v. United States*). In each instance, the courts rejected the takings claims, observing that the harm to private property resulting from the wildlife-protection measure was simply the "incidental result" of reasonable government action.

It is less clear how a court would evaluate a claim that the ESA or similar statute deprived the claimant of the use and value of his or her land in violation of the Fifth Amendment. Certain principles will likely guide a court's analysis of such a claim, however. One theory that may prove useful is rooted in the government's duty to protect wildlife for the benefit of the public good. A federal district court has suggested that this interest is so important that it rises to the level of a federal property interest. If this were the case, takings challenges to the ESA would have to be resolved by balancing competing private- *and public*-property interests.

Even if the ESA were analyzed under the traditional test used with ordinary land-use regulations, it would likely still survive a challenge. In *Mountain States Legal Foundation v. Hodel,* for example, a federal appellate court determined that, in light of the important public interest served by the Wild Free-Roaming Horses and Burros Act, no taking occurred despite evidence that the grazing habits of the protected wildlife had significantly diminished the value of the plaintiff's property.

It may be that wildlife-protection programs are better shielded from takings challenges than other environmental measures because of a legal tradition recognizing the importance of wildlife as a natural resource. But the Endangered Species Act has long been criticized for putting "birds and bunnies" before people. Representatives of extractive industries claim that the act is preventing land from being put to productive use for grazing, mining, and logging. Property rights advocates criticize the act for interfering with private and commercial development.

A number of bills designed to enhance private-property protections in the ESA were introduced in the 103rd Congress. The Endangered Species Act Procedural Reform Amendments of 1993 (H.R. 1490), introduced by Representative Billy Tauzin, would require that "A final decision of the Secretary ... that substantially deprives a property owner of the economically viable use of the property owned or held by the property owner is deemed, at the option of the property owner, to be a taking under the Constitution of the United States...."

If enacted, the Tauzin bill would effectively usurp the power of the courts to interpret the takings clause of the Fifth Amendment in the context of the ESA. Not only would it treat the ESA as an ordinary land-use regulation, but it would utilize a new standard that would be far more likely to result in takings awards against the federal government.

Representative Bob Smith's Just Compensation Act (H.R. 1388) would compensate property owners for "any diminution in value" to private property resulting from federal action under the ESA or other environmental programs. Representative James Hansen's Human Protection Act (H.R. 1414) would amend the ESA to prohibit any federal action under the ESA unless the economic benefits outweighed the economic costs. These proposals would also result in a dramatic departure from the present law.

A bill introduced by Representative Gerry Studds, the Endangered Species Act Amendments (H.R. 2043), would take a different approach. Studds' bill would offer private landowners cash incentives to undertake purely voluntary conservation measures on private property.

At the same time, the Department of Interior (DOI) has recently authorized a number of experiments aimed at preserving protected species such as the gnat-catcher and the desert tortoise while simultaneously allowing controlled economic development. The DOI hopes that these programs will balance the public and private interests at stake, thereby reducing the likelihood of protracted litigation.

CONCLUSION

On the federal level at least, much could change on the takings issue in the next few years. For example, two new justices have taken seats on the U.S. Supreme Court. While it is too early to say where Justice Stephen Breyer will be on the takings issue, Justice Ruth Bader Ginsberg dissented in the U.S. Supreme Court's most recent case, *Dolan v. City of Tigard,* a challenge to a municipal ordinance requiring a business to set aside a portion of the parcel on which the business was located for flood control and transportation needs as a condition of permission to expand the owner's business operations. The Court ruled that the city had an obligation to demonstrate a relationship of "rough proportionality"—both in nature and extent—between a dedication condition and the impact of development, and sent the case back to the city for further proceedings.

The 104th Congress will convene in 1995 with a Republican majority in both the House of Representatives and the Senate. Many Republicans on the

House side campaigned on the "Contract with America," which includes numerous proposals for rolling back Federal regulatory authority. Proposed legislation based on the contract includes a provision for "compensating" even minor limitations on the use or value of private property. During his time in office, President Clinton will fill at least one vacancy on the Court of Appeals for the Federal Circuit and scores of others throughout the lower federal courts. The president is also authorized to appoint a different Claims Court judge to be Chief Judge of the U.S. Court of Federal Claims. Finally, President Clinton has the opportunity to review the Reagan executive order on takings and to rescind or amend it. Each of these actions alone, and certainly cumulatively, could have a dramatic effect on the future of the takings equation on the federal level.

Lucas v. South Carolina Coastal Council

An Enigmatic Approach to the Environmental Regulation of Land

Tim Searchinger

The U.S. Supreme Court, unlike most other courts, can choose which cases it will decide. Its agreement even to hear a case can therefore arouse broad interest and speculation. In 1992, the Court created a furor among environmentalists, developers, and ideological warriors of various persuasions when it agreed to accept an appeal in *Lucas v. South Carolina Coastal Council*.[1] The case involved a South Carolina regulation that prevented new building on coastal beachfront land likely to erode away within 40 years. A developer, whose entire property lay within the setback, sued. He claimed that the law was constitutionally equivalent to a formal effort by the government to take over the ownership of the property, entitling him to compensation for the lost development value of the land.

The case aroused widespread attention in part because Lucas argued broadly that any law that has the effect of denying "economically viable" use of property requires compensation. Laws can occasionally affect the value of property: Federal agricultural programs can greatly increase the value of agricultural land, but the Federal Reserve Board, by raising interest rates, can trigger widespread farm bankruptcies and plummeting land values. By approving a new drug, the government can cause the value of a drug company to skyrocket; but a federal agency can also end a multimillion-dollar breast-implant business overnight by banning those implants. Granting a television license can create a profitable business, but new rules that result in the denial of a license can eliminate the business. New landfill standards can make modern landfills more profitable but, at the same time, close thousands of old landfills. Few of these laws have been subject to serious takings claims, but Lucas's theory appeared to put them in jeopardy.

Read more narrowly, the Supreme Court's decision to hear the case had at least broad implications for a variety of environmental laws that limit development of land. Since the nineteenth century, governments have occasionally restricted or prohibited development on certain parts of beaches and on other areas near water bodies. Over the last 30 years, however, government at federal, state, and local levels has recognized that these earlier restrictions were inadequate to the task. New wetland, stream preservation, and steep-slope regulations now prevent degradation of neighboring water bodies, and other regulations, such as those protecting endangered species, may also limit development of private land.

In many ways, these new laws imitate conventional zoning requirements for setbacks from streets and other kinds of restrictions, but their purposes somewhat differ. Unlike traditional zoning laws that protect neighbors from each other, these laws protect downstream users of natural resources. Unlike zoning and other government regulations, these environmental laws also have been subject to considerable takings challenges in state courts and lower federal courts. Those courts have rejected the overwhelming majority of demands for compensation, but previous Supreme Court decisions had primarily addressed these kinds of restrictions in procedural ways. *Lucas* provided an opportunity for an increasingly conservative Supreme Court to deal with attacks on these regulations more directly.

COASTAL ZONE DEVELOPMENT RESTRICTIONS

The South Carolina coastal restriction has ancient roots. The Bible itself refers to the "foolish man who built his house on sand[, for t]he rain came down, the streams rose, and the winds blew and beat against that house, and it fell with a great crash" (*Matthew* 7:26–27). Of all coastal areas, the most unstable are the 1.4 million acres of coastal barrier islands along the Atlantic Ocean and Gulf of Mexico. As one Senate committee report summarized:

> *Storms can wipe out whole sections of beach when they are overwashed and can just as easily close inlets as sediments are redeposited. The sands of the beaches continually move and are redistributed. In response to a rising sea level (about one foot per century along the Atlantic coast), these [barrier] islands are generally migrating landward. The combination of erosion and*

migration, as well as the effects of flooding from hurricanes and other storms, make these areas exceptionally hazardous places for permanent man-made structures and human habitation.[2]

Hurricane Hugo in 1989 illustrated these hazards. It caused $6 billion in damage and took 29 lives. Not only was sand-dune development on many barrier islands severely damaged or destroyed, but debris from those developments caused extensive damage to property further inland as well. In one case the storm blew a roof 1,000 feet inland.

Coastal development also contributes to environmental degradation of coastal habitat, which is disproportionately significant for fish and wildlife. Construction on sand dunes tends to enhance erosion rates. Construction also typically leads to seawalls, jetties or other artificial efforts to hold back the power of waves, and these structures tend to increase erosion and flooding in neighboring areas.

Despite the age-old awareness of these concerns, beachfront development has still occurred. In the United States, development along coastal barrier islands and shorefronts throughout the twentieth century has led to a regular cycle of destruction in storms followed by requests for federal disaster assistance that Congress found hard to resist.

In 1968 the federal government initiated its first effort to deal with this problem by creating the federal flood insurance program. Congress theorized that flood insurance would provide an alternative source of compensation to disaster relief. But the magnitude of risk involved generally limited the availability of private insurance. As part of a deal by which the federal government would make insurance available, Congress required communities to adopt land-use controls and other measures to minimize the impact of floods. The program forbade either insurance or disaster-relief funds for communities that had not adopted appropriate ordinances.

Over the years, this program proved effective in reimbursing landowners for flood losses, but the mandated land-use controls have been too lax to minimize flood losses or the costs of disaster relief to the federal government. As a result, Congress passed another series of laws designed to encourage local communities to toughen development regulations in coastal areas in part through setback requirements.

Reflecting this move toward increasing stringency in response to continuing damages, South Carolina in 1977, adopted its first coastal-development restrictions. These restrictions, however, were limited to the beach and sand dunes themselves. Faced with continued erosion problems, the state legislature established a commission in 1987 to make further recommendations. The commission found that more than a quarter of South Carolina's coastline was critically eroding, and that development close to the sand dune/beach area had accelerated that erosion. The next year the legislature responded by strengthening the law to require that development occur no closer to the water than the line at which scientists expect the water to be after 40 years of erosion.

LUCAS V. SOUTH CAROLINA COASTAL COUNCIL

The Isle of Palm lies north of Savannah, Georgia, in South Carolina. In the late 1970s and 1980s, David Lucas, a businessman, helped to construct several large residential developments there. In 1986, he purchased two lots on the island for $985,000. When South Carolina strengthened its coastal laws two years later, those lots turned out to be entirely within the setback line and therefore precluded from development. Today the lots are as far as 300 feet away from the beach. Reflecting the changing nature of the island, however, the lots were underwater between 1957 and 1962 and partially covered for half of the last 40 years.

When Lucas sued, the trial court found that the restrictions left his land valueless. Because of that finding alone, the court held that the law "took" his property and required that $1.2 million be paid in compensation.

The Coastal Commission appealed to the South Carolina Supreme Court, which reversed the decision. The court noted that Lucas had not challenged the legislative finding that coastal development within the setback area threatened lives, property, and the environment. According to the court, Lucas in effect conceded that the law was not a taking because of the precedent established in prior cases in which the U.S. Supreme Court has held that government may prohibit harmful uses of property without compensation.

When the U.S. Supreme Court agreed to review this decision, a wide range of interests on both sides filed briefs as friends of the court. The case essentially required the Court to reconcile two separate lines of cases. In one line of cases upholding zoning laws—even laws that enormously reduce the value of land—the Court has included the caveat that zoning regulations must continue to allow "economically viable" uses of property. In the other line of cases, the Court has held that even restrictions that largely eliminate the value of certain property (such as a beer distributorship, a livery stable, or a quarry) do not require compensation because the intent of the restrictions was to prevent harm. These cases have generally established what is known as the "nuisance" defense.

In *Lucas,* the arguments before the Supreme Court largely focused on the nature of the nuisance defense, which Lucas himself argued should not exist at all. Property rights advocates generally contended that the defense should only exist for activities that would be a nuisance under judge-made "common law"—law that has evolved from medieval England. The Bush administration argued that the exception should extend to some statutory or regulatory restrictions but only if they had "origins in the common law of nuisance," a vague standard the administration did little to explain.

On the other side, environmental advocates and others argued that the government should be able to prohibit any activity that is harmful to others. In previous cases, they noted, the Supreme Court had specifically rejected the claim that the nuisance defense should only apply to common law nuisances. The environmental advocates acknowledged that the Court might have a role in independently determining whether the legislative finding of harm was reasonable; but they argued that the *Lucas* case did not raise the question of how much second-guessing was appropriate because Lucas had not even challenged the legislative judgment that the coastal setback requirement was necessary to prevent harm.

The Decision

The Supreme Court's decision, written by Justice Antonin Scalia, included something for everyone: It contained rhetoric and hints favorable to property rights activists, but its bottom-line rule was more enigmatic than definitive.

The essence of the decision was the Court's creation of a new categorical rule for takings cases: the "total taking." The Court defined a total taking as a case in which a regulation denies "all economically productive use" or one that leaves land "valueless." According to the Court, those regulations are presumptive takings that require compensation. In such a context, courts must refuse to examine the legislature's reasons for believing the restrictions necessary to prevent harm.

Justice Scalia provided a variety of reasons for this ruling, arguing that at least from the standpoint of the property owner, a regulation leaving land without value and an actual seizure of title had little difference. He also stated that whether a regulation prevented harm or sought to achieve a benefit was a distinction in the eye of the beholder. Essentially, all actions that prevent harm provide benefits, and all actions that provide benefits prevent harm to the extent that they prevent the denial of a benefit. Justice Scalia was concerned that legislatures would go out and seize people's property through regulation simply by calling their actions harm preventing. He specifically expressed doubt about regulations that prevent development of land.

Despite rejecting the harm–benefit distinction, the Court immediately resurrected it. In addition to legislatures, courts, using the doctrine of nuisance, also prohibit uses of property that pose a harm to others. To the extent that a regulation reflected these judge-made law principles of nuisance, the Court ruled that it would not be a taking. Unlike statutory limits on property, the Court indicated that judge-made limitations on property were actually limitations of the underlying property right.

A vital portion of the decision involved an issue that had not actually received attention in any of the briefs. All of the significant briefs had assumed that the takings clause did not distinguish between property rights in land and rights to other kinds of property, such as cars, businesses, contracts, or patents. The Bush administration joined environmental organizations in pointing to a wide range of laws that can render many forms of property valueless, such as laws that make dangerous drugs illegal. Because the Supreme Court had never *explicitly* distinguished between land and other forms of property, these examples alerted the Court that their decision had the potential to invalidate significant areas of modern government.

In *Lucas,* the Supreme Court for the first time explicitly distinguished between land and other forms of property. Justice Scalia acknowledged that government regulation often made property other than land valueless. Because of that history, the Court concluded that owners of personal property should reasonably expect the possibility that regulations would leave property valueless. But the Court held that the takings clause commanded special protection for land and therefore limited its takings rule to land.

Based on these rules, the Court held that Lucas had established a presumptive taking by proving that the regulation had left his land valueless. Lucas did not need to attack the judgment of the legislature that this development would cause harm. Because the lower courts had not examined the law of nuisance, however, the Supreme Court did not rule for Lucas. The justices sent the case back to the lower courts for them to examine whether the regulation was consistent with the background principles of the state's law of nuisance.

Only five of the nine justices joined the opinion. Because one of those five, Byron White, has resigned, the opinions of the four other justices will help determine the long-term significance of *Lucas.* Those four justices offered four separate opinions—and one of the justices agreed with the decision of the majority—but all of the justices appeared less sympathetic to Lucas than the majority.

THE SIGNIFICANCE OF LUCAS

Lucas raised at least as many questions as it answered. How significant the case turns out to be for the law of takings depends on how these questions are answered. With the resignation of Justice White, the answers are even harder to predict.

How Will Courts Determine the Preexisting Property Right?

Regulations such as those at issue in *Lucas* will rarely prohibit development of an entire area of property. If Lucas's land had extended farther inland, Lucas could have built on part of the property and used the remainder as the sandy yard. The regulation would therefore certainly not have left all of his land valueless.

However, property rights can be conceptually subdivided. A court could view ownership of a 10-acre parcel of land as ownership of 10 one-acre parcels. The complete ownership of land can also be separated into the right to build, the right to walk or hunt on the land, the right to exclude others from flooding the land, and even such exotic rights as the conditional right to build a shopping center pending approval by local planning authorities. Seen this way, it is possible to view any restriction as the complete extinction of some property rights. For example, if zoning prohibits a shopping center in a particular area, it would completely extinguish the distinct property right to build a shopping center.

In past cases, the Supreme Court and lower courts have almost unanimously viewed property rights as a whole; in other words, they have focused on the entire contiguous area of land and all the rights possessed by the same owner. As a result, if the law restricted use of 10 acres of land on a 20-acre parcel, the courts viewed it only as a restriction of one-half of the parcel.

In a footnote in *Lucas,* Justice Scalia indicated a desire to reopen this question, which the lower courts have so far declined to do. If the Supreme Court does change its previous view, however, *Lucas* could have a broad effect. It could threaten even such conventional land-use requirements as setbacks and minimum-acreage zoning.

What Is Denial of "All Economically Productive Use?"

Lucas created a categorical rule to apply to a particular context—namely, to regulations that leave land without "economically beneficial uses," or as stated elsewhere, "without economic value." If "without economic value" is meant literally, *Lucas* will have limited impact. Few restrictions ever leave land valueless. Even restrictions that preclude development of wetlands or that impose coastal setbacks typically leave landowners the ability to develop a portion of the contiguous land area. Undeveloped land also typically has economic value. It can provide recreational opportunities and can often enhance the value of neighboring property. A footnote in *Lucas* made clear that a regulation that decreases the value of property by 95 percent would not trigger the *Lucas* rule. If *Lucas* means that land must literally be left valueless, it would likely have limited impact.

Despite this fact, some have tried to apply a different meaning to "economically beneficial." In one case since *Lucas*, a homebuilders' group has argued that any regulation that contributes to a situation in which a developer must sell property below what it originally cost requires compensation.

In addition to this implausible interpretation, *Lucas* also has potential impacts in several other circumstances. One involves mining prohibitions. Rules prohibiting mining in sensitive areas because of the impact on surface uses can deny all economic access to certain minerals. It is unclear whether the *Lucas* rule applies to mineral rights as well as to surface rights in land; but if it does, *Lucas* may sometimes have a significant impact.

Another question is how *Lucas* will be applied to land of marginal value. Developers tend to face a variety of restrictions when they build: they must meet fire codes, install adequate sewage treatment facilities, control stormwater. All of these restrictions impose costs. For land that has only minimal development value, or for land in a declining market area like a decaying urban city, those restrictions can temporarily leave land without value. Cities like New York struggle to deal with thousands of tax defaults by property owners who no longer find profit in maintaining their land. The same problems can arise from a new air pollution regulation whose cost, although not great in and of itself, contributes to the closure of a marginally profitable steel mill.

These restrictions have generally not been considered takings. If *Lucas* is interpreted strictly, however, it may have the odd effect of treating basic restrictions on marginally valuable lands as takings.

How Will State Courts Apply the Law of Nuisance in the *Lucas* Context?

The common law of nuisance is a branch of judge-made tort law, which evolved from ancient English court decisions in disputes typically pitting one individual against another. The law of nuisance is essentially the tort (civil injury) rules of land. But nuisance law is notoriously vague. It essentially provides courts broad leeway to decide whether they think some kind of uses of land should be allowed. According to the most authoritative statement of the law of nuisance: a nuisance can be any activity that involves "a significant interference with the health, safety, peace, comfort, or convenience of the public."

Essentially, nuisance law requires courts to engage in the same kind of analysis that legislators or regulators engage in when they pass statutes. The practical effect of *Lucas* is therefore to shift decision making regarding at least some severe restrictions on land use from legislatures to courts.

How will courts apply their new power? Although nuisance principles are extremely broad, environmentalists are concerned largely for one reason: Courts have difficulty dealing with cumulative harms and with activities that do not themselves cause harm but simply create unacceptable risks of harm. This difficulty occurs in part because it is generally impossible to bring before the court, in the search for a comprehensive solution, all the parties who contribute in small measures to a large problem. Courts also like causation to be direct and simple: Either a chemical gave the plaintiff cancer or it did not. A typical nuisance case might be one in which a smoky factory makes it impossible to live in neighboring houses.

In the real world, the toughest environmental problems are those in which many small, seemingly safe uses of property combine to cause serious harm or even an unacceptable risk of harm. Examples include the ozone hole, urban smog, and the degradation of great water bodies like the Chesapeake Bay. Even cancer can rarely be traced to a single source of a single chemical. Environmental protection began with judge-made law but shifted to legislative statutes long ago precisely because courts have difficulty recognizing and regulating such diffuse sources of harm.

Despite this problem, the basic nuisance principles are broad and can overcome these causation problems. Even Justice Scalia implicitly recognized that fact in *Lucas* when he acknowledged that it would be a nuisance to build a nuclear power plant on an earthquake fault, although doing so does not certainly or even probably cause harm; doing so simply creates an unacceptable risk of harm.

Another important feature of nuisance law that would minimize the likelihood of takings is that the law encourages judges to defer to legislative and regulatory judgments. In other words, a court is likely to consider a use of land a nuisance if the legislature or administrative agency considers that land use inappropriate. Indeed, the most authoritative analysis of nuisance law in all 50 states says explicitly that a nuisance includes conduct that "is proscribed by a statute, ordinance or administrative regulation."

Exactly how courts will deal with this heavy emphasis on deference to legislation and regulations is unclear. On the one hand, the *Lucas* decision ignores
that relationship. It seems to suggest that restrictions can be neatly divided into
those imposed by judge-made law and those imposed by legislatures and agencies. On the other hand, nuisance law in the real world relies heavily on
legislative and administrative standards and rules. Future decisions will have to
resolve this question.

The remand of *Lucas* itself theoretically provided an opportunity for courts
to address some of these questions. By the time the South Carolina Supreme
Court addressed the case on remand, however, the legislature had changed the
earlier statute. It now permitted variances from the regulation in hardship cases
such as that of Lucas. Because the legislature now permitted this development,
the government attorneys decided not to assert that the use was limited by the
law of nuisance. The South Carolina Supreme Court accordingly found that
Lucas had demonstrated a right to compensation.

A question still remains of whether Lucas has suffered any damages. Because
South Carolina will now probably permit Lucas the opportunity to build, it is
if he suffered damages for the intervening period. It may very well be that the
regulation saved Lucas money because the Isle of Palm has gone through a real-
estate slump. The trial court is now struggling with these issues.

How Will Courts Deal with the Case That Is Not a Total Taking?

Perhaps the largest question left by *Lucas* is how it will affect decisions outside
of its arena, i.e., regulations that do not leave land valueless. Commentators of
all persuasions, and even the Supreme Court, have admitted that the Court has
provided little practical guidance to analyze these cases. In general, the Court
has instructed lower courts to examine the "nature of the government action,"
the "magnitude of the economic impact," and the interference with "reasonable investment-backed opportunities." But these are vague terms that courts
have applied with very different meanings. How each inquiry interacts with
the others also remains unclear.

At its most general, the Supreme Court has stated that the takings inquiry
should be one of fairness: the takings clause prohibits "Government from
forcing some people alone to bear public burdens, which, in all fairness and
justice, should be borne by the public as a whole."[3] The problem with this
principle is that it provides no definition or standard of fairness. What determines whether a "burden" may be justly assigned to an individual rather than
to the public? The Supreme Court has never said. Furthermore, courts do not
normally overturn statutes simply because they think the statutes are unfair.
Legislators themselves consider fairness when they write laws. The real ques-

tion raised by the court is, therefore, which assignments of benefits and burdens are so unjust that courts may overrule them? Having failed to articulate a standard for "fairness," the Court has even less articulated a standard for judging when courts should impose their own judgment of fairness.

Historically, both the Supreme Court and the lower courts have rejected virtually all claims that regulations that diminish but do not eliminate economic value require compensation. In doing so they have offered a variety of rationales. In part, they have recognized that government actions so drastically shape property values that it would be impractical to require compensation for a select category of those actions. In part, the courts have recognized that many of the challenged regulations are designed to prevent harm to others.

Before *Lucas,* the Supreme Court had made an exception to this rule essentially only for those regulations that provide government or the public the right physically to occupy or walk over land. The Court has treated these regulations as the equivalent of government actions to condemn land for public highways and other infrastructure purposes. It therefore remains unclear whether, after *Lucas,* the Court will find that regulations which greatly diminish but do not eliminate the value of land are takings.

Despite these holdings, the new property rights movement in recent years has succeeded in convincing a few lower-court judges that severe land-use regulations should require compensation even if substantial economic value remains. The vagueness of the Supreme Court's guidance has left lower courts free to offer a variety of rationales for their diverse decisions. The different rationales could occupy many volumes, but two topics are worth highlighting.

To What Extent Was the Property Subject to Regulation Before Purchase?

Courts have generally held that property owners are entitled to compensation only if a regulation interferes with the property owners' reasonable expectations. In general, courts examine the reasonable expectations that existed at the time the land was purchased. According to most courts, if a land use was heavily regulated at the time of purchase, the purchaser has no reasonable expectation to use the property in violation of the regulations. For example, if a property owner purchases a wetland in the face of wetland regulations, most courts would agree that the owner has no reasonable expectation to develop the wetland. *Lucas,* with its heavy emphasis on expectations, is likely to reenforce this conclusion.

To What Extent Does a Regulation Prevent Off-Site Harm?

Justice Scalia's decision in *Lucas* criticizes the idea of distinguishing between a regulation that prevents harm to others and a regulation that provides a benefit. Despite this criticism, at the root of the judge-made law of nuisance just such a distinction lies, which the courts are unable to discard. Decisions by lower courts since *Lucas* suggest that whether the courts view a regulation as designed to prevent harm will continue to be a significant factor in their decisions.

How Do Courts Feel about the Environmental Land-Use Regulations?

Had Lucas's land in 1992 actually been underwater or only feet from the tide, it is hard to imagine that the Court's decision would have been the same—the safety hazard would have been too clear. The decision itself indicated that government can eliminate the value of land without compensation to stop a fire or prevent another imminent threat to public safety regardless of whether the court is stopping a judge-recognized nuisance. This language suggests that had the majority of the Supreme Court truly accepted the safety rationale for South Carolina's beach regulation, the result may have been different.

Environmental regulations, like those at issue in *Lucas,* have expanded because more limited regulations have failed. Protection of water quality started by limiting the pollutants that a factory could discharge through a pipe. But those limitations were not enough to prevent degradation. As wetlands were developed, water bodies lost the natural filter of pollutants at their borders with the land and became polluted. From the standpoint of the water body, the factory polluter and the developer of wetlands are the same. *Lucas* provided little rationale for treating them differently.

It is hard to escape the conclusion that the majority in *Lucas* simply doubted the reasonableness of environmental regulations that prohibit development of certain kinds of land. Interestingly, Justices Kennedy and Souter, who are conservative, did not join the majority's opinion. That may be because they only recently moved to Washington, having previously served in states in which these kinds of environmental laws have gained broad acceptance. How courts rule in the future is likely to reflect the extent to which judges accept the rationale for land-focused environmental regulations. If that is true, judges are also likely to treat these regulations less suspiciously in takings cases as their environmental rationales become better understood.

CONCLUSION

The reasoning of *Lucas* is portentous: Because legislatures are not to be trusted regarding people's property, courts rather than legislatures should be the arbiters of determining what activities are sufficiently harmful that they should be prohibited. Applying this reasoning broadly would put the courts in a position of second-guessing economic regulations—a kind of second-guessing that led the courts during the last century to strike down such basic regulations today as child-labor laws. The courts abandoned the field of economic regulation to the legislatures during this century. Justice Scalia's reasoning in *Lucas* does not have obvious limits.

Despite this potential breadth, *Lucas* only applies this reasoning to a small number of cases: regulations that leave land valueless. One senses that the majority as a whole doubted the full breadth of Justice Scalia's reasoning but wished to achieve the result in this particular case because of its doubts about this application of this regulation. Unable to gain a majority for a broader rule, Justice Scalia then salted *Lucas* with many suggestions about how the new approach could be expanded.

Lucas therefore has little impact of itself but raises questions. New appointments to the Supreme Court and cases over the next few years will likely determine whether *Lucas* turns out to be a sharp curve or a minor swerve.

Notes

1. 112 S. Ct. 2886 (1992).
2. S. Rep. No. 419, 97th Cong., 2d Sess. 1 (1982); reprinted in 1982 U.S.C.C.A.N. 3212, 3213.
3. *Armstrong v. United States,* 364 U.S. 40, 49 (1960).

"Absolute" Rights

Property and Privacy

Mary Ann Glendon

A man's home is his castle. That maxim (traditionally attributed to Sir Edward Coke) was Marvin Sokolow's defense when he was hauled into a Queens County court by his landlord after his downstairs neighbors had complained about the noise above them. They claimed that their peace and quiet were being destroyed by the Sokolow children, ages two and four. The landlord sought to evict the Sokolows on the basis of a clause in their lease providing that no tenant shall make, or permit any members of his family to make, "disturbing noises," or otherwise interfere with the "rights, comforts, or convenience of other tenants."

In rendering his decision, Judge Daniel Fitzpatrick went right to the heart of the matter. "The difficulty of the situation here," he said, "is that Mr. Sokolow's castle is directly above the castle of Mr. Levin." The judge sympathized with the Levins, a middle-aged working couple who cherished a quiet evening at home after a grueling day in Manhattan. He was understanding about the Sokolows' predicament as well. The judge opined that "children and noise have been inseparable from a time whence the mind of man runneth not to the contrary." He took a dim view, however, of Mr. Sokolow's claim that "this is my home, and no one can tell me what to do in my own home." The judge pointed out the obvious fact that modern apartment-house living brings us into a kind of "auditory intimacy" with our neighbors. Apartment dwellers in urban America are in a different relation with each other than lords and ladies living in an age "when castles were remote, separated by broad moors, and when an intruder had to force moat and wall to make his presence felt within."

Though he rejected the notion that Mr. Sokolow had the right to do anything he wanted in his home, the judge did not accept the equally extreme position of the landlord and the Levins that, under the lease, *any* disturbing noise provided grounds for throwing a family out of its apartment. Neither the property interest claimed by the tenant nor the contract language relied on by the landlord could be treated as giving rise to absolute rights. Both were subject to evaluation in the light of reason, and in that light the judge found that the noise made by the Sokolows was neither excessive nor deliberate. Noting that the Christmas season was approaching ("a time for peace on earth to men of good will"), Judge Fitzpatrick announced his solution to the problem: "They are all nice people and a little mutual forbearance and understanding of each other's problems should resolve the issues to everyone's satisfaction."

Nice people all over the United States, like Mr. Sokolow and his neighbors, often deploy the rhetoric of rights as though they and their particular interests trumped everything else in sight. So far as property is concerned, few of us have not maintained at one time or another that "it's mine and I can do what I want with it"—whether the "it" is a flag, a backyard, or our own bodies. If a neighbor complains about our stereo, our noisy party, or our late-night piano practicing, our automatic reaction is apt to be that we have a right to do as we please in our own homes.

In these sorts of situations, like Mr. Sokolow, we often try to clinch the argument by appealing to the ancient property rights of Englishmen, and by invoking these rights in the strongest possible way. Yet this careless manner of speaking cannot be blamed on our English legal inheritance, nor even on the American frontier mentality. Neither in England, nor even in Canada (where conditions were historically more similar to ours) is the idea of property or the discourse of rights so extravagant.

The exaggerated absoluteness of our American rights dialect is all the more remarkable when we consider how little relation it bears to reality. There is a striking discrepancy, as the *Sokolow* case illustrates, between our tendency to state rights in a stark unlimited fashion and the commonsense restrictions that have to be placed on one person's rights when they collide with those of another person. On any given day, in courtrooms all over the nation, harried judges use a chastened, domesticated concept of rights when they handle garden-variety disputes. Landlords' contract rights do not extend to evicting tenants for any disturbing noise; but tenants cannot make as much noise as they wish in the enclosed space that belongs to them.

Property, historically the paradigmatic right in England and the United States, has always been subject to reasonable regulation, despite the excited rhetoric that often attends its assertion. How then can we explain the persistence of absoluteness in our property rhetoric, and in our rights rhetoric in general? To find the beginnings of an answer, we must go back to the first great "moment" in the history of rights, when property became the template from which other American rights were cut.

Property acquired its near-mythic status in our legal tradition, in part, because the language and images of John Locke played such a key role in American thinking about government. To show that property rights were "natural" and prepolitical, Locke postulated a "state of nature" in which "every Man has a Property in his own Person," and in the "Labour of his Body, and the Work of his Hands." When a man "mixed" his labor with something by removing it from its natural state, Locke argued, he made the acorn—or the apple, or the fish, or the deer—his property, "at least where there is enough, and as good left in common for others." The same was true, Locke said, for his appropriation of land by tilling, planting, and cultivating. After spinning this famous tale, Locke went on to his next proposition—namely, that the essential reason human beings submit to government is to safeguard their "property." In a move that was to have great significance for Americans, he announced that he would use the word *property* to designate, collectively, *Lives, Liberties, and Estates.* According to Locke, the preservation of property, in this capacious sense, is "the great and *chief end*" for which men come together into commonwealths.

Locke's property theory entered into a distinctively American property story. It was mediated and reinforced in this respect by William Blackstone's lectures on law that were much more widely read and consulted in the United States than in England. Whereas for Locke property had been a means to an end (constitutional monarchy), it was for Blackstone a good in itself. And what a good! "There is nothing which so generally strikes the imagination and engages the affections of mankind," Blackstone wrote, "as the right of property; or that sole and despotic dominion which one man claims and exercises over the external things of the world, in total exclusion of the rights of any other individual in the universe." In this apostrophe to property, we find no *ifs, ands,* or *buts.* A property owner, Blackstone tells us, rules over what he owns, not merely as a king, but as a despot. Property rights are absolute, individual, and exclusive.

The strong property rights talk of Locke and Blackstone was in the air at the right moment to fuse with certain political factors that helped to make property the cardinal symbol of individual freedom and independence in the United States. Chief among these factors was the uneasiness felt by the framers of our Constitution concerning the potential threat posed to property rights by popularly elected legislatures. As Jennifer Nedelsky has put it, the Founding Fathers took property as the "central instance of rights at risk in a republic governed by popularly elected legislatures."

From the very beginning, the absoluteness of American property rhetoric promoted illusions and impeded clear thinking about property rights and rights in general. The framers' efforts to directly and indirectly protect the interests of property owners did not, and were not meant to, preclude considerable public regulation of property. The Fifth Amendment expressly recognized the federal eminent domain or "takings" power. In the nineteenth century, the takings authority was liberally invoked, especially at the state level, to promote economic development, and notably to aid railroads in acquiring land. Furthermore, traditional flexible legal limitations on the rights of owners (such as the broad principle that one should not use one's property to inflict harm on others) were routinely applied in the capillaries of private law.

Despite many limitations on property rights in practice, the paradigm of property as a specially important, and very strong, right continued to exert a powerful influence on the law. From the latter years of the nineteenth century up to the 1930s, the Supreme Court repeatedly invoked property rights (in an expansive form) to strike down a series of progressive laws that, taken together, might have served to ease the transition here, as similar legislation did in Europe, to a modern mixed economy and welfare state.

While the Supreme Court was thus according a high level of protection to the interest of owners of productive property, courts at the state level were diligently using the law of trespass to erect a protective shield around another kind of property: the family home. Legal historian Aviam Soifer has written that "the rhetoric surrounding legal doctrine from the middle to the end of the nineteenth century tended to reinforce [beliefs of most white male Americans that they were] entirely free to contract for, hold, and devise property as they saw fit."

The heyday of the absolutist property paradigm in American *law* came to an end more than 50 years ago when the Supreme Court, under heavy pressure to uphold the economic and labor legislation of the Depression and New Deal period, repudiated several earlier cases in which it had sacrificed progressive legislation on the altar of a broad notion of "property."

Nevertheless, the paradigm persists in popular discourse and still occasionally receives lip service even from the Supreme Court. The Court's now-common subordination of property to other rights makes it all the more remarkable that property continues to cast its spell and to entrance the minds of legal scholars as well as laypersons. In America, when we want to protect something, we try to get it characterized as a right. To a great extent, it is still the case that when we *especially* want to hold on to something (welfare benefits, a job) we try to get the object of our concern characterized as a property right.

There are Lockean echoes in the efforts of many persons on both the left and right of the American political spectrum to link "property" with liberty and independence. Each camp, of course, has a different understanding of property. Since land ownership can no longer serve to provide the majority of citizens with a protected sphere, jobs and their associated benefits (especially pensions) are the principal bases for whatever economic security most middle-class people possess. Welfare benefits have become the meager counterpart for a large part of the poverty-level population. As the importance of employment and social assistance for status and security came to be appreciated, Thurman Arnold, Charles Reich, and other legal theorists began to try to reconceptualize jobs and welfare as new forms of property. In the 1960s reformist lawyers launched a campaign to persuade the Supreme Court that welfare benefits, Social Security, and government jobs should be treated as property for constitutional purposes. This effort had only limited success in a series of cases that established that one could not be deprived of welfare benefits and certain other statutory entitlements without an opportunity to be heard. Conservative lawyers, for their part, have had equally modest success in trying to convince the Court that the takings clause should accord more protection to the type of property that interests them—the wealth produced by the free operation of market forces.

Much of the attention the Supreme Court once lavished on a broad concept of property, including the freedom of contract to acquire it, it now devotes to certain other liberties that it has designated as "fundamental." Remarkably, the property paradigm, including the old language of absoluteness, broods over this developing jurisprudence of personal rights. The new right of privacy, like the old right of property, has been imagined by the Court and lawyers generally as marking off a protected sphere that surrounds the individual. Indeed, much of the old property rhetoric has simply been transferred to this new area, and the Court has reexperienced familiar difficulties in working out principled limitations on a right that seemed for a time to have no bounds.

Though the "preferred" rights change from time to time, American legal discourse still promotes careless habits of speaking and thinking about them. Mr. Sokolow spoke for many of us when he claimed that no one could tell him what not to do in his own home. He must have known perfectly well that he could not print dollar bills, raise chickens, commit mayhem, or even have a late-night jam session in his Queens castle. When he spoke as he did, he was not speaking the language of the Founders. Still less was he speaking the language of the early colonists, who accepted much official (and officious) intrusion into their personal lives. The frontier offered more scope, perhaps, for the illusion of absoluteness, but the circumstances of those who opened the West were also conducive to a vivid awareness of human vulnerability and interdependence. Where then does this tough talk come from? Why do we Americans habitually exaggerate the absoluteness of the important rights we legitimately claim?

The starkness of some of the language in the Bill of Rights has helped to legitimate intemperate arguments made by those who have a particular attachment to one of the rights framed in such terms. But stark constitutional formulations alone cannot explain our fondness for absolute rights talk. For property rights appear in the Constitution only in an oblique and implicitly qualified form: "No person ... shall be deprived of ... property, without due process of law; nor shall private property be taken for public use, without just compensation." In the case of property, it was not the Fifth Amendment but the Lockean paradigm, cut loose from its context, that became part of our property story as well as of our rights discourse. Blackstone's flights of fancy about property as absolute dominion stuck in American legal imaginations more than his endless boring pages on what property owners really might and might not do with what they owned.

However, neither Lockean rights rhetoric as mediated by Blackstone nor constitutional language can account directly or fully for the illusions of absoluteness that are promoted by American rights talk. Another key piece of the puzzle is the pervasiveness of legal culture in American society. The strong language the Mr. Sokolow and the rest of us so frequently use is remarkably similar to a certain type of lawyers' talk that has increasingly passed into common parlance. A large legal profession, whose most visible members habitually engaged in strategic exaggeration and overstatement, was already having a substantial effect on popular discourse in Alexis de Tocqueville's day. The rank and file of the legal profession, it is true, spend the greater part of their professional lives in the humdrum business of adjusting one person's rights with another's. But we are not only the most lawyer-ridden society in the world, we are also the country in which the lawyer's role is the most adversarial. The careful, precise, professional jargon of the workaday office lawyer appears in popular discourse mainly in caricature ("whereas hereinbefore provided"), while the highly colored language of advocacy flows out to the larger society on the lips of orators, statesmen, and flamboyant courtroom performers. Courtroom law talk, it should be noted, rests on an assumption that is not generally to be commended in civil conversation: that when each of two disputants pushes his or her version of the facts and theory of law to the ethically permissible limit, some third party will be smart enough to figure out from the two distorted accounts what probably happened and how the law should be brought to bear on the case.

What's wrong with a little exaggeration, one might ask, especially in the furtherance of something as important as individual rights? If we always took care to note that rights are qualified, would we not risk eroding them altogether? Well, no. In the first place, no one can be an absolutist for *all* our constitutionally guaranteed rights, because taking any one of them as far as it can go soon brings it into conflict with another. Second, the rhetoric of absoluteness increases the likelihood of conflict and inhibits the sort of dialogue that is increasingly necessary in a pluralistic society. In the common enterprise of ordering our lives together, much depends on communication, reason giving, and mutual understanding. Even the legal profession is beginning to question the utility and legitimacy of the traditional strategic adoption of extreme positions by lawyers. Lawyers, as well as clients, are reckoning the social cost of our unique brand of adversary litigation. How ironic it would be if the American legal profession became more sophisticated about alternative methods of dispute resolution, yet the old hardball litigators' talk lingered on in the rest of society and continued to make it difficult for neighbors and family members to deal with the frictions inherent in everyday living.

Claims of absoluteness have the further ill effect of tending to downgrade rights into the mere expression of unbounded desires and wants. Excessively strong formulations express our most infantile instincts rather than our potential to be reasonable men and women. A country in which we can do "anything we want" is not a republic of free people attempting to order their lives together.

Absoluteness is an illusion, and hardly a harmless one. When we assert our rights to life, liberty, and property, we are expressing the reasonable hope that such things can be made more secure by law and politics. When we assert these rights in an absolute form, however, we are expressing infinite and impossible desires—to be completely free, to possess things totally, to be masters of our fate and captains of our souls. There is pathos as well as bravado in these attempts to deny the fragility and contingency of human existence, personal freedom, and the possession of worldly goods.

The exaggerated absoluteness of our American rights rhetoric is closely bound up with its other distinctive traits: a near-silence concerning responsibility and a tendency to envision the rights bearer as a lone autonomous individual. Thus, for example, those who contest the legitimacy of mandatory automobile seat belt or motorcycle helmet laws frequently say: "It's my body and I have the right to do as I please with it." In this shibboleth, the old horse of property is harnessed to the service of an unlimited liberty. The implication is that no one else is affected by the exercise of the individual right in question. This way of thinking and speaking ignores the fact that it is the rare driver, passenger, or biker who does not have a child, a spouse, or a parent. It glosses over the likelihood that if the rights bearer comes to grief, the cost of medical treatment, rehabilitation, and long-term care will be spread among many others.

V

The Economics
of Conservation

A prime theme of the Wise Use attack on the environmental movement is that the environmental agenda is incompatible with economic development and job creation. Moreover, the popular media frequently treat environmental issues as involving a stark trade-off between jobs and the environment. Increasingly, environmentalists are working hard to demonstrate the linkages between environmental quality and economic health.

John S. Gray III, a political consultant, debunks the jobs-versus-environment dichotomy in "Jobs and the Environment." Focusing on several arenas in which the jobs-versus-environment debate has played out, such as the Pacific Northwest, Gray examines the actual economic forces at work and the effect of environmental issues on the pace of economic activity.

In "The Wise Use Threat to American Workers," Donald R. Judge, the leader of the Montana AFL-CIO, provides a critical appraisal of the Wise Use movement from the perspective of the labor movement. He argues that some of the same companies that have provided financial support for wise use have been waging antilabor campaigns in the workplace. Using the example of the Lolo and Kootenai Accords, Judge explains how Wise Use forces successfully defeated a constructive labor–environmentalist agreement on management of public forest lands in Montana.

Contrary to Wise Use arguments, environmental regulation can actually promote job creation and economic growth by stimulating the need for clean technologies and pollution-control equipment. Environmental Business International's Grant Ferrier documents, in "Strategic Overview of the Environmental Industry," the continued growth of the $123 billion environmental industry, which now employs over 1 million Americans. Donald L. Conners, Michael D. Bliss, and Jack Archer, leaders in the effort to promote the export potential of the American environmental industry, describe the challenges and opportunities of this emerging field in "The U.S. Environmental Industry and the Global Marketplace for Environmental Goods and Services."

In "Science, Technology, Environment, and Competitiveness in a North American Context," Linda K. Trocki of the Los Alamos National Laboratory describes the economic functions and effects of environmental regulation. She argues for economically efficient environmental regulations based on a careful assessment of relevant costs and benefits. She concludes that pursuing environmental-quality goals is consistent with efforts to expand international trading opportunities across North America.

In Sante Fe, New Mexico, Henry H. Carey and Meria L. Loeks of the Forest Trust are establishing new relationships that seek to avoid the polarization that exists in the debate over our nation's forests. "Restructuring the Timber Economy" describes the Forest Trust's efforts to support locally controlled forestry practitioners that operate on a sustained-yield basis.

Jobs and the Environment

John S. Gray III

INTRODUCTION

If we are to believe many news sources, the world can either be a very unhealthy place where we are all simply concerned with economic growth and development or a natural paradise where people have no means of economic support. *Business Week, Time, Newsweek,* and other popular magazines, as well as television and radio, have run feature stories on the apparent clash between a healthy environment and a healthy economy, as though each must come directly at the expense of the other.

In the following discussion we will show that although difficult decisions about preferences must be made in any conservation effort, the issues involved are broader and more complicated than simply "jobs versus the environment." We will give a brief overview of how the economy and conservation of the environment are often put at odds, and show that the issue of jobs versus the environment is not always the most important issue behind many conservation battles.

HISTORICAL PERSPECTIVE

Since the first European explorers set foot in the Americas, a debate has raged about how the bountiful natural resources of this land should be used. Some settlers saw the land as a large inexhaustible source of gold, timber, range, and other resources to be controlled and exploited. Even at the earliest, however, there were others who viewed the land as a unique paradise to be savored. Writers such as Whitman and Emerson found the natural landscape as an important counterpoint to the developed world.

During the middle of the nineteenth century, Americans began to see the limits to their seemingly boundless wilderness. George Perkins Marsh published *Man and Nature,* a call for environmental awareness; later, in 1872, President Ulysses S. Grant signed legislation creating Yellowstone National Park; the Appalachian Mountain Club was founded in 1876, followed by the Sierra Club in 1892. Over the years, the conservation movement and its friends in the federal government have carved out a national system of parks and preserves that are respected worldwide.

The debate over preservation and development raged in the earliest days of the conservation movement. This longstanding debate is the nucleus of the jobs versus the environment issue.

SUSTAINABLE DEVELOPMENT

The issue of jobs and the environment extends beyond national boundaries; it is part of an international debate. With the increase in international trade concurrent with increases in worldwide poverty and hunger, jobs and the environment, one of the principle topics at the recent meeting of the United Nations Conference on Environment and Development (UNCED) in Rio de Janeiro, has clearly become an important international issue. At the UNCED, heads of state and negotiators from 170 countries considered a series of proposals to address global economic development on a scale that is sustainable under existing ecological limits. The concept of sustainability is based on the realization that environmental degradation and economic decline go hand in hand and that, therefore, environmentalism must not be viewed as an option but rather a necessity for economic growth. This understanding of the economic importance of a healthy ecosystem forms the basis for concern about the destruction of tropical rain forests and fear of the greenhouse effect.

To save our future from the consequences of overdevelopment, some proponents of sustainable development believe we should

- Improve the efficiency of industry by adopting technological advances that use fewer resources and produce more acceptable amounts and types of waste.
- Account for the benefits of conserving the environment more accurately, when determining the costs and benefits of development, by using economic valuation strategies, some of which are described in Appendix A, and by establishing appropriate agreements between countries to address international problems.

- Stabilize population growth.
- Encourage lifestyles that foster appropriate use of resources (particularly in industrial nations, which use a disproportionate share of the earth's resources).

Although widely accepted in the environmental community, the concept of sustainable development is still controversial in some sectors. Because of the broad-brush approach that proponents take on so many issues, many ideas can be made to fit under the umbrella of sustainable development—indeed some opponents of environmentalism have been known to adopt the language of sustainable development in order to persuade the general public to support their position.

SOME U.S. JOBS AND ENVIRONMENT CONTROVERSIES

The following are brief summaries of a variety of controversies in selected regions of the country involving the jobs and environment issue. Cases in any number of states could be presented; however, Americans for the Environment (AFE) believes these four are representative.

Timber Industry versus the Northern Spotted Owl and Old-Growth Forests

The saga of the northern spotted owl, old-growth forests, and the timber industry has become synonymous with the jobs-versus-environment topic. At issue is the harvesting of trees and the destruction of old-growth forests on federal lands that harbor an endangered owl species. (An excellent summary of this controversy can be found in a report by the Congressional Research Service of the Library of Congress [Order Code IB90094] by M. Lynne Corn.)

Conservationists argue that timber sales to private interests in old-growth forests could jeopardize the northern spotted owl. Timber-industry officials counter that a ban on harvesting of these forests could end thousands of jobs (estimates vary from 19,000 to 250,000). Since June 1990, when the spotted owl was listed as threatened throughout its range by the federal government's Fish and Wildlife Service, the already high energy of the battle has increased. Several suits and countersuits have been filed over the government's enforcement of the Endangered Species Act.

Measures have been introduced in Congress to address the issue from both sides (see Appendix B, "Congressional Initiatives"). Some feel that an exception or special accommodation to the Endangered Species Act should be made because the economic impact of a ban on harvesting these forests would be devastating to many people in the Northwest. Often left unstated by the supporters of this view is the underlying argument that human life and the livelihood of some humans should not be made subordinate to flora or fauna. However, others argue that because they are an integral part of the quality of life, the value of old-growth forests to the economy of the communities near them is greater than the revenue *generated by* the sale of these forests as timber. Other measures have suggested that the federal government should offer income support for workers dislocated by a ban on harvesting. Implicit in this alternative is the recognition that being good stewards of the environment has some short-term costs, but these costs do not outweigh the benefits gained by conservation of wildlife and the environment.

An added complication in this discussion about spotted owls is the troubled timber industry. The timber industry itself has long recognized that the supply of old-growth timber is being depleted. In the past, when old-growth forests were depleted in the Northeast and South, there was always another region to which the industry could move. These forests in Washington and Oregon are the last of the old-growth forests in the lower 48 states. One observer has noted that the real issue is not that the timber industry is matched against the spotted owl, but that it is up against the Pacific Ocean.

Salmon Fishing in the Pacific States

In California and two other Pacific states, Oregon and Washington, another conflict is taking place that at first glance appears to be a jobs-versus-environment issue. As in many other controversies involving conservation, more is at issue than the loss of jobs or the saving of the environment. Much of the friction arises from the question of which jobs will be lost or saved, and which way of life is more valued by society.

As in so many coastal states, California has a declining fish population. Over the last few years salmon found in waters off the west coast from Canada to California have declined dramatically. In 1991, commercial and sport salmon fishing combined amounted to $66.4 million of revenue for California, Oregon, and Washington, down 28 percent from 1990 and 58 percent below the 1976–1990 average. On April 10, 1992, the Pacific Fishery Management Council, a federal panel charged with setting fishing levels, decided to decrease the number of allowed salmon caught to one-half the 1991 levels. The panel came very close to banning all salmon fishing off the coast.

There are many reasons for the decline in the salmon population: Droughts in California and Oregon have reduced water levels and raised the temperature in many spawning streams; the warmer ocean current caused by a weather phenomenon called El Niño kills off the plankton on which salmon feed; clogged watersheds from the debris left from logging block the routes of spawning salmon; and dams hinder efficient spawning. Other factors include overfishing and the runoff of agricultural chemicals. The result of this decline is that several species of salmon are now considered to be endangered.

The effect of this new limit on salmon on the livelihoods of commercial fishermen is obvious. With the recent years of limits already having weakened their finances, many fishermen, claiming that they cannot survive, are trying to find other work. This can prove difficult in the rugged communities in which they live, where fishing has traditionally been the only game in town. To add insult to injury, when the fishermen do try to retool, they are unable to sell their fishing boats at anything but rock-bottom prices; fishing has been curtailed so dramatically that potential buyers of fishing boats are hard to come by.

Since everyone and no one is to blame for the decline in the salmon population, some fishermen feel they are unfairly being singled out for punishment. In their view, dams built for cities and farmers destroy the salmon spawning grounds, but fishermen are forced to pay the price by the imposition of limits. Fishermen mourn the decline of a way of life, a heritage that they have passed from generation to generation in much the same way that farming or ranching traditions are passed on. ·

Although the plight of the commercial salmon fishermen is one that evokes sympathy, there are some reasons why fishermen should be the most outspoken advocates for conservation to rebuild the salmon stock. They have the most to gain from increased stocks of salmon since their livelihood is based on catching them. Instead of fighting limits today, they might join with environmentalists who are trying to do something about the threat of agricultural runoff and some of the other man-made root causes of the decline in salmon.

Gold Mines and the San Luis Valley of Colorado

Most environmental controversies involve other issues apart from the obvious economy versus the environment tug-of-war. The controversy over the mining of gold in a small community in Colorado is an example.

The San Luis Valley is a beautiful region in the Sangre De Cristo Mountain Range of Colorado. Although this area has one of the higher poverty rates in the state (its per capita income of $12,707 makes it one of the five poorest counties in Colorado), it is an area rich in history. Founded in 1851, San Luis was the first town in the state to be settled by whites. Most residents have strong local roots. Of the 2,030 county residents, 700 have nonfarming jobs; half of this group is employed by some level of government. The next largest industries are mining and agriculture, followed by a small service sector.

The fact that the Battle Mountain Gold Company's (BMG) desire to operate a mine in the valley was met with great protest comes as no surprise. Some residents in this close-knit community were leery of an outside corporation (BMG is based in Houston) that wished to introduce a change in their lifestyle and community. Concerns about the environmental soundness of the cyanide vat leaching operation ranged from, Would the cyanide used in the mining process harm the water supply? to Would the operation destroy the typography of their beautiful valley or its wildlife?

Mining is not a stranger to this valley, in which the first mining claim was established in the 1800s. Over the past 40 years the farmers of this community have lived with mining; but the new BMG mine caused a strong reaction. From the time the company began feasibility studies, residents fought BMG in its attempts to get the permits and water rights needed for the mine's operation. In the community's eyes BMG lacked credibility. The company was unknown to the community and therefore unwanted.

Despite the opposition's best efforts, BMG opened its mine in the spring of 1991. Company officials estimate that it will operate for seven years. They estimate that there are 425,000 ounces of recoverable gold in the ore deposit, which, at $350 per ounce, is worth $149 million.

In an area of poor farmers and ranchers, the 94 workers employed by the 24-hour operation produce a sizable effect on the economy of the community. The ripple effect of the wages from these jobs is felt throughout the valley. San Luis faces the familiar dilemma of striking a balance between opposing an environmental threat and the loss of possible employment opportunities.

Texas Hill Country Preserves

In Texas a great experiment in compromise is being undertaken by The Nature Conservancy and many private and public entities in the Texas hill country.

Houston may be the largest city, and Dallas may have the state's favored sports teams, but in this state most residents think of the 26-county region in the center of the state containing The Nature Conservancy's new "bioreserve" as the heart of Texas. This area of rolling hills includes part of San Antonio and Austin and many small ranch and farming communities. It also includes some of the most delicate ecosystems in the country. Subterranean rivers spring up to feed wildlife. The hill country's most distinctive feature is the Balcones Escarpment, a 200-mile-long crescent of limestone that cross-cuts rivers, streams, and canyons. The underground reservoir collects rainwater from this region and is one of the largest and cleanest in the country. The region still supports many of the species that were found there before the first Europeans settled this area. It contains 70 species of endangered or threatened plants and animals.

During the past two decades, the population in the hill country region has grown dramatically. Austin and San Antonio have been among the fastest-growing cities in the country during this time. Some previously remote areas in the hill country have been discovered by developers creating suburban communities and business parks. The Nature Conservancy has become a key player in the design and implementation of a new planning initiative that will allow for some development but also will control the amount and type of development or land use. Strategists in this effort are assuming that when they can plan for an entire ecological region, preserving the most essential tracts of land, it becomes less necessary to protect every piece of habitat. The Conservancy is working with federal, state, local, and private entities on this approach, which has three basic priorities:

1. Set aside a few highly protected and carefully managed "core" reserves for native fauna and flora, in addition to existing park lands.
2. Surround the core reserves with ecologically friendly buffer zones, which would consist, for example, of ranches that maintain wild habitat for tourists as well as undeveloped areas of military installations.
3. Create ecologically healthy islands of wildlife habitat on the outskirts of cities, while allowing development to proceed around them.

Underlying this effort is the assumption that planned development is preferable to unplanned growth. If the most essential tracts of land can be preserved and adjoining lands developed in harmony with the preserves, then conservationists will not have to fight for every single bug and tree. There will be fewer fights between economic interests and environmentalists.

An important aspect of this effort is the fact that in Texas there has always been a strong culture of individuality and private-property rights. Although Dallas and Austin have relatively longstanding city-planning traditions, many of the urban areas in Texas until recently have had minimal commercial- and residential-zoning laws. Houston, the state's largest city, is only now constructing its first zoning plan. This is an indicator of the very strong private-property-rights climate that exists in the state.

The success of The Nature Conservancy and others at purchasing the land for the nature preserves and getting property owners to go along with restrictions on the use of their property to ensure ecologically friendly buffer zones will be watched all over the country as others attempt to find a way of negotiating between the pressures of economics and environmental conservation.

NEW MAJOR OPPONENTS

As we have seen in the cases described above, the traditional opponents of conservation forces in many of these controversies typically are industry groups: the timber industry in the spotted owl controversy; select private developers in some land conservation efforts; and farmers, ranchers, and fishermen in cases where they perceive their livelihood being put at risk. These groups can be most successful when their interests coincide with the local population's general interests.

In other words, when the opponent to a conservation initiative is a major employer in the community, it is more likely to win—a majority of the populace has a direct or strong indirect connection to the employer's interest. But even under these circumstances, opponents of conservation initiatives have the disadvantage of sounding selfish. The developers want the government to loosen environmental controls so that they can build and reap the profits, which, as a side effect, may also benefit society. Fishermen do not want limits set on the number of fish they can catch simply because they want to make a living. Conservationists, on the other hand, are at an advantage when they can make the case that they are looking out for the interest of the general public by preserving natural resources for present and future generations. The general public, not directly part of the discussion, can appreciate that the environmentalists' argument may be in their best interest, particularly if the environmentalists are a part of the community and have arisen directly in response to a perceived threat.

INDUSTRIES AND JOBS GENERATED
THROUGH ENVIRONMENTALISM

The employment opportunities provided by "green" industries are significant and often overlooked. In the past 20 years there has been tremendous growth in the tourism industry. In 1988 it was estimated that there were 400 million international tourist arrivals. Tourism revenues are third among all export industries. Tourism to protected areas is particularly on the upswing. This "nature tourism" is defined, in a recent report of the World Wildlife Fund, as tourism that consists of traveling to relatively undisturbed or uncontaminated natural areas with the specific objective of studying, admiring, and enjoying the scenery and its wild plants and animals as well as any existing cultural manifestations found in these areas. In the United States a 1988 U.S. Fish and

Wildlife Service survey indicated that a total of 29 million U.S. citizens participated in 310 million trips to natural areas. In other words, ecotourism is big business. And because it is a nonconsumptive value use of natural resources, ecotourism is particularly important in discussions of the jobs-and-environment controversy since it is among the alternative industries often proposed as a substitute for overexploitation of natural resources (see Appendix A for a discussion of economic arguments).

Another source of jobs is recycling. Although programs vary, on average one job is created for every 465 tons of material received for recycling each year. Compared to incineration and landfilling, recycling provides greater job opportunities because it is more labor intensive and cheaper than these other options.

A third source of job growth is pollution control and energy efficiency. Pollution control alone accounts for 2.5 percent of total employment in the United States. Although these industries make up a significant portion of the economy, some business analysts feel that they still have not been sufficiently capitalized on by American industry for development and expansion. There is actually a fear on the part of some U.S. analysts that these industries may be lost due to aggressive competition on the part of other countries.

A case in point is Japan. The Japanese suffered greatly as the result of two energy crises, which raised oil prices and placed oil products in short supply. These crises caused Japanese industry and government to implement severe measures mandating energy efficiency (which in turn leads to less pollution). Because of this early investment, Japan is ahead in many green technologies, including:

- **Waste incineration.** Japanese manufacturers are building powerful, low-emission incinerators for most solid and liquid waste.

- **Automobile fuel efficiency.** Toyota, Nissan, Honda, and Mazda are making strides in decreasing the amount of fuel burned by their automobiles, which results in less carbon dioxide released. They have also been experimenting with lighter body materials and better catalytic converters.

- **Recycling at steel plants.** Some plants are being designed to recycle, thus reducing waste from steel production, Japan's major industrial-waste producer.

- **Wastewater treatment.** Currently Japan is exporting sewage-control and sludge-treatment equipment and expertise to other Asian countries.

- **Alternative energy development.** Japan leads the world in solar and fuel-cell technology.

APPENDIX A: SELECTED ECONOMIC ARGUMENTS

According to economists, there are several underlying reasons why natural resources are often overexploited. Americans for the Environment has selected one source dealing with the area of biological resources, *Economics and Biological Diversity: Developing and Using Economic Incentives to Conserve Biological Resources,* by Jeffery A. McNeely, and has paraphrased some of McNeely's points as follows:

1. Biological resources are often not given appropriate prices in the marketplace. When a biological resource is traded in the market, it may have additional associated values that are not reflected in the market price. Individuals and industries can consequently make a private economic gain without paying the full value, creating a subsidy at the expense of the general public.

2. The benefits of protecting biological areas are seldom fully represented in cost–benefit analyses. The social benefits of conserving biological resources are often intangible, not fully reflected in the price. However, the short-term economic benefits of exploiting biological resources are very easy to quantify and thus receive greater emphasis in these analyses. Hence, cost-benefit analyses usually overestimate the net benefits of resource exploitation.

3. Exploiters of natural resources pay only part of the cost of the benefit they receive; the rest of the cost is paid by society. The use of biological resources creates "external costs," which are considered accidental side effects and not taken into account during cost–benefit analysis, thus creating a high cost for future generations.

4. The weaker the ownership of the resource (i.e., open–access resources and resources in economically deprived areas), the higher the chance that the resource will be exploited.

5. Measures of national income (such as per capita Gross Domestic Product) do not include the depletion of natural resources as a loss of wealth. Just the opposite is true—these economic measures actually include the loss of natural resources as income. For instance, revenue from the sale of timber from ancient forests is included in the GDP. What is not taken into account is the fact that depletion of those forests now will result in future economic loss.

In order for governments and society to place more appropriate value on natural resources, a combination of the following assessment methods should be used.

1. Direct values are those concerned with the enjoyment or satisfaction directly received by consumers of biological resources. These are divided into consumptive-use value and productive-use value. Consumptive-use value is the value placed on a natural resource that is consumed readily without passing through a market. The consumptive-use value of going berry picking is the value that one gives the entire recreational experience, not the value of the berries picked. Consumptive-use value is very rarely quantified but clearly important. On the other hand, productive-use value is the value assigned to products that are commercially harvested. This value is often the one used in determining national income or other measures of wealth.

2. Indirect values are those that reflect the value of a natural resource to society at large, rather than to an individual or corporation. Although indirect values are not often included in traditional measures of wealth, they may far outweigh direct values when quantified and computed. Indirect values include nonconsumptive-use value and option value. Nonconsumptive-use value is the value of the resource to humankind because of its existence. Often this includes its value in supporting other natural resources. Many nonconsumptive values have considerable economic impact. Option value, on the other hand, is the future unknown value of a natural resource. The salmon species that becomes extinct may actually hold the key to some very important future discovery. In many cases, overexploitation of a resource ends our option for future use of that resource.

The Wise Use Threat to American Workers

Donald R. Judge

The Reverend Martin Luther King Jr. had great dreams for America.

He dreamt that, one day, this nation would live up to its creed and that all people would indeed be equal.

He dreamt that, one day, his four black children "would not be judged by the color of their skin, but by the content of their character."

He dreamt that, one day, there would be racial peace across the land.

If he were here today, I believe he would also dream of peace among those who live, work, and play in the nation's forests and other public lands. I believe he would dream of the day when mill workers and loggers would sit down at the table with conservationists and talk out their differences.

But, even today, as during his lifetime, Martin Luther King Jr. would find real bigots in his way. The people who call themselves the "Wise Use movement" would do all they could to prevent his dream from becoming a reality. Our experience at trying to reach environmental peace in Montana's troubled timber country is proof that the "wise guys" don't want that peace.

It has long been said that conservation extremists want no solution to Montana's continuing wilderness debate so that all the possible wilderness lands would remain "locked up" and managed as wild lands pending a solution.

If that is true, then I believe there is an equal axiom on the side of the wise guys: They want no solution to the wilderness debate so that public frustration and disgust will rise so high that, ultimately, the solution will be to open all public lands to all uses.

We saw that frustrated reaction to a certain extent in the 1988 elections, when Montanans defeated their incumbent Democratic U.S. Senator, John Melcher, who was beat over the head mercilessly with the wilderness issue.

The wise users ignored the fact that Melcher carved boundaries in ways that drove the extreme environmentalists nuts, but catered to the wishes of industry and recreational groups.

All the wise guys saw was that John Melcher favored some wilderness somewhere, and that was too much for them. They painted him as the state's leading "greenie," as being out of touch with real Montanans, and so on. As a result, they turned much of his traditional electoral support from the moderate political spectrum against him.

And on the other end, the extreme environmentalists also tore him up. They criticized him for not pushing stronger environmental protections, for not including more land in wilderness proposals, for caving in to too many industry demands, and so on. And so Melcher lost much of his traditional electoral support from the more liberal end of the political spectrum, as well.

What we got as a result of this political warfare over the environment was Conrad Burns, a conservative Republican senator who publicly embraces the Wise Use movement and spurns workers and environmentalists routinely. He has voted against the interests of workers at every turn, and he wouldn't even support protection for the geothermal wells that make Yellowstone National Park the crown jewel of the National Park System.

Obviously, what we got as a result of this political warfare over the environment was a victory for the Wise Use movement. They won against an incumbent—almost unheard of—and even against a conservative Montana Democrat—again, almost unheard of.

What were we to do?

That's where Dr. King's ideals came in. We decided that we better try to make peace, because by fighting, we were both losing the war.

We decided to bring mill workers and conservationists together in the same room and have them talk to each other—not as adversaries, but as neighbors, as Montanans, as citizens whose best interests would be served by peace in the forests.

It worked.

After years of often bitter debate over how best to manage the public forests in Montana, timber workers and conservationists set aside past differences and hammered out agreements in the fall of 1990 that spelled life for both groups—and many others.

In an unprecedented example of direct citizen action and cooperation, timber workers and conservationists sat down together in lumber towns like Libby, Superior, Thompson Falls, and Missoula to strike agreements on what should and should not be designated wilderness. Local labor officials met with leaders of state and local conservation groups and over a period of six months, wrote what have come to be known as the Lolo and Kootenai Accords.

The Accords, which drew national press attention, were compromises on the wilderness status of lands that make up the Kootenai National Forest in northwest Montana and the Lolo National Forest in southwest Montana.

The Accords proposed wilderness legislation that would "lock up" only about two percent of the timber suitable for harvest in each of the two forests. Roughly 98 percent of the timber suitable for harvest would be released from the current wilderness study "limbo" and would be available for Montana's lumber mills. On the other hand, conservationists were able to protect more public land than in any pervious wilderness proposals for those forests.

In short, the Accords meant jobs for our timber workers—and the communities reliant upon them—and wilderness protection for those who wanted it.

Partly as a result of Senator Melcher's defeat, reasonable people on both sides of what had been a 15-year wilderness debate in Montana realized that continued inaction was going to spell disaster for both. And so they settled down to talk to each other.

And when they did, they realized that they really agreed on many issues and were able to discuss compromises where they didn't agree. They were able to sit down at the table and look at the maps and point out specific drainages, timber stands, wildlife areas, and so forth that might be affected.

Timber workers were able to point out places where logging was actually going to be beneficial in the long run. Conservationists were able to point out areas where vital habitat would be jeopardized. Together, they moved boundaries and drew maps and redrew them until the Accords came together.

The Accords they hammered out represented those groups' opinions about how best to manage the lands on those two public forests that make up so much of Montana's timber country.

The groups that ended up supporting the accords process were diverse in origin but unified in purpose. From the worker community came

- Lumber, Production, and Industrial Workers local unions in Libby, Thompson Falls, Bonner, and Missoula
- International Woodworkers of America local union in Superior
- United Paperworkers International local union in Missoula
- The Montana State AFL-CIO

From the conservation community came

- Missoula Backcountry Horsemen
- Concerned Citizens of Superior Ranger District
- Great Burn Study Group
- Montana Wildlands Coalition
- Western Montana Fish and Game Association
- Montana Wilderness Association
- Cabinet Resources Group
- Libby Sportsmen
- Kootenai Wildlands Alliance
- Montana Audubon Council
- American Fisheries Society
- Montana Outfitters and Guides Association

The Accords even drew initial support from Champion International Corp., the employer of many of the union members involved, as well as the American Smelting and Refining Company (ASARCO), which operates and has proposed several mining and smelting ventures in Montana.

When the Accords were made public, widespread public acclaim took almost everyone by surprise. This acclaim and support created a kind of domino effect among other like-minded groups that were not directly involved in the Accords process.

The state's generally conservative press was also supportive, reflecting the growing public sentiment to "do something" on the wilderness issue. The conservative *Helena Independent Record* called the Accords the "first glimmer of hope" in years, while its somewhat more liberal sister paper, the *Montana Standard,* wrote that the Accords "should be implemented and politics should not be allowed to subvert it." Even the nationally respected *San Francisco Examiner* followed the Accords process and editorialized that, "When the history of environmental policies is written, this tiny logging town (Libby) may figure as the place where divisive hysteria gave way to useful compromise. It was here that environmentalists and sawmill workers—among the most bitter enemies—quietly worked out a precedent-setting accord."

About then is when the trouble started. Public acclaim was so broad and so exciting that the wise guys got scared—scared that the Accords might work and that Montana's wilderness debate might finally have an end, at least on two forests. And they got scared about the precedent that might be established for other forests to consider in the rest of the state as well as throughout the Northwest. That's when the Wise Use movement went into high gear.

Extremist groups that want "not one more acre" of wilderness started complaining that they had been left out of the Accords process. Some public-land-user groups complained that their voices had not been heard. Some sportsmen's groups cried that their needs weren't being met. And despite innumerable meetings with many and varied groups, and many adjustments to the Accords boundaries to satisfy their concerns, the attacks continued.

Long lists of groups whose members weren't at the Accords meetings were published in the press, and the impression was created that the Accords were dreamed up by a handful of unions and elitist groups who purposely chose to ignore the wishes of all others. Little attention was paid to the simple reality that to get something moving, a small group had to start the work and had to be willing to make some tough choices. And even less recognition was made that several of the complaining groups had been asked to offer suggestions for changes to the Accords but chose, instead, to simply call for their rejection.

As a result, the Accords were successfully derailed. Congressional legislation to institute the Accords was held up by Montana's new Wise Use senator,

Conrad Burns. Conservative Republican Ron Marlanee, long a labor and environmental enemy and now a private-sector lobbyist for the Safari Club, also contributed to the Accords' congressional blockage.

The result is easy to see:

- we continue to have no wilderness solution in Montana
- we continue to have millions of acres locked up in wilderness study limbo
- we continue to have timber shortage problems that are exploited in the press by Wise Users
- we continue to have a rising public frustration over Montana politicians' perceived inability to solve the dilemma

These continuing problems will surely have an effect in the 1994 elections, when Wise Use Senator Burns comes up for reelection. The wise guys will be working hard to see that he's reelected, but perhaps more importantly, they'll be working to get state and local candidates elected on what they hope will be Wise Use coattails.

Now, even given all this information, it's still puzzling to some folks why labor is involved in opposing the wise guys. We've heard many sincere questions about why we aren't just jumping aboard with the corporations that employ many of us and, in turn, finance the Wise Use movement.

For us, the answer is at once simple and difficult. It's difficult because the companies that own the means of extracting timber, ore, and other natural resources say we're arguing against our own jobs, or our kids' jobs. We don't want to do that—we believe we can have both jobs and a healthy environment, the same healthy environment that attracted us all to this area in the first place.

But we believe in even more than that.

We believe we can have jobs that are safe, where workers are treated fairly, where compensation is sufficient to provide for our families' needs.

In many cases, the same companies that have been financing the Wise Use movement have been financing antilabor campaigns at the workplace or operating unsafe workplaces that literally kill workers.

And yet they want us to jump aboard the Wise Use train with them. We say "NO."

ASARCO has fought unionization as its mine in ecologically sensitive northwest Montana, and despite a positive union vote by the workers in the first election resisted so vehemently that the union lost by eleven votes in a second election.

ASARCO just recently announced the closure of one of its mines in Montana, perhaps hoping to leverage the permit process for a nearby proposed mine. That leverage attempt will put hundreds of workers out on the streets in an area where unemployment already is among the highest in the region.

And yet they want us to join the ASARCO-financed Wise Use movement. We say "NO.

NERCO, one of the largest funders of this new movement, forced its unionized workers at Decker, Montana, into a two-year strike. And, following an administrative judge's ruling ordering them to give these workers back their jobs, NERCO appealed the decision and did not come to a settlement until two years later.

And yet such corporations wonder why labor refuses to join with their Wise Use agenda?

In the timber industry, one of the most antiunion companies in the nation is Louisiana-Pacific, also a big funder of the Wise Use movement.

Businesses, chambers of commerce, the Farm Bureau, and others work together in the so-called "right-to-work" movement, which is a stake aimed right at the heart of workers' democratic rights to organize. They pump time, in-kind expenditures, and money into the right-to-work movement and the National Right to Work Committee. They set up state committees to push their antiworker agenda, and they funnel money in from across the nation.

And yet they still ask why we're not joining them in the Wise Use movement.

Corporations in the extractive industries across the state—and the nation—are joining in coalitions that fight working families' interests economically, socially, and politically, and yet still they want us to join them in the Wise Use movement.

We say "NO!"

That's when this difficult question gets simplified: when you look at all the things the Wise Use companies are doing to hurt workers' interests. That's when we're able to work past the immediate rhetoric and say "NO!"

The only option is for workers and conservationists to quit warring with one another and start talking. Start drawing maps, debating boundaries, discussing wildlife habitat, reviewing snowmobile trails, and so forth. And to start compromising—compromising in ways that preserve our environmental heritage as well as our economic heritage.

If the cry goes up "not one more acre of wilderness" from the industry side, we'll lose. If the cry goes up "not one more acre given up" from the conservation side, we'll lose. And the wise guys will have won.

Determined and dedicated citizen action led to the Accords. They can lead to more accords in more areas, and they can lead public opinion away from the wise guys and back towards compromise and results. They can lead to economic and social stability. And they can lead to people living, working, and sharing together the vast natural resources that make up this country of ours.

Strategic Overview of the Environmental Industry

Grant Ferrier

Addressing the world's environmental concerns has created an emerging and growing portion of the private sector devoted to cleaning up and protecting the environment. The environmental industry is a $150 billion business in the United States and employs more than one million individuals. Not bad for an industry that generated less than $10 billion in revenues 20 years ago, when it consisted mostly of waste hauling and sewage treatment. The turning point was undoubtedly the dawn of the environmental regulatory era with the formation of the EPA in 1970. EPA's debut was followed closely by the first Clean Air Act, the Clean Water Act, and later by RCRA, CERCLA, and a number of other acronyms that have become all too familiar with pollution generators and the businesses that seek to serve them.

What is the environmental industry today? How has it developed in North America? And how fast is it growing? The following charts the results of more than five years of analysis of the entire industry by Environmental Business International (EBI).

The relative novelty and fragmentation of the various environmental segments make it hard to identify all the companies doing environmental business. Indeed more than half the industry is made up of relatively small companies. Privately held companies contribute more than two-thirds of environmental-industry revenues in the United States, but publicly traded environmental firms (there are 250 in the EBJ Stock Index) are increasing their share every year.

The recession in 1991 and 1992 sent chills through revenue growth and profitability in the environmental industry. Combined with other factors, it fired a warning shot of continued decelerating growth throughout the 1990s. Despite the fact that industry growth is projected to be above that of the economy at large, trends point to the sobering truth that the environmental industry cannot sustain itself in its present form. In other words, the vast majority of business in the environmental industry today is related to cleaning up for "sins of the past" or controlling emissions from now outdated facilities, both of which have a finite life cycle. Environmental companies have always

Table 1   The U.S. Environmental Industry in 1992

Segment	Revenues ($ billion)	Companies	Avg. rev. growth (%)
Solid waste	28	5,200	6
Resource recovery/recycling	16	5,100	7
Water treatment/equipment	13	2,500	5
Hazardous waste management	14	2,800	6
Engineering/consulting	14	6,800	8
Private water utilities	12	24,000	2
Waste management equipment	11	6,000	7
Air pollution control	6	1,200	11
Asbestos abatement	3	2,500	1
Analytical services/environmental testing	2	1,500	5
Instrument manufacturing	2	300	6
Alternative energy	2	1,800	13
Total	**123**	**59,700**	**6**

had to cope with being in a very dynamic and unpredictable industry, but the emerging "paradigm shift" in the pollution- and waste-generating community from pollution control and cleanup to pollution prevention and waste minimization mandates a similar shift in the environmental industry.

Nevertheless, most companies will find plenty of business in enhancing environmental quality, particularly those with the foresight to start positioning for work in the still embryonic global market. Continually redefining the environmental industry remains a challenge. Table 1 shows total numbers and revenues of U.S. environmental companies.

Annual industry growth has fallen from 15 percent in 1989 to 10 percent in 1990 and down to 2 percent in 1991 and 3 percent in 1992. However, with the economy rebounding, the Clinton administration showing greater emphasis on the environmental industry, and the quest for environmental quality at a reasonable cost continuing, growth is expected to average 6 percent over the next five years.

RECESSION'S EFFECT RUNS DEEP

Three years ago EBI concluded its annual industry overview report with the prediction that composite annual growth for the entire environmental industry would average 11 percent for five years, but that growth would be subject to two unknowns: regulations and the economy. Little did we know that the latter would play such a dampening role. Besides postponing environmental work and reducing demand for environmental services, the economy also delayed the evolution of regulation, the primary driver of the environmental industry.

The recession has affected the pace of regulation not only by imposing a thinly veiled "moratorium" on new regulation but more significantly by putting the squeeze on government budgets, particularly at the state level. State governmental departments are often the first line of enforcement, and there is evidence of some relaxation in state activities. In most constituencies, political emphasis has shifted in favor of the economy at the expense of the environment, although no politicians have spoken from platforms that are overtly anti-environmental.

Despite the recession, most industry analysts believe there is reason for environmental companies to be bullish, at least for the next five years. Like regulation, other industry drivers, such as fear of liability and the importance of cultivating a clean corporate image, will not disappear. But industry growth is no longer strong enough to carry all environmental companies. In the 1980s, companies thrived on the basis of good project management. In the 1990s, companies will only survive with the addition of good business management.

Solid waste management continues to be the largest and most mature environmental-industry segment, but it cannot rely on business as usual. The vast majority of the more than $28 billion in revenues result from collections (about 76 percent), but the operation of transfer stations and landfills represents growing proportions of revenues.

Declining landfill capacity increases transfer station business, where flatbed trailers are loaded from conventional garbage trucks, enabling large volumes of waste to be hauled over longer distances. Landfill shortages have understandably led to higher tipping fees, up 6 percent in the Northeast and 32 percent in the West from 1988 to 1990, according to a recent survey by the National Solid Wastes Management Association (Washington, D.C.). Landfill costs will continue to increase due to more stringent regulations, namely RCRA Subtitle D, which is expected to result in the closure of half of the country's 6,000 remaining landfills.

The trend toward fewer and larger landfills plays into the hands of the larger competitors, which historically have grown through acquisition. In fact, 80 percent of environmental-industry acquisitions from 1985 to 1990 were in solid waste, a total of nearly 1,400. And the binge doesn't appear to be over. Joan Berkowitz of Farkas & Berkowitz Co. (Washington, D.C.) said that with numerous small private operators still in business, there is "plenty of room for further consolidation." Berkowitz also notes that more companies are showing financial muscle, with 10 firms going public in the past couple of years.

Despite the advantages enjoyed by larger firms, the recession ensured that 1991 was no banner year in solid waste. Volumes of waste were down, particularly in the commercial/industrial sector, which provides almost 70 percent of collection revenues. Some companies suffered unexpectedly poor quarters, and overall operating margins of publicly traded companies in 1991 fell to 15 percent from 20 percent in 1990. EBJ Index company revenue was up 23 percent in 1991 (over four times our estimated total segment growth), highlighting the advantages of larger players, but acquisitions account for much of that revenue growth.

A key trend facing solid-waste companies is what William T. Lorenz & Co. calls a "major structural change in the solid-waste business." Solid waste's broad-based adoption of integrated waste management will divert more waste from landfills into recycling and waste-to-energy programs. Companies not offering alternatives to landfills will find it difficult to renew municipal contracts and compete for privatization contracts from the more than 25 percent of the business that still remains in the public sector. But integrated services don't come cheap, and the expense of adding recycling programs was a major factor in the erosion of earnings of many solid-waste leaders.

Resource recovery includes companies in postindustrial recycling, postconsumer recycling, waste-to-energy programs, and the recovery of chemicals or other materials from industrial wastes. Resource recovery experienced the largest revenue drop of any segment in 1991–92 as the market value of the materials recycled by the scrap and postconsumer businesses diminished, most by 20–50 percent.

The year 1991 was tough for manufacturing, making it doubly tough for recyclers already struggling with unstable demand for their recovered materials. Prices for virtually all materials plummeted as demand was weak and oversupply was commonplace. Prices paid by end-users, however, remained more than twice as high as prices paid by processors, lending credence to our assertion that processors are in the most stable sector of the recycling business. Niche players like Imco in aluminum cans, Allwaste in glass, and a number of firms in the established steel scrap business managed to scrape by.

Besides the creation of a manufacturing infrastructure to use recycled materials at home, a worldwide recovery is needed to rebuild demand as much of America's waste product go abroad. More than 6.6 million tons of waste paper was exported in 1991 (20 percent of that recovered), and it is consistently one of our top exports by volume. Numbers on domestic plastic recycling are elusive, but shipments of plastic waste overseas reached $100 million in 1991.

The waste-to-energy business has been up and down in the last few years. More than 100 projects have been canceled, but new projects under construction and in planning are expected to provide the added capacity to handle nearly 25 percent of municipal solid waste by the year 2000. Some projects have been put on hold, however, as municipalities await the results of the favored alternatives of source reduction and recycling. Waste-to-energy was a $2 billion market in 1991, with two firms, Wheelabrator and Ogden Projects, splitting about 40 percent of the market.

Chemical recovery is a blossoming business for a number of companies, and opportunities will continue to emerge. Horsehead Resource Development, a $70 million firm, recovers zinc from furnace dust. Regenex recycles industrial polymer waste and spent antifreeze into ethylene glycol for new antifreeze. Molten Metal Technology uses catalytic extraction to reclaim metals from a variety of waste streams. These few examples illustrate the growing opportunities for services and technology demanded as a result of land-ban regulations requiring further separation of chemical wastes.

Accelerated recovery of chemicals, more stringent regulations, and interstate transfer limitations pose a threat to companies in traditional forms of hazardous-waste management, a $13.7 billion business in 1991. Off-site services, construction and disposal associated with remediation, and on-site management of ongoing waste streams make up most of the chemical-waste market. Nuclear waste and medical waste each provide markets of over $1 billion. Business for disposal leaders Chemical Waste Management, Laidlaw, Rollins, USPCI, and others was fairly flat in 1991; and with some exceptions, prospects for 1992 are much the same. Growth will return with economic recovery, but forces changing the nature of this segment (discussed later) and the ability to diversify will be key to each company's success.

Environmental engineering/consulting was the only segment to maintain double-digit growth in 1991, but it flattened to only 4 percent in 1992. The market reached $14.2 billion in 1991. Gross revenues of the top 30 engineering/consulting (e/c) firms topped $5 billion, and the top 10 environmental contracting/construction firms topped $4 billion. However, the latter figure did not contribute entirely to the revenues in this segment.

The federal market showed the strongest growth, thanks mostly to cleanup agendas at the Department of Defense and the Department of Energy. These markets are partially responsible for introducing new competition into the e/c segment in the form of construction firms, defense contractors, and other diversifying companies. The municipal market was slow in 1991 due to financing problems from the recession. The recession also affected the industrial market, though more selectively and on a regional basis.

Industrial customers represent 62 percent of the e/c market, and some notable business trends are occurring in this sector. Major corporations are increasingly seeking national agreements with e/c firms. Examples of *Fortune*

100 companies cutting their environmental consultants from more than 50 down to fewer than 20 are not exceptional. Like other segments, the advantage is tilting in favor of larger national firms; but even tiny e/c companies can thrive in focused niches.

Competition for business will be the focus of the 1990s. Alan Farkas of Farkas Berkowitz & Co. comments that competition has gotten more "heterogeneous" in the 1990s. Distinct types of engineers and firms and their respective markets are blending together and also are having to take on new entrants from other industries. "With increased heterogeneity comes the basis for stronger competitive intensity," said Farkas. Although it is not yet prevalent, "we will see stronger competition in the years ahead."

A segment that has experienced intense competition is analytical services. An overcapacity of labs has made pricing pressure the main challenge for managers. The recession also has slowed demand, yielding a flat 1991 with revenues of $1.7 billion. Growth should return following some consolidation but will not near the rates of the mid-1980s.

We have traditionally viewed analytical services as a forerunner for the entire environmental industry. Most work in projects and services, as well as equipment purchases, follows some form of environmental testing. Rapid growth in the 1980s came ahead of other segments, and it stands to reason that other environmental services will follow a similar course. Overcapacity in the testing business could foreshadow oversupply in other services, leading to price pressures and growth rates below expectations.

Instrument manufacturing revenues grew to $2.1 billion. Instrumentation expenditures follow more of a regulatory and product development cycle than an economic one, contend manufacturers. Nevertheless, growth has slowed considerably over the past two years. New regulations will continue to provide markets for monitoring and analysis. Recent stormwater regulations maintained sales for many manufacturers.

About 57 percent of the market in analytical instruments is for laboratory use, estimates a report by Strategic Directions International Inc. (Los Angeles). Air analysis (24 percent), water analysis (12 percent), radiation, and others make up the rest. The report also estimates that the United States represents about half of the total global market.

The revenues of 25 publicly traded companies selling water treatment/infrastructure equipment grew 8 percent in 1991 despite flat capital expenditures by municipalities and very modest increases by industry. Construction costs make up more than half the expenditures in wastewater treatment systems (63 percent as estimated by a William T. Lorenz & Co. report), and much of these are not counted in the $12.9 billion we estimate for segment revenues.

Equipment, chemicals, repair, and specialized services represent most of the water infrastructure segment, but clearly much more is spent on water and wastewater management each year. A report by Richard Miller & Associates (Norcross, Ga.) puts the total market at over $30 billion—$6 billion for industrial capital expenditures, $12 billion for municipal capital expenditures, $5 billion for industrial operations and management (O&M), and $9 billion for municipal O&M. Obviously, a majority of these costs do not make it into the environmental industry.

Air pollution control is another equipment segment that has been flat recently as capital expenditure is postponed. The wait for final Clean Air Act regulations is an even more significant factor in holding off the anticipated burst in market growth. Consultants have been the first to benefit, but equipment manufacturers, installers, and materials providers all anticipate good times.

Asbestos abatement suffered the most dramatic losses of any environmental industry segment in 1991 but leveled off somewhat in 1992. Industry revenues plunged 25 percent in 1991, and the revenues of EBJ's 13 still-consolidating publicly traded firms were down 14 percent. The recession had a major impact on the asbestos industry, notably discretionary jobs not associated with renovation or demolition. Weakness in the property market also delayed work associated with commercial renovation.

The number of players also showed a sharp decline, with the number of $250,000 businesses falling from 1,500 to 700, according to Neil Wernick of Rifkin-Wernick Associates (Jenkintown, Penn.). Diversification into such areas as underground storage tank (UST) cleanup, indoor air pollution control, and lead paint abatement has been on many lips for the last few years but pursued successfully by relatively few firms. In 1991 the much-talked-about market for lead paint abatement was about $900 million, but it's an opportunity that's not yet quite ripe, said Wernick.

Waste-management equipment serves as a catchall segment for environmental products and technologies not specifically associated with water and air pollution control. The majority are purchased by generators, but some are used in the waste-management segments. Products include waste storage and containment units like drums, tanks, and liners, and waste handling and compression equipment like protective clothing and heavy equipment. Products for spill response, indoor air quality, noise abatement, and occupational safety also are included. The category with the highest growth potential may be environmental software and information management systems.

Diversified companies are defined as companies deriving a clear majority of their revenues from the environmental industry, but with a majority of those revenues not residing in a particular segment. Air & Water Technologies serves as a good example. In 1991 it completed purchase of Metcalf & Eddy, the number-three engineering/consulting firm, and maintained its ownership in Research-Cottrell, the number-one seller of air pollution control (APC) equipment in the United States last year.

Environmental industry giant Waste Management Inc., with revenues topping $7.5 billion, may yet migrate from segment 2 to segment 13. With links to Chemical Waste Management in segment 3, Brand in segment 4, SEC Donohue and Rust International in segment 7, its own recycling subsidiary, Recycle America, and waste-to-energy leader Wheelabrator in segment 8, and National Seal, the number-two landfill lining company, in segment 11, Waste Management has nearly all the bases covered. No other company has cast its net as wide as Waste Management, but no doubt more than a few business plans call for diversification.

Conglomerates continue to play an increasingly important role in the environmental industry, as evidenced by the growth of firms tracked in segment 14 of the EBJ Index. From 8 companies two years ago to 17 last year, up to 25 major corporations are listed today. Originally we defined environmental conglomerates as multimillion-dollar corporations with divisions or subsidiaries generating at least $25 million in environmental revenues.

Conglomerates own a number of top engineering firms, including Radian Corp. (No. 11 on our engineering/consulting list; owned by Hartford Steam Boiler), Environmental Science & Engineering (No. 13, owned by Cilcorp), and United Engineers & Constructors (No. 5 on our contracting/construction list; owned by Raytheon Co.). Publicly traded construction conglomerates include Fluor (No. 2 on our contracting/construction list), Dresser Industries (owns No. 3, M. W. Kellogg, as well as the No. 5 APC equipment firm, Lodge Cottrell), Foster Wheeler (No. 4 and in the top five in waste-to-energy), and Morrison-Knudsen (No. 7).

Other segments also were represented. Alcoa controlled 41 percent of the aluminum-can recycling market, and some paper manufacturers entered the wastepaper business. Hewlett-Packard, Perkin Elmer, and Varian are all significant players in the environmental instrumentation market. Corning owns Enseco, the nation's leading environmental testing business, with $82 million in revenues in 1991. Union Pacific owns USPCI, a $250 million hazardous waste management firm, and is one of a handful of railroad companies in the waste business (Conrail and Burlington being two other notables). Westinghouse has been making moves recently, selling its engineering/consulting subsidiary and going ahead with aggressive plans in the hazardous waste disposal, incineration, and remediation construction businesses.

Chemical industry leaders DuPont, Dow, Amoco, Rhone-Poulenc, and others are leveraging their expertise into the hazardous-waste business. DuPont and Dow have contrasting strategies, however, for subsidiaries that will both top $50 million this year. Ted Fischer, president of DuPont Environmental Remediation Services, says that his company is mainly "servicing internal needs" and endeavoring to do project management at all DuPont sites. Barry Naft, president of Dow's subsidiary, AWD Technologies, says its goal is not to serve its parent but be a leader in the commercial market, also an eventual goal shared by Fischer. Both companies surely benefit from the technical expertise, capital base, and R&D budgets of their parents.

OVER THE HORIZON

The year 1991 was unpleasant for environmental-industry executives, and the burning question remains: Was it just a hitch in the growth curve, or a sign of times to come? How does the environmental industry as we know it fit into the "sustainable economy" envisioned by futurists and embraced by progressive policymakers?

The question that will determine whether we move in the direction of a more sustainable economy is: will our economic system ever fully value our ecological system? Environmental regulation is the first step in this long process. Internalizing environmental costs into the price of all our goods and services, however, will take more than just a politically popular paradigm shift.

The writing on the wall is that the environmental industry will be folded into the strategic development of industry in general, the result being that some services will be absorbed and some will remain distinct.

Although the recession has taken a toll on the environmental industry, many companies anticipate a return to business as usual. Growth will, of course, pick up for environmental companies, as portrayed in Table 2. Results in 1991 were "a recession-induced blip," agreed Alan Farkas. In fact, there may even be a recovery-induced spike in the curve, but it is unlikely to be big or sudden enough to be noticed. There will be some releasing of pent-up demand, but only in those segments driven by compliance and liability, like remediation and air and water quality. Farkas also agreed with our assertion that the environmental industry would, in general, be "a lagging indicator" coming out of the recession.

The environmental industry will make up for lost time, but forces are already at work that will contribute to a gradual deceleration in most segments. Analysis of net revenues in publicly traded environmental companies in the

Table 2 Projected Growth and Revenues
for the Environmental Industry

Industry segment	Avg. ann. growth (%)	Projected revenue ($ billions)					
		1992	1993	1994	1995	1996	1997
1. Analytical services	5	1.8	1.8	2.0	2.1	2.2	2.3
2. Solid waste management	5	28.2	29.8	32.0	33.8	35.7	36.9
3. Hazardous waste management	6	14.6	15.4	16.6	17.7	18.6	19.5
4. Asbestos abatement	1	3.1	3.2	3.2	3.3	3.3	3.3
5. Water infrastructure	5	13.0	13.7	14.5	15.3	16.0	16.6
6. Water utilities	3	21.8	22.4	23.2	24.0	24.9	25.5
7. Environmental consulting	8	14.2	15.2	16.7	18.1	19.4	20.9
8. Resource recovery	8	16.1	17.1	18.6	20.2	21.9	23.5
9. Instrument manufacturing	7	1.8	1.9	2.1	2.3	2.5	2.6
10. Air pollution control	10	5.4	5.9	6.7	7.4	8.2	8.9
11. Waste management equipment	6	11.5	12.2	13.3	14.1	14.8	15.3
12. Environmental energy sources	14	2.2	2.4	2.8	3.2	3.7	4.2
TOTAL	**6**	**133.7**	**141.2**	**151.7**	**161.5**	**171.1**	**179.5**
Composite annual growth rate (%)			3.9	5.6	7.4	6.5	6.0	4.9

Source: Environmental Business International Inc.

ENVIRONMENTAL INDUSTRY SEGMENTS

Analytical Services   Environmental laboratory testing and services (sampling, lab pack)

Solid Waste Management   Collection, transportation, transfer stations, disposal, landfill ownership/management

Hazardous Waste Management   Remediation contracting, on-site and off-site management/construction/ownership of TSDR (transport, storage, disposal, and recycling) facilities, transportation, industrial services/cleaning: tanks and facilities (includes the above for medical, nuclear, and SQG waste)

Asbestos Abatement   Cleanup of asbestos contaminated material/sites/buildings

Water Infrastructure/Treatment   Infrastructure/treatment equipment for wastewater treatment and water purification. Includes delivery and discharge equipment such as pumps, pipes, and valves and treatment materials such as chemicals, carbon, separation, biological, thermal, and oxidation treatment equipment— plus maintenance and repairs

Water Utilities   Private and public sector water delivery

Environmental Engineering/Consulting   Permitting, compliance, design, project management, O&M, audits, risk analysis, site assessment, impact statements, industrial hygiene, litigation support, pollution prevention, etc.

Resource Recovery   Postindustrial recovery/recycling/scrap, postconsumer recycling, waste-to-energy

Instrument Manufacturing   Analytical testing/lab instruments, continuous monitoring instruments, portable test kits, hand-held or field instruments

Air Pollution Control Equipment   Stationary source emission control equipment

Waste Management Equipment   Equipment for handling, storing, or transporting solid, liquid, or hazardous waste and recyclable materials. Also includes information systems and software

Environmental Energy Sources   Solar, wind, geothermal, small-scale hydro, efficiency

EBJ Index over the past three years shows a leveling off and even a halting of growth. As mentioned, these results are not entirely attributable to the recession. Now it is time for the wake-up call: The sum total of trend analysis in each of the 12 environmental industry segments shows a deceleration of growth and an inevitable, gradual diminishment of the environmental industry as we know it today.

THE WRITING ON THE WALL

Remediation of existing sites, no matter how long the list, is clearly a business with a finite life cycle. Undoubtedly, new standards of cleanup or containment will also be hammered out, which will influence the lifespan of the business. Does anyone really believe that the University of Tennessee's projected costs of $750 billion to remediate the nation's contaminated sites to current standards will be spent?

The remediation market will be strong for at least a decade and maybe two; but like other cleanup markets such as asbestos abatement and underground storage tanks, it has to end sometime. We are making more USTs (albeit better structured and monitored), but we certainly are not making much asbestos and, hopefully, not many more Superfund sites.

Also affecting the hazardous-waste management segment are the already diminishing volumes of hazardous waste to be managed. A number of large-quantity generators have made immense strides in cutting waste flows by merely correcting design, operation, and material inefficiencies that did not account for environmental costs.

Northrop Aircraft Division (Hawthorne, Calif.) is one example of many companies from many industries that are in the midst of successful waste minimization programs. By mid-1991, Northrop reduced its hazardous waste by 50 percent from 1989 and aims for a 90-percent reduction from 1989 levels by 1996 while increasing production. Gary Freeman, Northrop's deputy for environmental management, admits that the first half of the reductions will be the easiest, most resulting from correcting what now appear to be glaring inefficiencies that were once standard operations. Large, avoided disposal costs have kept management in support of going ahead with the more expensive waste minimization investments needed to achieve Northrop's goals, according to Freeman.

While Northrop is by no means unique, the majority of industrial companies have yet to make even the easy waste reductions; however, these companies will increasingly reduce hazardous-waste volumes available for commercial management in the next few years. Off-site services will always have a market in the form of reclamation, recycling, incineration, and, to a lesser extent, storage and landfilling, but the volumes available for commercial handling will be smaller. It is said that the manufacturing sector rebuilds its factories every 20 years, and the new generation already coming on line shows a significant decrease in waste output.

Hazardous waste management is an area in which new technology can hurt business for vendors—not only by diminishing waste volumes and facilitating alternative treatment, but by helping to internalize waste management for generators. A company will choose to obtain a product to treat its own waste, particularly if the product can be built into a new facility, rather than incur the ongoing expense of hiring a hazardous-waste management firm. It is no secret that disposal firms in both hazardous and solid waste have not been strong promoters of waste minimization.

Analyst Hugh Holman of Alex. Brown & Sons sees the 1990s as the decade in which technology will significantly alter the hazardous-waste industry. Besides the obvious trend toward avoiding the generation of pollution in the first place, Holman anticipates a shift from physical waste management to chemistry-based approaches, anticipating that the segment in the year 2000 will resemble the chemical industry more than the hazardous waste management business of today. Another trend is the "unbundling" of waste streams as both technology and regulation increasingly target specific wastes.

By the same token, waste reduction will affect solid waste management firms, but reductions in volumes will neither be as easy nor as immediately apparent. A variety of studies, blinded to some extent by past numbers, project per capita generation of municipal solid waste (MSW) to grow steadily over the next 20 years. EPA's numbers indicate that Americans generated 2.7 lb of MSW per person per day in 1960, growing to 3.8 lb in 1986 and 4 lb in 1990. EPA's projections for the future are for 4.4 lb in 2000 and 4.9 lb in 2010.

Not all those who look at the market agree. A recent solid-waste report by William T. Lorenz & Co. (Concord, N.H.) states: "The actual growth rate in per capita generation, with all source reduction and waste minimization programs in place, could be even slower than forecast by the EPA. It is even conceivable that the daily generation rate could actually decline between now and the year 2000." We agree and even forecast a reduction in the rate in our 30-year model. Products and consumer habits are changing rapidly enough to reverse the trend in this decade. The United States currently generates *twice* as much MSW per capita as Germany, Japan, France, and the United Kingdom.

Equally important to solid waste companies is the shift in how the waste will be managed. Landfilling peaked in 1985 at 83 percent, according to the Lorenz report, and the MSW management mix moved to 68 percent landfill, 17 percent waste-to-energy incineration, and 15 percent recycled in 1990. By 1995 Lorenz predicts that landfilling will be down to 55 percent, waste-to-energy up to 22 percent, recycling up to 22 percent, with composting starting to play a role. The consensus top end for recycling is 25–30 percent of MSW. Some proponents believe that composting could eventually manage almost half the waste stream, but most projections put composting's share at 6–10 percent in the year 2000.

Many solid waste management companies have undertaken the shift to integrated waste management services by offering recycling and by increasing their interest in the waste-to-energy business. Although volumes of waste may not grow as many expect, prices to manage each unit volume will surely rise. Revenues in the solid waste segment will continue to grow, though portions of revenues of individual companies will gravitate toward resource recovery. Despite maintaining revenue growth, the capital expense for industry leaders to create the infrastructure of integrated services demanded by the public and governments will show up in lowered earnings throughout the decade.

Companies in the postconsumer and postindustrial recycling side of resource recovery will benefit from the creation of another infrastructure: the one that uses recycled materials as a feedstock. Recyclers have been perpetually plagued by unstable demand, and thus unstable prices, for their material.

Paper provides a good example of the cycle recovered materials go through. In 1990, 79 million tons of paper and paperboard products were produced in the United States, and 37 percent, or 29 million tons, of scrap paper was collected (6.5 million tons of this was exported). Old newspapers represented 6 million tons of the scrap paper collected in 1990, but only 1.8 million tons were bought by newsprint producers. At the time, operating mills in North America had the capacity to recycle only 3.6 million tons of old newspapers. No wonder it wasn't difficult for buyers to convince sellers of the "glut" and receive rock-bottom prices.

The addition of recycling capacity, partially in response to oversupply, has been dramatic recently, and an additional capacity for more than 3.7 million tons of old newspapers was completed by the end of 1992. The pulp and paper industry is also slowly discovering that, once de-inking and other equipment is capitalized, making recycled paper can save money.

State recycled-content laws, however, will be the strongest long-term driver behind the addition of recycling capacity. Since most laws requiring certain percentages of recycled content will be introduced in stages on into the next century, and virtually every state and possibly the federal government plans such measures, demand for paper looks likely to stabilize for recyclers.

Chemical recovery promises to be a mainstay of the resource-recovery business, although it does not currently represent a large portion of resource-recovery revenues. Much of the business will be transferred from the hazardous-waste management segment as reclamation technologies take hold for many hazardous waste streams.

Revenues for the resource-recovery segment should average double-digit growth well into the next century. As mentioned, a significant portion will be cannibalized from other segments, but the relative value of reclaimed materials will also increase appreciably.

Water infrastructure and water utility companies will not encounter diminishing demand for clean water but will reach a level of stable growth. The nation's infrastructure is in need of repair and this will continue to drive the market for equipment and specialty services. Construction of new treatment facilities has been flat, but an eventually upgraded Clean Water Act, along with more funding, will spur new secondary and tertiary treatment systems. New infrastructure projects for using reclaimed and gray water should also emerge in the next century. In the meantime, a number of equipment manufacturers should find receptive international markets as water quality issues penetrate the developing world.

CONCLUSION

Technical services in the environmental industry have historically been focused on righting the environmental wrongs of the past. We have not made up for 100 years of industrial neglect in a decade, and much work in waste management and cleanup remains; but there is only so much time remaining in which we can make up for those years of neglect. Eventually the balance of work will shift to applying technology and services to mitigating future environmental problems rather than cleaning up old ones. It is up to the environmental industry to lead the shift or find itself being absorbed by industry rather than complementing it.

Acknowledgments

Environmental Business International, located in San Diego, California (619-295-7685), has been the nation's leading research and publishing firm focusing on the environmental industry since 1988. As in any research project, we first compile all existing data, and we are grateful to all those who have cooperated with our research efforts. Specific citations to data are made in the text, but industry figures are mostly the product of primary research by the author and the staff of EBI.

The U.S. Environmental Industry and the Global Marketplace for Environmental Goods and Services

Donald L. Connors • *Michael D. Bliss* • *Jack Archer*

INTRODUCTION

For many Americans, and particularly for those in the environmental movement, "business" and "the environment" have for too long appeared to be on
opposite sides of the debate over environmental quality. In this view, business
has been seen as part of the problem. Indeed the U.S. approach to environmental regulation over the past two decades has in large part focused on laws
and regulations affecting the way businesses in the United States operate.

We want to suggest in this chapter that the time is ripe for a new way of
thinking about the relationship between business and the environment. We
suggest that business is an important part of the solution to global environmental problems. Whatever once were the merits of the view that saw business
and environmental interests as ultimately antithetical, we believe that the time
has come to recognize and seek institutional support for the important positive
relationships between business and the goal of sound and sustainable global
environmental management.

There are two critical elements that must be taken account of in thinking
about the relationship between business and the environment: (1) the U.S.
environmental industry itself, which is made up of enterprises whose business
is achieving sound environmental management and who, in doing this work,
create economic growth and jobs; and (2) the fact that the United States was
the first, among the world's nations, to get into the business of environmental
protection in a serious and systematic way, and that accordingly as a nation we
have an unprecedented fund of know-how and experience available to the
nations of the world.

In short, there is, for the U.S. environmental industry, an extraordinary market opportunity presented by the growing global interest in sound environmental management and sustainable development. If this opportunity can be effectively realized, we will have achieved *both* economic growth *and* increased protection of the global environment. We think this is a classic win-win situation. A national trade association for the U.S. environmental industry, the Environmental Business Council of the U.S. Inc. (EBC-U.S.), has recently been established to provide support for and implement this analysis by working with the U.S. environmental industry, government, universities, and nonprofit organizations. There has also been established, to work in conjunction with EBC-U.S., a not-for-profit organization, the International Environmental Business and Technology Cooperation Institute. The institute will work to foster the use of appropriate environmental management technologies and strategies globally and to implement these goals through private sector, business-to-business initiatives.

We believe that EBC-U.S., the institute, and, more important, the analysis of the relationship between the U.S. environmental industry and the goal of improved global environmental management that informs them represent an important new way of thinking about the relationship between business and the environment. We also believe that this analysis deserves the support of all those interested in the goal of sustainable development.

This chapter analyzes the historic opportunity for the export of U.S. environmental goods and services over the next 20 years and describes a strategy for linking business initiatives and government programs through the catalyst of a national association for the U.S. environmental industry. This strategy takes its force from a variety of powerful economic, political, and social trends currently at work in the United States and worldwide. It harnesses and directs existing federal and state governmental programs, proposed initiatives of the Clinton administration, legislative proposals in Congress, and the historic expertise of the U.S. environmental industry to create an unprecedented opportunity for the United States to become a leader in the global marketplace for environmental goods and services, a marketplace that is projected to undergo tremendous growth over the next 20 years.

The U.S. environmental industry includes companies that manufacture products or provide services in the environmental and energy areas, as well as educational and research institutions. It has for some time existed in relative obscurity. Yet, there are around 60,000 environmental companies concentrated in as many as 15 "clusters" throughout the United States that, in 1991, had revenues of $120 billion. We believe that the U.S. environmental industry will have a critical and expanding role to play in the future in both protecting the environment and promoting economic growth.

The continuing development and adoption of less polluting and more efficient products, manufacturing processes, and services is a critical strategy for accommodating, without irrevocably altering, the planetary life-support system and the doubling of global population, as well as the five-fold increase in economic activity projected by the mid-twenty-first century. Industry analysts also project that the worldwide market for environmental goods and services will grow by 51 percent, to $408 billion, by 1996. America's world-class universities, vigorous environmental regulations, sophisticated high-technology manufacturing and environmental service companies, highly skilled labor force, and capable management all give us a significant competitive advantage in the industry. However, our dominant share of the global environmental marketplace is slipping, and important opportunities are being missed. We must encourage environmental and energy technology innovation, improve its diffusion, and facilitate the export of environmental goods and services.

STRATEGIC OPPORTUNITIES FOR THE U.S. ENVIRONMENTAL INDUSTRY

Several developments have created a unique opportunity for the U.S. environmental industry to expand, but there are obstacles to overcome first.

The Global Environmental Market

According to a number of experts who track the environmental industry, the current dominance of U.S. companies is giving way to competitive pressures from European as well as Japanese environmental companies as the global environmental market develops.[1]

The global market for environmental goods and services is substantial, and it is predicted to undergo tremendous growth in the next 20 years. According to studies prepared by the Organization for Economic Cooperation and Development (OECD), the size of the worldwide environmental market, which in 1990 was estimated to be $200 billion, will reach $300 billion by the year 2000, making environmental protection one of the world's fastest growing industries.[2] The *Environmental Business Journal* (EBJ), a newsletter that tracks the U.S. industry, estimated the size of the 1991 worldwide environmental market at $270 billion, based on analysis of 12 environmental sectors. EBJ projects a 51-percent growth in that market, to $408 billion, by 1996.

Grant Ferrier, the editor of EBJ, believes that although the United States, with about 44 percent of the world environmental market, is exhibiting the slower growth typical of a mature industry, he estimates U.S. share of this market will grow about seven percent annually until 1996, while environmental industries in other countries serving the global market, including Canada, Mexico, Latin America, eastern Europe, and Southeast Asia, will grow at double-digit rates.

According to Ferrier's estimates, revenues from the U.S. environmental industry, which accounted for 970,000 jobs in 1991, will account for 280,000 additional jobs in 1996. Ferrier also estimates that in 1992 the U.S. market share of the international environmental industry was 5 percent. He believes that this share could be increased to 15 percent with a comprehensive government–business program to develop this market. According to Ferrier's estimates, implementing such a program could create 312,000 new U.S. jobs in the environmental industry by 1997.

Over the next five years, Ferrier estimates that the U.S. share of the worldwide market will drop from 44 to 40 percent, while western Europe's share will rise from 30 to 32 percent. Japan, which Ferrier estimates had about 8 percent of the 1991 global environmental market, is projected to remain approximately at that level through 1996.

Only a coordinated strategy for the U.S. environmental industry will reverse its predicted decline in the global market. We believe that a failure to act now may result in the loss of existing and future market share, such as the United States has experienced in the consumer electronics, machine tools, textiles, and other once-powerful industries.

Long-Term Market Trends

The global environmental market is driven by the following factors:

- Expanding population and economic activity, which use more resources and create more pollution and waste
- Heightened public awareness of environmental issues and growing demand for environmental quality
- Business recognition that proactive environmental management, pollution prevention, and energy efficiency are basic elements of business strategy
- Heightened business concern about environmental liability, corporate image, and pressure from investors[3]
- Linkage of trade and the environment, such as that occurring in the North American Free Trade Agreement (NAFTA)[4]
- Linkage of official development assistance (ODA) with export of U.S. environmental goods and services

- Future multilateral trade negotiations, such as the General Agreement on Tariffs and Trade (GATT)
- International agreements, such as the Montreal Protocol for Chlorofluoro-carbons (CFCs), those adopted at the Earth Summit in Rio in 1992, and others that will be adopted as the extent of global environmental problems is better understood

The initiatives adopted at the Rio summit are especially important for their impact on the global environmental marketplace. Six action points resulted from the summit, at which 172 nations were represented. These action points were

1. to adopt Agenda 21, a comprehensive program for sustainable development
2. to direct the United Nations to establish a Commission on Sustainable Development to oversee implementation of Agenda 21
3. to adopt the Rio Declaration, a nonbinding statement of 27 broad principles for guiding environmental policy
4. to adopt a legally binding treaty to safeguard biological diversity and genetic resources
5. to adopt a legally binding treaty on climate change
6. to adopt a statement of forest principles

The Commission on Sustainable Development has been established by the U.N. (December 1992), and 53 members have been elected to serve (February 1993). The commission's first meeting was held in June 1993, and it focused on ways in which an international environmental management system can be developed to implement Agenda 21.

Among the specific goals of Agenda 21 is the transfer of environmentally sound technology. Chapter 34 specifically recognizes that such technology transfer must be built on joint efforts by business and government, with the goal of building global capacity for sound environmental management ("capacity building") through education, training, and technology cooperation.

This mechanism for achieving the goals of Agenda 21 through global technology cooperation and capacity building, to be implemented by a partnership of private enterprise and government, offers the U.S. environmental industry an extraordinary opportunity to participate in and shape the new global environmental management structures and institutions that will emerge over the next decade.

Related to these developments are foreign-policy analyses suggesting that the U.S. foreign-aid program, which historically was Cold War based, be restructured to address global environmental and sustainable development needs. Such a program—which has been called the Sustainable Development Initiative—would also provide vigorous government assistance for the export of U.S. environmental goods and services.[5] The U.S. congressional Office of Technology Assessment (OTA) undertook an assessment on trade and competitiveness implications of environmental policies for U.S. industry. In connection with this assessment, the OTA prepared a background paper examining the increasing potential for linkages between Official Development Assistance (ODA) and environmental export promotion. A related OTA background paper, "Trade and Environment: Conflicts and Opportunities," was issued in May 1992.

Collectively, the Rio initiatives and the other factors set out above will help shape the global business environment for the environmental industry. These and other factors accelerate the demand for improved environmental management, which in turn creates the need for environmental goods, services, education, training, information, and advice.

Over time, these forces and newer, incentive-based regulatory programs will lead to new environmental regulations and a favorable climate in many nations for environmental investments. This will result in increased business for the U.S. environmental industry if the necessary resources are mobilized so that the industry is able to (1) maintain and enhance its edge in many environmental technologies and (2) identify and take advantage of the global opportunity that lies ahead for the sale of goods and services abroad. These business opportunities will also be realized by environmental organizations establishing business-to-business relationships with decision makers from other nations.

Simply stated, economic opportunities will be created by the transfer of the experience, training, and technology needed for sustainable development from those who have it to those who require it. The Rio summit described this process as technology cooperation, which relies principally on private initiatives and depends in large measure on business-to-business relationships between firms in the developed world and firms in the developing world. This cooperation will be critically enhanced by support and cooperation from governments and other institutions, including multilateral lending agencies, like the World Bank and the regional development banks.

Competitive Advantage of the U.S. Environmental Industry

In his important book, *The Competitive Advantage of Nations* (Free Press, New York, 1990), Michael Porter of the Harvard Business School has identified clusters of competitive industries, such as the U.S. environmental industry, as a critical feature of national and international economic competitiveness. In this five-year study of 10 leading trading nations, Professor Porter concludes that the traditional sources of competitiveness have been superseded by the changing nature of international competition.

These clusters of nationally or internationally competitive industries are groupings of industries linked together through customer, supplier, or other relationships. Once a cluster forms, the industries that comprise it become mutually reinforcing. Aggressive rivalry in one industry spreads to other industries in the cluster through spin-offs or related diversification. Information flows freely, and innovation spreads rapidly through the relationships among customers and suppliers. Institutions such as colleges, universities, and public infrastructure adapt to cluster needs. Through a cumulative process that often occurs over several decades, and has occurred with the U.S. environmental industry, the state or nation becomes a unique repository of specialized expertise, technology, and institutions for competing in a given field.

CHALLENGES FACING THE
U.S. ENVIRONMENTAL INDUSTRY

Access to International Markets

Many U.S. environmental firms lack both experience and established customer bases in the international market. On the other hand, such firms often possess the environmental technology, the expertise, and the scientific and management skills needed abroad. As we have pointed out, U.S. preeminence in the environmental industry is based on more than 20 years of national experience under the most demanding environmental regulations in the world. Further, U.S. spending on environmental goods and services is estimated to be between 2 and 3 percent of GDP, a figure that no other nation approaches.

This lack of experience presents obstacles to American firms seeking to do business in the international marketplace. Some of these obstacles are as follow:

- Many U.S. firms are reluctant to consider export prospects and voluntarily exclude themselves from new markets because they perceive exporting to be too risky, complicated, or not profitable.[6]

- International firms and governments that might be customers are subject to different environmental laws and regulations, as well as different technical standards, than those prevailing in the United States. For instance, the ISO 9000 standard adopted by the European Community is also being adopted by a number of other non-EC nations. Many U.S. companies are unfamiliar with this and other international standards—and their implications.

- Nationalized enterprises, cartel-like organization, labor-union participation, political and governmental influence, and difficulties in penetrating traditional networks of referrals and reciprocal trading patterns may in effect bar entry to American environmental firms.

- Identifying and gaining access to key decision makers may often require social, commercial, political, and personal contacts that new American entrants in foreign markets often lack.

- Financing is difficult to obtain, while foreign competitors often have attractive (often government-sponsored) financing support. Further, learning how to effectively utilize the various trade-financing mechanisms available from, among others, the Departments of State and Commerce, USAID, the EPA, and the Export–Import Bank is difficult and time-consuming.

- Putting together the full package of goods and services that potential customers need may require teaming up with other suppliers. U.S. firms with expertise in a particular area of environmental services will often need to provide complementary services (for instance, education and training, which could be provided in coordination with an academic or governmental training institute) in order to provide effective and useful programs in a foreign context. Moreover, U.S. firms will be in competition with business firms and governmental enterprises from other countries seeking to sell environmental goods and services abroad, sometimes in an integrated, well-funded "team" approach.

- Access to foreign firms and governments is often best obtained through centralized "official" trade associations, particularly in Latin American and Eastern European countries with a history of centrally organized states.

- In many cases, bureaucrats will either have sole control or a veto over purchases of environmental goods and services. Thus, close personal contacts will often enhance success.

The U.S. environmental industry needs a central voice to address these problems. Moreover, the Clinton administration has indicated its interest in using environmental exports as one of the critical industries for economic growth and the generation of new jobs. However, if this interest is to bear fruit, the private sector must organize itself to effectively shape government policies and programs.

We believe that a nationally organized, highly mobilized U.S. environmental industry can be very helpful in reaching the Clinton administration's goals to expand the number of high-wage jobs in our economy and to promote better environmental management globally. By increasing the export of

U.S. environmental technologies, products, and services, we can dramatically and quickly expand employment in the U.S. industry. More important, this growth would occur in areas of the nation (e.g., California and the Northeast) that have been hard hit during the recent recession and the defense cutbacks. Our estimates, based on research provided by the *Environmental Business Journal,* is that by 1996 approximately 200,000 jobs will be created in the U.S. environmental industry serving the domestic market. We believe an aggressive government–industry program of export promotion of environmental goods and services, including the activities we propose, could create an additional 100,000 to 300,000 jobs.

Technological Competitiveness

According to the World Resources Institute,[7] many industrial countries are now devoting larger amounts of research and development resources to the search for new environmental technologies, not only to solve environmental problems at home but also to strengthen the competitive position of their industries internationally. In the United States, however, where national security has dominated the technological agenda for half a century, public priorities have been slower to shift. Despite the U.S. head start in environmental protection and technology, Germany, Japan, and other OECD countries have gained an edge in many environmental technologies, such as air pollution equipment. In these countries, industry and government often cooperate in developing advanced technologies, including those with potentially critical environmental advantages.

Many in the environmental industry believe that their technological progress is being impeded by a lack of direction in public policy. Many also believe that government regulatory policy often inhibits innovative solutions. We believe, however, that there are two additional factors that in fact inhibit the environmental industry's ability to maintain and improve its competitive advantage.

First, the lack of a long-term technology development vision in U.S. environmental policy casts a fundamental uncertainty over investment strategy in U.S. industry and has erected barriers to environmental technology innovation. In this regard, we believe there are substantial opportunities for employing defense-related expertise and technology to provide both structural assistance to the nation's defense-conversion program and to stimulate advances in environmental technology.

An extensive study published in 1991 by the EPA's Technology Innovation and Economics Committee concluded that the barriers in state and federal environmental and compliance policies are slowing technology innovation for environmental purposes. The study, which involved stakeholders in the public and private sectors, recommends major areas for improvement and concludes that fundamental changes to the environmental regulatory system will also be needed to encourage technology innovation.[8]

But innovation alone is insufficient if the opportunities for commercialization and environmental protection in the domestic and international markets are to be realized. A second factor also must be involved: the diffusion of technology, which is accomplished by the spread and adaptation of a technical idea following early commercial use. This diffusion can be accomplished by such activities as technical assistance, publications, training, licensing policies, and other technology transfer programs. A clear government policy must be adopted and implemented for improving technology diffusion. In a recent report, the EPA's Technology Innovation and Economics Committee concluded that the environmental regulatory system could expand environmental progress and improve economic competitiveness if processes that diffuse environmentally beneficial technologies are used to effectively complement regulations. The report makes several important policy recommendations, including, among others, making diffusion an EPA mission by building relationships with industry, supporting research, and expanding support for the international diffusion of environmental technologies to help meet U.S. environmental and competitiveness objectives.[9]

The U.S. environmental industry, working cooperatively with the federal and state governments, can play an effective role in encouraging and facilitating innovation and diffusion of environmental and energy technology. Fortunately, some American leaders in and out of government are beginning to address these technological and economic challenges. Moves are afoot in Congress to create national initiatives to support environmental research and development and to stimulate technological advances. If properly designed and implemented, with strong input from a national industry association, such initiatives could effectively support the export of U.S. environmental goods and services into the global marketplace.

LOCAL AND REGIONAL ENVIRONMENTAL ASSOCIATIONS

A number of local environmental-industry associations have been organized across the United States over the past several years. One of these is the Environmental Business Council (EBC), headquartered in Boston, an association of environmental and energy firms organized to foster the development of an effective and competitive environmental industry and to enhance and maintain a clean and productive environment.

The New England EBC's mission is to bring member organizations together with public- and private-sector organizations throughout the world to promote business development, resource protection, and modern environmental management for industry and government. To carry out its mission, the New England EBC conducts member activities and has organized committees that offer programs ranging from seminars on human-resource issues to international business development.

The Agreement of Cooperation, which the New England EBC recently entered into with Mexico's industrial trade association, CONCAMIN, illustrates how an organized U.S. environmental industry can collaborate with industry in other nations in developing new market opportunities within the context of the international movement toward sustainable development. Under this agreement (which the New England EBC entered into at the invitation of CONCAMIN), the New England EBC assists CONCAMIN and its member companies to implement modern environmental management through information transfer, educational programs, training, and technology cooperation. By the end of 1992, nearly $100 million in contracts for new business had been committed or was under proposal. The New England EBC is currently working to replicate this Mexican initiative in Canada, Latin America, Poland, and Eastern Europe.

Other local environmental-industry associations include the Oregon Environmental Technology Association (OETA) and the California Environmental Technology Partnership (CETP). OETA, which was founded in 1991 to more effectively address the unique opportunities and challenges facing the environmental industry, is committed to providing effective and responsible environmental management, products, and services that enhance economic and business objectives. OETA is also committed to working with other organizations in establishing the Northwest, and the United States, as the world's primary supplier of environmental goods and services.

CETP, created in 1992 by California Governor Pete Wilson, is a cooperative effort organized by the California Environmental Protection Agency and the California Trade and Commerce Agency (formerly the Department of Commerce). Its primary mission is to involve state government, industry, academia, financial institutions, and public-interest groups in efforts to support the California environmental industry and to maintain and expand the state's strong position in the national and global environmental market.

Other state and regional associations have been established in the past few years or are currently being organized. These associations indicate the strength of the U.S. environmental industry in the various regional clusters and represent an important resource for implementing this strategy for domestic economic development and improved management of the global environment.

U.S. GOVERNMENTAL PROGRAMS AND INITIATIVES:
THE NEED FOR STRONG INDUSTRY LEADERSHIP

Government policies and programs on a number of fronts are necessary for the continued vitality and growth of the U.S. environmental industry. The industry's current strong position is due, in significant part, to the advanced state of federal and state environmental regulatory requirements. This, as Michael Porter has pointed out, has been a key ingredient in creating the competitiveness of the American environmental industry. As Professor Porter also points out, formal government programs on other levels, including export assistance and financing, are critical to enabling this key cluster to maintain its competitiveness advantage.

At the federal level, there are a number of existing programs and initiatives to support the growth of the U.S. environmental industry and the export of U.S. environmental goods and services. Similarly, there are many comparable programs on the state level, such as in California and Massachusetts. We believe that such government support is essential. We also believe that to be truly effective, this initiative needs to be shaped and directed in a partnership with the private sector.

Federal programs and initiatives supporting the U.S. environmental industry currently suffer from lack of focus and coordination. The following are examples of some of these programs:[10]

- The Agency for International Development (AID) has allocated about 9 percent of its total funding (or approximately $600 million) for energy and environmental projects. Many observers feel that these projects have been a low priority for AID.

- The Department of Energy (DOE) undertakes or coordinates numerous export programs for energy technologies and provides technical assistance in several countries, including Mexico, Thailand, Egypt, India, and China.

- The Environmental Protection Agency (EPA) has several technology cooperation activities, including an international clearinghouse for environmental technologies, as well as training programs. The EPA also is currently developing new export initiatives, including the U.S. TIES program (U.S. Technology for International Environmental Solutions), which provides information, testing, demonstration projects, and research and development in environmental technology.[11]

- The Trade and Development Agency (TDA) funds feasibility studies for energy and environmental infrastructure projects and undertakes other market development activities.

- The Export–Import Bank (Eximbank) provides loans, guarantees, and insurance to finance U.S. exports. Eximbank has funded a number of energy-related loans.

- The Overseas Private Investment Corporation (OPIC) provides political-risk insurance, loans, and other guarantees to U.S. companies investing in developing countries. OPIC is currently seeking to capitalize an environmental investment fund authorized at $100 million.

- The U.S.–Asia Environmental Partnership (U.S.-AEP) is an interagency initiative seeking to facilitate private sector entry into the Asian environmental and energy markets.

- The Department of Commerce has a number of programs that promote exports of energy and environmental goods and services.

As this list demonstrates, a number of federal programs have been created; however, they are not effectively coordinated. The need to coordinate such programs is one of four key strategy recommendations of a recent Roundtable Report of the Center for Strategic and International Studies (CSIS), a Washington, D.C., independent public-policy research institution. We believe that a national environmental association will be in a unique position to work with the Clinton administration to reshape and refashion these government programs into an effective, proactive government–business partnership that will allow U.S. environmental industries to compete with industry competitors in Japan, Germany, and other countries where effective government support is a way of life.

The Clinton administration and Congress are currently working on a number of important policy and legislative initiatives that grow out of or complement this analysis. In his Earth Day address on April 21, 1993, President Clinton directed the Department of Commerce to develop an interagency strategic plan for the export of U.S. environmental technology and to improve the competitiveness of these technologies. The Secretary of Commerce will work cooperatively on developing this plan with the Department of Energy and the EPA.

The initial goals of the administration's environmental technology initiative are to ensure that technology research dollars are used to develop competitive environmental products and to expand markets for U.S. environmental products. This includes developing partnerships with key industries and government laboratories to assess the environmental impacts of proposed new technologies and to market environmental technologies to other nations. The administration's initiative, recognizing that the United States is a leading innovator in developing environmental technologies, seeks to help ensure that U.S. manufacturers are at the forefront in selling environmental technologies in the global marketplace.

Congress is currently considering a variety of new legislative proposals, all of which recognize the importance of the U.S. environmental industry to both U.S. economic development and the long-term goal of improved global environmental management. Among these are the National Environmental Trade Development Act of 1993 (H.R. 2112), sponsored by Representative Gerry Studds, which would establish up to six Regional Environmental Business and Technology Cooperation Centers to assess international needs for environmental goods and services and to provide export assistance to U.S. companies. This legislation would also establish a new senior level Environmental Service Corps within the Peace Corps to provide technical advice and assistance on environmental problems to developing nations. The House Science, Space, and Technology Committee currently is working on proposed "Green Technology" legislation. The concepts behind Green Technology include using technology to clean up pollution, designing products that are less polluting over their useful lives and in their eventual disposal, and changing the way products are designed and manufactured so that their manufacture is less polluting. These various legislative proposals will, we believe, be most effective if they reflect the views of the U.S. environmental industry in both their drafting and their implementation. Finally, there are a number of existing federal programs in the environmental area that we believe should be fully implemented.

JOBS AND THE ENVIRONMENT: OPPORTUNITIES FOR THE U.S. ENVIRONMENTAL INDUSTRY

We believe that it is the responsibility of government to organize its various departments and agencies to support environmental technology development, innovation diffusion, and the export of environmental goods and services. It is, however, the responsibility of business to create, organize, and manage the national environmental industry association needed to achieve these goals. Both must cooperate to fund and conduct the necessary research about the industry, the global markets, and the other activities, including training and information transfer, needed to achieve these goals.

We believe that creation of a national association is essential if the industry is to meet these challenges and realize its potential. This association will work with its members to identify the necessary pools of skills, work-force training programs, technology, and infrastructure required to enable its industries and firms to sustain long-term global competitiveness. It will interact with other related and supporting industries and associations. It will promote environmental regulation that pressures firms to innovate, and it will encourage company formation to provide the products and services necessary to help industry meet domestic and international environmental standards. It will work with its membership to encourage innovation, sustained investment, and vigorous competition among local rivals. In so doing, with both government and the private sector, the organization will strive to form and further develop nationally and internationally competitive clusters of environmental industries across the United States.

Fundamental to our analysis is the recognition that the private sector—the U.S. environmental industry—is a critical engine for introducing and maintaining increasingly higher environmental standards and achieving the goal of sustainable development throughout the world. This vital role of business-based technology cooperation was acknowledged in Agenda 21, which recognized that technology cooperation between developed and developing countries "involves joint efforts by enterprises and governments, both suppliers of technology and recipients." Finally, by meeting this emerging global demand for improved environmental management, the U.S. environmental industry will contribute to substantial growth in the domestic economy. In short, we believe that the U.S. environmental industry has before it an extraordinary opportunity both to contribute to the goal of increased protection of the global environment and to create economic growth and jobs in the U.S. economy.

Notes

1. Collins, Charles. 1992. Europe eyes major share in global environmental market. *Winslow Environmental News* 3(2). Winslow Management Company, Boston.
2. Much of this industry is concentrated in the United States, Germany, and Japan, but it is now growing rapidly in other countries.
3. See generally Stephen Schmidheiney, *Changing Course*, MIT Press, Cambridge, Mass., 1992; Bruce Smart, *Beyond Compliance: A New Industry View of the Environment*, World Resources Institute, 1992; Lester R. Brown, *State of the World*, 1993 (esp. Chapters 9 and 10), World Watch Institute, Norton, New York, 1993; *Columbia Journal of*

World Business, Corporate Environmentalism (Fall/Winter 1992), Columbia Business School, New York, 1992; Joseph J. Romm, The Once and Future Superpower (esp. Chapter 5, pp. 170–176), Morrow, New York, 1992.

4. U.S. Congress, Office of Technology Assessment, Trade and Environment: Conflicts and Opportunities, OTA-BP-ITE-94, Washington, D.C., U.S. Government Printing Office, May 1992. See also Lally, Esty, and Van Googotstratem, Environmental protection and international trade: Toward mutually supportive rules and policies. Harvard Environmental Law Review 16(2), 1992. For analysis of the gravity of the challenge facing the global environment, see Our Common Future, Report of the World Commission on Environment and Development, Oxford University Press, 1987; Al Gore, Earth in the Balance, Houghton Mifflin, New York, 1992; Shridath Ramphal, Our Country, the Planet, Lime Tree, 1992.

5. Clad, James C., and Stone, Roger D. New Mission for Foreign Aid, Foreign Affairs: America and the World 1992–1993; Vol. 92, No. 1.

6. Nothdurft, William E. 1992. Going Global: How Europe Helps Small Firms Export. Brookings Institution, Washington, D.C.

7. Heaton, George, Repetto, Robert, and Sobin, Rodney. 1992. Backs to the Future: U.S. Government Policy toward Environmentally Critical Technology. World Resources Institute, Washington, D.C.

8. Permitting and Compliance Policy: Barriers to U.S. Environmental Technology Innovation—Report and Recommendations of the Technology Innovation and Economics Committee. U.S. EPA 101-N-91-001, January 1991.

9. Improving Technology Diffusion for Environmental Protection—Report and Recommendation of the Technology Innovation and Economics Committee. U.S. EPA 130-R-92-001, October 1992.

10. This list of programs is drawn from Developing a U.S. Strategy for Environmental and Energy Technology Cooperation and Trade, Center for Strategic and International Studies, Draft Round Table Report, February 1993.

11. See Global Markets for Environmental Technologies, U.S. EPA Task Force on Technology Cooperation and Export Assistance, Washington, D.C., December, 1992.

Science, Technology, Environment, and Competitiveness in a North American Context

Linda K. Trocki

All sectors of the economy produce pollutants: industries and businesses produce waste products through their processes; autos and trucks release significant pollutants in their emissions; most electric utilities produce gaseous or solid wastes with fuel combustion; and the household sector produces municipal waste and, through less-efficient use of energy, demands more electricity, which produces more waste. Other than waste-collection fees for solid wastes, these emissions historically had either no or low associated costs. Beginning in 1970, increasing numbers of environmental regulations began to impose costs or limits on pollutants in the United States. These regulations were necessary because a livable environment—clean air, water, and other natural resources—is a public good, like national defense or education. We all derive a benefit from it but cannot afford individually to provide it.

What types of incentives or regulations are needed to protect the public good, our environment? What is the role of environmental economics in policy formulation? How is this role affected by uncertainty? Will the environmental costs make us less competitive? What should we do as a continent to prioritize and solve current environmental problems and to prevent future ones?

THE ECONOMIC PROS AND CONS OF ENVIRONMENTAL REGULATIONS

Why Environmental Regulations Can Help Competitiveness

Economic competitiveness is defined here as the capability to produce goods and services at a lower *total* cost than other states or nations. The emphasis on *total* costs implies that these costs should include pollution-abatement costs. If they do not, the total cost of the good in the country where it is produced may exceed the price at which it is sold. If our goods undersold those of another country and did not include pollution abatement, they would do so at the expense of degrading our environment, which ultimately will extract a real cost. Where transboundary environmental effects are caused by the production of the good, both nations must receive adequate compensation or protection for the degradation of their environment while maintaining sovereignty.

Environmental regulations therefore do not always hurt competitiveness.[1] Indeed, efficient ones *never* degrade competitiveness if one considers a long time horizon. Efficient regulations, i.e., where the marginal cost of pollution abatement equals the marginal benefit, help competitiveness in at least the following four ways:

1. We're in it for the long term. Regulations should ensure that natural resources are preserved for future generations, so that the long-term factors of production exist to support future generations. An example is the adequate preservation of the Great Lakes so that fishing, transport, recreation, and health interests are protected for the future.

2. Regulations should encourage waste (and pollution) minimization, which results in more output of a salable good per unit of input and prevents costly future cleanups. Energy efficiency poses a good example—many efficiency measures have a quick payback, result in lower long-term costs of production, and emit fewer greenhouse gases. Pollution minimization also avoids putting hazards into our environment that will later require costly cleanups. Given the short time horizon of interest to corporations and businesses, economic incentives such as tax breaks and subsidies should be considered to stimulate investment in longer-term efficiency and environmental improvements.

3. Producers minimize expenditures required to comply with environmental regulations by devising new, cheap technologies for compliance. These technologies may then be sold competitively on international markets. Examples are clean coal technology, which the U.S. Department of Energy expects to be salable abroad.

4. Environmentally conscious manufacturing or production can be a form of product differentiation or advertisement. Faced with equal or even higher prices for a good produced by an environmentally conscious firm, many consumers will choose it over goods produced by polluting firms. Examples include tuna advertised as "kind to dolphins" and the boycott against Exxon by some consumers after the *Valdez* oil spill.

Why Environmental Regulations Might Hurt Competitiveness

Inefficient regulations that set emissions limits too low or high, or that rely on too many command and control measures, can cause the following effects:

1. As mentioned above, the cost of compliance could be greater or less than the benefit received from compliance. This inefficiency will cause the cost of the good produced to be too high or too low, respectively. Krupnick and Portney's (1991) analysis of the Clean Air Act Amendments, described below under "Same Lessons Learned," illustrate this situation.

2. Command and control measures are unlikely to result in cost-minimizing pollution abatement. Therefore, the amount of pollution abated per dollar spent under command and control measures is likely to be less than the amount abated per dollar under more market-based incentives, such as taxes and subsidies.

3. If other countries have more efficient regulations, their costs of production will be lower and their goods more competitive. Also, it is argued that the cost of production is lower (and, hence, competitiveness greater) in countries where environmental laws are lax. This is the "pollution haven" hypothesis that polluting industries use to oppose environmental regulations. It is discussed later in this chapter under the section on trade effects.

4. The transaction costs of compliance (monitoring, permit fees, litigation costs, etc.) are money spent on nonproductive goods. The more we spend on them, the less we spend on investment in productive capital. A current example is the hundreds of billions of dollars that the U.S. Department of Energy is planning to spend on environmental restoration; since their total budget is kept fairly constant, every dollar that goes into environmental restoration is one dollar less spent on research and development of products that may make the U.S. competitive.

CAN WE MEASURE ENVIRONMENTAL COSTS AND BENEFITS?

What to Count?

Environmental regulations are often designed with the best intentions of informed policymakers, but the transformation of policies during the political process can result in a "do-nothing" regulation or, worse yet, create a monster. More economic–impact analysis during all stages of regulation design, debate, passage, and implementation, coupled with education of the public, are critically needed to prevent expensive mistakes.[2] Economic analysis, i.e., determination of costs and benefits and the prediction of the impact of a policy on supply and demand, can be difficult to quantify. Although environmentalists express concern about the ability to accurately quantify benefits, these concerns may be overstated. Economists have made progress in valuing social goods, and the production functions (equations that describe the quantity and relations of inputs to outputs) for a single industry can be approximated.

The key costs include the following:

- capital costs (plants, equipment, and construction)
- operation and maintenance of pollution-abatement processes (materials, equipment leasing, parts and supplies, direct labor, fuel and power, private contractor services, and research and development)
- pilot tests
- permit fees
- life-cycle reporting and monitoring costs
- expected costs of litigation and insurance
- overhead
- health and safety protection
- community-relations program
- government enforcement costs
- contingency (proportional to the uncertainty of performance of the abatement measure)
- macroeconomic effects (changes in the level of income, employment, and final prices for the whole economy)
- trade effects
- changes in social welfare, including distributional effects (consumer inconvenience costs and decreases in consumer surplus[3])

The benefits that must balance these costs are generally measures of the value of the environmental improvement, or the value of preventing further environmental degradation (i.e., costs that society avoids), such as the following:

- avoided health-care costs
- avoided morbidity costs
- avoided litigation costs
- avoided environmental damage costs
- the value that consumers place on the preservation of a resource (such as recreational-use values, or an existence value[4])

Measuring the up-front costs of an abatement measure is not enough information to determine if the costs are comparable to the benefits. We are dealing with a very complex natural system—the environment—or fairly complex machinery that may not be adequately maintained. One needs to know how the measure will perform in both the short term and the long term and what its effectiveness will be in reducing or eliminating environmental problems. Measurement of the costs and benefits may require sophisticated atmospheric or groundwater modeling and risk analysis to predict the effect of a pollution abatement measure. For example, shutting down a refinery in Mexico City is probably a good idea to lower air pollution and reduce health risks. But its effect on air quality must be balanced against the number of jobs lost, construction of a replacement refinery elsewhere, and possible increases in the cost of transporting refined products to Mexico City. Neither the effect on air quality nor the effect on the economy is easy to measure. The joint studies of the Mexican Petroleum Institute and Los Alamos on air pollution abatement in Mexico City rely on atmospheric dispersion and chemistry modeling to predict how a measure that reduces release of pollutants effects Mexico City air quality. Input–output modeling is one way that economists have measured economy-wide impacts. In other studies being performed by Los Alamos, we apply groundwater modeling to optimize remedial measures and compare the cost-effectiveness of alternative measures. Health-risk analysis is commonly performed to evaluate alternative environmental remediation alternatives.

Although environmental economists have made progress in quantifying costs and benefits, most analyses require the prediction of future events, which is fraught with uncertainty. Uncertainty levels exist for nearly every variable in the equation: compliance costs, costs of noncompliance, effects of compliance, measures of benefits, and the time frame during which effects will occur. Levels of uncertainty are clearly visible in the international controversy over what should be done to abate greenhouse gases. Thus, a policy analyst does not compute a deterministic number, but reports an expected monetary value that represents the probability distribution of a variety of possible outcomes. Other important reporting requirements include results of sensitivity studies and the size of the uncertainty of results.

Another complicating factor in the analysis is the choice of an economic discount rate. One typically discounts the sum of multiyear costs and benefits to obtain a net present value in constant dollars. The choice of discount rate is controversial. High rates tend to discount the effects on future generations, while low rates assume that new solutions will not be available to future generations, which requires us to value their utility almost equally to ours.

The choice of a pollution control level, and an environmental regulation in general, is often like buying an insurance premium—one never knows exactly how much to buy or how much will be used, but most people agree that they need some insurance.

Some Lessons Learned

Costs of analyzing policy options. Rubin (1991) offers a critical analysis of the 10-year National Acid Precipitation Program (NAPP). The study began in 1980 with the goal of addressing five key questions, including "What are the estimates of future environmental conditions based on realistic assumptions about the effects of acid rain abatement alternatives?" and "What do comparisons of the effects of alternative scenarios mean?" Rubin finds that the massive study reported much scientific data but failed to interpret the results in a form that the policymaker could understand, i.e., the dollar value of benefits. He also criticizes it for failing to adequately address uncertainties:

> *The assessment does not take the lead in posing other questions. For example, as in Europe and Canada, one could first ask what critical loads or changes in deposition are needed to avoid effects, and then work backwards to determine the appropriate emissions reductions. . . .By not asking some of the right questions to begin with, the NAPP assessment simply missed the boat in terms of influencing key public policy decisions. (p. 919)*

Rubin implies that a complex effort that cost tens of millions of dollars had no effect.[5]

The U.S. Clean Air Act Amendment (CAAA). The value of this amendment has yet to be determined, and the jury will be out on this one for a long time. The U.S. Congress passed the amendment in 1990 to require sharp reductions in sulfur dioxide emissions by electric power plants, to impose state-of-the-art control technology to prevent release of air toxics, and to impose more stringent measures on districts that are having difficulty with ozone compliance. Krupnick and Portney's (1991) evaluation of the costs and benefits of the CAAA estimated that control costs in the South Coast Air Quality Management District (the Los Angeles area) would amount to $13 billion per year and the benefits, $4 billion (based on avoided premature mortality, avoided ozone- and particulate-related morbidity, and material damages). They compared these costs and benefits with returns from alternative health investments, where "In the health area alone, $10 billion invested in smoking cessation programs, radon control, better natal and neonatal health care, or similar measures might contribute much more to public health and well-being" (p. 526).

Krupnick and Portney's conclusions on the applicability of environmental cost-effectiveness analysis reaffirm the theme of this chapter:

> *Finally, implicit in our discussion is discomfort with the premises on which our national air quality standards are now based. If, as seems likely, there are no pollution concentrations at which safety can be assured, the real question in ambient standard setting is the amount of risk we are willing to accept. The decision must be informed by economics. Although*

such economic considerations should never be allowed to dominate air pol-
lution control decisions, it is unwise to exclude them. (p. 527)

The Comprehensive Environmental Response, Compensation, and Reliability Act
(Superfund) and Superfund Amendments and Reauthorization Act. Superfund regu-
lates cleanup of hazardous land pollution caused by past activities. It assigns
responsibility and cost to owners who may not have even caused the pollution,
which stifles potential investors. In addition, it has been implemented so poorly
that the U.S. Office of Technology Assessment, in a report entitled "Are We
Cleaning Up?," concluded that although $11 billion had been spent on cleanup
or containment of a small fraction of the Superfund sites, little had been
accomplished in eliminating the hazards; the remediation would likely have to
be done over again because the initial attempts were inadequate.

Abandoned Superfund sites will require a total of $80 to $120 billion to
remediate, and federally owned sites will require an additional $75 to $250 billion. Estimates for the nuclear weapons complex cleanup total $300 to $700
billion over 30 years (Passell 1991). Are the resulting reductions in health risks
worth the benefits? Many think not.

> *To be sure, the problem of weighing the cleanup benefits against the costs is*
> *complicated by a lack of information about how dangerous individual chem-*
> *icals are, and in what concentrations. Nonetheless, experts insist that what*
> *began as a crusade against polluters has become a diversion, siphoning*
> *money and technical expertise from more pressing environmental concerns.*
> *(Passell 1991, p. 1)*

WHAT DO THEORY AND LESSONS LEARNED MEAN FOR COMPETITIVENESS, AND FOR CANADA, MEXICO, AND THE UNITED STATES?

Trade Effects May Not Be Significant

Studies of the effect of environmental regulation on trade and competitiveness
were stimulated by the "pollution haven" hypothesis, which holds that jobs
and exports will be lost in countries with stringent environmental regulations
as polluting industries relocate to countries where environmental regulations
are less stringent or nonexistent (i.e., developing countries) and whose environments, as a result, will suffer. This hypothesis has largely proven wrong for
several reasons. Leonard (1988) found that patterns of investment in industrialized and industrializing countries could not be correlated with relative

pollution-abatement costs in the countries. Tobey (1990) examined trade patterns and found similar results. Several other studies conclude that environmental regulations and pollution-abatement costs are similar in industrialized countries; and even where relative costs differ, other determinants of trade, such as relative labor rates, interest rates (i.e., cost of capital), the price of inputs, exchange rates, and political and economic stability, are far more important in determining competitiveness and levels of foreign investment in a country (U.S. Congressional Budget Office 1988; Cropper and Oates 1991). A number of multinational corporations make it a practice to install state-of-the-art pollution-control equipment in countries in which they invest, regardless of the national environmental regulations. This "premium" invested in good environmental practices protects them against future changes in environmental regulations and establishes good community relations.

Another reason why environmental-control costs are not critical to competitiveness is that they are not very large. Cropper and Oates (1991) cite average control costs as "only 1 to 2½ percent of total costs in most pollution-intensive industries" (p. 41). They cite another author's work that listed the highest cost to an industry as 5¼ percent of total costs for electric utilities.

The EPA estimates that annualized pollution-control costs[6] in the United States averaged 1.7 percent of Gross Domestic Product (GDP) in the 1980s and are expected to increase to 2 percent in the late 1990s. EPA cites a study by the Organization for Economic Cooperation and Development (1990) that reported annual[7] pollution-control costs as a percentage of GDP[8] were highest in the former West Germany. With the exception of Norway, where annual costs were 0.82 percent, the relative costs are comparable among the countries included.

Based on the studies cited above, the United States, Canada, and Mexico should not concern themselves with the effect of environmental regulations on competitiveness.

Who Pays for What along Borders?

Possible transboundary pollution problems facing the United States, Canada, and Mexico include the following: air pollution from industries on both sides of the border, pollution of rivers in the United States that deteriorate the water quality available to Mexico, Great Lakes pollution, pollution of groundwater along the border, potential offshore oil spills that affect coastal waterways, inadequate waste treatment and migration of pollution to neighboring countries, and pollution caused by industries of one country operating in a neighboring country.

The country from which the transboundary pollution originates should pay for damages created by that pollution in neighboring countries. This is the equitable arrangement, but it is impossible to implement. One cannot conclusively prove that acid rain damage to a forest along the U.S.–Canada border came from the Sudbury smelter or from U.S. industry along the Great Lakes. We should, however, be able to allocate relative responsibility for damages caused by transboundary pollution by knowing total emissions from industries on both sides of the border and atmospheric conditions that determine a pollutant's direction of travel. The European Economic Community is considering the following options, which may offer some solutions to Canadian–U.S.–Mexican border issues: introduction of international pollution controls, such as the "national bubble" (a pollution quota within an imaginary bubble drawn around a country), establishment of critical loads (pollution standards for a given area), and payments from one country to another to reduce transboundary pollution (Wood et al. 1989). In addition, the state implementation plans to redress ozone pollution in New York, New Jersey, and Connecticut may provide some other models or mechanisms for dealing with transboundary problems.

We do not necessarily have to look to other regions or states to provide examples of how to solve border pollution issues. A working group for each environmental medium was formed to study pollution under the Binational Environmental Agreement between the United States and Mexico. The United States and Canada have made great progress in solving disputes over acid rain. In their study of pollution from the maquiladora assembly plants in Mexico, Perry et al. (1990) note that Mexico's *Ley General del Equilibrio Ecológico y la Protección al Ambiente* and associated regulations of 1988 specify that any hazardous waste generated by a maquiladora industry must be returned to the country of origin. Since the maquiladoras are becoming "higher tech" and use increasing amounts of hazardous solvents, the number of maquiladoras exporting waste and the volume of the exports should grow. However, EPA records show that only 1 percent of maquiladoras operating in northern Baja California and Sonora requested shipment of hazardous waste to the United States. The percentage of maquiladoras producing waste is much larger. The low number of shipments is either an information tracking problem or a lack of compliance. The Hazardous Materials and Waste Management Work Group, one of the Mexican–U.S. work groups formed under the Binational Environmental Agreement, is addressing this problem.

While we do not yet have many of the solutions for who pays for what along borders, nor how much they should pay, we are making significant progress in cooperative studies of the problems. In the future, more cooperation, compensation, and incentives are needed to minimize transboundary pollution.

Beyond the Borders: A North American Agenda
for Environmental Cooperation

"Regionalism" seems to be the theme of many national-security conferences these days. With the dissolution of a bipolar national-security environment defined by two superpowers, analysts project increasing economic and political ties that strengthen regions. European economic integration of 1992, combined with the diminished role of the United States and Canada in the North Atlantic Treaty Organization, may weaken North American ties to Europe and possibly make North American goods less competitive in Europe. The Europeans more actively address shared environmental problems than do North Americans. In contrast to our "foot dragging" over Global Climate Change, Europeans are actively considering stabilization of greenhouse gas emission by curtailing the use of fossil fuels in Europe. The Japanese are developing clever new technologies to minimize carbon dioxide emissions from fossil fuel combustion. Leasing arrangements offered by the Japanese even mitigate the large, up-front capital costs required for energy and environmental efficiency improvements. When and if we decide to do something about carbon dioxide emissions, we will perhaps be following Europe's lead in fuel efficiency and diversification of energy supplies and buying Japanese equipment to accomplish these measures.

The global climate change issue is a prime example of the uncertainty surrounding the formulation of an environmental policy, and a joint approach will require much time, effort, and concessions to develop. The three countries can, however, increase cooperation soon in several areas that might lessen emissions of greenhouse gases and solve other common environmental problems. Several examples of cooperation already exist because they made economic sense: exploitation of Canada's hydroelectric power to avoid further reliance on more polluting fossil fuels in the northeastern United States, and active consideration of a natural gas pipeline that could allow more replacement of other, dirtier fossil fuels.

We should immediately begin sharing information and providing technical assistance to one another to avoid the perils and pitfalls of environmental policy formulation discussed earlier in this chapter. At a time when the Canadian government is doubling environmental expenditures under the new Green Plan (Anonymous 1991) and the Mexican government is implementing its new environmental law, joint studies to maximize preservation of our continent's rich natural resources at reasonable cost are ripe for implementation. None of us can afford to waste any more resources on inefficient environmental programs, such as the mistakes made under Superfund. Each of us alone would have to spend vast sums of money developing the tools to measure environmental costs and benefits. These tools should be shared among the countries.

Other areas besides policy formulation ("talking") and enforcement ("policing") can perhaps yield much larger benefits. The recent free-trade agreements present an excellent opportunity to increase the flow of "environment-friendly" technologies across borders. One area is more market penetration of energy-efficient technology. Since energy consumption causes many of the negative environmental side effects, increased energy efficiency becomes increasingly important from an environmental as well as an economic point of view. Much energy-efficient technology is already available, but it has not been adopted because consumers do not appreciate its potential savings. We could cooperate on educating energy consumers through public-information campaigns. We could also jointly consider the difficult political issues of increasing energy prices or imposing a carbon tax.

Another area for possible cooperation exists: the huge, polluted natural laboratories of Los Angeles and Mexico City. We should increase joint studies of air pollution, such as the one between the Mexican Petroleum Institute and Los Alamos. Expensive models and technologies to characterize and abate air pollution can be shared. Texas and Mexico have begun to work together to solve air pollution problems in the adjacent cities of El Paso and Juarez.

Most important, beyond joint policy formulation and information sharing, we can encourage North American leadership in pollution-abatement equipment manufacturing by opening a large regional market to such equipment and jointly producing the equipment. Joint venture arrangements among Canada, Mexico, and the United States should be considered.

The global nature of greenhouse warming and the regional nature of acid rain and water pollution mandate a coordinated North American approach to these environmental problems. None of us can afford to act alone to curtail pollution if neighboring nations cancel our efforts by continuing to pollute.

CONCLUSIONS

To preserve and increase quality of life and to protect our productive, economic resources, we need environmental regulations. These regulations should be implemented in an economically efficient manner, using taxes, subsidies, and pollution permit trading where possible. Since environmental regulations seek to control very complex systems, it is hard to predict if the full life-cycle costs of controls will equal the full life-cycle environmental benefits. Health-risk analysis and equity issues deserve strong consideration in formulation of plans. Public education is also needed to focus attention on the most damaging hazards. Economics, risk, uncertainty, and equity analysis are all critical ingredients in the formulation of effective environmental regulations.

However, lack of perfect information is no excuse for inaction. Given the magnitude of the possible economic effects of environmental damage, we must take an expected value approach and begin to ensure ourselves against these damages.

To date, costs of environmental controls have not been shown to affect economic competitiveness because these costs are relatively small and are overwhelmed by the cost of other production factors. However, spending several billion dollars annually on environmental controls and cleanup means several billion less will be spent on more productive private and social investments. Given the magnitude of the costs involved, it is critical to share knowledge and control technologies to maximize the amount of pollution abatement per dollar or peso spent. Diplomacy, good scientific and economic information, and equity analysis should govern our negotiations over transboundary pollution prevention and cleanup. Canada, Mexico, and the United States should place environmental technologies high on the priority list under the free-trade agreements. These technologies can help us to minimize our continent's pollution, to become more efficient producers, and to compete in world markets in a growing technology area.

Acknowledgments

The idea for this chapter originated with John Wirth, founder of the North American Institute. Some of the ideas expressed were presented at a meeting of the North American Institute entitled "Harmonizing Economic Competitiveness with Environmental Quality: A North American Challenge," in Santa Fe, New Mexico. The author gratefully acknowledges the comments by Peter Emerson, Chuck Robinson, Mason Willrich, Charles McMillan, Fraser Wilson, Dianna MacArthur, Jesus Reyes-Heroles, and others at the conference, which have been incorporated.

Notes

1. The possible exception where differences in environmental regulations may hurt competitveness is agriculture. Some environmental regulations preclude use of important, but possibly harmful, inputs to agricultuure, such as growth hormones, fertilizers, and pesticides. Countries where use of these substances are allowed may gain a substantial competitive advantage.
2. From U.S. Environmental Protection Agency (1990), Portnoy and Krupnick (1989), Booth and Trocki (1991), and U.S. Congressional Budget Office (1988).

3. Consumer surplus is the sum of the incremental amount above the market price that each consumer would have been willing to pay for a good. For example, the more competitive market for petroleum allows a consumer who would have been willing to pay $30 per barrel to buy it for $20 per barrel. The resulting surplus for that consumer is $10 per barrel. If pollution abatement costs increase the market price to $23 per barrel, the consumer's surplus decreases to $7.

4. An example of a recreational-use value would be the amount that people are willing to pay to camp in a national forest campground or the cost of a fishing license. An example of an existence value is the amount that people are willing to pay to prevent extinction of an exotic plant or animal that they may never see.

5. Of course, the money was not entirely wasted—the opportunity still exists to quantify costs and benefits. However, since the alternatives and abatement measures that received so much analysis may not be the optimal ones, a considerable amount of work might need to be repeated to determine optimal levels of emissions control.

6. To compute annualized costs, capital costs are spread out over an amortization period and include depreciation and interest. Annual operation and maintenance costs are added to the amortized capital costs to obtain the annualized costs of pollution control.

7. Annual costs include all capital, operation, and maintenance expenses for pollution control incurred in a given year. Capital costs are not amortized.

8. The household sector is excluded from the GDP, except for France and the United States, where percentages are reported relative to GDP with and without the household sector.

References

Anonymous. 1991. Canada's green plan: Blueprint for a healthy environment. *Environment* **33** (4), 18.

Booth, S. R., and Trocki, L. K. 1991. Cost-effectiveness analysis of new environmental technologies. Proceedings, HAZMAT South, September, Atlanta, Georgia.

Cropper, M. L., and Oates, W. E. 1991. Environmental economics: A survey. Resources for the Future Discussion Paper QE90-12-REV.

Krupnick, A. J., and Portney, P. R. 1991. Controlling urban air pollution: A benefit–cost assessment. *Science* **252**, 522–527.

Leonard, H. J. 1988. *Pollution and the Struggle for the World Product,* Cambridge University Press, Cambridge, England.

Organization for Economic Cooperation and Development. 1990. Pollution control and abatement expenditure in OECD countries: A statistical compendium. OECD Environment Monographs, No. 38, November, p. 40.

Passell, P. 1991. Experts question staggering costs of toxic cleanups. *New York Times,* September 1, p. 1.

Perry, D. M., Sanchez, R., Glaze, W. H., and Mazari, M. 1990. Binational management of hazardous waste: The Maquiladora industry at the U.S.–Mexico border. *Environmental Management* **14** (4), 446–7.

Portney, P. R., and Krupnick, A. J. 1989. The benefits and costs of Superfund cleanups: An information assessment. Illinois Institute of Technology/IIT Research Institute Report No. IITRI N08020-IV.

Rubin, E. S. 1991. Benefit–cost implications of acid rain controls: An evaluation of the NAPAP integrated assessment. *Journal of the Air Waste Management Association* **41** (7), 914–921.

Tobey, J. A. 1990. The effects of environmental policies on patterns of world trade: An empirical test. *Kyklos,* Fasc. 2.

U.S. Congressional Budget Office. 1988. Assessing the costs of environmental legislation. Staff Working Paper No. PB90-202698.

U.S. Environmental Protection Agency (EPA). 1990. Environmental investments: The cost of a clean environment. EPA Report No. EPA-230-11-90-083, p. 1–4.

Wood, W. B., Demko, G. J., and Mofson, P. 1989. Ecopolitics in the global greenhouse. *Environment* **3** (7), 16.

Restructuring the Timber Economy

Henry H. Carey • *Meria L. Loeks*

For the last 10 years, the forestry arena has been characterized by intense tur-moil and conflict. Timber-dependent communities have suffered loss of jobs and out-migration. The Wise Use movement has been quick to point a finger at a single scapegoat, environmental regulation, as the cause of these ills. Focusing on this easy target, however, clouds the multiplicity of serious prob-lems confronting timber-dependent communities.

Traditionally, rural economies have been based on agriculture and export of natural resources. As a result, these economies have been linked inextricably to national and global trends. In the early 1980s, a downturn in the housing in-dustry sent the timber industry into its greatest recession since the Great Depres-sion. This recession persisted for almost 10 years as a result of a variety of factors.

In the 1980s, the timber industry was only one of many affected by a general trend toward the deemphasis of raw materials in the production process. For example, Peter Drucker, business management expert, reports that Japan used 60 percent less raw material in 1984 to produce the same level of output as a decade earlier. This trend resulted in a global decline in the demand for raw materials. At the same time, wood-products manufacturers found that prof-itability was inextricably linked to reducing labor costs through mechanization. Improved efficiency in the production process reduced the number of timber-related jobs while increasing supply. Increased production and declining demand for timber resulted in depressed prices that accelerated sawmill failures.

Drucker suggests that the structure of the natural-resource economy has changed forever. If this is true, development strategies based on increasing exports of raw materials from rural areas are doomed to failure. On the other hand, a variety of recent studies indicates that alternative development strate-gies may provide a significant basis for hope for rural communities. These strategies include methods for enhancing the quality and increasing the diver-sity of products manufactured in rural areas. They also address ways to improve the sensitivity of rural businesses to the global market and to link rural areas to regional supply and labor networks.

FOREST-BASED, RURAL DEVELOPMENT PRACTITIONERS

Over the past 10 years, a new breed of forest-based community development organizations has evolved to utilize alternative development strategies. These organizations, known as forest-based, rural development practitioners, have their roots in forest-dependent communities scattered across the United States. The common threads linking communities where practitioner organizations have formed are open space, natural beauty, economies dependent on natural resources, poverty, and depressed social conditions.

Practitioners address social problems in their communities through a variety of development strategies. Some seek to improve the broad economic base of the entire community, while others focus on specific sectors. The diversity of strategies is reflected in the structure of the organizations themselves. Most are nonprofit, some are small businesses. Some of the nonprofits are associated with for-profit ventures. All share a willingness to get their hands dirty in some market-based venture.

Forest practitioners generally tend to have the dual goals of building sustainable communities and protecting the environment. Practitioners assist individuals and communities to harvest the forest in ecologically appropriate ways. They work in Chehalis, Oregon; Vallecitos, New Mexico; Berea, Kentucky; Centerville, Iowa; and Montepelier, Vermont. They serve diverse client populations, including African-American, Hispanic, Native American, and Caucasian communities. Some openly profess environmental advocacy as their prime motive, while others are grappling with environmental issues to achieve economic objectives. Their projects range from furniture making to stream restoration, mushroom and berry wildcrafting to fish farming, hardwood coffin manufacturing to tourism.

Forest practitioners help communities band together to bid on timber sales. They assist communities and individuals to gain new skills or market existing abilities by creating "value-added" products, such as flooring and furniture, which are manufactured within the community—increasing community resources and creating jobs. This chapter describes the programs of four of these groups, the Forest Trust, the Mountain Association for Community Economic Development (MACED), the Plumas Corporation, and the Institute for Sustainable Forestry (ISF).

Forest Trust

The Forest Trust is a nonprofit forest protection and rural development organization based in Sante Fe, New Mexico. The Trust's mission is to protect forests and foster productive relationships between human and natural communities. Among the many programs sponsored by the Trust are a wood-products brokerage and a forestry-services project. The wood-products brokerage is a go-between for rural timber cutters and the construction industry. The forestry-services project trains rural youth in forestry and business skills and provides employment on a forestry crew.

Rachel Siegel, an intern from the Yale School of Management, told a story that prompted the creation of the Trust's brokerage. On a busy corner on the outskirts of Sante Fe, woodcutters from nearby rural communities wait to sell their products, which include building supplies and firewood. One early morning in 1989, Luis, a woodcutter who worked hard to cut and hand peel a truckload of vigas (ceiling beams), drove to Sante Fe from his mountain village. He waited on the corner all day for a buyer. Unfortunately, his vigas were the wrong species of wood and the wrong length for local builders. By late afternoon, after having had no luck selling them, he took the vigas around to local lumber yards, where he found the prices too low and the cultural barriers to communication too high. Discouraged, he returned home and cut up the vigas for firewood.

With individual variations, this story is true of many local timber cutters waiting at woodcutters' corner. To address this dilemma, the Forest Trust created the wood-products brokerage. The Trust contacted rural woodcutters with latillas (ceiling cross pieces) and hand-hewn vigas for sale, and then found Santa Fe contractors building adobe homes who sorely needed these products. With the Trust as an intermediary, a flow of communication between producer and contractor was established. The Trust also helped producers with quality-control and delivery requirements.

In the first year of operation, brokerage sales exceeded $55,000; in 1993 they were projected at $120,000. Ninety percent of this income is returned directly to the local community.

The Forest Trust also helps local communities develop the necessary skills to maintain sustainable relationships with surrounding ecosystems. With grants from the Ford and Arca Foundations, the Trust opened its Mora Forestry Center in June 1986. The center trains approximately 20 young people each summer in forest property management, fire fighting, and business skills, including job counseling and advice on résumé writing. Students from the summer program have the opportunity to join the Trust's forestry crew.

A common target for discussions of employment opportunities in forested areas is the enormous amount of work contracted to private businesses by federal and state agencies. Thinning, tree planting, erosion control, and stream restoration are only a few of the many tasks that these agencies let out for competitive bidding. Local businesses, however, are poorly organized to capture such opportunities. Most federal and state contracts are captured by large regional or national companies.

In 1986, the Trust formed a forestry-services crew and began bidding for timber-stand examination, trail construction, and erosion-control contracts with the U.S. Forest Service and the Soil Conservation Service. The crew, which also builds dams and controls erosion for private landowners, is now self-supporting and no longer requires foundation funding.

The Forest Trust's wood-products brokerage and forestry-services crew respect the high cultural value placed on community and land stewardship in the Hispanic and Indian communities of the Southwest. These projects are making successful and significant contributions toward balanced relationships between human communities and the forest.

Plumas Corporation

The Plumas Corporation, founded in 1983, derives its name from Plumas County in the Sierra Nevada Mountains of California. This beautiful area has two diverse populations: retirees, who are not dependent on income sources in Plumas County, and out-of-work miners and loggers. Not surprisingly, these groups have different needs and interests regarding the environment and employment opportunities.

Over the years, the primary land uses in Plumas County have been mining, livestock grazing, and timber harvesting. Natural wildfires occur frequently. The consequences of traditional land uses and of wildfires have been the degradation of 152,000 acres of wetlands, meadows, rangelands, and forests. In addition, 770 miles of streams are in poor condition. Feelings run high in Plumas County when there is talk of further development or, on the other hand, of continued unemployment.

This polarized scenario was highly charged when Plumas entered as an economic-development corporation. After lengthy discussions about shared goals and interests, county residents resolved that they wanted development that was environmentally healthy and that expanded recreational uses. Plumas Corporation took the lead in securing this sort of development and has been remarkably successful in linking financial resources with land management opportunities.

One of the most successful projects has been restoring Wolf Creek. The project employed out-of-work loggers, using their bulldozing skills to restore the natural meander of the creek, which had been cemented into a straight course by the U.S. Army Corps of Engineers and had subsequently become a town dump.

Other successful Plumas projects include 33 riparian and wetland restorations, the first junior college "watershed management technician" program in the nation, and two high school programs undertaking geomorphic stream restoration. On the projects old enough to allow monitoring, waterfowl populations have increased 700 percent, trout populations have increased 500 percent, and stream-bank erosion has decreased 70 percent. Perhaps most important, the community is healing wounds caused by bitter divisions and is learning to work together for the common good.

Mountain Association for Community Economic Development (MACED)

MACED, founded in 1976 in Berea, Kentucky, has as its single-minded purpose the improvement of the lives of Appalachian Kentuckians. Bill Duncan, MACED's founder, stated the association's purpose as assisting "low-income people and their communities to take self-reliant initiatives which solve the immediate problems directly and, in the long run, increase their freedom to make choices and share in the region's wealth." MACED's projects include a wood-products business, a bank loan program for low-income, fixed-interest-rate mortgages, educational initiatives, and water quality control.

Early on, MACED saw Appalachian Kentucky's vast and underutilized forests as a vehicle to create jobs and improve the well-being of Appalachian Kentuckians. One board member described the decision to target wood products: "When we decided to focus on wood products, all we knew was that there were a hell of a lot of trees in eastern Kentucky that no one was cutting or harvesting."

Kentucky has almost 12 million acres of commercial forest land owned by more than 400,000 landowners. Over 90 percent of its timber volume is hardwood, concentrated in the Appalachian Mountains of eastern Kentucky. While 72 percent of the region's land is forested, less than one-third of the new growth is harvested each year.

Appalachia's miners and small farmers have supplemented their incomes with back-lot sawmills for more than 100 years. These mills, often only a saw sheltered from the weather by a roof and four poles, are scattered throughout even the most isolated of the region's mountain hollows. Many small mills can saw only a half truckload of wood in a day, and the largest saw only five truckloads. In 1975, the majority of Appalachian Kentucky's small mills were cutting all grades of logs for low-value pallets and railroad ties. Moreover, little of the high-grade lumber suitable for furniture or veneer was processed in state; instead, it was exported to other states or overseas. While the wood-products industry employed more than five percent of Kentucky's industrial workers, the furniture industry employed a fraction of one percent. Other ways of making value-added products, such as kiln drying the wood or turning sawdust into fuel, had not been explored.

In sum, Appalachian Kentucky's hardwood industry was inefficient at all levels. The industry was underharvesting, foregoing premium prices for high-grade lumber, and allowing other states and countries to realize the profits from value-added manufacturing.

For MACED, developing the hardwood industry seemed a logical means to help improve incomes. The area's many small sawmills could be the mechanism to turn the underutilized forest resource into new employment for the region. For example, Morehead Pallet Company came to MACED after its loan requests were refused by several local banks. The company's owner, who had grown up in an isolated mountain hollow, was a man with ideas and dreams, stubborn determination, and a willingness to take risks. When MACED started working with him, he owned a six-year-old, marginally efficient sawmill employing 10 to 15 workers on a part-time basis. A small site and inadequate working capital made it impossible for him to expand. MACED helped develop detailed expansion plans that showed an investment of $750,000 would be needed to move the plant to a larger site, improve the sawmill, and provide working capital sufficient to employ 15 workers full-time. When the state finance authority laughed at its projections, MACED committed $225,000 to the project. To make the business more credit worthy, MACED helped develop and set up an accounting system. MACED worked with the firm's timber buyers, lumber graders, and sawyers to find ways to improve the business's profitability. As a result of these activities, the owner was able to get financing for the rest of the project.

MACED has made grading and pricing information readily available to Appalachian Kentucky's hardwood industry. By this simple act, MACED has shifted the balance of market power throughout the industry. Grade and price information are no longer kept secret, so large operators cannot skim easy profits at the expense of small, disadvantaged loggers and sawmill operators. Armed with this once-secret information, disadvantaged loggers and sawmill operators are asking questions and learning from each other, and they are demanding a fair price. The fact that they can realize an economic gain is persuading them to invest in better equipment and adopt improved management practices.

As a result of MACED's strategic interventions in the market, many back-lot sawmill operators and loggers have become savvy buyers and sellers, and they have become better able to earn more stable and higher incomes. New jobs have been created because of MACED's targeted technical and financial assistance to these small-scale entrepreneurs.

Institute for Sustainable Forestry (ISF)

The Institute for Sustainable Forestry in Redway, California, is located among the redwood forests. ISF is dedicated to promoting the ecological and economic sustainability of the earth's forest resources by creating new forest management practices, as well as educational and research and development opportunities. ISF sponsors community workshops on topics such as fire hazards and thinning, and it publishes informative bulletins. One of ISF's first projects is development of a certification process for forest products that support sustainable forestry. Wood products labeled "Pacific Certified Ecological Forest Products" will guarantee consumers that harvest and manufacture have been conducted without harm to the forest ecosystem.

ISF is a nonprofit outgrowth of Wild Iris Forestry, a for-profit, small business founded in 1985 by Jan and Peggy Iris. Wild Iris's goal is to keep the process of lumber production within the Humboldt County community. Wild Iris wholesales wood to local carpenters and furniture makers, and it also mills, dries, and manufactures hardwood flooring and molding. By adding value to raw timber, local employment and control of the quality of production increases.

CONCLUSION

In 1990, the Forest Trust began searching for groups like MACED, Plumas Corporation, and the Institute for Sustainable Forestry, which are working with forest-based rural development. In June 1991, the Trust hosted a two-day "practitioners' working session" to explore common ground and build a foundation for future collaboration. Twenty-five organizations from 15 states were represented at the session. Practitioners coping with problems in isolation suddenly discovered that they were not alone and that they could share problems from culturally, organizationally, and geographically diverse perspectives. Today, this network has grown to over 50 organizations.

Forest practitioners are important from the local to the national level. Locally, they provide hope for communities dependent on diminishing natural resources; nationally, they provide models for community development based on sustainable resource management. These groups are leading the way beyond the resource-based export economics of the past to a new vision of rural vitality and self-determination.

VI

People and Wildlife

For environmentalists, protection of species in danger of extinction should be one of our society's highest objectives. To others, though, the Endangered Species Act is a prime example of conservationists placing the welfare of wildlife over that of people. They also object that the act unreasonably interferes with private-property rights and economic development. The challenge facing environmentalists is to demonstrate the connection between species protection and human welfare.

In "Winning and Losing in Environmental Ethics," Holmes Rolston III directly challenges the idea that anyone could "lose" by living in a clean, healthy, natural environment. Our society is engaged in a false struggle, he contends, to the extent we assume that any restraint on satisfaction of human desires is either unnatural or harmful to us.

In "Economic and Health Benefits of Biodiversity," testimony delivered to the Senate Committee on Environment and Public Works, Thomas Eisner of Cornell University describes the public health and scientific benefits of preserving biodiversity. He points to such important plant-derived drugs as quinine and morphine and emphasizes that the "chemical exploration of nature" has just begun.

In "The Endangered Species Act: A Commitment Worth Keeping," Randall D. Snodgrass of the National Audubon Society describes the efforts of Wise Use groups to challenge the Endangered Species Act. He discusses both the history of America's commitment to the protection of endangered species, outlining various ways in which the current act could be strengthened, and the debate over the act's reauthorization.

"The Tragedy of the Oceans," first published in *The Economist,* describes how overfishing and pollution are exhausting the once seemingly inexhaustible supply of fish from the sea. The article advocates innovative government action and forceful persuasion to restore and maintain the world's fisheries.

Winning and Losing in Environmental Ethics

Holmes Rolston III

Will people lose when they do the right thing by way of care for nature—animals, wildflowers, endangered species, old-growth forests? We typically hold two beliefs in tension:

1. Values are in conflict—acting to do A brings more for the resource users, less for the preservationists, vice versa, acting to do B brings more for some people, less for others. What some gain, others lose. Decisions are a win–lose game. With a consumable resource, if you use it one way, you cannot use it another way. You cannot eat a piece of pie twice. Either a resource is put to one use or another. Either an acreage is plowed farmland or it is wetland for waterfowl hunting, not both. There must be winners and losers. Humans gain or lose vis-á-vis one another, and also they gain or lose vis-á-vis nature. If the wetland is drained and plowed, the fauna and flora lose: humans gain. Here we may wonder how much humans ought to win—all of the time or part of the time. Humans cannot lose all of the time; but, at the other extreme, we may also hold that humans ought not invariably be the winners.

2. The right solutions are all win–win solutions—isn't it really in the human self-interest to conserve a decent environment? A bumper sticker reads "Recycling: Everyone wins." That is almost an aphoristic model for the whole human–nature relationship. If we are in harmony with nature, everyone wins.

Socrates, the father of philosophy, said that he knew with certainty that "no evil can come to a good man" (*Apology,* 41). He argues that doing the wrong thing ruins one's character, the worst harm of all. So, even if considerable other harms come in result, the just person never loses because he or she gains virtue. No accumulation of resulting harms can weigh negatively more than doing the right thing weighs positively. Doing the right thing more than compensates for other losses, such as one might have in business, political, or social affairs.

Consider abolishing slavery. Although slave owners lost in the short term, they and their society gained in the long term. When the right thing was done, the result was win–win in the long term. Similarly with the liberation of women. Some men lost job opportunities; others have to do housework they did not have to do before. Males lost their dominance, they lost power. But relationships are now more just and humane; interpersonal relationships—male to female, white to black—are more genuine. The talents and skills of women and blacks, formerly often wasted, now are fully utilized in the work force; family incomes are higher, marriages are richer, and so on.

In the course of learning morality, we come to be corrected from a misperception. We win because we get our values right. The loser will be worse off by his lights, but his lights are wrong, and if he or she gets things in the right light, there is no loss, only gain. It doesn't do any good to win if you're wrong; the win isn't a win. Consider a parallel in environmental ethics: The person reforms, re-forms his or her values, and becomes a winner because he or she is now living in a richer and more harmonious relationship with nature.

Some will protest that we insist that humans can win but then redefine winning. We win by moving the goalposts—and that's cheating, like showing a net positive balance in your checkbook by revising the multiplication tables. You will win, by losing at the old game and playing a new game. Some persons did lose, in the sense that losing had when our argument started. They lost timber, or opportunities for development, or jobs. But now you redefine winning, and they do not lose.

Yes, you do have to move the goalposts to win. That might be cheating if the game is football. But in environmental ethics, there is a disanalogy. You move the goalposts because you discover that they are in the wrong place, and you get the goalposts in the right place. And that is really to win, because getting to the wrong goal is not winning. With the new goalposts, people find more values in the natural world than before. We stop exploiting nature and become a member of a human and a biotic community, residing on a richer, more meaningful earth.

The person who is doing the wrong thing will, quite likely, not think it is wrong. We can couple this with another of Socrates' seemingly startling beliefs: that those who do wrong do so involuntarily because they act in ignorance (*Protagoras,* 352). Indeed, Socrates was sure that the person doing the wrong thing thinks that the decision and action is right, else the person would not do it. That is the famous Socratic paradox: that no person does wrong voluntarily. It makes no sense to do, voluntarily and knowingly, the wrong thing. We only do evil by mistake. Many have thought that Socrates here goes too far: some people, acting selfishly, do knowingly do the wrong thing. Still, he is at least onto a half-truth, and certainly many of those who wish to do the wrong thing environmentally are in fact well intended. They think they are making a wise use of the environment.

Whoever acts in a way that jeopardizes species must think that the action does not really jeopardize species, or, if jeopardy is known, that there are over-riding considerations. Loggers who press to cut more old-growth forest in the Pacific Northwest must think something like this. The action has got to seem good to the person who does it. Jobs and timber for houses are really more important than owls and ancient forests. One way or another, the person has calculated what seems right, and he or she expects to win. And this is not always just self-interest; the person wants humans to win, to optimize their values in their uses of the natural world.

If such a person is wrong, the goalposts, misperceived, will have to be moved. But that is not cheating to win, that is facing up to the truth: what was before thought to be winning is losing. In the Pacific Northwest, there will be some losers, in the sense that some persons will have to change jobs. They will, meanwhile, come to reside in a community that is stable in its relationship to the forests in which it is embedded, and that makes them winners. They once lived in a community with a worldview that saw the great forests of the North-west as a resource to be taken possession of, exploited. But that is not an appro-priate worldview; it sees nature as commodity for human gratification and nothing else. Its idea of winning is to consume, the more the better, and to make profit for those who satisfy consumers. Consumerism is the name of the game. But, moving the goalposts, these "losers" at the exploitation game will come to live in a community with a new worldview, that of a sustainable rela-tionship with the forested landscape, and that is a new idea of winning. What they really lose is what is a good thing to lose: an exploitative attitude toward forests. What they gain is a good thing to gain: a land ethic.

In the course of learning morality, we come to be corrected of a mispercep-tion. We win because we get our values right. The issue is not trade-off; it is error correction. You can't win wrong. Really, you can only win right. People who do right have more character, more ability to value outside themselves and more noble values within themselves. Deciding whether we win or lose, we need a dynamic rather than a static view of interests. Our desires change over time, shaped and reshaped by the affiliations of our careers. The goalposts are constantly moving. It may take a decade or two to know whether you won or lost, because interests and values shift over time. In a society that is already per-haps the wealthiest in the world, environmental integrity is likely to become more valuable over time. The consumerist mentality will become satiated and increasingly interested in the things that money cannot buy, increasingly inter-ested in the biological richness that is increasingly jeopardized. Chances are those who lost opportunity for development really won natural values that they, their children, and grandchildren will come to cherish.

Here a different aspect of the matter strikes us. A win–win ethics is not much ethics at all, because to be self-interested in a trade-off is not to be particularly ethical; it is simply to be prudent. No doubt there are win–win situations, and these are to be delighted in, but they are not ethical situations. If I purchase a new car, I get what I want, the car; the automobile salesman gets what he wants, my \$12,000; and we are both happy, the deal is a good thing. But it is not an action in which either of us is to be praised for our charity, or even our morality, though the trade does require minimal honest dealing.

We are uncomfortable with saying "good ethics is good business" and stopping at that. We may think that good ethics and good business are compatible enough; but, still, if I have good ethics only because it is good for business, because it pays off, then am I not being more prudent than moral? Extrapolating, we now say: Doing the right thing environmentally, you may not gain in business at all. But you will gain elsewhere more than you lose in business. There is still a payoff. You will gain all those noneconomic natural values: recreational opportunities, the pleasure of bird-watching, opportunities for solitude and aesthetic appreciation of nature, and so on. You will gain your higher quality of life, plus your more excellent character.

So now, winning quality of life and excellence of character has become the determinative thing, although gains to nature are close-coupled with gains to excellent character. Gains to nature are always gains to the person with a lofty character and a high-quality lifestyle—win–win. Why be moral? Because it offers me the best chances for happiness or, better, the most excellent character. Environmental ethics pays off.

Here the economists may insist, against the ethicists, that humans cannot really be expected to behave as losers in the economies in which they operate. Indeed, the very definition of a "rational" person, as an economist uses this term, is that a person acts to maximize self-interest. By managing money, for example, we expect that persons will earn the most money they can; and by spending money, that they will get the most they can for their outlay. It is irrational to do otherwise. The economy is fueled by persons acting in intelligent self-interest. No economy can work if people are intent on being losers. No ethics can expect people to be steady losers; that flies in the face of what people have to do to eat, clothe themselves, put shelter over their heads, look out after their offspring, and, generally, look out after themselves.

Nor ought an ethics expect them to lose so. If you want to get people to do the right thing, you will have to give them incentives. If you want them to do the right thing by way of saving endangered species, or recycling their wastes, or controlling their pollutants, you will have to make it to their advantage to do these right behaviors. Else you are doomed to fail. Probably you can persuade a few people to do these things out of charity, some of the time, but if you are expecting behaviors of most of the people most of the time, these will have to be behaviors where people can do right by themselves at the same time that they do right by the environment. It will have to be a win–win situation. We must not say, of course, that an ethics has to be popular to be right; to the contrary, ethics has often set ideals that are only partially attainable. So perhaps there are only a few people who are prepared to sacrifice for the environment. Meanwhile, most ordinary citizens will remain ordinary selves, with an interest both in taking care of themselves and in doing right by the environment.

True, we cannot expect people to be steady losers. But neither must we expect them to be aggrandizing maximizers. Self-interest is not the only rule in the game, though it is one of the indispensable rules. It may be, for instance, that self-interest is satisfied with "enough" (the root, etymologically, of "satisfaction"), and that thereafter, with enough for self, self becomes more interested in its relationship with others, in the community the self inhabits, from which it increasingly draws meanings and further satisfactions. In this community "right" relations are what is most satisfying, though they need no longer add to personal property accumulations.

The human self is interested in excellence, but that is not the only determinant of behavior. The self finds its satisfactions, first, in capturing enough values from the natural world to have vital needs met, to be prosperous; that is a consumer self. The self finds satisfactions, second, in meaningful relationships within the cultural world that the self inhabits as citizen, and, third, in the natural world in which the self resides, a resident of a landscape. This is the communitarian self. Winning involves more than one set of goalposts. We reach points where we do shift goalposts. Human development reaches levels where we say "Enough!" and shift our value focus because to win more of what we already have enough of is not any longer to win. To the contrary, it is to begin to lose.

This view of human nature does not require that persons be particularly excellent, noble individuals. Nor does it see them as full of selfish economic drives and nothing more. Human nature has multiple satisfactions, multiple values that the person can take an interest in defending, multiple goalposts on the field of play. There are multiple natural values in which humans can and ought to take an interest. The possibilities in human nature and the possibilities in nature are such that, in the culture we now inhabit, no one needs to lose when doing the right thing in environmental ethics, though many will have to learn different satisfactions. Winning is here redefined from the "scoring the most points" of the aggrandizing self to the "satisfied life" of the person enjoying an optimal value richness in his or her community. If you want to call that Wise Use, then call it Wise Use. But many will prefer to say that this is not so much a use as a deeper wisdom, reached by *Homo sapiens,* literally the wise species, where humans find their place by building a sustainable culture on a landscape, one that is in harmony with the many natural values carried in their value-laden world.

By this account, in the old-growth forests in the Northwest, we have long since cut past "Enough!" Loggers with an insatiable timber appetite will lose, but the Northwest will not, if it can find a sustainable relationship to its forests, if it can find a lifestyle that optimizes the mix of values carried by its forests. That will be satisfactory.

It is not that what we choose is satisfying, and that brings our good. Rather, what is satisfying *is* our good; and the environmental component is that we find the ecology we inhabit satisfying. This ecology can be satisfying to use if and only if it is both resource and residence, not only if we use it, but also if we live in it in meaningful community. We are not choosing it for our happiness, but our happiness is bound up with it.

Would we choose these things without our happiness? Would we then lose? Ought we to do so? These are difficult questions, not because we think we ought to answer yes, or are reluctant to say no; rather, we do not know how to answer either yes or no. We are constituted in these relationships of harmony with our landscapes, as well as with our participation in our cultures, and we find such a constitution to be satisfying. And we also find these natural things, the fauna and flora, satisfactory fits in their places, whether or not we are there to be satisfied with our experiences of these relationships. We do want to say: Yes, we want the animals and plants to flourish whether or not we are around to be happy; we want them there without our happiness.

If we answer: No, we would not choose these things without our happiness, then just that not choosing of them makes us unhappy, unsatisfied. Having moved the goalposts to where they now are, constituted in significant part by our ecology, there is no other happiness to be chosen elsewhere. There are other ingredients to happiness, such as the many cultural components, but they now are conjoined with this ecological one. Repudiating the natural world in which we reside, repudiating our ecology, is itself unsatisfying. Not choosing these ecological goods in order to gain happiness otherwise is a logical and empirical impossibility. All the other nonnatural goods of culture, whatever they are, are undermined with the loss of these natural values.

Two kinds of satisfactoriness constitute this relationship of doing right by nature and its protection: (1) The satisfactory character of the natural world, a complex web of adapted fits in a prolific ecosystem, is continued. That would be so without us. (2) Humans taking satisfaction in this natural world is likewise continued. These things have a good of their own, they are located in a good place, they are desired for their own sake, *and* desiring them is my satisfaction. That is a win–win situation. Oppositely, losing them is losing the satisfaction that comes based on them, as well as their being lost in their own right; that is a lose–lose situation.

When we are ethical we sometimes have to place the interests of others above our own, and that means that certain of our interests will not be satisfied, not in the degree that they might have, had we no ethical concern. If our interest is in making a profit, that interest will not be satisfied in the degree below. If our interest is in building a cabin on a parcel of bayshore land that the state wishes to include in a nature conserve for eagles, we lose that opportunity. Do we lose? Yes, if there is no other way to make a profit. Yes, if we have no shelter over our heads. No, if there are other sectors of the economy in which these desires can be satisfied. No, if my enlarged value set means that I subsequently find higher satisfactions than I did before I had this newfound opportunity to reside on a landscape replete with the native fauna and flora.

One thing we want to do, in addition to promoting our personal self-interests, is to be responsible members of a community with integrity. That sense of belonging to a healthy society and, in environmental ethics, of belonging to a healthy ecosystem—that too is part of our self-interest, but now the self is entwined with the community destinies. You cannot be healthy if the ship on which you are sailing is sinking. We win when we assume responsibility for heritages that are greater than we are.

We make a mistake if we have too private a view of interests, too dualistic a view of winning. Certain things have to be won together. Our sense of what is our interest is smeared out into the welfare of the community we inhabit. Environmental ethics is not inclined to focus just on the human community or, if that fails, to retreat into the isolated self with its excellence and justice. Valuing others, including valuing nonhuman others, is itself a satisfactory act. That is what is wrong with the quality-of-life, human-excellence view; it has fallen into concern with what is a satisfactory, satisfying view of my life and my self. But what we are really satisfied by is not just the excellence of an own self, but also by the display of excellences in the surrounding world. We are so satisfied by the flourishing of these others that there is no sense of loss at all. Your gain is my gain, not my gain in any selfish sense, but my gain in living in a richer, more value-laden, meaningful world. That is real quality of life.

Is there some peculiar human excellence that requires that nature be harmed? When culture wins, must nature lose? That question has a time-bound answer; and I fear that the first answer to this question has to be: Yes. Culture is the peculiar human excellence, and advanced agricultural and technological culture is not possible except as it is superimposed on nature in such a way that it captures natural values and redirects them to cultural use. Take forestry. Civilization on earth over the last 20 centuries is almost unthinkable without the use of wood for structure and for fuel. The scale of timber and fuel needed to support a developing civilization will invariably modify forest ecosystems adversely. Hopefully, such an extractive resource use can be put on a sustainable basis. The trees can perhaps be well tended, fertilized, and sprayed. But even so, when a forest is made a resource for culture, the natural forest as a wild ecosystem will be harmed. The integrity of the primeval forest ecosystem will be sacrificed, more or less, when it is harnessed to such culture.

Or consider agriculture. Plowed soil will disturb the native forest or grassland that preceded it. In this sense, all agricultures will harm the ecosystems upon which agriculture is superimposed. The ecosystem can perhaps retain its health; an agriculture can be intelligently fitted into the ecological process of a landscape. Nevertheless, agriculture proportionate to its extent disturbs and harms the pristine integrity of the landscape. It rebuilds the landscape to meet the needs of the farmers and those they feed. The farmers win; the pristine grasslands and forest are sacrificed to their benefit. And the city folk have bread in their supermarkets.

Or consider animals reared both for food and for other products, such as their skins. Where animals are domesticated, as with cows, sheep, and goats, the animals must be tended. The welfare of the cows is entwined with the welfare of the cowboy, that of the sheep entwined with that of the shepherd, but the animals become artifacts of culture. They are bred for the qualities humans desire, tender meat or soft wool; their reproduction is manipulated by breeders; they are traded in markets; and so on. They are often not particularly unhappy animals; the chickens that I remember on my grandfather's farm in Alabama rather liked it where they were. Nevertheless all domestic animals are captured for human uses. We butchered in the fall, sheared sheep in the spring, and ate chicken every Sunday.

Consider beasts of burden. It is difficult to think that civilization could have developed to its advanced state without beasts of burden. Humans would not have figured out how to build motorcars and trucks without ever having built buggies and wagons, without ever having ridden a beast or laid a load on its back. It is true that a horseman attends to the welfare of his horse, and that most of these animals would never have existed without their breeders; nevertheless they became artifacts of culture.

The point is that culture does require the capture and sacrifice of certain kinds of natural values. The cultural phase of human history not only must be superposed on natural history, it must also adapt and rebuild that natural history to its own benefit. And from here onward, any society that we can envision must be scientifically sophisticated, technologically advanced, globally oriented, as well as (we hope) just and charitable, caring for universal human rights and for biospheric values. This society will try to fit itself in intelligently with the ecosystemic processes on which it is superimposed. But it will also have to redirect those process to its benefit. In that sense nature must be harmed if culture is to continue. Culture is a postevolutionary phase of our planetary history; it must be superimposed on the nature it presupposes. At the same time, humans should build sustainable cultures that fit in with the continuing ecological processes. So the first principle of culture is that it rebuild wild nature; the second principle of culture is that culture ought to be sustainable on the ecological processes that support it.

When Iowa is plowed up to plant corn, the bison must scatter, and there will be fewer bobolinks—sacrificed so that Europeans may build their culture on the American continent. The most we can say is that Iowans can and ought to sustain their agriculture within the hydrology, soil chemistries, nutrient-recycling processes, and so on, that operate on the Iowa landscape. But there is no sustainable development of Iowa agriculture that leaves the natural history of Iowa umblemished. Legitimate human demands for culture cannot be satisfied without the sacrifice of nature. That is a sad truth.

But that is looking past. What's ahead? Must we further harm nature to develop culture? The answer to that question, once again time bound, is, at least in the developed countries: No, a satisfactory culture is quite possible without further degrading nature. Indeed, further degrading nature is likely to make culture less satisfactory. This is an empirical claim. About 2 percent of the contiguous United States is wilderness (1.2 percent designated; 1 percent under study); 98 percent is developed, farmed, grazed, timbered, or designated for multiple use. Another 2 percent might be suitable for wilderness or semi-wild status—cutover forests that have reverted to the wild, or areas as yet little developed. On the 96 percent that is domesticated, there often remain vast natural processes—rainfall and streamflow, soil fertility, photosynthesis, nutrient recycling, native fauna and flora—though these processes have typically been much degraded—pollutants in the streams and soils, soils lost, native fauna and flora decimated, species endangered, exotics introduced.

Remembering the root of "satisfactory," we are far past the point where enough is enough, and the mix of cultural and natural values ought not to be further skewed in the direction of the cultural. It is already so disproportionate that in many areas of the nation the natural values are in short supply, not the cultural ones. These natural values ought to be preserved for their own sake, but when they are preserved for their own sake they simultaneously enrich the culture that is otherwise impoverished of natural values. When Columbus arrived in the Americas in 1492, there was a vast amount of wilderness. In the 500 years since, there has been an explosion of European culture rebuilding the landscape, and that rebuilding has now reached a point where further expansion of culture at the price of nature will be counterproductive, even for culture. The next 500 years simply cannot be like the last 500 without a tragic loss of natural values that will harm humans as well as harming what nature today remains on the landscape.

That is the way to interpret what is happening in the Pacific Northwest. The old-growth forest has been massively cut, and further cutting is not going to be good for the fauna and flora, not good for the spotted owl; but it is not going to be good for the culture in the Pacific Northwest either, because it will throw the natural values there into an increasingly short supply, and it will only further prolong an already unsustainable culture, increasing the disaster when the crash comes.

The end of ethics is more life, increased quality of life, more experience of neighborhood. It is a sad truth that life preys on life, culture does have to eat nature, but that is not the only truth; there is a glad truth that culture can be satisfied, can only be satisfactory, in entwined destiny with nature. I do not say that there is no further cultural development needed, only that we do not need further cultural development that sacrifices nature for culture, that enlarges the sphere of culture at the price of diminishing the sphere of nature. Nor will culture be harmed if we do not get it.

Can and ought humans lose? The world is a complicated place. There is no simple answer; the answer is first yes and later no; sometimes yes, sometimes no; in some ways and places yes, in others no; superficially yes and at depth no; yes for self-aggrandizing humans, no for communitarian humans; yes for humans caught up in the inequities of culture, no for humans doing the right thing by nature. Perhaps the proper response is not to be dismayed that the question is so elusive, but to be glad that the answers are so open ended. We have a great deal to gain by doing the right thing; and even when it seems that we lose by doing the right thing, we typically do not—not if we get our goalposts in the right place, not if we can refocus our goals off the narrow self and enlarge them into the community we inhabit. There is always a deeper, philosophical sense in which it seems impossible to lose; that is all the more incentive to do the right thing.

Socrates did not think he could be a loser in Athens, and we have discovered a bigger truth. Humans ought not to be losers on Earth; they belong on their home planet. Earth is a planet with promise, a planet of great value. Our human experience has characteristically been devoted to the promise of culture, in which we live and move and have our being. But our human experience must also devote itself to the promise of nature, in which we also live and move and have our being. For not only are humans the only species capable of enjoying the promise of culture, humans are also the only species capable of enjoying the splendid panorama of life that vitalizes this planet.

In humans, the richness on Earth has become conscious of itself. Humans can appreciate this richness as no other species can. That enriches the richness even more. Humans can also creatively produce their own novel diverse and complex cultures, eminently a rich thing. But would it not be indeed a tragic failure of human culture, especially of our prized and so-called modern human culture, if it were further to degrade the biodiversity achieved over the millennia, leaving a depauperate Earth? We would not only be impoverishing ourselves, we would be impoverishing the planet. We would not be *Homo sapiens*, the wise species.

Economic and Health Benefits of Biodiversity

Thomas Eisner

Mr. Chairman, Honorable Senators, Ladies and Gentlemen:[1]

My name is Thomas Eisner. I am the Jacob Gould Schurman Professor of Biology at Cornell University. I am a member of the National Academy of Sciences, a former president of the American Society of Naturalists, and a former elected chairman of the Section of Biology of the American Association for the Advancement of Science, the largest scientific organization in the United States.

I am a chemical ecologist. I work on the chemicals of nature, the myriad of substances produced by animals, plants, and microorganisms in the course of their natural activities. These substances have played a major role in our own survival. Since the dawn of civilization, humans have turned to the living forms of nature in their search for chemicals of use, and that search has had an extraordinary record of paying off. Nature has provided us with spices and perfumes, solvents and glues, pesticides, fungicides, insect repellents, and countless other agrochemicals. But most importantly, it has provided us with medicines. Fully one-third of medical prescriptions given out annually in the United States are based on substances derived from nature or synthesized in imitation of natural substances. It is therefore in large measure the inventions of nature, rather than those of chemists, that have given us drugs. Witness for example such common medicinals as digitalis, quinine, morphine, reserpine, and curare, used in treatment of such diverse conditions as heart disease, malaria, pain, hypertension, and muscle spasms. All are derived from plants, plants already known and put to use by primitive peoples who discovered their therapeutic properties centuries ago. Even aspirin has an indirect botanical origin. It is chemically related to a substance in the bark of white birch, which in traditional medicine was used for preparation of an analgesic infusion. The important point, however, is that the quest for medicinals is ongoing and continuing to be rewarding. The discovery of penicillin only a half century ago launched the search for drugs from microorganisms, a search that led to the discovery of all our major antibiotics, as well as such miracle drugs as cyclosporin, an immune suppressant used in conjunction with organ transplants, and ivermectin, a worm killer dispensed worldwide in veterinary and human medicine. Unusual drugs continue to be discovered from the most unexpected sources. The well-known vinca alkaloids used in treatment of leukemias and Hodgkin's disease were isolated from a Madagascar periwinkle plant, and taxol, the widely heralded antitumor agent effective in ovarian and other cancer therapies, was obtained from the bark of the Pacific yew tree.

Sales of medicinals worldwide generate upward of $100 billion per year. A single drug such as ivermectin can generate over $1 billion in annual sales for its manufacturer. To those of us aware of the chemical potential of species, nature represents a veritable treasury. We view biodiversity as a vast chemical resource, and species extinction as a curtailment of that resource. Simply put, and quite aside from aesthetic and other measures of worth, species have chemical value.

A point that cannot be overemphasized is that the chemical exploration of nature has only just begun. Most species have never been examined chemically, and those that have been studied have been screened for only a fraction of their potentially useful constituents. Even those organisms best studied, the plants, remain for the most part chemically unknown. Similarly, millions of species of microorganisms exist, yet only thousands have been screened. Like that vast plurality of lower animals, the invertebrates, they remain mostly to be discovered, let alone examined chemically. Insects, for example, of which one million have been named but millions more are known to exist, have hardly begun to be screened. Yet the few that have been studied have yielded highly interesting substances, including hormone and birth-control analogues, cardiotonic factors, wound-healing promoters, and antiviral agents. The chemical treasury of nature does indeed hold infinite promise. It is a treasury yet to be revealed.

Species extinction takes on special meaning in this context. Species are disappearing at an ever-increasing rate, faster than rates of evolutionary replacement, and faster certainly than the rate at which they are being studied chemically. Nature's chemical treasury is literally vanishing before it has been appraised. I find this reality appalling. We are losing the options for chemical exploration, options from which we could benefit for centuries to come. The tide of species extinction will need to be stemmed. To the extent that the Endangered Species Act provides a means for monitoring the decline of biodiversity in the United States, and a mechanism for saving important habitats where these are threatened, that act fulfills a vital function. Reenactment of the act should be a matter of high national priority.

Before closing my testimony, I would like to address some points that are sometimes raised in discussions pertaining to the chemical evaluation of nature.

Why, one is sometimes asked, should more than one population of a species be saved? Is it really necessary, say, to preserve both an Arizona and a Wyoming population of a given plant? The answer is that one should indeed strive to save multiple populations. The chemical composition of a species is a reflection of its genetic makeup. At different portions of their range organisms tend to differ genetically, and consequently to differ chemically as well. Compounds produced by a plant in Arizona may be absent from its relatives in Wyoming, and vice versa. Preserving more than one population of a species is therefore the prudent thing to do if we are to maximize the chance of uncovering new chemicals from organisms.

Why, one is also asked, should a species be preserved in the wild? Could it not be maintained in cultivation, either in a greenhouse or other artificial setting? The answer here is that species in captivity may not produce all the chemicals they synthesize in the wild. Species often produce certain compounds only when induced to do so by specific environmental factors. Plants sometimes produce defensive chemicals only when "provoked" to do so by enemy attack (for example, insect attack). We may therefore miss out on the discovery of chemicals of interest if an organism is no longer available in the wild.

Does a species lose its value once it has been studied chemically? Does it then matter if it becomes extinct? The answer here is that our chemical knowledge of a species is essentially never exhaustive. What we know today about the chemistry of a species is a reflection of the state of the art of our analytical techniques and of the focus of our chemical search. Species contain literally hundreds of compounds of potential interest. What we find in our chemical searches today is what present technology enables us to detect, and what our state of chemical knowledge tells us to look for. Even the best known of species are bound to contain a broad range of chemicals discoverable only by future techniques. There is therefore no such thing as chemical obsolescence of species, any more than there is genetic obsolescence. Indeed, preserving species for their intrinsic genetic value is in itself of paramount importance. The very genes which in an organism are responsible for production of a desired chemical might some day be put to "work" in a biotechnological setting to manufacture that chemical for an industrial laboratory. Or one might transfer such genes to another organism, thereby conveying upon the recipient the capacity to synthesize the chemical. Crop plants, for instance, artificially endowed with genes which in other plants encode for production of insect repellents, might with such genes wage their own defensive battles against insects, without help of pesticides. If for no other reason than to keep open such chemical and genetic options, species will need to be preserved as effectively as we can possibly do so.

My final point is one that I would like to illustrate by example. When we speak of species extinction and of the need to preserve biodiversity we tend often to focus on the tropics and to ignore the problem as it pertains to our own nation. Our fauna and flora are extraordinary. They are diverse. They are aesthetically beautiful. And they are chemically very largely unexplored. In the course of my research, I commonly visit an area in central Florida, the so-called Lake Wales Ridge, that is biologically unique and is rapidly disappearing. Many lesser-known species may already have been wiped out in the area, and many others doubtless are at the brink of extinction. One plant that caught my interest there, a small, relatively inconspicuous mint plant, is *Dicerandra frutescens*. This plant has a potent odor, and I noted its leaves to be virtually free of insect injury. Its odor, I thought, might provide it with protection against insects. So I teamed up with colleagues at Cornell, who proceeded to characterize the chemicals responsible for the scent of the plant. The principal constituent, *trans*-pulegol, turned out to be a new compound, powerfully repellent to insects. The finding was worthwhile since there is considerable interest these days in insect repellents of natural origin. The point worth noting is that *Dicerandra frutescens* is an endangered species. It was discovered only in 1962, and it survives precariously today on an area no larger than a few hundred acres. Had most of this acreage not been part of a protected site—a field research establishment called the Archbold Biological Station—*Dicerandra* might already have disappeared and its chemical might never have been discovered.

The case of *Dicerandra* is illustrative of that of countless species in our nation. There are many reasons for protecting these species. Foremost, perhaps, are aesthetic reasons. But as I have tried to point out, there are practical reasons as well. We cannot afford to turn a blind eye to the chemical value of nature. We must protect our biodiversity. Reauthorizing the Endangered Species Act is an imperative.

Note

1. Testimony by Dr. Thomas Eisner, Division of Biological Sciences, Cornell University, Ithaca, N.Y., before the Subcommittee on Environmental Protection of the Senate Committee on Environment and Public Works, on the occasion of hearings on reauthorization of the Endangered Species Act, April 10, 1992.

The Endangered Species Act

A Commitment Worth Keeping

Randall D. Snodgrass

In the mountains of Southern California, a great bird spreads its enormous wings and soars effortlessly through the sky. It peers down on a landscape it has never seen before, though its ancestors have flown here for thousands of years. The California condor, North America's largest bird, once stood perilously close to extinction. For several years, none of these birds has known freedom; all were in captivity, part of a last-ditch effort to rescue this majestic species from extinction. Now this rescue effort has reached a dramatic milestone. Several condor chicks, offspring of the last birds brought in from the wild, have been released into their rugged mountain habitat northwest of Los Angeles. Against incredible odds, the Endangered Species Act (ESA) is succeeding in turning the condor's road to extinction into a road to recovery.

The success of the condor does not stand in isolation. In the fall of 1991, 50 young black-footed ferrets were released on a high, windswept plain in south-central Wyoming. Only a decade ago the species was thought to be extinct. Thanks to the success of a breeding program funded under the ESA, there are more than 300 of these masked weasels in captivity, and biologists have recently discovered that the ferrets have produced young in the wild.

The red wolf, bald eagle, whooping crane, brown pelican, peregrine falcon, alligator, Pacific gray whale, and many other plants and animals, both in the United States and abroad, have also benefited from recovery programs under this landmark 1973 law.

The ESA not only protects critical wildlife habitat and vital ecosystems, it also preserves biological diversity. Since the Declaration of Independence was signed in 1776, we have lost to extinction 480 plants and animals on this continent alone. Gone forever are the eastern cougar, silver trout, passenger pigeon, Carolina parakeet, the dusky seaside sparrow, and 30 other birds.

Today, there are more than 700 species in danger of extinction in the United States and thousands worldwide. Protection afforded these species by the ESA is our best hope for recovery.

The ESA, whose stated purpose is to conserve endangered species and the ecosystems on which they depend, is our most effective legal mechanism, for it enjoys primacy in the courts. (A 1978 Supreme Court decision upheld the constitutionality of the law.)

LOSS OF BIODIVERSITY

Most scientists agree that the world is now undergoing its first genuinely catastrophic extinction. Professor John C. Briggs sounded the alarm in the journal *BioScience:*

> *[Extinction] is taking place so fast that evolutionary response and ecosystem reorganization is impossible. One cannot reasonably compare the Cretaceous–Tertiary extinction (when dinosaurs and thousands of other species died out) with the current human destruction of the biosphere. The first was a relatively minor setback in the continuum of evolutionary change; the second, if it is carried on for another 30 years, will result in an impoverished world that will not begin to recover until the human population pressure is relieved. Such a recovery, if it is ever achieved, will take millions of years and will not restore the species now being lost.*

Dr. Edward O. Wilson, the famed Harvard entomologist and Pulitzer Prize–winning author, predicts in his book *The Diversity of Life* that we could lose one-quarter of the species on earth within the next 50 years. Wilson says he is often asked why we should worry, since evolution always brings biodiversity up to the mark. His caustic response:

> *Our descendants will be mightily peeved to learn that they are going to have to wait 10 million years or five times . . . the entire history of the human species . . . to see [nature] recover from what we are doing in less than 100 years.*

The Endangered Species Act is our country's way of trying to stem the loss of biological diversity. The ESA is also a model for other countries around the globe struggling to protect their natural heritage.

REAUTHORIZATION

Now Congress must "reauthorize" the Endangered Species Act, as it does periodically with the Clean Air Act, Clean Water Act, and other statutes. Reauthorization increases the funding authorization to implement the law—but it also subjects the act to substantive amendments. Reauthorization was scheduled for 1992 but has been postponed for two reasons: (1) 1992 was an election year and (2) the ESA, having become a target for developers and so-called Wise Use groups, is controversial.

The Opposition

In past ESA reauthorizations, the process resulted in a net benefit for endangered wildlife because many of the amendments adopted in 1978, 1982, and 1988 fine-tuned and strengthened the law. But this reauthorization may be different unless the environmental community bands together to defend the act from the onslaught of amendments expected from a powerful, well-funded coalition of the timber, mining, and shrimping industries, real-estate developers, the Farm Bureau, the National Inholders Association, western water interests, off-road-vehicle enthusiasts, and Wise Use groups. Joined by their ideological allies in Congress, these groups are determined to gut the Endangered Species Act.

Their message is "the act isn't working," "it is out of balance," or "it puts wildlife needs ahead of those of people." Their intention is to

1. eliminate protection for subspecies such as the northern spotted owl, Florida panther, and Mojave Desert tortoise and for vertebrate populations such as the bald eagle, grizzly bear, and wolf, which have healthy populations in Alaska but are endangered in the contiguous 48 states
2. require expensive and time-consuming analysis of private-property rights when promulgating regulations under the ESA
3. impose economic considerations in the decision to list a species as threat-ened or endangered

Conservative western lawmakers introduced bills in the 102d Congress that, if passed, would have required that the potential economic benefits of pro-tecting a species under ESA outweigh potential economic costs. In the early 1980s, former Interior Secretary James Watt tried this through administrative decree, and the result was that it brought the process of listing species as threat-ened or endangered to a virtual halt. The Watt legacy lives on today with nearly 4,000 plants and animals being listed as "candidates" for protection under the Endangered Species Act.

Under current law, economic considerations are taken into account in recovery efforts, but a determination of whether to list a species is based solely on biological factors. Amending the act to require federal agencies to consider the economic impacts of listing a species would fundamentally abandon the reasons Congress enacted the law 20 years ago—to prevent species from becoming "extinct as a consequence of economic growth and development" and to preserve their "aesthetic, ecological, educational, historical, recreational, and scientific value to the Nation and its people."

Let's explore the real economic impacts of the Endangered Species Act. In a *Wall Street Journal* op-ed piece (February 20, 1992), John C. Sawhill, chief executive officer of The Nature Conservancy, wrote:

> *In the past five years, some 34,600 development projects were evaluated by the U.S. Fish & Wildlife Service for their impact on endangered species. Only 23—less than one-tenth of one percent—were halted because they put species in jeopardy.*
>
> *To put this in perspective, in the same period 29 airplanes crashed into commercial or residential buildings in the U.S. That means that a developer faced a greater chance during that time of having an airplane crash into something he built than having a project stopped by the Endangered Species Act.*

The Conservation Agenda

The best defense against opponents of the act is a strong offense! In the 102d Congress, Representative Gerry Studds (D-MA), chairman of the House Merchant Marine and Fisheries Committee, which has jurisdiction over the ESA, introduced reauthorization legislation that the conservation community united to support. The bill, H.R. 4045, which enjoyed bipartisan support in Congress from 109 cosponsors and was reintroduced to the 103d Congress, would (1) double the funding for implementing the ESA, (2) expedite recovery of listed species, and (3) broaden the scope of the act to make it more preventative.

Dramatically increasing the funding for the ESA is justified for many reasons. The act has been so underfunded during the past two decades that it cannot achieve the recovery goals Congress intended. A staggering 43 percent of the listed species do not have recovery plans. And without a plan for recovering the species, there is little hope it will ever be taken off the endangered list, the primary objective of the act, unless the species becomes extinct.

To expedite the recovery process, Studds' bill would impose on the U.S. Fish & Wildlife Service and other federal agencies deadlines for developing recovery plans. In addition, the legislation would require agencies to issue multiple species recovery plans so that in ecosystems like Yellowstone or the Everglades, where there are numerous threatened or endangered species, habitat could be restored and protected for all of the imperiled species.

There also is a utilitarian reason for increasing funding for the act—protecting and improving the quality of human life. In the past, Congress has not provided enough money for federal agencies to protect "candidate" species. The result is that 57 candidate plants, with known medicinal values, could become extinct before their medical properties are fully explored. People discovered the therapeutic values of plants centuries ago. Fully one-third of medical prescriptions come from substances derived from nature—digitalis, quinine, and morphine used in the treatment of heart disease, malaria, and pain, respectively, come from plants. Unfortunately, we may never realize the full potential for these candidate plants to save lives or improve our health.

The ESA also must be broadened to make is more proactive. The Studds bill would improve the law to prevent as many as possible of the 4,000 candidate species from ever having to be listed as threatened or endangered. The amendment would expand and increase funding for the Habitat Conservation Planning function of the act to include candidate species rather than just listed species. By restoring and protecting habitat for candidate species, the conflicts that sometimes arise once a species is listed could be avoided.

ORGANIZATION

The conservation community has organized an alliance of over 150 environmental, scientific, business, religious, and animal welfare organizations united in support of reauthorizing and strengthening the ESA. The role of the Endangered Species Coalition is to transform and mobilize the public support for endangered species into activism for votes in Congress. That support has always been solid. The National Audubon Society and The Nature Conservancy commissioned a national poll in December 1991 that indicated that the majority of Americans support protecting endangered species. Out of 1,000 registered voters, 66 percent favored the Endangered Species Act and only 11 percent opposed it. The poll was updated in January 1993 and supporters of the act increased to 73 percent, or almost three-quarters of Americans.

It is well established that there will always be a minority of people with different environmental values from those shared by conservationists. It is our intention to defeat the Wise Use groups on an issue they identify as their priority—the ESA. By defeating them on ESA, ancient forest, wetlands, and the

1872 Mining Law, we can dry up their corporate funding and erode their political base.

A lobbyist for the Farm Bureau said recently that their efforts to weaken wetlands provisions in the Clean Water Act were just a warm-up exercise for what they plan to do to the Endangered Species Act. Conservationists need to show opponents of the act what they are up against. These are the themes we should emphasize:

- Focus on the success stories of the Endangered Species Act, the species whose populations are recovering.
- Emphasize that the act also benefits people by helping to ensure clean air and clean water, protecting open space and recreational opportunities, and maintaining chemical and genetic options for food crops and new medicines.
- Economic prosperity and progress—jobs, a strong regional economy, and a better quality of life—depend on maintaining a sustainable environment, including protecting endangered species.
- The act helps protect vital ecosystems: Species in danger of extinction are warning signs from damaged ecosystems. The ultimate consequence of loss of species and reduction in biodiversity is a threat to our own survival.

You can help make a difference by taking the following actions:

- Send a letter to your representative to urge him or her to cosponsor the Studds–Dingell ESA bill and to support greater funding by the Appropriations Committee to implement the law.
- Meet with your representative when he or she is at home in the district. Conservationists need to educate politicians about biodiversity and the need to protect it.
- Utilize the information in this chapter to write a letter to the editor or an opinion piece for your hometown newspaper.
- Contact the Endangered Species Coalition and sign up on ESA mailing lists to receive alerts.

Frantic last-ditch efforts to save a species like the California condor or the black-footed ferret from extinction are expensive and labor intensive, but they are necessary if we are to protect the diversity of life on this planet. Restoring and protecting ecosystems is a major challenge and critically important.

By passing the Studds–Dingell bill, Congress now has an opportunity to strengthen the Endangered Species Act and require federal agencies to take a more proactive, multispecies, ecosystem approach aimed at preventing species from becoming threatened or endangered. This is easier and makes far more economic sense than forever racing to save individual species from the brink of extinction.

The Endangered Species Act is truly a commitment worth keeping. The law benefits all the environmental issues we care about. Let's keep it strong.

If you would like more information on the reauthorization of the Endangered Species Act, please write to National Audubon Society, Endangered Species Campaign, 666 Pennsylvania Avenue N.W., Washington, D.C. 20003, or call (202) 547-9009.

The Tragedy of the Oceans

The Economist

Sea fishing grew rapidly in the decades after the second world war. Mechanised fleets increased the fishermen's catch in traditional grounds and then carried them to distant waters for more. After the catch had trebled to over 60 million tonnes in only 20 years, fishing developed more slowly in the 1970s and 1980s, like the rest of the oil-shocked world economy. In 1989, when the sea catch topped 86 million tonnes, the growth stopped.

In 1990 and 1991, the two most recent years for which the Food and Agriculture Organization (FAO) has figures, the world catch began to shrink. It has not been a dramatic fall—only a few percent overall. But experts at the FAO, in common with many fisheries scientists, now believe that the limit to sustainable landings of wild fish was exceeded decades earlier. In more and more waters, too few fish have been left in the sea to maintain spawning stocks. Fishermen are living off capital, consuming the resource that should yield their catch.

When catches of the most valuable fish in northern waters, such as turbot and halibut, started to fall, fleets began instead to chase other species that had been thrown back as "trash" only a generation before—whiting, spiny dogfish, and others. They also fished distant waters and found massive catches of a few low-value species. The FAO notes that it was these short-lived fish—such as Alaska pollack, Peruvian anchovetta, and Japanese pilchard—that swelled the world catch in the 1980s. But the trend was masked because catches were measured in tonnes, not dollars.

The world's 3 million or so trawlers, purse-seiners, and gill-netters cannot hope for further gains of that kind. There are no more waters and few species that have not been explored. The world's fleets say they operate at a loss: $22 billion in 1989, not counting capital expenditure or profit from unreported illicit catches.

Almost all of the 200 fisheries monitored by the FAO are fully exploited. One in three is depleted or heavily over-exploited, almost all in the developed countries. Although fishermen still catch relatively few of the 15,000 species of fish extant, most of the remainder are expensive to catch, unappetizing, or both.

New technology means that fishing is no longer limited by the captain's skills and the crew's strength. A vessel can now trawl four nets where once it set only one. With cheap nylon filament, it can set (albeit illegally) up to 40 miles (65 km) of gill nets a day. Thanks to refrigeration, mother ships can freeze and process hundreds of tonnes of fish before returning to port. Spotter planes and helicopters search out fish. Directional sonar lets captains "see" shoals of fish and even distinguish between species. Satellites help vessels lay their nets precisely where fish have schooled in the past.

The rich countries' fleets have outstripped their fishing grounds' capacities by such a long way that Iceland and the European Union could cut their fleets by 40 percent, Norway by two-thirds, and all three would still catch as much fish as they do today. Governments have encouraged this excess by subsidising fishing fleets, often as a form of regional aid and in response to falling catches.

MUDDYING THE WATERS

Overfishing is not the only threat to the world's fisheries, although it is the most severe. Development and pollution are also reducing stocks. According to Paul Brouha, director of the American Fisheries Society, 11–15 million salmon once spawned in the Columbia river system. Now there are only 3 million of which 2.75 million come from hatcheries. So much of the river system has been dammed that only 250,000 salmon can find their way back to old spawning grounds.

According to a recent study[1], three-quarters of the American catch comprises species that depend upon estuaries (often as a habitat for juveniles, which can safely feed in the shallows). But estuaries are themselves vulnerable. Almost a third of the world's 5.5 billion people live within 60 kilometers of the sea, polluting inshore waters with effluent from industry and farmland. Lagoons and wetlands are filled to make land; mangrove forests are cut down; fresh water is siphoned off upstream, affecting the salinity of estuaries and the growth of young fish.

For all the damage that they cause, overfishing and pollution rarely lead to extinction (though even this is possible for a few large, slow-growing and valuable species, such as the bluefin tuna). Nor, at least for many years yet, will fish be off the menu for those who have enough money. Indeed, as the price of fish climbs and biotechnology develops, the most valuable fish will increasingly be farmed. Aquaculture yielded more than 12 million tonnes in 1990, and is growing by more than 10 percent a year. Fin-fish make up almost 70 percent of the total; shellfish, a quarter; and shrimp about 6 percent. But intensive fish farming tends to damage coastlines. And, though the technology is developing rapidly, the FAO doubts whether farmed fish will account for more than 12 percent of world fish consumption by the end of the century.

It would be wrong, however, to think that "wild" fish matter only to fishermen. A shortage has other economic and social consequences. Fish prices have been rising since the early 1980s. Fish is the most important source of animal protein in some countries, especially poor ones. Moreover, as overfishing spreads to poorer countries, the effects may be more severe than in the richer ones. This is partly because overfishing threatens to engulf local fisheries more rapidly, and partly because more jobs are at stake: artisanal fisheries employ 20 times as many people as the industrial fisheries that are replacing them, according to London's Panos Institute; and fishermen tend to live in places where few other jobs are available.

CUTTING NET LOSSES

It is an avoidable problem. Overfishing is waste on a grand scale. American fishery managers estimate that the U.S. catch is almost half as valuable as it could be if fish stocks in federal waters were allowed to recover. The EU has said that its waters could, if properly regulated, yield a further $2.5-billion-worth of fish a year. The FAO has estimated the annual loss worldwide at $15–$30 billion.

Such figures have strengthened the arguments of resource managers and fisheries economists. But until 1976 most world fish stocks were open to all-comers, making conservation almost impossible. Then, an international agreement extended some aspects of jurisdiction from 12 to 200 nautical miles offshore, to create areas now known as "exclusive economic zones."

Because most commercially attractive fish live near the shore, the 1976 agreement brought many fisheries under the control of the nearest country. Marine biologists were then able to set quotas based on the maximum catch that would leave enough fish to spawn next year; and managers could try to limit fishing by licensing boats, restricting fishing times, and regulating fishing gear—such as the size of boats and of nets' mesh.

And yet, even so, after 18 years of management, overfishing in developed-country waters is worse than ever. Too often, politicians have been reluctant to conserve stocks, for fear of reducing fishermen's income; and managers have been unwilling to follow scientists' advice. When countries have banned unregulated foreign fleets from their exclusive zones, domestic fleets have expanded to take their place.

The catch in developed countries has fallen back to the levels of the early

1970s. Catches of Atlantic cod off the northwest American coast peaked at 800,000 tonnes in 1968 and collapsed in the 1970s. In 1992 managers recommended a catch of less than 50,000 tones; Canada closed the fishery altogether. In the North Sea, the spawning cod stock fell to 66,000 tonnes in 1990, barely a third of the FAO's safe minimum.

In some waters, management has merely brought the foolishness of over-fishing into the open. In 1975 the Alaskan fleet enjoyed a season for Pacific halibut lasting 120 days. The fleet can now take the year's entire catch in one or two 24-hour "derbys." If fishing went on longer, there would be too few halibut to spawn future catches. (The Alaskan herring-roe fishery is open for a mere 40 minutes a year.) Boats queue to sell their catch to processors, who gut and freeze the year's supply as quickly as they can.

Having failed in Europe and America, fisheries management threatens to fail in developing countries too. A few, such as Namibia, are introducing sensible management early on, even before the fleet is overcapitalized. More, however, are repeating the mistakes made in the rich countries by building up fleets without regard to the size of their fishing stocks, sometimes with subsidies from development agencies.

Fishermen are not happy with overfishing, but see no alternative. Few have any faith in the government managers who have curbed their independence but have not delivered the plenty that was promised. They (correctly) see that fisheries science is inexact, but (wrongly) deduce that the scientists' estimates of a safe catch are always too low. Even if they trusted the fisheries managers, many fishermen would worry more about paying the mortgages on their boats.

So conservation usually seems to happen only when it is too late—when there is no doubt that stocks have collapsed. To assume that stocks can always recover would be a mistake: it is quite possible that the near elimination of a species can change the ecology of a fishing ground permanently. And yet, so far, most stocks have shown a remarkable recovery when the fishing stops. During the 1970s, for example, the stock of North Sea herring collapsed from several million tonnes to 52,000 tonnes in 1977. Fishing was banned temporarily, allowing stock to rise back to 1.3 million tonnes and the catch to 646,000 tonnes.

THE HUNTER'S LOGIC

Managing fisheries has proved hard not because fishermen are foolish, but because many boats are kept in business by subsidies, and each boat has a powerful motive to overfish. Like hunters, fishermen will try and take what they can when they can, before anyone else catches it. A fisherman who tries to conserve the stock by leaving fish in the sea has no reason for thinking that he will gain by his investment: the fish he has spared, or their offspring, will probably be caught by someone else. On the contrary, if he catches more fish now he will be the richer for it. Although there will be fewer fish next year, the cost will not be borne by him alone, but spread over the entire fleet. Without regulation, in other words, fishermen have an incentive to overfish.

With regulation, though, they have an incentive to twist the rules or to cheat. Fisheries scientists, looking at the stocks, the species, and weather, can predict the number of fish that can be caught safely that year, but this is no good if their advice is ignored. Enforcement is expensive and it is hard to stop landings of so-called "black" fish. Although nobody can be sure of the size of the illegal catch, some estimates suggest it is 30–50 percent of the reported catch (a figure which helps explain why much of the world fleet continues operating, officially, at a loss).

The unintended effects of regulation can be severe. A boat licensed to catch only a limited amount of a particular species has an incentive to throw back any fish that it does not find valuable—even fish that might have some value to other fishermen. Poor specimens of the target species are thrown back, because the fishermen want to fill their quotas with the highest-quality fish they can find. The by-catch of nontarget species is enormous. Gill nets in the north Pacific catch 200 unintended species—40 percent of the total catch weight. One study estimates the annual by-catch of fin-fish in the world's shrimp trawls at 8.2–16 million tonnes.

If regulation is to work, it must be supported by effective surveillance and heavy penalties, says John Beddington of Imperial College, London, who runs the Fisheries Management Research Programme for Britain's Overseas Development Administration. Governments that have both those weapons can pay for administration by charging large license fees to reflect the difference between the value of fishing inside and outside the licensed area.

Mr. Beddington's group helps to run the fisheries around the Chagos archipelago in the Indian Ocean: when an unlicensed fishing boat was fined $2.25 million recently, revenue from license fees promptly shot up. It has also helped the government of the Falklands to install a licensing regime. After howls of protest from countries that had been fishing the waters cheaply for years, fisheries now provide 50–70 percent of the islands' total revenue.

Such policies are much easier to introduce if the fishing industry is foreign. Countries with powerful and overcapitalized domestic fishing industries need a different approach. New Zealand has tried to encourage its fishing industry to take a long-term view, by sharing out quotas in the catch and then encouraging fishing companies to trade their quotas with each other. If a fisherman regards a certain stock of fish as his property, the theory runs, he will want to protect and conserve it, just as a farmer would try to improve the productivity of his land. The quotas can be bought and sold, so fishermen leaving fishing will have something to show for it. This is one way to help reduce today's massive overcapacity.

New Zealand's scheme, introduced in 1982 and expanded in 1986, has not been without its problems. There were long arguments over the size of each fisherman's quota. Then, quotas set in terms of an absolute tonnage of fish proved too high to be sustainable. The overestimate was most serious in the case of the orange roughy, a fish discovered only in the 1970s. Once it had been established that this oddity took 20–30 years to reach maturity and lived for up to 150 years, it was clear that its quota had been set too high. Rather than buy out the fishermen, the government changed the rules and set quotas as a proportion of future catches.

These unforeseen changes made fishermen slow to trust the scheme. According to Philip Major, of New Zealand's Ministry of Agriculture, it was six years from the expansion of the scheme in 1986 to the point at which behavior started to change. Now, Mr. Major can point to several small signs that fishermen are starting to act like owners and not hunters. They are voluntarily helping to finance the policing of valuable inshore shell fisheries, for example. Trawlers are paying more attention to the quality of their fish, ensuring that those at the bottom of the nets are not accidentally pulped and so squeezing more revenue from each catch. In 1993 fishermen were offered the chance to catch an extra 50,000 tonnes of hoki. But the market was glutted. So the industry refused, hoping to catch more hoki in future years. "It's the first group of fishermen I've ever encountered who turned down the chance to take more fish," says Mr. Major.

The most elaborate scheme to regulate fisheries was unveiled in January 1994 by the Australian state of New South Wales. The state proposed to give fishermen shares (which would be registered, like land titles) in each fishery, distributed as a proportion of their past catch. Each year, owners would hand back 2.5 percent of their shares to the government, which would sell them and keep the proceeds, to reinforce the concept that the fisheries remained a communal resource even though the right to fish was owned by the individual fishermen.

Under the Australian scheme, fishermen should be able to sell all or part of a year's fishing rights easily and cheaply. That way, they could buy quota from other boats to cover fish in their catch of the wrong quality or species, not just throw the fish away.

One of the terms of the shares would be the accepting of restrictions, set for 10 years, on fishing inputs, such as the kinds of nets and boats fishermen could use. Penalties for cheating would be steep. If the rules were changed early, fishermen could fish under the old rules up to the end of the ten-year period already under way, or accept the new rules for a new 10-year share. The aim is to ensure that the scheme can evolve in tandem with scientific understanding of different fisheries; but also to make changes in the rules gradual and predictable, so that they do not undermine faith in the system.

The fisheries of New Zealand and New South Wales are tiny, compared with those of the north Atlantic or northwest Pacific. That makes experiments easier to design and police. But effective regulation will always be difficult, expensive, and resisted more often than not by fishermen themselves. Schemes to trade quotas will spread only slowly even to fisheries that are already overexploited, and will work only when they command the confidence of the fishermen. In the developing world, it is hard to imagine that investment in fisheries management will match that in fleet capacity.

If the FAO is right, fish will become scarcer and dearer over the coming years. High prices will curb consumption and stimulate fish farming, but not enough to deter overfishing so long as subsidies remain in place. Until now, only the dramatic collapse of local stocks has persuaded individual groups of fishermen and individual governments of the need for radical, tough regulation. That harsh lesson has had to be learned afresh, time and time again. While some fishermen realize that the age of the unbounded ocean is already over, and that fisheries must be managed, the question is how to persuade all fishermen, and all governments, of the urgency of that need.

Note

1. *Global Marine Biological Diversity,* edited by Elliott Norse. (Washington, D.C.: Island Press, 1993).

VII

Effective Activism

Some observers maintain that the neglect environmental groups have shown to their own grassroots constituency is at least partly responsible for the successes of the Wise Use movement. The perception by some that environmental concerns may not be representative of the actual concerns of affected citizens is a major threat to the conservation agenda. The reality is that environmental progress is simply impossible without effective grassroots involvement and action.

Beyond simply "rallying the troops," however, conservationists also must reach out to individuals and groups who share common interests in order to combat the Wise Use agenda and advance environmental goals. Building coalitions with natural allies, as well as reaching out to form new relationships with other groups, is key to broadening and strengthening the environmental cause.

To Janet Ellis, president of the Montana Audubon Council and a prime organizer in the recent Yellowstone wolf reintroduction hearings, opposing the Wise Use movement means being misrepresented, harassed, and intimidated by Wise Use supporters at public hearings. Her advice to activists, in "Taking on the Anti-Environmentalists: Step by Step," is to draw public attention to Wise Use tactics of intimidation and deception and to become better organized, getting groups and individuals to focus on specific events and messages.

In "Building Broad-Based Coalitions to Oppose Takings Legislation," Dana B. Larsen of Arizona Common Cause describes the successful efforts by Common Cause, the Sierra Club, and other groups to organize a citizens' petition drive to place Arizona's takings legislation on that state's 1994 ballot. The legislation would require state agencies to conduct elaborate reviews to determine whether their proposed actions might result in a taking under the Fifth Amendment. Larsen emphasizes the importance of creating a broad-based coalition to work to defeat state takings legislation.

In "Finding the Ties That Bind: Coalitions with Agricultural Groups," Teresa Erickson of the Northern Plains Resource Council describes her organization's long-standing efforts to build a true coalition of environmentalists and farmers. Using their appreciation for and dependency on the land as a common bond, conservationists, farmers, and ranchers frequently cooperate in Montana to fight threats to their common interests.

In "Countering the Resource Abuse Movement," Douglass North, an attorney and river conservation activist in the Pacific Northwest, offers specific practical advice on how to counter the fears and distortions that undergird the Wise Use movement. He explains the movement's appeal and suggests how conservationists can respond effectively to it.

Taking on Anti-Environmentalists

Step by Step

Janet Ellis

"It's people! People from all walks of life. It's businesspeople and workers, loggers and backpackers, ranchers and wildlife photographers. It's mothers and fathers, kids and seniors. It's members of every community."

The above quote sounds like a description of members of the Audubon Society, right? Instead, it is an excerpt from a membership publication for Communities for a Great Northwest, an organization that is more apt to describe Audubon members as "preservationists" and "obstructionists."

A new force is flexing its muscles in Montana. It is well financed, well organized, and vocal. And it paints you and me as "preservationists that care more about wildlife than people."

We began to experience this anti-environmental force in Montana in 1991: on January 24 in Bozeman, 670 people gathered to oppose the Greater Yellowstone Coordinating Committee's "Vision Document"; on April 1 in Helena and May 13 in Great Falls, 500 people gathered to oppose wolf reintroduction; and on June 7 in Missoula, 1,000 people gathered to protest the Lolo-Kootenai Wilderness Accords.

This anti-environmental campaign, organized by the conservative Western State Public Lands Coalition, is called "People for the West!" Montana groups involved in People for the West! include Communities for a Great Northwest, Montana PLUS (Public Lands Used Sensibly), the Montana Mining Association, Montana Woolgrowers, Montana Stockgrowers, 4×4 clubs, and WETA (Western Environmental Trade Association).

FEAR AS A TACTIC

Although the corporate funders of the campaign are motivated by profits, the grassroots members appear to be motivated by fear: fear of the loss of their jobs, homes, and communities.

A glimpse of the kind of fear tactics being used is provided by Lillian Herne of Gardiner, Montana, who attended the premeeting rally against the Greater Yellowstone Coordinating Committee's "Vision Document":

> *The spokesman for People for the West! stated that the purpose of the "Vision" was to drive people off the public and private lands. No wonder people were angry. If I had not read the document myself, I would have been angry too. However, I had read it cover-to-cover, not just the few sentences they recommended we read. I know the accusations were false. . . . I kept wondering if People for the West! had not really read the "Vision" and were whipping us up over something they had not fully researched (as irresponsible as that is) or if they had read the document and were deliberately misleading us.* (Livingston Enterprise, *February 27, 1991*)

How would you feel if you were told that someone was going to take away your job and destroy your community? Angry and scared. And when these citizens arrived at the Greater Yellowstone Coordinating Committee meeting, they made their anger known. Bob Barbee, Superintendent of Yellowstone National Park, said, "You can't imagine the virulence of the outcry. . . . I was Saddam Hussein, . . . a communist, everything else you could think of. One lady got up there, jaw quivering, used her time to say the Pledge of Allegiance, then looked at me and called me a Nazi" (*Washington Post,* May 16, 1991).

CONSERVATIONISTS FEELING INTIMIDATED

How would you feel walking into one of these anti-environmental hearings? Picture yourself as a conservationist about to attend a public hearing. You have spent time researching the issue and writing your prepared statement. There have been several hearings on this issue before, so you are comfortable with the issue and what you think you are getting involved in. But when you arrive at the hearing, you are startled to find yourself at an anti-environmental rally. You are outnumbered ten to one. The crowd is hostile.

This situation happened to the president of the local Audubon chapter in April 1991. Although he and his wife thought they were going to a public hearing on wolf reintroduction, they found themselves at a hostile, antiwolf rally. They were not prepared for the emotion—and the intimidation, the hissing, and the applause. They also felt that the other side was capable of violence.

The intimidation even followed them home. Someone complained to Beth's supervisor that she had attended the hearing to support wolf reintroduction. Consequently, when another wolf reintroduction hearing was announced for the summer of 1992, Tim and Beth cringed—they didn't want to be subjected to the same intimidating experience.

CONSERVATIONISTS BEGIN TO FIGHT BACK

For most environmental hearings in 1991, Montana environmentalists were outnumbered and outpowered. From reintroduction of black-footed ferrets to wilderness hearings, the crowd was generally anti-environmental, very vocal, and hostile.

In an effort to reverse this trend, a number of conservation leaders and staff sat down to take a look at what was happening. We realized that we all felt overwhelmed and beaten up, but we had no idea what to do to try to reverse the new anti-environmental trend.

Individuals acting as individuals can make a difference. But individuals organized around a common purpose can make a substantial difference. The basic principles of grassroots organizing teach us to develop a strategy to win on an issue.

People for the West! is an issues campaign, and we began our work by looking at their campaign strategically: their goals, their allies and potential allies, their opponents and potential opponents, and the tactics that they have been using to accomplish their goals. From there we could begin to develop our own road map to countering their effort. The results we came up with include the following:

Their goals: preventing reform of the 1872 Mining Law, allowing industry to control natural resources, weakening environmental laws, building political power (elect candidates who will support their efforts), and privatizing public resources.

Their allies/potential allies: mining industry, small miners, off-road-vehicle users, timber industry, loggers, agricultural organizations, ranchers, oil and gas industry, and private landowners.

Their opponents: environmentalists, national conservation organizations, progressive elected officials, proponents of the 1872 Mining Law reform, and federal and state regulatory agencies.

Their tactics:
- Using fear ("you're going to lose your job")
- Painting issues in a manner that polarizes, as black and white, with their side portrayed as "the voice of reason." Because black-and-white issues are easier for the media to pick up, it is easier for them to get their ideas across to the general public.
- Using basic grassroots organizing techniques to get people involved.
- Thinking strategically in terms of picking fights that broaden their constituency. Opposition to any reform of the 1872 Mining Law was the original focus of the campaign. In Montana they have used wolf reintroduction and water issues to bring agriculture into the movement. They have gotten the timber industry and 4×4 clubs involved by using wilderness issues as a focal point. The result is that they are uniting many conservative people against environmentalists and environmental regulation.
- Emphasizing patriotism and traditional family values; they say that they care about jobs and families.
- Using intimidation—of environmentalists and public officials.
- Being very vocal (the squeaky wheel gets the grease).

In turn, we went through the same exercise to try to develop an effort to counter their campaign:

Our goals: reforming the 1872 Mining Law, retaining and electing progressive candidates, working toward a sustainable economy, exposing the power of corporations, putting "public" back into public lands, redefining the political climate.

Our allies/potential allies: environmental organizations, progressive economic development groups, progressive candidates, progressive corporations, workers (particularly organized labor), churches, Native Americans, the tourism industry, seniors, agricultural groups, and progressive funders.

Our opponents: the industry groups listed above and anti-environmental candidates.

Our tactics:
- Researching the who, what, and how of the Wise Use movement in Montana.
- Educating our membership and the public about the research we have done.
- Building a diverse coalition to work on issues and/or this movement.
- Working to present our side of issues as "the voice of reason."

- Watching for their events and taking them on, one at a time.
- Continuing to analyze how we have set ourselves up for this anti-environmental movement.
- Working to stand in the other person's shoes; trying to look at the legitimate parts of their arguments.
- Getting back to the basics: using standard grassroots organizing techniques.
- Getting conservationists active in politics.

With our strategy outlined, we began to divide up responsibilities and set up a structure to help organizations continue to work together on this issue. We realized that our resources were very limited, and that we needed to do the best job we could with our limited time and money.

The most important part of our effort has been to work cooperatively with other members of the environmental community. We have a long way to go, however, to change the political climate. But by working together on specific tasks, we have made slow but steady progress to counter our state's anti-environmental movement.

RESEARCH

Our research in Montana has centered around who is behind the movement, what they are doing, and where their money is coming from. We have been able to document the answers to these questions with some Montana-specific information. For example, the state Office of Political Practices keeps records of lobbying expenditures. When the anti-environmental groups begin to shout about the "big, green propaganda machine" and the "environmental elite," we have been able to counter their calls with compelling statistics about the "big, brown propaganda machine": in Montana, conservationists were outspent 12 to 1 and outnumbered 6 to 1 during the 1991 Montana legislative session (industry spent $920,300 with 117 lobbyists; conservationists spent $75,800 with 19 lobbyists). Similar trends were reported for the 1993 session (Montana's legislature meets every other year).

We have also researched the issues that our opponents are working on, such as the private-property-rights legislation now before the Montana legislature. We have spent a lot of time analyzing this issue, articulating our perspective, and working strategically on ways to kill the legislation.

We have tried to educate our members and the public regarding the research that has been compiled on who is behind this movement, the issues they are working on, and the tactics they are using. Our outreach has included newsletter articles, presentations at meetings, press conferences, letters to the editor, and meetings with editorial boards.

COALITION WORK

We have worked to form a coalition with other interested individuals and organizations. The AFL-CIO, for example, has researched the connections between the corporations and the individuals involved with People for the West!, and it turns out that some of these anti-environmentalists are also anti-union, which has cemented our efforts to work together with organized labor to oppose this conservative force. Conservationists and the AFL-CIO also are presently working together against the private-property-rights movement in Montana.

Largely because of the coalition we have developed to support us in our efforts, one of Audubon's main issues during the 1993 Montana legislature put the real-estate industry on the defensive: the enactment of stronger subdivision- and land-use-planning laws. In the process we have made a concerted effort to reach beyond our traditional allies, and subsequently to get new allies actively involved.

Our subdivision-reform coalition is diverse and includes county commissioners; rural fire fighters; sportsmen; agricultural groups, including the Montana Stockgrowers (a People for the West! group) and the Montana Dairymen's Association; and professional planners. It has taken a lot of effort—and creativity—to develop, work, and nurture this diverse coalition. But because of the broad-based support we have developed, we are optimistic that we will finally reform Montana's weak subdivision laws—after fighting the real-estate industry on this issue for 20 years.

EVENTS

We are now at the point where we can spot the anti-environmentalists' "events." Our efforts are focused on taking them on, one event at a time. For example, in August 1992, a wolf reintroduction hearing requested by the anti-environmental movement was scheduled in Helena. As mentioned earlier, the movement had two successful antiwolf hearings in 1991. We realized that this was not just another wolf hearing: we knew that it was going to be a symbolic place for us to take a stand.

Months in advance, conservation leaders from around the state began planning for that hearing; we knew we needed to get a lot of prowolf supporters to attend.

Our task was difficult because of our limited resources (to make telephone calls and mail alerts) and the fact that the hearing was on a weekday afternoon—when most of our members were working. We also had a difficult time getting members excited to come to a wolf hearing: there had been so many hearings on the issue that this one didn't seem critical.

To prepare our members for the hearing, we organized a prehearing rally with speakers, lunch, and music. Alerts were sent out to let members know how important this hearing was going to be. We also got a lot of people to call members and encourage them to come. The lunchtime rally allowed many local people who could not attend the hearing because of work an opportunity to show up and voice their support. We also worked hard to get the media to cover the event. In the end, we had 200 people at our rally, to the 70 people at the antiwolf rally. We were heartened to learn that the attendance at their rally was so poor that the speeches by the governor and an anti-environmental congressional candidate were canceled. The hearing took testimony from 100 people, of whom 60 favored wolf reintroduction and 40 opposed it—a small, but important moral victory for the environmental community of Montana.

POLITICAL ACTION

The final front we have begun to work on is getting conservationists more involved in political campaigns. In 1992, a political action committee (PAC) named Montana Conservation Voters was formed. The purpose of the PAC was not to donate large sums of money to candidates; rather, it was to get volunteers to work on campaigns. We learned the rules and regulations governing PACs, assembled a list of officers, and endorsed several candidates. Most of our energy went into trying to get conservationists involved in campaigns—and making sure that candidates knew that conservationists were working for them.

Our long-term goal is to educate members about elections, and how important individual efforts can be toward electing conservation-minded candidates. We also want to get more conservationists interested in political action and, potentially, in taking the next step: running for office.

A FINAL WORD

Right now we are involved in another round of battles. The mining industry has introduced a lot of strong, anti-environmental legislation in the Montana legislature. We are also fighting a private-property-rights bill that could significantly weaken current environmental laws. On the federal level, we are facing another potential People for the West! event: a federal hearing on raising grazing fees on public lands.

A noted conservationist has said that "conservationists are sometimes perceived as holding whooping cranes in higher esteem than people. It is up to us to clarify that the choice is not between wild places and people. Rather, it is between a rich or an impoverished existence for people."

We have a long way to go before we change the political climate in this state away from anti-environmental sentiments. However, I'm more optimistic now than I was a year ago about our ability to succeed. We have taken the time to stop, think, and plan our strategy to win this "mother of all" conservation battles. And slowly, steadily, we are making progress.

In some ways, the People for the West! campaign has been good for Montana conservationists. It has united us and made us more thoughtful and deliberate in our actions. We have also made a new commitment to strengthening our grassroots activists. The Montana conservation movement is rich in people who deeply care about this state. Perhaps we should name our new campaign "Westerners for People!"

APPENDIX

Three Ways of Dealing with People for the West!

1. If you see that an environmental position has been painted as all bad, begin scrutinizing it. Look at the facts and arguments on both sides of the issue. Try to determine what is a legitimate concern and what is based on misinformation.

2. Before you speak, know your facts. Accuracy and thoroughness are the hallmarks of successful environmental campaigns. If an issue is emotionally charged, there is always a temptation to overstate your case. Succumbing to this temptation is bad: your long-term credibility is much more important than any temporary gain you might make by overstating facts. If you make a mistake, correct it as soon as it is discovered.

3. Although you should take your role as an environmentalist seriously, you can't afford to take yourself too seriously. You must understand that if attacks are made against you, it is merely business—don't take it personally. And above all, maintain your sense of humor—you'll need it.

Building Broad-Based Coalitions to Oppose Takings Legislation

Dana B. Larsen

On June 1, 1992, over the objections of public-interest groups, environmentalists, and nearly every newspaper in the state, Governor J. Fife Symington III signed into law the deceptively labeled Private Property Protection Act, making Arizona one of a few states to pass comprehensive legislation ostensibly designed to protect private property from burdensome government regulation. The passage of this law set the stage for a massive coalition effort by over 40 community organizations and activists to oppose its final enactment through a statewide referendum drive. During the summer and early fall of 1992, this coalition, the Take Back Your Rights Committee, collected more than 71,000 signatures in 90 days, forcing a public vote on the issue and thus suspending the law's enactment and implementation.

The most difficult, yet most important, aspect of building a coalition to fight the takings legislation was to forge an understanding of how broadly sweeping its implications truly were. The experience of the Take Back Your Rights Committee in Arizona underscores the necessity of creating and maintaining a broad-based coalition in fighting and defeating takings legislation. This chapter is offered to assist citizens in other states in preparing for and successfully defeating such assaults on public health and safety protections.

PASSAGE OF TAKINGS LEGISLATION IN ARIZONA

During the 1992 Arizona legislative session, conservative Republican legislators led by Representative Mark Killian (House Majority Leader and now Speaker of the House) joined with a few conservative and rural Democrats led by Senator Gus Arzberger in introducing a number of bills that dealt with defining and expanding property rights. When such takings legislation was first introduced rather late in the legislative session, no one in the public-interest or environmental community fully understood its complexity or its full implications until Sierra Club activists and David Baron, an attorney for the Arizona Center for Law in the Public Interest, began to sound the alarm, alerting the rest of the public-interest community.

Effects of Takings Legislation

This legislation would require state agencies to account for and assess any possible adverse effect on the profitable use of property before taking action to protect the environment or public health and safety. Then, if some adverse effect were identified, the agency would be required to estimate what the state budget impact would be if the state were required to compensate affected property owners for their loss of profitability.

The proponents argued that this law would only create new levels of review. On the contrary, it would do far more: It would change the basic standards for action by a government agency so as to avoid having any act to protect public health and safety become a taking.

New Standards Created

The legislation stated that "the mere assertion of a public health and safety purpose is insufficient to avoid a taking. Therefore, actions that are purportedly to protect public health and safety shall be (1) taken only in response to a "direct & substantial threat" to public safety, (2) designed to advance "significantly" the health and safety purpose, (3) no greater than necessary to achieve the public health and safety purpose, and (4) "proportionate" to that property's contribution to the overall problem. These are entirely new standards put forward by this law and exist no where else in Arizona law.

As David Baron noted, the practical effects of these requirements would be to shut down any state agencies that get in the way of unlimited exploitation of natural resources, uninhibited industrial and other pollution, and unchecked hazards to public health. It could paralyze those agencies that attempt to address every conceivable impact they might have on the "profitable use of property." The net effect would be a dangerous chilling and choking off of any actions involving regulations, permits, licenses, and other protections designed to safeguard our communities.

If the legislation didn't succeed in killing legitimate state agency actions, the special interests could then move to the courts to try to win financial compensation for their lost profitability. Their expectation would be that the courts would be pressured to grant compensation—at taxpayer expense—and that gradually taxpayers would revolt against environmental and public health protection regulations. If this law were allowed to stand, it could either bankrupt the state by underwriting corporate profitability or mean the end of environmental and public health and safety protection.

The Proponents of Takings Legislation

Because the environmental community was late in fully understanding the impact of takings legislation, and the fact that its supporters were already fully mobilized, passage of the legislation was practically assured. In addition to the expected rural and extractive industries, such as the Arizona Farm Bureau and the mining, timber, and grazing industries, the takings supporters also included urban allies in the Arizona Chamber of Commerce. Additionally, and perhaps uniquely in Arizona, takings proponents captured the state AFL-CIO support, which proved critical in their winning legislative passage. Organized labor's endorsement was instrumental in winning a few key Democratic votes by assuring them that takings legislation would not have any effect on workers' health and safety conditions.

The proponents of the takings legislation had their arguments and slogans well prepared and well rehearsed. The Arizona Chamber even distributed campaign buttons that read "I Love Private Property," with the little heart symbol. They stressed over and over that this legislation would merely codify existing case law and simply require government agencies to assess their rules and regulations for takings implications before implementation. The legislation was characterized as "getting big government off the back of the little guy" and, most important, as "protecting private-property rights." The proponents argued that small businesses are being strangled by government regulations, causing Arizona to lose important jobs. Their slogans and rhetoric clearly captured the imagination of a majority in the legislature. Additionally, their preparation in building their coalition isolated and marginalized the opposition.

The opponents of the takings legislation were left to fight a defensive battle, using only logic and reason in trying to explain why the supporters' arguments were inaccurate. Those who work in the legislative process know that it rarely is moved by mere logic and reason—it is not like an appellate court. The opponents at first could only argue that the legislation was too costly and unnecessary, and that the supporters had not presented any evidence that a state regulation had resulted in a taking. We were in a position of being characterized as opposing the protection of private property.

BUILDING THE TAKE BACK YOUR RIGHTS COALITION: THE ARIZONA EXPERIENCE

Preparing a Challenge to the Law

Those of us who opposed the legislation met several times in the following two weeks to examine our options. After Governor Symington signed the bill, it would become law within 90 days unless successfully challenged. The Arizona Constitution allows for a voter referendum on laws that are not passed with an emergency provision. To force a referendum on a law, within 90 days of legislative adjournment, opponents have to gather signature petitions from at least five percent of those who voted in the last gubernatorial election. In our case, that meant we needed to collect 53,000 valid signatures from Arizona voters during the 90 days of the Arizona summer. It seemed like an especially daunting task. Our only other options were either to let the law stand, demonstrate how bad it was, and seek its eventual repeal or to seek relief through the courts, which we were advised was at best problematic.

The handful of people who had been involved in opposing the bill in the legislature knew that we would be unable to gather the required number of signatures in such a short time on our own. If we were to have any hope of success, we would need the support of a much larger group.

Personal Contacts

Building a successful coalition on this or any other issue is largely the result of personal contacts and connections with individuals and organizations. In Common Cause, we follow the guideline that we have no permanent friends and no permanent enemies. This applies to our lobbying efforts with legislators and with other community groups. On some issues there is a natural and obvious convergence of interests, while on other issues the possibilities for alliances are less obvious. The lesson here is not to assume that other groups will support or oppose your efforts on the takings issue, or on any other issue for that matter. You cannot overestimate the importance of maintaining open lines of communication and building on personal relationships.

Over the past few years in Arizona, we have tried to build an on-going and formalized interconnection between some of the major public-interest and environmental organizations. For instance, Arizona Common Cause has recruited members of the Sierra Club, the Center for Law in the Public Interest, and consumer and neighborhood advocates to its Governing Board. It was this formalized relationship that brought Common Cause into the fight and helped expand the coalition.

Rob Smith of the Sierra Club made a request of the Common Cause State Governing Board that it oppose the takings legislation, and this request was bolstered by an analysis of the legislation by David Baron of the Arizona Center for Law in the Public Interest. Both of these men are known and respected by the Board, and when they explained the impact of the legislation, the Board was convinced.

After receiving final approval to adopt this issue, I was able to go to the individuals and organizations that I am familiar with in the public-interest community, and the Sierra Club was able to mobilize the environmental groups. However, we recognized that in order to stop this legislation, we needed to expand beyond those groups. The issue needed to be understood and adopted by a much larger population.

Reshaping the Message

Our coalition had to explain a message that was more than simply an argument against the need to protect private property—no one can successfully argue against wanting to protect private property. We had to argue the bill on our terms, not theirs. We developed a message based on what is wrong with the legislation, i.e., what would happen if the law were allowed to go into effect. Our message focused on how takings legislation would undermine not only environmental protection standards but also the state's ability to enforce public health and safety regulations. We also stressed the financial aspects of the legislation, such as the new levels of bureaucracy that would be created and who would have to pay the cost of cleaning up the pollution under such a system.

Once we were able to articulate a clear and concise message about the negative impact of this legislation on various communities of interest we could then go to these communities to enlist their support in fighting the takings legislation.

Reaching beyond the Traditional Environmental Groups

It is important to be able to speak to prospective coalition members about an issue in terms of their concerns, whether it is for environmental, health care, or zoning concerns. Why is this issue important to them? How does it affect them? Second, it is most helpful if you have some personal contact or connection with the group you wish to enlist. Just as it was helpful for the Common Cause board to have people they knew and trusted explain the issue, it was critical to have people that were known and trusted speak to the groups we wished to join the coalition. Once again personal relationships are the key to successful lobbying efforts, whether with the legislature, the media, or with coalition partners.

When asking for their help, it is important to be specific and clear on what you want them to do and for them to know how they can make a difference. By the time we got to the referendum campaign to keep the law from going into effect, we were asking coalition members to endorse our efforts to stop the law, to help gather signatures on petitions, to provide financial support to the campaign committee, to print information in their newsletters, and to go to their individual members for support. When the issue is still in the legislative arena, coalition members can be asked to testify on the bill and to have their individual members write and call specific legislators.

In addition to the array of environmental organizations, and the public-interest groups like Common Cause, the Arizona Center for Law in the Public Interest, the League of Women Voters, and Arizona Citizen Action, we also received support from the Arizona State Democratic Party and the Maricopa County Democratic Party as well as the Arizona Green Party.

Some of the key community groups that joined our coalition to oppose the takings legislation were members of the religious community, particularly the peace and justice committees (Arizona Ecumenical Council and the Unitarian Universalist Church), senior citizen groups (Valley of the Sun Grey Panthers), neighborhood associations in Phoenix and Tucson, health care workers from organizations such as the Arizona Public Health Association, the Arizona Consumers Council, ACORN (Association of Community Organizations for Reform Now), and the Arizona Heritage Alliance. The Heritage Alliance is an affiliation of organizations that won passage of an initiative to provide state funds for environmental protection and development of parks and historic preservation. This group helped us to reach a whole new audience of historic preservation and archeological groups.

Speaking Their Language

One example of how we engaged a community of interest outside of the non-traditional environmental groups was with the religious organizations in the state. This experience provided important lessons on how to present our issues in the language that is most familiar to a specific audience. Once again, personal relationships are tremendously valuable in making contacts and appointments. It is important to know your audience, not just in terms of their issues but also in terms of their culture—that is, their values and language.

Within certain religious groups there is a strong tradition of environmental concern, a respect and reverence for the earth; a belief in the idea that the natural environment is a gift and a blessing not to be abused and that we have a responsibility for stewardship of this gift to ensure that God's handiwork (nature) is still there for our children and grandchildren and all future generations. Additionally, many religious organizations also are directly involved in child day-care operations and elder-care facilities and are familiar with regulations protecting health and safety. With that in mind, we were able to speak to various religious groups about takings legislation from the aspect of its threat to environmental protection as well as its impact on health and safety regulation.

Fully Utilizing Coalition Partners

Most of the environmental groups were relatively easy to persuade to join the coalition once we were able to present the issue in familiar terms. What was important after that was how to get them fully involved in the fight. How do we let our own members know what we want them to do? After mailing out alerts and newsletters, how can we make the most effective direct contact with individual members?

For instance, the Sierra Club sponsors numerous hikes, outings, and events each month. We made a point of providing information about the takings legislation and our campaign, including petitions to sign, that outings leaders could pass on to the people on the hike. We even had volunteers set up at trail heads on weekends to pass out information to hikers and campers and obtain their signatures. We tried to be sure that coalition partners engaged and involved their members in similar ways whether through church or neighborhood events.

Providing Information to Members

We found that our coalition partners needed for us to provide them with written information that could help them explain takings legislation clearly and concisely to their members. Having simple one-page fact sheets about the legislation was most welcome; some groups, however, wanted the more detailed legal analysis that we provided. Additionally, we found that supplying them with copies of news articles and editorials on the topic was effective because it demonstrated that other people saw the issue in much the same way. We could then point to the news stories and editorials and say, don't just take our word for it, here's what the *Tribune* or *Star* has to say, which added to the credibility of our arguments. We also provided new groups with the growing lists of coalition partners to demonstrate the breadth and depth of support for our side.

Some Benefits of a Broad-Based Coalition

By expanding beyond the nontraditional environmental groups, the Take Back Your Rights Committee was able to reach the much wider audience critical to our petition drive. It helped us to learn to develop the necessary vocabulary for explaining the implications of this legislation to the general public, which is vital in winning at the ballot box. Moreover, it helped us to combat the image that our opponents try to paint of us—that we are just another special-interest group or that we are more concerned about trees and animals than we are about people. By speaking to a wide range of people of diverse backgrounds and concerns, we always needed to keep in mind the human dimension of our undertaking: what will be this legislation's impact on human life.

By the time we finished with the successful signature-gathering part of the campaign, more than 40 organizations and 30 public officials had become partners in fighting the takings legislation in Arizona.

LEARNING FROM THE ARIZONA EXPERIENCE

While each state legislative battle over takings has its own distinctive character, a few key lessons appear to have emerged from our experience in Arizona.

Anticipate. We can expect to see takings legislation in most every state, and certainly every western state. It is coming, so be ready for it. If you are prepared, and know the rhetoric and slogans of the takings/Wise Use proponents, you will know how to offer effective counter arguments.

Start early. Without a doubt, our late start hurt our legislative efforts. Don't wait until the takings legislation is in front of you before you start building your coalitions. Get a jump on the other side. Also, let friendly legislators know what to anticipate and provide them information with which to fight the legislation.

Enlist organized labor. The takings battle in the Arizona legislature was narrowly lost because early on the proponents captured the state AFL–CIO, which was persuaded that environmental deregulation would translate into economic growth and job creation. Nationally, the AFL–CIO opposes this kind of legislation in Congress; in many other states, such as Montana, organized labor is active in fighting takings legislation. In fact, most labor organizations recognize that the net effect of this kind of legislation would be to seriously undermine regulations protecting worker health and safety.

Get cost estimates on implementation of takings legislation. If you can, get estimates from government agencies on what they expect it to cost to implement this legislation, including both the cost of doing the regulatory review for takings implications as well as the expected costs for paying takings claims. In Arizona, three state agencies estimated their costs for simply doing the takings assessments would be at least $500,000. That was just three agencies out of nearly 40. The Arizona Department of Transportation estimated that it would cost them as much as an additional $10 million to do their current projects under the takings guidelines. After those figures came out, the governor directed the rest of his agency heads not to release any further information.

If agencies or departments can provide that information, and legislators, the media, and the public know its real costs to taxpayers, it could be critical in defeating this legislation. Where and when it is possible, ask friendly legislators to seek cost analysis for such legislation.

CONCLUSION

At the end of the 90 days, the Take Back Your Rights coalition turned in more than 71,600 signatures to the Arizona secretary of state's office. Such an effort would not have been possible without the support and efforts of a large and broad-based coalition. The signatures were sent to the county recorder's office, which verified a sufficient number to validate our petition drive. The secretary of state has certified that the issue will be on the November 1994 general election ballot. Hoping to challenge our place on the ballot, the Arizona Farm Bureau went through our petitions, looking for any irregularities; but after weeks of review, they abandoned their effort.

The Take Back Your Rights coalition is currently organizing and trying to raise money to fight the battle to defeat the takings legislation in November 1994. [*On November 8, 1994, the voters in Arizona decided by a 60–40 margin to repeal the Arizona takings law. Eds.*]

Finding the Ties That Bind

Coalitions with Agriculture Groups

Teresa Erickson

Over 20 years ago, a group of ranchers and farmers organized themselves to fight strip mining in Montana. These people didn't wear birkenstocks or read *Mother Jones.* They were (are) redneck cowboys (girls), individuals who drove pickup trucks and ate big steaks, but who exhibited a strong sense of stewardship to the land. They raised money, read environmental impact statements, organized lobby trips, wrote letters, made phone calls, staged actions against regulatory agencies, and did all the things more closely identified with environmental activism. At the same time, these people earned their living raising livestock and planting and harvesting grains.

This handful of people grew into the Northern Plains Resource Council (NPRC), an enduring organization that to this day fights for clean water, clean air, unabused land, and social justice. The membership is still primarily made up of families earning their living in agriculture.

What has kept the NPRC together is a focus on people's self-interest. The term *self-interest* wears the negative connotation of selfishness. Yet, it is the cable that holds together all successful coalitions. And, for purposes of this writing, is the secret to forging an alliance between agriculture and environmentalism.

In the case of NPRC, the agrarian membership took up the cause of clean water, clean air, and land stewardship because it was in their best interest. Grass doesn't grow well, or at all, in contaminated soil. Livestock abort, contract diseases, and have lower survival rates when drinking contaminated water. Communities become tumultuous, unsafe, expensive, and hostile when rapid "boom" growth occurs from mining. If a rancher wants a decent life, and has the moxie to fight for it, then he or she is a natural born environmentalist.

In the 21 years of NPRC's existence, the organization has gone on to tackle other natural-resource issues besides coal strip mining. Today, one of the organization's primary focuses is reform of the notorious 1872 Mining Law. The enthusiasm to change this law is coming from ranchers who live in areas affected by hard-rock mining. They are people whose springs and wells have dried up when a tunnel-boring machine pierced an underground aquifer, consequently draining it and altering its behavior forever. They are people who live near abandoned mine sites oozing acid drainage into surface and groundwater. They are people who have found traces of cyanide in their wells. And they are people whose lifestyle and values have been threatened by boom conditions and the resulting social disorders. Again, they are people whose self-interest is in getting the law reformed.

Another example of agri-environmentalism is rural people fighting to reform waste policy. Why? Because sparsely populated areas that are semiarid are the bull's-eye for mega landfills and incinerators that import solid and hazardous wastes from everywhere else. Because it is *their* air and groundwater that are put at risk just because the city council of some distant metropolis decided that disposal in the West is easier than implementing a decent waste-reduction program at home.

NPRC finds that the issue most effective in tying together agriculture and environmentalism is water. Water is so precious in the West that threats to its quantity or quality can bring together interest that may have nothing else in common.

Local, state, and national environmental organizations have been allies with NPRC in most of its efforts. To avoid the seemingly inevitable skirmishes that break out among organizations, care was taken to communicate and divide up responsibilities. Of particular concern was establishing agreements on who got credit for victories and who took the heat for controversies. Without such agreements, and they haven't always been made, coalition efforts between agricultural and environmental interests have been thorny and unproductive, even when self-interest was present.

STAYING LOCAL

A phenomenon that will always exist between local and national organizations, ranging from friction to outright conflict, is how decisions are made in public-policy fights. Local groups contend (and this is the perspective of NPRC) that those who must live with the direct consequences of a law or rule should have at least equal say in legal and legislative negotiations. National environmental groups are often guilty of shaping policy that affects agriculture and rural areas without any knowledge of practical application. Further, because the Washington, D.C., beltway is largely insulated from public opinion in the heartland, national groups develop policy without regard for how it sells back home. We contend that perception is almost as powerful as reality, and if the locals don't understand something that they are going to have to live with, it invites fear, confusion, and rebellion. Local groups then become the cleanup crew or scapegoat for such misunderstandings. Much of this conflict can be avoided with honest and frequent communication between national and local groups.

Offered here is some proof for these contentions about local opinion. In late 1991, NPRC commissioned a poll in Montana to gauge public opinion regarding a host of mining, water protection, and waste issues. Overall the results were interesting as well as encouraging, but one question in particular raised a point worth fleshing out here. The question read as follows:

I am going to read you a list of organizations and types of people and for each one I want you to tell me whether you think they have too much power, not enough power, or about the right amount of power in influencing environmental policy in Montana.

The following are the results (in percentages):

Power	Too much power	Not enough
Montana citizens	3	64
State government	39	20
Montana corporations	20	28
Out-of-state environmental groups	54	10
Montana environmental groups	24	24
Farmers and ranchers	8	51
Federal government	52	12
Out-of-state corporations	60	11

We concluded that Montanans see good and bad actors on both sides. But they know who the bad guys on both sides are: out-of-state organizations. There is little doubt that the most effective actors will be those who most accurately represent average, ordinary people in Montana. Voters resent out-of-state corporations, organizations, and the federal government, all of whom lack credibility on environmental issues in Montana. They will be ineffective, if not detrimental, for either side.

With this question and others in the poll, there was no doubt who voters want to see more involved in the decision-making process: Montana citizens, especially farmers and ranchers. Nearly two-thirds, 64 percent, think Montana citizens do not have enough influence on environmental policy, and only 3 percent think they have too much power.

The poll data were clear—lasting environmental policy accepted and even embraced by the people whom it affects should be shaped by local people.

VYING FOR AGRICULTURE

Farmers and ranchers are angry, hurt, and lashing back. It is virtually impossible to pick up an ag publication without finding articles that condemn environmentalism.

Extractive and disposal industries are in hot pursuit to win over the agricultural constituency. Polarization is occurring and, for certain industries and for the right wing, it is a condition to be wished for and actively pursued. For with polarization, environmental protection reforms in coal and hard-rock mining will not happen; and garbage trains will carry the wastes of eastern cities west to be dumped on the plains.

The mining, waste disposal, timber, and other industries that impose environmental costs on the rest of society are eager to block almost any environmental protection measure. The waste-disposal industry, scared to death of local control, fights any measures that would allow local citizens some control over siting plans. The mining industry has gone so far as to create its own political movement. The Wise Use movement is largely a concoction of mining industry groups, from which, at least in Montana, it has received the vast majority of its money.

These firms are anxious about the mounting pressure for mining-law reform and have realized that they need a broader political base in order to keep stifling such legislation. So their hired organizers go from group to group, decrying government interference in their lives, and involving farmers, ranchers, and even snowmobile groups. You can bet your bottom dollar that massive mining firms, often controlled from Canada, Australia, and Japan, don't give a damn about some Angus rancher in Rosebud County, Montana. But if they can get that rancher to speak against mining-law reform, maybe write to his or her congressman, then the Wise Use charade will have paid off for these corporate giants.

If that rancher is already feeling hostile toward environmental groups, then the Wise Use agenda has an easy target. But if that rancher is familiar with local environmental or citizen groups and is a member of one, then he or she won't be easily used by the Wise Use people. That rancher will know that environmental protection doesn't mean a bunch of people he or she will never meet and with whom there is nothing in common. And when a rancher who knows that environmentalism means protecting water and a rural way of life is told that environmental protections are only advocated by San Francisco and Washington, D.C., socialites, then that lie will be exposed.

The mining industry has learned the value of developing a political base at the local level. One could argue that some of the national conservation groups have something to learn from them.

INDIVIDUALS VERSUS ORGANIZATIONS

Agriculture is a word that encompasses a broad assortment of people and economies. There is no one self-interest that applies to all of agriculture; and in fact, something that is good for one may be bad for another. So it is difficult to pin down the "who" in agriculture. Though used liberally throughout this writing, the word *agriculture* pertains to individuals whose livelihoods are in agriculture.

It is significant to note that NPRC's success in ag/environmental alliances has not been with ag groups. In fact, the Montana Stockgrowers Association, the Montana Wool Growers Association, the Montana Farm Bureau, and the Montana Grain Growers have almost always been our opposition, even on nonenvironmental issues. A lot of futile effort has gone into seeking coalition with formal organizations. No good explanation for this situation can be offered because it is difficult to fathom. NPRC surmises, because of our own experience with the vigilance required to remain grassroots and member-controlled, that the leadership of these groups is out of touch with the membership. The executive directors are an easy target for an industry "win-over" strategy. Often, the staffs of these ag groups are lobbying on behalf of the mining and oil and gas industries, and yet their efforts are not reported in their legislative newsletters. Resolutions passed at some of their annual meetings do not authorize them to take up the cause of industry giants, but they do it anyway. On many occasions, NPRC has witnessed these groups actually campaigning for policy that would be disastrous to certain individuals in agriculture.

NPRC has had some success, however, with more populist ag groups, such as Farmer's Union and National Farmer's Organization, mainly because these groups tend to be closer to their membership. But overall, the most fruitful efforts take us back to the principle of self-interest of the individual. Through individuals who hold membership in one or more of the aforementioned groups, we have neutralized the opposition by agitation from within. For example, in the mid-1970s, NPRC members who were also Stockgrowers went to their annual convention with a resolution supporting strip-mine reclamation. Following a heated debate, a proreclamation resolution passed. The Stockgrowers leadership didn't lead a charge for reclamation, but they did get their wings clipped from weighing in on behalf of the coal industry, which they have a propensity to do.

Most of the ag groups have local chapters that meet from time to time. When some of our own membership also hold membership in an ag group, we have had success in raising environmental reform issues at the chapter level. Though not always successful in winning chapter support, we've created debate and cleared up misconceptions.

This strategy will be crucial in the reauthorization of the Clean Water Act. Agricultural publications and organizations are in a panic mode over the non-point pollution issues. Unless a workable solution that is gradual in its implementation is ultimately developed, the embers of hostility toward environmentalism will burst into flame.

SUMMARY

As the farmworker organizer Cesar Chavez once said: "When people ask me how I organize, I think it is a silly question. Why of course, I talk to one person, then I go talk to another, and another." There is no substitute for face-to-face communication and building personal relationships. Agricultural people tend to be very polite and practiced in dealing with honesty. People with an environmental purpose who take the time and care to communicate in a nonhostile way with farmers and ranchers *will* gain ground.

Coalitions and alliances between environmentalists and agricultural people are based on the principle of interest, one-on-one communication, and a willingness to try and understand how environmental regulations and policies affect the farmer and rancher. Through these principles the ever-fraying thread between the two interests can be strengthened.

One last thought. NPRC also believes that farmers and ranchers must try to understand the thoughts of the environmentalist. And if this writing were to be going to an agricultural audience, the reverse would be true in virtually every statement. That is to say, it is in the self-interest of farmers and ranchers, because they are in the minority, to seek coalitions with environmental groups. It must work both ways for truly lasting and positive public policy to happen.

Countering the Resource Abuse Movement

Douglass North

To counter the resource abuse movement's attack on conservation, it is helpful to think about the movement's appeal to rural Americans. This chapter describes those elements of appeal and provides some practical advice about countering them in the context of river conservation efforts. The Wise Use appeal rests on four basic elements:

1. Fear of unknown regulations
2. Fear of the government
3. Fear of limitations on private-property rights
4. Lies

FEAR OF UNKNOWN REGULATIONS

Property owners are not intimately familiar with all the laws and programs available to protect rivers. They are understandably concerned that a conservation proposal could impose onerous regulations on them. Their fear of the unknown is often greater than any concern they might have about a real program. The best counter to fear of the unknown is education. The people who may be affected by a conservation program need to have information on it so they can understand it. It is important to get information to people *before* the resource abuse movement becomes active in the area. Once the resource abuse movement has had an opportunity to scare everyone with its lies, communication becomes very difficult.

Educate People in the River Valley

Getting the necessary information to the people in a river valley can be difficult. There are no readily available mailing lists or periodicals which everyone is sure to read. If the population of a river valley is small enough, it may be possible to reach nearly everyone through a series of public meetings and some articles in the local paper. You could even go door-to-door with information to reach everyone with land along the river. If your conservation effort is directed to a broader region or a populous river valley, it may be impossible to reach people in this manner.

Work with the Media

For broader campaigns, it is particularly important to educate the media. You must get to know the reporters who cover conservation and environmental stories at all the regional and local newspapers, radio and TV stations. They must have your information and know how to get in touch with you when a story breaks. You must also educate them about the resource abuse movement, so the reporters are aware of how deceptive and misleading most of the information put out by the movement is. Collect articles from other media to use to educated your media. They won't fall for the resource abuse movement's propaganda without checking out the facts first.

FEAR OF THE GOVERNMENT

Most Americans, particularly those living in rural areas, have a fear and distrust of the government, particularly the federal government. To them, the federal government consists of faceless bureaucrats enforcing strict regulations which do not apply to their local situation.

Disassociate Your Effort from the Government

Unfortunately, most river-protection programs involve laws or the government in some fashion, so the resource abuse movement plays upon rural fears of the government to stir up opposition to any conservation proposals. There is simply no way to win the battle for people's hearts and minds if you are saddled with being an apologist for everything the government does. The only tactic which can help neutralize the government bashing engaged in by the resource abuse movement is to refuse to allow them to saddle you with the government on your side of the debate.

It's best to agree that you can't trust the bureaucrats and that's exactly why you want to enact the conservation program you are promoting. Point out that the river protection program you are promoting tells the bureaucrats exactly what to do instead of giving them a lot of discretion to decide how to resolve issues. Point out that it is the resource abuse movement that wants to leave the bureaucrats with the broad discretion allowed by current law. This will not completely negate the resource abuse movement's antigovernment appeal, but it should reduce it.

FEAR OF LIMITS ON PRIVATE-PROPERTY RIGHTS

Wise Use advocates do have a point here. Most conservation programs do place limits on what a private landowner can do with his or her land. What they fail to note is that such limits are essential to maintaining the value of everyone's property rights, including the affected landowner's. What good are your unfettered property rights if you have no clean water, clean air, or access to your property because unfettered development has fouled the air and water and clogged all the roadways with congestion?

Clearly Define the Takings Issue

Resource abuse advocates are often concerned about governmental takings which may occur when the value of private property may be reduced due to regulations restricting its use. It is important to note that not all conservation programs involve a takings issue. Certainly, simple land acquisition from willing sellers presents no such problems. Similarly, National Wild & Scenic designation presents no takings issue because designation has no effect on private property unless the government pays for any deed restrictions placed on the property.

Include Diminution of Public Property

Resource abuse advocates frequently champion legislation to require compensation to landowners for any diminution in value of their lands due to environmental regulations. This legislation addresses only one side of the equation. The other side is the diminution in value of public property that belongs to all citizens due to actions taken by private landowners. When a private landowner builds roads and clear-cuts his or her land, his or her actions increase the amount of silt in the water and raise the water temperature, harming fish and shellfish habitat downstream in the bay or ocean into which the water empties. If we are to have legislation requiring compensation to landowners for the impact of environmental regulations, then the same legislation should require private landowners to compensate the public when the actions they take harm the public's fish, wildlife, clean water, and clean air. Not to mention neighboring private landowners.

LIES

The resource abuse movement's appeal relies heavily upon exaggerations, distortions, and outright lies. This tactic is very effective in the short run because it allows the movement to quickly inflame the public's passions about the supposed gross injustices done to rural people by government and urban environmentalists. In the long run, however, the lies and distortions come back to haunt the resource abuse movement. Once the real information is brought before the public, and particularly before decision makers, they realize that they have been had. At that point the resource abuse movement ceases to have very much credibility.

"Weather the Storm"

The resource abuse movement is frequently successful in stopping conservation legislation in the short term because its wild claims can mobilize opposition very quickly. Based on our experience in Washington, their effectiveness usually peaks at about three to six months. After about six months, people begin to discover that they have been had by the resource abuse distortions and the movement's effectiveness levels off. After about nine months, its effectiveness begins to decline.

Consequently, in many cases, conservationists simply have to disprove the resource abuse movement's wild claims and wait it out. The movement may well be able to prevent any legislation from passing in any given year. But if conservationists refute the misleading claims and continue to work their proposal, they are likely to be successful the next year or the year thereafter. The resource abuse movement makes conservation more difficult and often delays good legislation, but it rarely defeats good conservation in the long run.

APPENDIX: OTHER WINNING STRATEGIES TO FIGHT RESOURCE ABUSE RHETORIC AND TACTICS

Get Involved and Get Others Involved

Our voices need to be heard. If concerned citizens speak out in support of wildlife and the environment, the resource abuse movement will be hard put to change laws and regulations that protect all of us, in favor of a few special interests.

- Establish a strong and constant presence at local planning meetings and hearings.
- Coordinate with other environmental groups in your community.
- Contact civic, business, political, educational, and religious leaders in your community. Recruit spokespeople from the ranks of those groups the resource abuse people claim to represent, such as farmers.
- Identify potential Wise Use converts and reach out to them. Show them why protecting the environment is good for them and their children. Be careful not to alienate them with statements that make sweeping generalizations that include them such as "all ranchers and farmers are antienvironment."
- Go on the offensive; be proactive and positive. Don't be forced into apologizing for an environmental position. We are not antipeople, we are for an improved quality of life for all. Get accurate information on issues about which the resource abuse movement is likely to spread misinformation— before they do so.

Expose Resource Abuse Rhetoric

A common tactic of the resource abusers is to distort the facts or make up facts so that they sound reasonable.

- Read what they are saying and research the correct facts. Get on their mailing lists. Pay particular attention to the economics of environmental protection. Point out how environmental protection and conservation results in increased long-term economic security. Emphasize quality of life issues—imagine a future without clean air, clean water, trees, and wildlife.
- Find out and publicize who the resource abuse groups in your area actually represent. Most are supported by industry.
- Explain what would happen if we follow the recommendations of the resource abuse groups. Describe how differently your community might look if there had been no environmental regulations in place over the last 20 years.

Reach Out to the Mass Media

Some newspapers and magazines seem to be taking the side of resource abusers due to their emphasis on jobs and supposed grassroots clout.

- Unearth the facts that contradict the resource abuse platform. Share this information at public meetings and meet personally with editorial boards.
- Start simply. One easy first step is to write a letter to the editor or a piece for the op/ed section. Recruit someone well known in the community to also write such a letter.

- Develop a relationship with your paper, radio, or local television station. Be a source of accurate and interesting information about environmental issues and the resource abuse movement.
- Keep your messages simple, personal, and related to reader/viewer concerns. Back up passion with facts.

Other Suggestions

- Stand strong in the face of the intimidating tactics of resource abusers. If you set the example, others are likely to support you.
- Stake the moral high ground. Don't let yourself be drawn into a shouting match. Continue to counter hyperbole with facts.

VIII

Message and the Media

The successes of the Wise Use movement are due in no small part to its leaders' effective use of television and newspapers to communicate their message. The success of environmentalists' efforts to combat Wise Use and advance their own agenda will depend on understanding the appeal of the Wise Use message and how it is communicated, as well as understanding how the general public perceives environmental issues and environmentalists.

In "Working with the Media," Jim Bernfield explains the importance of activists learning how to utilize media outlets to get their views before the general public. He offers practical advice on communicating with the media, obtaining coverage in newspapers, radio, and television, and getting editorials and letters to the editor published.

One of the great success stories of the Wise Use movement was the defeat of added protections for Yellowstone Park through the weakening of the Greater Yellowstone Vision Document. In "Wise Use and the Greater Yellowstone Vision Document: Lessons Learned," Robert Ekey of the Greater Yellowstone Coalition attributes this victory to the Wise Use movement's ability to get its message out and control the debate in the media. Based on this experience, Ekey offers various strategies for countering Wise Use activities and for effectively communicating the environmental message.

Understanding how the media perceive the debate is also important. The media are the primary means by which both the Wise Use movement and conservationists reach the general public. Part VIII concludes with "Working Journalists Speak Out on Wise Use," a panel discussion held at the 1992 annual conference of the Society of Environmental Journalists. Two prominent journalists who cover the environment, Keith Schneider of the *New York Times* and Turner Broadcasting's Sharon Collins, offer their perspectives on the Wise Use movement both as a "story" and as a political phenomenon.

Working with the Media

Jim Bernfield

You must have the tools at hand to build your case before the people. The media, wisely used, provide one of the most important tools to communicate with the public. But just as you need the media to sell your agenda, the media need you to fill out their stories.

Good media coverage must be earned. The only way to do that is to make the media campaign a high priority, considered at every step of your efforts. On a strategic level, you must craft bankable soundbites, assiduously work reporters, and spend time to determine how best to frame your issues. On a tactical level, you must plan, support, and execute your media campaign as carefully as one might build a court case or a run for public office. If you aggressively pursue news coverage, it will come. If you are waiting for the press to come to you, have a good book handy—you'll be waiting for a while.

This section describes how to use the media to spread the message. First is an overview of your job of outreach as a public interest advocate. Next is a description of the role of a media contact within your organization. Finally, the basic tactics of gaining media attention are provided.

MEDIA AND MESSAGE

The first critical step to designing your media campaign is to define your message. Then, at all costs, stick to the message. Use any argument that delivers that message, but stick to the message. Consider your audience and adapt your arguments to their interests. Consider the news atmosphere and adapt your arguments to the times. But stick to the message.

One of your most difficult jobs will be coming up with new news pegs on which to hang the stories. The peg is the salient news item that draws reporters to listen to your message. Your message should never vary, but you can make news again and again by working similar stories off of different pegs. Your efforts will only succeed if the right message is brought to the right audience. Remember that different media have different audiences, and target accordingly.

Additionally, national environmental groups need to get into the habit of communicating to various local groups effective means of getting reporters' attention and the national groups' upcoming agendas. If you can show local impact from an issue in the national news, you will get the attention of the local media.

Every invitation to speak and every news event is an opportunity to discredit and marginalize Wise Use. An indictment of the Wise Use movement—sharp at certain times, subtle at other times—should be woven into every speech, interview, and news release.

NETWORKING

The first step to good media relations is selecting a single person who will cultivate relationships with the professionals in the media—a local press secretary who will interact with the local media. It's important to have varied spokespeople who represent all aspects of your network of allies, but people in the media want to deal with someone with whom they have dealt before— someone they are sure understands their special needs. This person ought to be friendly and helpful, while having a firm understanding of the technical issues and how best to convey your message.

The people who work in media are professionals. They come to their jobs with the expectation that they can get the information they need to write their stories, and they are appreciative when the professionalism of the groups they deal with make it easier for them to do so.

One can't call the newsroom out of the blue and effectively plant a story. The press person should contact the news directors and appropriate reporters in the region, introduce the campaign and him- or herself, and send a packet of information about the local group. From then on, this person should lead all press contacts for the group. The media should know that this is the person with the authority to speak for your organization, the person who can give interviews on the record, give accurate background information, and speak authoritatively when he or she goes off the record.

The most important media tool is the ever-changing list of reporters and producers the press person must create and continually update. If your relationship with the media is carefully nurtured, the press will take calls from that person when you have a newsworthy event or your group has a comment to make on breaking news.

Building trust is the key to a good relationship with the media. That can be as simple as providing interviews long before deadline, to producing real news at news conferences about which the press can write a story, to returning favorable stories with better access to newsmakers. It can be as complex as providing a single reporter who will be in attendance at the Wise Use press conference with penetrating questions. Trust pays off.

A Few Tips

You spend a great deal of time familiarizing yourself with your issues while the press spends at most a few days or hours on it. You and your organization are real experts, relative to news reporters. This means that you can't expect a reporter to see through Wise Use propaganda as easily as you might. The better you educate reporters, the better story you will see in print or on television. Relay information to reporters with authority, and make your story as clear and simple as possible. But if you overstuff a reporter with abstruse detail, the story will most likely be muddied or garbled.

There is a market for information. Sometimes you are in a buyers' market, sometimes in a sellers' market. But only reporters know for sure. Part of the cultivation of reporters is to learn what kind of market you are in and use that information to get better results. There's no reason to have a press conference on an issue shared among three other environmental groups; promising an exclusive advance copy of a newsworthy report can have reporters practically bidding against one another to have the first story. The press contact's role is to use his or her connections to recognize each situation.

Press people can be gregarious, but being friendly is part of their job. Don't mistake camaraderie for friendship and pass along information that should not be seen in print.

Set up a system to monitor all aspects of the media for positive and negative attention. Newspaper and television coverage is easy to assess because it is so limited, but monitoring radio is a job for several listeners. Yet radio is critical because of the new politics of call-in shows.

Some of the best ideas for news actions come from studying the coverage of other news actions. If it worked once, chances are good that it will work again. Apply the principles that you see in other stories to the news actions you are considering.

Good stories can be praised to their authors as "fair and balanced," but every piece of skewed reporting should get a response. If the Wise Use movement seems to be dictating the agenda of a news source, a strong and swift response of calls and letters must be orchestrated showing the station or paper that you are a force to be considered.

COMMUNICATING WITH THE MEDIA

A good deal of effort goes into a news action. Basically, you must put yourself into reporters' shoes and consider what questions they could possibly have, no matter how off-base. Then you should attempt to answer every one of these questions by bringing the topic back to the message you are trying to send. There are some traditional avenues to answering all of the reporters' questions, from where and when an event will be held, to who the participants are, to what they are trying to say. The following section describes each one.

Advisory

Before any news event, the media must be alerted. The standard form is the media advisory, which should be faxed to reporters and the wire services' day-book no later than the day prior to an event. In as clear and as short a form as possible, an advisory should state the time, location, and purpose of an event. It should always list a phone contact so that reporters with questions about the event can call someone they know they can trust for information. After an advisory has been sent, it is always advisable to call the recipients and urge their attendance at the news event. These calls can have an ulterior purpose, as well, providing your organization with early insights into how the media view your proposed action and allowing you time to fine tune accordingly.

Press Release

The press release is the news story you would write if you were covering your news action for the press. Across the top of the page in all capitals, large letters reading "NEWS RELEASE" should be printed. A contact person who can speak authoritatively for the group, along with his or her phone number, should be listed. This person must be readily accessible, so that a reporter who needs to flesh out a story can do so. For example, an attorney who wrote the brief but has to appear in court the week of its release should not be selected as the lead contact on a story about a challenge to takings expansion legislation.

Then write a "slug" or proposed headline that is as provocative as possible. The rest of the release should be written in standard newspaper style. The lead paragraph should be a single sentence that provides the five W's and the one H. A message-driven quote should be as high in the story as possible; it should be no lower than the second paragraph. The rest of the story should be in inverted pyramid style, concluding with a paragraph describing your organization.

The News Action

Make life easy for reporters—make your news accessible and tangible with a news action. The news action is essentially a peg on which to hang your message, some reason for reporters to come listen to your message. It is typically best to make news as early in the day as possible for two reasons: (1) so that reporters have time to get reactions and file their stories before their deadlines and (2) to control the news day by staking the news cycle's first claim, off of which all other information must relate.

The press conference is the most straightforward of all news actions, but even a press conference can run from civil disobedience to the opening of a technical meeting. Creativity attracts the media, but care should be taken not to let creativity distract from your message or demean the serious intent of your program. Given environmentalists' special need to appear as moderate as you really are, careful consideration should be taken before some of the traditional green news actions are taken.

The practice of finding a message-driven site cannot be overemphasized. Television cameras can tell the story in pictures, reinforcing the words of the speaker. If background material is provided, the written press and radio will reinforce the speaker's claim by explaining the importance of the site. If it is appropriate, your group's logo can be prominent enough to be in the television shot or newspaper photo.

The news action is appropriate at every step of the process of shaping public policy. When grassroots action first brings an issue to the attention of government officials or opinion leaders, a media event should further the argument. When local legislators or other leaders are contacted or sign on to your proposals, there is a story to be had. When the Wise Use movement takes action against you, you should have a press event to expose them. Editorials written on the issue can be cause for an event. If your recommendations become law or your legal case is won, there is a news story to be advanced with a media event. Finally, media events can chronicle implementation of new laws or present the deleterious effects of bad policies.

Press Kits

Press kits are the meat of many stories. They usually begin with the press release, which describes the event. Fact sheets follow, providing detailed information to back up every claim made in the news action. Issue papers or other documentary evidence follow the fact sheets. These should offer additional substantiation and provide documents that might make good visuals on the news or in the paper. At the back of the kit, positive clips about the organization, a biography of the speaker, or other "flesh" should be provided.

Making reporters' lives easier will bring about better results for your organization. Make press packets available in advance of the news action as well as at the news action itself. This will lead to well-educated reporters and better stories. In addition, some reporters will write their stories straight from the press packet, and some won't even show up for the event itself. These reporters ought to be offered the packet by fax or delivery and provided a telephone interview if possible.

NEWS VENUES

Understanding the strengths and weaknesses of each news medium is essential to wise use of the media. Your press contact should be intimately familiar with the strengths and weaknesses of each venue. Provided here are thumbnail sketches of the major news venues.

A newspaper's greatest strength is its influence over opinion leaders—it is often where they get their news and insights, as a written story can be more thematic than radio or television. Radio is the workhorse for a low-cost public-information campaign. Especially in remote areas, radio gives the best return for the investment of work a public-interest group puts into media relations. Talk radio is an easy place to gain a forum—sometimes it only takes a phone call. Television is the most emotional of the media, and the most difficult to control. Properly used, television can tell your story better than any other medium.

Narrowcasting

Op-eds in the *New York Times,* articles in *Harper's,* or interviews on "All Things Considered" are helpful in reaching opinion leaders and creating a credible clips file. But the people who make up your target audience probably do not get their information from these sources. You need to reach these people using *Field and Stream,* local weekly papers, and venues like your regional "PM Magazine" show. That is not to say, for instance, that you should ignore the *Atlantic* if it were to repeat its horribly slanted "Wise Use" issue from winter 1991. Nor would you ignore an invitation to appear on "McNeil-Lehrer." But that's not the place to wage the brunt of the battle against Wise Use. It must be fought at the grass roots, with local issues and local heroes.

Newspaper

The newspaper offers many avenues of communication. There are hard news and features, the op-ed page, editorials, and letters to the editor to consider. Newspapers, especially smaller papers, continue a great tradition of concentrating on local coverage.

Letters to the Editor

Letters to the editor are a first step into the media. The letters the paper prints are widely read as a barometer of public opinion. Papers will publish more than one letter on a single subject, offering the well-organized group a way to be perceived as strong. A campaign of letters to the editor, though, should be well thought out. Letters from average citizens give the impression that local people care about an issue. Letters from noted leaders of groups suggest the organization is on top of the issues. A single letter from a coalition of groups can send a message of power. But editors, who hate form letters that clearly come from organized groups, can keep an opinion off their pages if they think they're being manipulated. Finally, letters should be pithy—definitely limit the length of letters to three hundred words.

Features

Done well, the soft news story, or feature, can earn a group significant support without confrontation. The feature is a seemingly apolitical item about people or happenings in a community. This is the second place to build a media presence. Consider the bumper crop of a local farmer who uses no pesticide, the reconstruction and preservation of a historic home by a young couple, the 75th anniversary of a town's incorporation, a day in the life of the retiring librarian—each can transmit your message. The best way to get such a story published is to pitch it—fully matured—to the features editor of the local paper. You need not be explicit about the message you are trying to get into the paper, just convey the human interest that the story provides. Especially in smaller towns, where human-interest features are the basis for the newspaper's existence, this can be a very successful effort.

Op-Eds

Op-eds must be concise, and are most widely accepted and read when pegged to breaking news. An op-ed piece offers an author wide latitude. Humor, well-reasoned arguments, attacks or counterattacks are all possible within the framework of the op-ed. But before writing, read several issues of the paper to make sure that your submission meets the format and style criteria of the paper.

When writing an op-ed, remember that once the article appears in print it will be taken by readers to be the agenda of the movement. That means that staying on your message is vital. A misguided op-ed can provide the opposition with fodder for attacking you with the most powerful weapon there is—your own words.

Hard News

In the end, the hard news story carries the majority of the weight of a political fight; letters and features offer the subtle introduction of your perspective. After the completion of careful research, and the careful grooming of spokespeople and media contacts, should come the hard news story. If the timing of your entrance into the hard news beat can be chosen, it ought to come after the introduction of your group through letters, features, and op-eds and should coincide with the introduction of your positive agenda. But once your opponents have forced issues upon you, the time for the hard news story is at hand.

The hard news story tells of the creation of important news, and it is where your message will directly clash with that of the Wise Use movement. Stay moderate but dictate the terms of the debate. Here you can put forth your positive message of health, public safety, and protection of our future.

Editorials

The most coveted space in the newspaper is the editorial. It puts the power of an entire newspaper on one side of an issue. A meeting with editorial boards can earn a supportive editorial or quash a negative one—it is an endeavor worth seeking.

After your group has earned a reputation for effectiveness, or if it has something newsworthy to share, the editorial-page editor of the local newspaper should be called and a meeting requested. The most respected leaders and spokespeople of the organization should attend. Consider this meeting an important public speech for a small, select audience. Have a clear message and practice making a case for a positive editorial. At the meeting, distribute fact sheets, much like a press packet, to buttress all of the claims that are made. If at the conclusion of the meeting the editors have not offered to write an editorial, request that the paper publish one on the subject of the meeting.

Radio

Radio can be delivered by adapting the techniques that work for newspaper reporters. The most singular difference is that radio reporters try to capture the signature sound of a live event on tape for inclusion in their story. Sometimes the radio reporter will ignore such atmospherics and simply pull bites from your speaker's works. This can add a dimension to radio advocacy by diminishing the importance of location.

Increase the odds of getting news coverage by calling radio stations after they have received your news advisory, explain your event, and offer a spokesperson for a telephone interview. Just by saving work for the news staff you may earn a story. But be prepared to do the interview when you call. Have your message honed and two or three examples ready before the call is made. After the interview, fax the press packet from the event to the radio reporter so that he or she can flesh out the story you've told in the interview.

Should a particularly hot story break, one technique for responding is to record an "actuality"—a taped statement that reporters can broadcast by calling a rented phone number. In the case of an actuality, you record a statement or an interview and send out an advisory informing reporters that an actuality has been prepared for their use. This technique can get expensive, unless someone is willing to donate the technology.

Call-in shows are radio's version of the newspaper's letters to the editor, and the same tactics apply here. Don't sound canned, but the more calls from your side the better. Radio hosts try to avoid recycling the same callers again and again, so a phone tree of listeners helps to alert activists when the other side gets on the air and helps get more of your voices involved.

Television

Although television stories are different from stories in other media, the same rules hold true. Stories must be simpler, and good TV stories include elements that make them especially visual. Personal stories are essential for good television. In addition, television newspeople are not as portable as print or radio reporters. They have far more equipment to carry, more to do back at the studio, and only 22 minutes to report a full day's news. If you burn them with a story that has no news value or little visual impact, you can lose an important media contact.

A few television tips: Relax. Always arrange for the participants at your events to stand—it adds energy. Create or find backdrops that help explain the story, so that even if a viewer is not following your verbal argument, the story nonetheless gets through. If you do a studio interview, you will be asked to sit. Sit forward in the chair. Smile and try to be engaging rather than combative. In taped interviews, if your first answer is not successful, try it again. If you garble the soundbite, say it again. The story's producer wants the best story possible— he will present your best effort if given the choice.

Cable TV

There is a relatively cheap-to-use resource that is sorely underutilized by the public-interest community—cable television. Because most localities insist that communications companies trade some of their commodity—airtime—for the right to local service monopolies, public-interest groups can sometimes get access to the airwaves with regularity.

One of the strongest features of cable is its incredible ability to narrowcast to your supporters. Because so many options exist for cable viewers, the audience for any show is self-selected with great precision. Still, it is important to remember two parts of the audience who can be overlooked—channel surfers and your opposition. Surfers should be considered persuadable, and the show should be targeted to holding and entertaining these uninitiated viewers. And your Wise Use opponents, who will inevitably be taping the shows, should be considered brakes on any stridency a producer might be inclined to include in a television piece.

A regularly scheduled public-access cable television show is worth pursuing. Of course, each show should remain on the message, but regular access to a cable show offers a breadth of exciting options. First, the local environmental agenda can probably be best highlighted through videotape. Present the natural beauty of the locality with narration, or explain the environmental devastation of an area. Do supportive "street" interviews with opinion leaders and average folks. Tape environmentally supportive bites from celebrities when they pass through the area. Present entertaining public actions, like creative news actions or fund-raising benefits, in edited form. These are just some tried-and-true video techniques; local activists will have fresh suggestions.

Second, with regular airtime, various members of your network can share the focus. Over time, each group can be given a soapbox on which to present its case to viewers. In addition, live roundtable discussions allow spokespeople from diverse sections of your coalition to offer your argument to the segments of our audience with whom they identify. When your spokespeople's skills are well honed, your opponents can even be invited to join these discussions to defend themselves.

It can be hard to fill even a half-hour each week. Inspire the public to become involved. Videotaping is a growing American avocation, and video is the medium of choice for many young artists. The interest of these people should be tapped, and their on-message submission should be shown as part of your show. On occasion, the use of work by other partisans is an option. Geographically neutral segments, used by local shows to explain breaking issues or issues that are national in scope, can be used again and again in different areas. Local activists could then tailor a local segment to follow the prerecorded package.

Finally, there is no reason why local bands, scenes from local community theater, or local comedians cannot be showcased in between environmental segments. Variety adds immeasurably to video. These sidelights can both fill space and boost viewership. It is just important that these acts do not contradict your message or your interest in a broad appeal.

Paid Ads

Paid advertisements have recently been used regarding President Clinton's timber summit and the cause of reforming the 1872 Mining Law. Thirty-second political spots have been driving electoral politics for a generation, and they seem to be the wave of the future in issue politics, too. While expensive relative to other media—advertisements must be both produced and the air-time bought—they have proven to be effective. Environmental advertising must be measured in tone and its appeals framed in ways that all sides of the political spectrum can associate to their own values.

Cable can also be used to get real results from painfully small advertising budgets. Consider this scenario: watchers of the Discovery Channel are skewed to the upper end of the educational spectrum and are more environmentally inclined than most TV watchers. Were you to run a single ad on Discovery for a short time, an ad that explained a pending environmental vote, described its impact on the locality, and urged viewers to call their elected officials—with a number provided on the screen—one can assume that your voice would be heard.

The hidden element to paid advertising is coordination of the grassroots response. Paid advertising does not occur in a vacuum. Even with the most persuasive, evocative advertising, you must organize to ensure that the response you want actually happens. That means, for example, setting up telephone trees to instigate the calls to elected officials that your spot urges viewers to make. The fact is, you can rest assured that your opposition is doing the same.

Public Service Announcements

Some radio and television stations provide time for public-interest statements, called Public Service Announcements (PSAs). These broadcast op-eds provide a forum for your ideas and should be used to further your message in quick speeches by the most accomplished, message-driven communicators who will appeal to the station's target audience. Of course, these minutes are often run between infomercials at the close of the day, but the venue should not be discounted.

PSAs are unlike most other media vehicles: Because they are free airtime, you cannot count on their schedule or target their audience; they run infrequently on television and radio as a service to the community; many are innocuous, with messages like "quit smoking" and "buckle up"; but they can be used to your advantage.

Timing is essential. If environmentalists and their opponents are already at loggerheads, stations will refuse to run the PSA—so it needs to be produced and delivered to stations before anti-environmentalists enter the community. The nonpolitical organizations that are allied with the environmental movement can cheaply produce PSAs. Stations will not run the PSA if it is combative; it should stress the public benefits of conservation. If a national organization offers to produce a PSA, remember that the more generic the message, the more locales in which it can run, and the cheaper it is per area to produce.

Wise Use and the Greater Yellowstone Vision Document

Lessons Learned

Robert Ekey

During the winter of 1990–91, flyers began circulating around the Northern Rockies, warning people of plans to place a "buffer zone" around Yellowstone Park. If people didn't act soon, the flyers said, their rights to hunt, fish, and recreate on national forests would be revoked, timber jobs would go down the drain, and they might not be able to visit Yellowstone National Park by car in the future. Also at stake were private-property rights and ranching, oil and gas development, and mining.

The flyers were written by groups like the Wyoming Heritage Society and People for the West!, groups tied to the Wise Use movement. The alerts and flyers were aimed at the debate over the Greater Yellowstone Vision Document, a proposal by the U.S. Forest Service and the National Park Service to improve coordination and management of public lands in the Greater Yellowstone ecosystem. While the original draft Vision called for federal agencies to recognize a sense of "naturalness" in the region, it allowed for some commodity development to continue, including mining, logging, and grazing on federal lands.

The Vision was essentially the government's first foray into ecosystem management. It would not have changed any designations or use of federal land, but it did encourage federal agencies to take a coordinated ecosystem approach to their management activities. What the Vision did not call for was any kind of buffer zone around Yellowstone Park, nor would it have resulted in many of the outcomes predicted by the Wise Use groups.

The Vision gave the Wise Use movement a high-profile issue to use in its organizing efforts throughout the region, which served as a template for other Wise Use campaigns in the region. The all-too-familiar pattern is for groups to use misinformation to rally support or opposition to an issue.

In the case of the Wyoming Heritage Society, their alert encouraged people to attend public hearings and oppose the Vision Document, after characterizing it as an attempt to prohibit hunting and fishing on national forest lands, jeopardize private-property rights, eliminate cars in Yellowstone, and stop all commodity development and ranching.

People for the West! (PFW) made similar claims. According to a PFW newsletter, "The 'Vision' proposed goals to place some 19 million acres of land around Yellowstone Park under national park management standards." The newsletter went on to quote people as saying the Vision "was the biggest land grab since the Oklahoma land rush."

The campaigns accomplished what they intended. More than two-thirds of the 700 people at the public hearing in Bozeman, Montana, were angry and riled up in opposition to the plan. Many had never read the draft Vision Document, depending instead on "fact" sheets distributed by Wise Use groups.

A hostile mood dominated the Bozeman hearing. Yellowstone Park superintendent Bob Barbee was surprised by the crowd's anger. "You can't imagine the virulence of the outcry," Barbee said. "I was Saddam Hussein, a Communist, a Fascist, everything else you could think of. One lady got up there, jaw quivering, used her time to say the Pledge of Allegiance, then looked at me and called me a Nazi."

Following the hearings and additional political pressure from conservatives in the Wyoming, Montana, and Idaho congressional delegations, the National Park Service and Forest Service reduced the Vision from a 60-page document to 10 pages of platitudes. Not only were the concepts of coordinated ecosystem management shot down, but key people who endorsed them were transferred and ultimately resigned, including Forest Service regional forester John Mumma and Park Service regional director Lorraine Mintzmyer.

The defeat of the Vision Document was a blow to the conservation community in the Northern Rockies, which was surprised by the level of organization and support the Wise Use movement carried with it. However, an important lesson was learned: In addition to debating the real issues, be prepared to counter misinformation offered by Wise Use groups.

STRENGTHS OF THE WISE USE MESSAGE

The campaigns by People for the West! and the Wyoming Heritage Society during the Yellowstone Vision process are prime examples of the strategy Wise Use groups frequently use to organize their members.

Common themes of Wise Use campaigns include claims that rights are being taken away and livelihoods put in jeopardy, when in fact the people most likely to profit when land-use decisions swing in their favor are members of Wise Use groups. For example, when People for the West! organizes opposition to reform of the 1872 Mining Law, organizers rarely brag that they are heavily funded by mining companies—corporations that have the most to gain by stalling mining law reform.

One of the ways in which the Wise Use movement has been most successful is by creating the facade of a grassroots base. The image the movement has projected is of hard-working rural people trying to scratch a living from a raw but plentiful landscape. At the same time, they paint the environmental or conservation community as "preservationists" trying to kick them off the landscape, either by shutting out commodity extraction or denying access to public land.

The movement has garnered media attention because portraying a grass-roots image—especially as underdogs—fits the context of stories sought by some reporters. The media today rely on using people to tell the news story and illustrate a point, rather than bureaucrats and politicians talking about a problem. In addition, it is easy to romanticize people who make their living off the land, especially ranchers and farmers, but also loggers and miners—never mind that these "rugged individualists" reap large federal subsidies. The media are willing to perpetuate the myth, and Wise Users are aware of that and take advantage of it. *New York Times* reporter Keith Schneider calls the Wise Use movement "one of the most compelling stories that I cover."

It is the conservation community's job to expose the Wise Use movement for what it is. In the case of People for the West!, it is an attempt by a group of mining companies to fight reform of the 1872 General Mining Law; in the case of the National Federal Lands Conference, it is a land-grab attempt, reminiscent of the Sagebrush Rebellion, that encourages rural counties to attempt to exert more control over federal lands by adopting ordinances that appear to have no legal basis.

GETTING THE WORD OUT

The conservation community needs to more aggressively counter the Wise Use message. The mechanics for carrying the message to the media are the same here as in any other case:

- Communicate a simple message, based on fact and fueled by passion. Keep the message short—try to think in terms of soundbites, headlines, or sentences. The gist of almost any idea can be explained in less than 30 seconds.
- Educate reporters and editorial boards on the issue, in this case the financial backing of the Wise Use movement. Continue to build a rapport with reporters and lobby them for stories.
- Use all media outlets available, ranging from letters to the editor and op-ed pieces to radio talk shows and television interviews. Work with all the media in your area.
- Develop your message so it is relevant to people—explain why they should care about the Wise Use movement and what its leaders are trying to achieve.

COUNTERING THE WISE USE MESSAGE

While the methods of using the media to carry your message outlined above usually stay the same, the message can change daily. There are as many responses to the Wise Use movement as there are issues raised. In many cases, conservationists have been successful in challenging the Wise Users head-on. In other cases, shifting the debate to another level can be successful, such as discussing what really drives the local economy. For example, in the Northern Rockies, educating the public on how the economy is in transition from one based on resource extraction to one based on service can change the way an entire debate is framed.

Responding to Distortions

One effective response in the Northern Rockies has been to link local Wise Use groups with Ron Arnold's national agenda for the movement. Many local groups—even national groups—quickly distance themselves from the Arnold agenda, with its recommendations for allowing mining and oil and gas development in all national parks and wilderness areas, weakening the Endangered Species Act, gutting the Wilderness Act, and logging all old-growth forests to ameliorate the effects of global warming.

For example, in a 1992 Idaho controversy, the group Grassroots for Multiple Use (GMU) was active in challenging a plan by sportsmen and conservationists to protect the Henry's Fork River and its tributaries from hydroelectric developers. A Greater Yellowstone Coalition (GYC) board member who had been working in support of the river protection plan tied the GMU supporters to Arnold's radical agenda, even though they claimed they did not endorse it.

But after conservationists proved that other GMU groups in Montana had supported the Arnold agenda, the local Idaho group retreated.

In another case, at a rally of loggers and lumbermill workers at a lumber mill in Livingston, Montana, in 1992, an organizer hired by the Western Environmental Trade Association Ad-Hoc Committee (WETA) told the crowd that the GYC's goal was to shut the mill down. WETA, a Montana-based group comprised of utilities, timber and mining companies, and other pro-development interests, has frequently called for wilderness areas to be opened up for snowmobile use and has opposed designation of any additional wilderness. The WETA organizer, Dennis Winters, already had a statewide reputation for polarizing issues and communities, employing an evangelistic speaking style to accuse environmentalists of everything from closing down the Livingston mill to promoting domestic problems.

Such accusations deserve a swift and sure response. This was an opportune time for conservationists to launch an aggressive counterattack. Winter's assertion that GYC was out to shut the mill down was such a blatant lie that, after prodding from the coalition, even the mill managers the next day conceded to the media that GYC was not out to close the mill—in fact, the managers had been working with GYC and the Forest Service to address some timber and road-building conflicts.

In addition, in interviews with reporters, GYC accused Winters of polarizing the community, pitting neighbor against neighbor and friend against friend, and said what the community needed most right now was to work together to solve problems, rather than exacerbate them.

The result was that GYC and the rest of the conservation community gained the high ground by being perceived as carrying the reasonable message. Winters, on the other hand, was portrayed as an extremist. One local newspaper editorialized against Winters' tactics, characterizing him as an "Elmer Gantry–style snake oil salesman," and pointing out some of the positive aspects of conservationists' programs.

Effective Research

Researching Wise Use groups in your region before an issue arises facilitates a quick response to their claims. In Idaho, for example, being able to link a group to Ron Arnold's agenda damaged its credibility. In other instances involving People for the West!, describing its history of mining company funding dilutes any influence that organization might have.

Research allows one to be specific. We are all guilty at times of painting broad-brushed strokes in the media, using phrases like "this is an industry-backed effort," to describe the Wise Use movement. Engaging in such broad references not only tarnishes the good operators in that industry, but it also allows the bad operations—the ones actually funding the Wise Use movement—to hide behind anonymity.

For example, there is no secret why Chevron USA donated at least $45,000 to the People for the West! campaign. One of the primary missions of People for the West! is to organize opposition to reform of the 1872 Mining Law. That antiquated law allowed Chevron to buy 2,000 acres that comprise the Stillwater mine, located 40 miles northeast of Yellowstone National Park, for a total sum of $10,180—or $5 an acre—according to the Mineral Policy Center. Meanwhile, the platinum and palladium reserves at the mine are valued in the billions of dollars. Under the current but 120-year-old law, Chevron pays no royalties for the minerals it takes from what was once public land.

When encountering the Wise Use movement, it makes sense to conduct some basic research of who the players are—and who stands to gain. Abide by the old investigative reporters' axiom: Follow the money. Generally when the Wise Use movement is active in an area, someone stands to gain, whether through reduced regulation or continued public subsidies of private enterprises.

In addition to pegging mining companies for supporting People for the West!, other examples of following the money include the BlueRibbon Coalition, which receives heavy funding from manufacturers of all-terrain vehicles, and the National Wetlands Coalition—another green-sounding group out to weaken protections for wetlands—which is sponsored by developers and agricultural interests.

While working to highlight the industry operators supporting the Wise Use movement, it is also important to bring recognition to good operators in your area who act in a responsible manner and who are not Wise Use supporters. Helping the media find and report on ranchers who embrace a conservation ethic when grazing their cattle can help quiet ranchers fighting enforcement of grazing standards on lands they lease. Mining companies with poor environmental or reclamation records appear even worse when juxtaposed with one of the few companies that comply with environmental standards. In most cases, ranchers, individuals, and companies who pursue a land stewardship ethic do not support the Wise Use movement. Their efforts can serve as a guide for the public confused by claims that conservationists are trying to steal their life away.

Changing Economy

Organizers of the Wise Use movement realize that the economy in the Northern Rockies is making a slow, steady transition. While the resource-extraction industries are in a steady decline, other sectors of the economy, such as the service sector, are growing at a steady pace. The commodity industries are not being driven out—the shift only reflects larger regional trends. To help document the change, there have been several economic-trend studies completed for our region. A study by The Wilderness Society illustrates the overall shift away from resource industries. GYC supplemented that study with a series of economic profiles that found similar trends in 10 individual counties. Working with both studies, it is possible to educate people that the economy of the entire region is changing and that their counties are experiencing similar changes.

Two important points came out of the economic studies. First, much of the growth in the economy was attributed to individuals and businesses that were moving to the region because of quality-of-life considerations, including easy accessibility to the wildlands and recreational opportunities. By pitching stories to business and feature writers and others outside of the normal environmental beat, GYC tries to educate people about the changing economy and how their jobs are dependent on a healthy environment. Part of the message is that not all new jobs are in tourism, which provides us another opportunity to explain by example.

A second point illustrated by the county profiles is that the extractive industries—logging and timber mills, mining, oil and gas, and even agriculture—account for only a small fraction of the region's economy. Even in counties where there is a relatively large and visible presence, say a lumber mill, manufacturing still accounts for a tiny fraction of the overall economy. It is dwarfed by the service industry and a category showing income from retirement and outside investments. Taking this information to editors and news directors, one could argue that the resource-extraction industry has a voice in the media that is disproportionate to its importance to the regional economy.

Not every story you pitch to reporters and editors needs to be about your particular issue. By working hard on stories about the changing economy, we try to alter the context of the debate from a story that paints timber and logging as major influences in the Northern Rockies to one of the overall economy changing and how people and communities in the region are responding to that change. In pitching these stories, it is always beneficial to let people who are living the changes tell the story. People are more inclined to listen to their neighbors than to experts and spokesmen. A series of different voices telling your story is often more likely to be heard.

Private-Property Rights

One place where the Wise Use movement has been successful in having people tell a story is the issue regarding the "taking" of private property. The takings issue is often one of the most difficult to challenge in the media. The concept of private property is unquestionably popular, and Wise Use claims that private-property rights are in jeopardy often evoke a visceral response from the public. Takings of private-property claims make great soundbites, while countering a private-property-rights argument is often lengthy, complex, and difficult to communicate.

An example of a private-property claim in Greater Yellowstone was raised by the Church Universal and Triumphant (CUT), a Montana religious sect that wanted to develop a geothermal well on its ranch along the northern boundary of Yellowstone National Park. The National Park Service has opposed any geothermal development adjacent to its boundaries, contending it cannot be proven that such drilling and pumping would not have detrimental effects on Yellowstone's famous geothermal features.

GYC and other local activist groups have been lobbying for Congress to pass The Old Faithful Protection Act, a measure that would effectively prohibit geothermal development within 15 miles of the park's boundaries. The measure passed in the House but stalled in the Senate, largely because of CUT's claims that such a bill would represent a taking of private property. Claiming that the bill would prevent it from pumping hot water from a well it drilled, the religious sect demanded up to $500,000 in compensation from the treasury if it could not develop its well. Although other private-property owners in the area had not drilled wells and had remained silent on the issue, the Park Service feared that CUT's actions could prompt other landowners to drill or seek compensation.

CUT's claims prompted congressional conservatives to stall the bill. Media coverage of the bill focused not so much on the effort to protect Yellowstone's geysers as it did on the private-property-rights issue. It was difficult to shape a short, effective argument to counter their private-property claims. Arguments that the bill would result in the greater good or that responsibility accompanies rights fell on deaf ears with the media. Arguments that no rights are absolute— the First Amendment guarantees free speech but does not allow one to yell fire in a crowded theater—and that private-property rights don't condone Yellowstone's neighbors jeopardizing geothermal features also failed.

Two arguments, however, did prove effective. Progress was made when we argued that a taking did not exist because the legislation did not preclude CUT from using the surface flow off a hot spring on land where it owned water rights. Another effective message in countering CUT's private-property claim was that the sect was greedy—it seemed more interested in pumping from the federal treasury than from the geothermal aquifer. Focusing attention on the amount of money that CUT was requesting shifted the debate somewhat. Even so, the bill's future remains in question.

SUMMARY

The Wise Use movement has been effective in using supporters to carry a message to the media that appears to be grassroots, but whose real roots are a small group of people who stand to profit off public lands and at public expense. Their message of "holdouts for handouts" can be effectively countered, often to the advantage of conservationists.

Working Journalists
Speak Out on Wise Use

Society of Environmental Journalists

SHARON COLLINS

I think that when we made the decision to follow Ron Arnold—I spent about a week with him—it was because we didn't understand why the Wise Use movement was gaining so much ground. That was our goal—to understand the movement. Not to necessarily tear it apart, not necessarily to say it is good or bad. But just to understand it. In fact, the name of the piece was "Know Thine Enemy."

I think that what has happened is that "not in my back yard" no longer refers to just a waste dump, it refers to environmental regulations as well. And much of the support has been gained because of that feeling. If I can depart from Ron Arnold for just a moment. When I lived in Virginia, I served on an economic-development board. I was the only media person on the board, and why I was there—I think it was just to be a thorn in the side of the bank presidents and that sort, because we were always at odds over things like cogeneration facilities that wanted to locate and things like that. The one issue that always amazed me involved interbasin water transfer, and it had to do with a Virginia Beach plan to withdraw water out of the Roanoke River basin, down around Lake Gaston, North Carolina—the lake that borders both North Carolina and Virginia.

I lived in a small city about 45 minutes away from my station—called Danville—and this city pumped hundreds of thousands of dollars a year, over a period of years, to fight this on an environmental basis. They said, this is environmentally wrong—you ruin the river basin, fish will suffer, you will completely destroy an ecosystem here. However, this same body that spent hundreds of thousands of dollars to support the fight against interbasin water transfer completely reversed its position and went from being an environmentalist organization in position to a Wise Use organization, because all of a sudden the largest plant there—Goodyear—wanted to locate a cogeneration facility on the river.

I said, "Guys, doesn't this seem a little strange to you, that you're screaming 'you can't take our water downstream' and yet you're supporting not just this cogeneration facility, which sucks thousands of gallons of water a day, but you're also supporting about four other [plants] in a 20-mile radius? Don't you think that's a little contradictory? Do you see what I'm saying?" No, they did not see that at all. All of a sudden, someone was telling that city they could not locate a cogen facility. How dare anyone say that. And I think that on a local level, that's what's happened.

Everyone is a strong environmentalist, until you say, "Well, I don't care if you spent several hundred thousand dollars on that beachfront property, you can't build a house there because it's been labeled wetlands now,"—or there are new zoning restrictions there. So, I began at that level, to understand why people were joining the Wise Use movement.

When I started following Ron Arnold, though, it became a little more difficult because I was hearing things like "Let's drill for oil in Alaska's arctic region; let's tear up the national forests and let anybody log there." And I thought, now why would anybody go for this argument—I really want to understand this. So I set out to try to follow him and understand how he organized. First we went to a site owned by Georgia-Pacific. This was their "star" facility. He was gathering data for his next book. He writes a lot of books, and, I found out later, industry buys many of them. And we walked around, he carried his tape recorder and interviewed landowners about why they were so happy to have Georgia-Pacific manage their land. We spent some time with a widow, who could not handle her land. And I was asking her questions like what about your children, don't you want to leave this land to your children? Doesn't it bother you that this timber company is taking out trees? And she said, "They just want the money anyway. You know, I don't care. A tree's a tree. They can chop them down, I don't care. They leave enough trees for it still to look okay." And that was the way she felt about the matter.

So we went from there to California. And I thought, OK, in California I'm going to get some radical response. I'm going to get my soundbites here. So we started out. We went into a radio station, and the talk-show host—not Rush Limbaugh—this was a pretty tame-looking fellow, and he looked—if you'll excuse my generalization—kind of yuppielike. And I thought, this will be good, he's going to give Ron a run for his money. Not so. On the air, as he was asking Ron questions, he started agreeing with him. And so as we were rolling tape I said, "Gee, you know, you sound like a convert here." And he said, "I happen to believe that people are more important than animals." And I said, "But can't there be a balance?" And he said, "I agree with what Ron Arnold says; I think the balance is tilting in the other direction."

So we then went to a rally, largely organized by the tuna fishermen, but also attended by people in the housing business, people who run skeet-shooting operations, various occupations. And I saw Ron in operation. Chuck Cushman and I were talking about this earlier. He is a performer. He's the first to admit it. He stands up and says, "How many of you tuna fishermen have had to sell your boats?" And, of course, screams and shouts. "How many of you are sick and tired of those environmentalists cramming their stuff down your throat? You can't even fish anymore, can you?" And, of course, they start getting worked up and by the time it was all over, he starts talking about the War, and, of course, the name of one of his books is *Ecology Wars*. He stands up and says, "This is a war. One of the things you have to do in a war is fight with the best weapons you have [and the best weapon you have] is the court system. Sue them. Take them to court. Tie it up in litigation. The environmentalists can't move that way." He said, "This is your sword. What do you do with a sword? You stab the bastards." Then everybody was real worked up. And I thought, "Good grief, I'm not an environmentalist, really." You start getting kind of worried, because they're all worked up. The tuna fishermen are all worked up. A hairdresser said, "You know, I'm getting worried, because the next thing you know they're going to outlaw hair dye, those environmentalists." And then all the women started getting nervous.

And so I began to see what happens at these rallies. A lot of people there considered themselves environmentalists, because that word is so broad anymore, and there isn't really any other word to cover it. So all of these people who considered themselves to be environmentalists suddenly got a little angry when the environmentalists' position stepped on their toes. This is one of the little things that one of the tuna fishermen gave me. He came up after the rally and said, "I just want you to read this [letter]. They took my boat away." And the letter said, "I speak for all the fishermen in California. Men who sense and feel a very strong resentment and a censorship from the American public. The only crime they committed is they were fishermen." And that is the way they feel. Right or wrong, that's the way they feel. They told the story of the fisherman who was trying to get a dolphin out of a net and was killed by a shark. They told stories of how they had gone overboard in trying to save dolphins and no one in the media had reported it. Of course, Greenpeace was always the culprit in many of these arguments, but bottom line, they all felt that they had been taken advantage of in some way or fashion by environmental regulations.

So I really thought about how did this happen? And let me say, also, before we even began this story I talked to a lot of so-called environmental organizations about Ron Arnold. I said, "I'm getting ready to follow Ron Arnold."

Much of what I got from those discussions was "Oh, you know, Ron Arnold's a nut. Why are you even following him? Don't pay any attention to him." And I think that for a long time, folks did not pay much attention to Ron Arnold—until he had whipped up a lot of crowds, and had already gained the support, and touched on some very emotional issues that those in the environmental world had perhaps ignored. It really became obvious to me that we used to—when I was talking about environmental issues in the '70s—we were talking about Love Canal and babies dying from chemicals, and what people hear now is spotted owl and snail darter and it's not as emotional. You don't have the human quality, and that is where Ron Arnold and the Wise Use movement have moved right in. They have, as I think you mentioned, they took the PR book and they tore it apart—and they said, "Hey, we can do this, too." It's interesting to me because, I think, more than ever, the Wise Use movement is going to be very active and it's going to be difficult to cover. James Watt was the rallying cry for the environmental movement. Al Gore is [Ron Arnold's] rallying cry. And I would simply say that when covering the Wise Use movement, it's sometimes difficult, too, because as I was ending my interview with Ron Arnold, I said, "Ron, what if you're wrong? Let's just say: What if? I know you think NAFTA's crazy, you don't like George Bush, you don't like any of these guys. There's no acid rain, there's no ozone. But what if you're wrong? And then it's too late." And he said, "Well that's a stupid question, and I refuse to answer it. I'm not wrong." And that is how the interview ended.

And that is, sometimes, the difficulty in covering the Wise Use movement. You're dealing with emotion, and you're dealing with a right, seen by many people as just as important as free press, and that is the right to own, and control, private property. I think our work is cut out for us. In trying to be fair to both sides, you sometimes get caught up in a lot of emotion, and it sometimes becomes difficult to pull yourself back.

KEITH SCHNEIDER

I stumbled on the Wise Use movement in a story done [for] our paper by our Seattle correspondent. But I first talked to Chuck Cushman about this time last year, covering his movement to boycott GE and the Audubon Society specials on TV, and was really struck by what he was telling me, and decided to delve in, and what I learned—I don't want to be seen as a supporter of the Wise Use movement, but I think that the movement is maybe one of the most important and interesting movements to arise in environmentalism in a long time because it is prying into the environmental questions that we've all grappled with for two decades. Is there really global warming? Is there really an ozone problem? Does toxic-waste cleanup really represent the best use of public financing? What are the best uses of public lands? Is the government protection of land the best way to protect land for the environment? They are causing me, and I hope causing you, to take a second look at what I call sort of an environmental orthodoxy that's been adopted in the last 25 years.

We now have more information about who's being hurt and who's not being hurt by environmental problems, toxic waste. Had there been a bona fide Wise Use movement 12 years ago, with Love Canal, we may have taken a second look. The environmental movement and environmental journalism may have taken a second look at the real risks from abandoned toxic-waste sites and is it really necessary, and is it the best public use of funds to be spending $11 billion in federal money right now cleaning them up, or maybe we should just fence them off and wait for new technologies. These are the kinds of questions I'm asking, and they were brought to me in large part because of the multiple layers of the movement.

It's not a heterogeneous movement. I find it almost laughable that in the environmental press—*Audubon* magazine, *Sierra Club* magazine, I've read some others—that the rap on the Wise Use movement is that it's corporate funded. Well, the largest corporate donations that I know of in the environmental movement is the million dollars that General Electric gives the Audubon Society to support their Audubon Society specials. Now, General Electric's environmental record has a lot to be desired. They have more toxic-waste sites, Superfund sites than any industrial corporation in the country. I've covered General Electric messes from Hanford to Schenectedy, New York. For the Audubon Society magazine to be criticizing the Wise Use movement for corporate funding seems to me to be the height of hypocrisy.

The movement has also brought forward some very interesting legal ideas that are giving Congress fits. One of them is the takings legislation and the battery of legal theories about takings. Developed at the University of Chicago, [it] basically says that any government action—environmental regulation or actual seizure of land or property from a private owner—should be compensated by the government. Two years ago, a Wyoming coal company won $150 million from the Interior Department because under the Strip Mining Law the Interior Department barred them from mining coal reserves in an alluvial plain. That case prompted a flood of claims to come through the Claims Court, which is a little-known Washington court that is now deciding what really is the responsibility of the government when it comes to directing how private property is used. It's an important constitutional issue that has not been brought to the fore, except for the legal theories that have been brought by the Wise Use movement or the property rights movement.

There are questions to be asked about wetlands regulations. The property rights groups that I know of have no corporate funding at all. They are basically Mom and Pop type community environmental groups working on the other side. And they're asking some legitimate questions like, why is it on the Delmarva peninsula there [was an] actual prosecution and jailing of a property owner for filling in a wetland when down the road DuPont is polluting a river wantonly without any kind of prosecution of its corporate officers or managers.

In a political sense, I think that this year the movement reached a real pinnacle on the question of how are they going to lobby. The Bush administration—Vice President Quayle and Secretary Lujan—primarily developed a strategy for piggybacking on this movement, particularly in the West, and that's why you've heard a lot about the spotted owl, that's why you've heard a lot about CAFE in Michigan, and that's why you heard a lot about Al Gore's book and its proposals for taxing timber and virgin materials in New England. All of those arguments—everywhere the Bush administration used those arguments in their political campaign—particularly on radio—were rejected. Clinton swept New England, he swept the upper Middle West, and he swept the Northwest and California. Nevertheless, this movement attracted considerable attention at the top levels of the government in the Republican Party, and I think that they're going to continue to piggyback on this movement. What we have to be mindful of is that the fringe of the movement is not where the Wise Use movement is going to move. I don't think the Ron Arnold view of things is going to be paramount. However, the property rights view is the real strength of the movement. It's where the—they call themselves the Alliance for America—these are the Peggy Riegles of the world. She is a former *Daily News* vice president for finance in New York who bought a farm in Maryland and wanted to develop it in 10-acre plots and was barred from doing so because of wetlands regulations. And she and others like her all over the country have organized themselves through computers and faxing—it's a tremendous use of technology to stay in touch, and that's where the real movement is. Because it's the restrictions on property—that constitutional issue—that's driving the heart of the movement, and that's, I think, what we need to watch.

I don't think the Sea Shephards of the environmental movement [was] where the strength of the environmental movement was, nor do I think that the Ron Arnold view of things is where the strength of the Wise Use movement is—it's going to be in the center. They're going to be around to stay—they're getting larger, they're tremendously well organized. I met a Harvard-educated physicist and computer specialist in Lexington, Massachusetts, who is organizing the

Washington County Alliance in Maine, which is fighting National Park Service expansion of a wildlife refuge and some proposals for National Park lands in Maine. This guy's name is Eric Vail, and he has the best library on environmentalism I've ever seen, all computerized, annotated, computer discs—he's in touch with you, I'm sure, hourly—and they are tremendously well organized. Better organized, I think, at this point, than the environmental movement, because they're angrier, they're hungrier. And I think they're taking advantage of what I see as a moribundness in the intellectualism and the idea making within the national environmental movement. They're hungry, they've got new ideas, they've got legal, scientific, political arms that are moving forward; they're represented in Washington. They are coming on at a time when the national environmental movement is in some disarray, there's some sort of—it's just that the national environmental movement, I think, has to raise how it's thinking about these things, and one of the reasons they're being challenged is the Wise Use movement. They're being challenged on their right in a way they've never been challenged before. As an environmental journalist, it is one of the most compelling stories that I cover. I wish I could do more of it.

About the Authors

Jim Baca is the former New Mexico Land Commissioner and former director of the Federal Bureau of Land Management.

Jim Bernfield has served as a communications consultant for the American Resources Information Network.

Philip Brick is an assistant professor of political science at Whitman College in Walla Walla, Washington.

Henry H. Carey and Meria L. Loeks are with the Forest Trust in Sante Fe, New Mexico.

Donald L. Connors is president of the Environmental Business Council of the United States, Inc. Michael D. Bliss is an environmental lawyer practicing with the Boston law firm of Sullivan and Worcester. Jack Archer is professor of environmental science and the director for Environmental Policy and Programs for the University of Massachusetts.

Sharon Dennis is a staff attorney for the National Audubon Society and is directing its project on property right and the environment.

Raymond Booth Eby is a graduate student in the liberal arts at St. John's College in Annapolis, Maryland. He is a former truck driver, Marine, fishmonger, steelworker, TV repairman, waiter, butcher, bagel baker, camp counselor, freelance writer, and National Audubon Society staffer.

John D. Echeverria is general counsel of the National Audubon Society. He directs the environmental law program in the Society's Washington, D.C., office. He has written and spoken extensively on property rights and the environment.

Thomas Eisner is the Jacob Gould Professor of Biology at Cornell University. He is widely known for his work with insects and promoting the preservation of natural biodiversity.

Robert Ekey is a former Los Angeles newspaper reporter and is currently the communications director for the Greater Yellowstone Coalition.

Janet Ellis is active in natural-resource issues in Montana and throughout the Northwest. She is currently the president of the Montana Audubon Council.

Teresa Erickson is an organizer with the Northern Plains Resource Council. She is active in promoting reform of the 1872 Mining Act.

Grant Ferrier is the president of Environmental Business International. He is also the editor in chief of the *Environmental Business Journal,* a publication dedicated to providing strategic information to the environmental industry.

Mary Ann Glendon is professor of law at Harvard Law School.

John S. Gray III is a graduate of Rice University and the University of Texas. He is currently a political consultant in Washington, D.C.

Neil D. Hamilton is a professor of law at Drake University.

Donald R. Judge is the executive secretary of the Montana State AFL-CIO. He has long been a champion of labor, environmental, and public-interest coalitions.

Margaret Kriz is a staff correspondent for the *National Journal.*

Dana B. Larsen is a longtime activist in Arizona state politics. He is currently the executive director of Arizona Common Cause.

Marianne Lavelle is a staff reporter for the *National Law Journal.*

Thomas A. Lewis is a freelance investigative journalist based in northern Virginia.

Douglass North is the former conservation chair of the Rivers Council in Seattle, Washington. He is also one of the founding board members of River Network.

Eve Pell is a staff reporter for the Center for Investigative Reporting.

Thomas Michael Power is professor of economics and chairman of the Department of Economics at the University of Montana. He has served as a consultant on economics issues for the federal government and for state agencies.

Tarso Ramos is a researcher with the Western States Center on the Wise Use Public Exposure Project, a joint initiative of the Center and the Montana State AFL-CIO. The purpose of the project is to expose the corporate and ideological interests behind the Wise Use movement.

William E. Riebsame is associate professor of geology at the University of Colorado at Boulder. Robert G. Woodmansee is a professor of ecology at Colorado State University in Fort Collins, Colorado. Their work focuses on regional resource sustainability.

Holmes Rolston III is University Distinguished Professor of Philosophy at Colorado State University in Fort Collins, Colorado. He is the author of five books and over 70 articles.

Jon Roush is a rancher, environmentalist, and author. A former member of The Nature Conservancy's Board of Directors, he is currently president of The Wilderness Society.

Carl Safina is a marine biologist with the National Audubon Society. Suzanne Iudicello is an attorney with the Center for Marine Conservation.

Tim Searchinger is an attorney for the Environmental Defense Fund, specializing in water resource and wildlife issues.

Randall D. Snodgrass is director of wildlife policy with the National Audubon Society. He also currently serves on the steering committee of the Endangered Species Coalition.

James Gustave Speth is the former president of the World Resources Institute. He is currently the director of the United National Environment Programme.

Linda K. Trocki is with the Energy and Environmental Analysis Group at Los Alamos National Laboratory.

T. H. Watkins is a vice president of the Wilderness Society and the editor of *Wilderness* magazine. He is the author of a soon to be released book on the Great Depression.

Florence Williams is a former reporter for *High Country News*. She is currently pursuing her masters of fine arts while continuing to write freelance.

Grateful acknowledgment is expressed for permission to include the following previously published material.

"Cloaked in a Wise Disguise" by Thomas A. Lewis, *National Wildlife,* Oct./Nov. 1992. Copyright © the National Wildlife Foundation. Reprinted by permission.

"Stop the Greens: Business Fights Back by Hook or by Crook" by Eve Pell, *E Magazine,* Nov./Dec. 1991. Copyright © Center for Investigative Reporting.

"Land Mine" by Margaret Kriz, *National Journal,* Oct. 23, 1993.

"The 'Property Rights' Revolt: Environmentalists Fret as States Pass Reagan-Style Takings Laws" by Marianne Lavelle, *The National Law Journal,* May 10, 1993. Copyright © The New York Law Publishing Company. Reprinted by permission.

"Sagebrush Rebellion II" by Florence Williams. This chapter originally appeared in *High Country News,* P.O. Box 1090, Paonia, Colorado, 81428. (303) 527-4898.

"Not All That Glitters" by Thomas Michael Power, Ph.D, published by Mineral Policy Center, Washington, D.C.

"The Value of Land: Seeking Property Rights Solutions to Public Environmental Concerns" by Neil D. Hamilton, *Journal of Soil and Water Conservation,* vol. 48, no. 4. Copyright © 1993 Soil and Water Conservation Society.

" 'Absolute' Rights: Property and Privacy" by Mary Ann Glendon. Reprinted with the permission of Mary Ann Glendon.

"Winning and Losing in Environmental Ethics" by Holmes Rolston III. A longer version of this chapter was published in Frederick Ferré and Peter Hartel, eds., *Ethics and Environmental Policy: Theory Meets Practice* (Athens, GA: University of Georgia Press), 1994.

"The Tragedy of Oceans" copyright © 1994 The Economist Newspaper Group, Inc. Reprinted with permission. Further reproduction prohibited.

"Countering the Resource Abuse Movement" by Douglass North. Previously appeared in *River Voices,* published by River Network.

"Working Journalists Speak Out on the Wise Use Movement" excerpt of a taped panel discussion from the Second National Conference of the Society of Environmental Journalists, Nov. 6–8, 1992, University of Michigan at Ann Arbor.

Index